"Well, here we go again. In yet another ger_____ being called into question. This time the issues are often more subtle, but they represent a clear and present challenge for those who would defend and affirm the perfection of the Holy Scriptures. *Defending Inerrancy* is a much-needed work and one that will start an important and timely conversation. This is a book that cannot, must not, and will not be ignored."—**R. Albert Mohler Jr.**, president, The Southern Baptist Theological Seminary

"In the following pages Norman Geisler, who contributed as much as anyone to International Council on Biblical Inerrancy's [ICBI] original legacy, and William Roach interact with evangelical hypotheses that have the effect of confusing that legacy. They are masterly gatekeepers, and I count it an honor to commend this work to the Christian world."—**J. I . Packer,** from the foreword

"Even in the days of the ICBI, Norm Geisler knew that every generation would have to address the question of the faithfulness of God's Word. After all, the earliest attack of Satan was on the question of whether or not God had really said what our first parents understood him to say. In this superb volume, Geisler and Roach have demonstrated once again that the attack, though an old one, must and can be answered. Anyone engaging the culture needs to read this book."—**Paige Patterson,** president, Southwestern Baptist Theological Seminary

"The biblical doctrine of inerrancy is both true and of crucial importance for the life and health of the church. Geisler and Roach provide an excellent, up-to-date treatment of the recent history of the doctrine, an analysis of what it does and does not mean, and a response to recent attacks against it. I am glad to see this book come out and happy to recommend it."—**J. P. Moreland,** Distinguished Professor of Philosophy, Talbot School of Theology; author, *The God Question*

"Norm Geisler and I both served on the ICBI for the ten years of its existence. What Dr. Geisler has now written in his new book is certainly a masterpiece and worthy of careful attention by all who are interested in dealing with the inerrancy of the Word of God."—**Earl D. Radmacher,** president emeritus, Western Seminary, Portland, Oregon

"This volume is a call to consider the trustworthiness of Scripture. It is written by one of framers of the seminal Chicago Statement on Biblical Inerrancy, 1978. I maintain that everyone interested in spreading the message of the Bible should read and absorb Geisler's treatment of this subject. It will strengthen your conviction that God's Word is truth and that it will stand forever."—**Phil Roberts,** president, Midwest Baptist Theological Seminary, Kansas City, Missouri

DEFENDING INERRANCY

AFFIRMING *the*
ACCURACY *of* SCRIPTURE
for a NEW GENERATION

NORMAN L. GEISLER
AND WILLIAM C. ROACH

FOREWORD *by* J. I. PACKER

BakerBooks
a division of Baker Publishing Group
Grand Rapids, Michigan

Published by Baker Books
a division of Baker Publishing Group
P.O. Box 6287, Grand Rapids, MI 49516-6287
www.bakerbooks.com

Printed in the United States of America

Library of Congress Cataloging-in-Publication Data
Geisler, Norman L.
    Defending inerrancy : affirming the accuracy of Scripture for a new generation / Norman L. Geisler and William C. Roach.
      p. cm.
    Includes bibliographical references (p.   ).
    ISBN 978-0-8010-1434-5 (pbk.)
    1. Bible—Evidences, authority, etc. I. Roach, William C. II. Title.
BS480.G45 2011
220.1′32—dc22
                                                         2011031846

The internet addresses, email addresses, and phone numbers in this book are accurate at the time of publication. They are provided as a resource. Baker Publishing Group does not endorse them or vouch for their content or permanence.

We wish to thank Joel Paulus for the many hours
he spent improving the manuscript of this book.
For his diligent and scholarly efforts we are very
grateful. He greatly improved the final text.

Contents

Foreword

The two decades between the twentieth century's world wars were years of eclipse for English-speaking evangelicals on both sides of the Atlantic. Liberalism was in the saddle in the major Protestant churches, and liberalism remained as John Henry Newman had defined it:

> Liberalism in religion is the doctrine that there is no positive truth in religion, but that one creed is as good as another. . . . It is inconsistent with any recognition of any religion as true. It teaches that all are to be tolerated, for all are matters of opinion.[1]

The virile Reformational orthodoxy of earlier days had been elbowed out to the sidelines, and what we nowadays refer to as the guild—that is, the theological teaching community in universities, colleges, and seminaries—seemed finally to have closed its ranks against conservative scholarship and conservative scholars. Licking its wounds, evangelicalism had withdrawn into modes of premillennialism, mainly dispensational, on the one hand and pietism, mainly of the Keswick type, on the other. In North America, the biggest of these recessive groupings took the name fundamentalism, on the ground of its strict adherence to the fundamentals of biblical faith.

During the Second World War, however, a strong sense of need for a renewing of biblical and theological scholarship that would outthink, outflank, and outlast liberalism established itself in evangelical circles in both Britain and North America. The outcome was that Tyndale House, a biblical research center, was founded in Cambridge, England, in 1943 as an extension of the ministry of the Inter-Varsity Fellowship, and in 1947 Fuller Seminary, an academic spin-off from Charles Fuller's *Old Fashioned Revival Hour* broadcast, opened its doors. Both institutions aimed to be change agents and committed themselves to essentially the same vision: evangelical scholarship revivified, evangelical scholars finding a

9

place for themselves in the guild, and evangelical believers and congregations being resourced by biblical truth and wisdom at every point of need.

Both Tyndale House and Fuller Seminary took their primary academic and ecclesiological task to be the vindicating and reinstating of the canonical Scriptures as the fully inspired and authoritative Word of God, the multiform utterance of God in the words of some forty selected penmen, the church's criterion of true faith and godly practice, and the epistemological foundation of all authentic, Spirit-given knowledge of God. In the outworking of this agenda, however, differences of context have led to different particular concerns, with different outcomes. Tyndale House has given priority from the start to nurturing career academics, teachers, and writers who would gain status in the world of historically oriented and technically accomplished biblical studies at the university level. In the providence of God, it has been able to pursue its goals over the years in comparative peace, and while the inerrancy of Scripture—that is, the Bible's total truth and trustworthiness—has been a basic assumption in all the scholarship the House has sponsored, as it has always been of evangelical preaching and Bible teaching in Britain generally, it has never been the storm center of controversy in the way that it became for Fuller Seminary.

This is not the place to track the ups and downs of the ongoing debate at and around Fuller and its ripple effect on North American evangelicalism as a whole as Fuller graduates scattered to serve as pastors in mainline churches. Suffice it to say that out of this spreading confusion came the founding of the International Council on Biblical Inerrancy (ICBI) in 1978. The organizers of this body were convinced that the then current doubts and uncertainties about the Bible's total truth reflected inexact scholarship that could be diagnosed and corrected. ICBI's first purpose, then, was to announce this, and its second was to demonstrate it in particular cases in as much detail as was necessary. During the council's ten-year active life, conferences were called, books were written, and consensus statements produced, and ICBI's output as a whole seemed to achieve something like landmark status for evangelical people generally.

The essence of what ICBI stood for appears in "A Short Statement," produced at the Chicago conference in 1978:

> 1. God, who is Himself truth and speaks truth only, has inspired Holy Scripture in order thereby to reveal Himself to lost mankind through Jesus Christ as Creator and Lord, Redeemer and Judge. Holy Scripture is God's witness to Himself.
>
> 2. Holy Scripture, being God's own Word, written by men prepared and superintended by His Spirit, is of infallible divine authority in all matters upon which it touches: it is to be believed, as God's instruction, in all that it affirms; obeyed, as God's command, in all that it requires; embraced, as God's pledge, in all that it promises.
>
> 3. The Holy Spirit, Scripture's divine author, both authenticates it to us by His inward witness and opens our minds to understand its meaning.
>
> 4. Being wholly and verbally God-given, Scripture is without error or fault in all its teaching, no less in what it states about God's acts in creation, about the events

of world history, and about its own literary origins under God, than in its witness to God's saving grace in individual lives.

5. The authority of Scripture is inescapably impaired if this total divine inerrancy is in any way limited or disregarded, or made relative to a view of truth contrary to the Bible's own; and such lapses bring serious loss to both the individual and the Church.

Methodologically and strategically, the thrust of all this is clear and, indeed, inescapable. The warrant for accepting inerrancy as an article of faith is, first, the unquestioning acceptance of the Old Testament as authoritative teaching from God, leading up to Christ, that we perceive in Jesus himself and, following him, his apostles; plus the apostles' strong insistence on the divine authority of their own teaching; plus the church's certainty down the centuries of the canonicity of all the sixty-six books that make up our Bible, a certainty the God-givenness of which cannot rationally be doubted. The axiom of inerrancy as a guideline for biblical interpretation expresses and safeguards the belief that in all the inspired texts, whatever their literary genre and style, God speaks his mind to us in and through what the human writer articulates, so that whenever the interpreter takes up a passage to work with it, it is as if God says to him, in the shining words that William Blake (with less justification, be it sadly said) used of his own compositions:

> I give you the end of a golden string,
>   Only wind it into a ball;
> It will lead you in at Jerusalem's gate,
>   Built in Jerusalem's wall.

And the same maxim teaches that any who suspect biblical statements of inaccuracy should dig further into the conventions of culture and communication that operated when the statements were made, for it is here that the solution of their problems will be found. (For example, at a scholars' conference on Scripture in pre-ICBI days, Jesus's reference in Matthew 13:32 to the mustard seed as the smallest of all seeds was treated as problematical, being seen as a botanical inaccuracy. Knowing already that the mustard seed was the smallest of seeds that grew in Palestine and could be seen with the naked eye and had become proverbial for smallness, I was surprised. But I do not think that Jesus's statement would seem problematical to any group of scholars today.)

In each of these ways, then, belief in inerrancy determines the basic attitudes and procedures of exegetes as they do their detailed work, and so exercises a formative and stabilizing influence on the faith of the church.

In the following pages Norman Geisler, who contributed as much as anyone to ICBI's original legacy, and William Roach interact with evangelical hypotheses that have the effect of confusing that legacy. They are masterly gatekeepers, and I count it an honor to commend this work to the Christian world.

J. I. Packer

Prologue

The doctrine of the total or unlimited inerrancy[1] of Scripture has a venerable history (see John Hannah, *Inerrancy and the Church*). It is rooted in the early fathers of the church, expressed emphatically in Augustine and Aquinas, expressed explicitly by the Reformers, and continued into the nineteenth century without a major challenge within the church (see chap. 1 below). Since the time of Darwin (ca. 1860), however, there has been a constant challenge to it both from without and from within, with major eruptions from time to time.

The first of these came near the beginning of the twentieth century in the Warfield/Briggs debate when Charles A. Briggs, a professor at Union Theological Seminary in New York, denied inerrancy. B. B. Warfield and A. A. Hodge responded strongly with both books and articles. Together they wrote *Inspiration* (1881). Warfield penned essays (1894) now in *The Inspiration and Authority of the Bible* (1948) and in *Limited Inspiration* (1961).

Another major crisis came in the 1960s when a major evangelical institution, Fuller Seminary, took inerrancy from its doctrinal statement, which occasioned the exodus of many of its name teachers. This led one of them, Harold Lindsell, to blow the whistle in his book *The Battle for the Bible*. In the wake of this, nearly three hundred scholars gathered in Chicago in 1978 as the International Council on Biblical Inerrancy (ICBI) and formulated the famous Chicago Statement on Biblical Inerrancy. For the rest of the twentieth century, this detailed statement (see chap. 2 below) became the norm for the vast majority of evangelicalism. It was a strong influence in the major reversal of the Southern Baptist Convention on this issue. During this same period the major scholarly society based on the inerrancy of Scripture, the Evangelical Theological Society (ETS), experienced a rapid growth from a little over one thousand members to over four thousand members to date.

With the dawn of the twenty-first century, however, a major disruption has occurred in the ongoing inerrancy debate. A noted evangelical, Clark Pinnock

(*Scripture Principle*), challenged the traditional view of unlimited inerrancy and defended a view of limited inerrancy, which allows for minor errors in nonredemptive matters (see chap. 4). This led to a vote to expel him from the ETS, which garnered a solid majority of over 63 percent yet fell just short of the two-thirds majority needed to dismiss him from the society.

Meanwhile, many young evangelicals trained in contemporary higher criticism have grown increasingly dissatisfied with the traditional view of unlimited inerrancy that was embraced by Warfield, the ETS founders, and the ICBI. Many of them had joined the ETS since that society made a conscious decision not to challenge the consistency of each member's views with what the ETS framers meant by the statement. Instead, each member was allowed to follow his own conscience to judge whether his views were consistent with the ETS statement "The Bible alone and the Bible in its entirety is the Word of God written, and therefore inerrant in the autographs."

Inevitably, this "open" view on membership has led to two camps within ETS. The vast majority (80 percent) voted (in 2003) to accept the ICBI Chicago Statement as the ETS definition of what is meant by inerrancy, that it means unlimited inerrancy and that the Bible is totally without error in any matter on which it speaks (see Geisler, *Inerrancy*). As the ICBI Short Statement put it, "Holy Scripture, being God's own word, written by men prepared and superintended by his Spirit, is of infallible divine authority in all matters upon which it touches."

The other camp contains those who do not believe in unlimited inerrancy as meant by the ETS and ICBI framers. This came to light in 1976 when the ETS Executive Committee confessed that "some of the members of the Society have expressed the feeling that a measure of intellectual dishonesty prevails among members who do not take the signing of the doctrinal statement seriously." Further, an ETS Ad Hoc Committee recognized this problem when it posed the proper question in 1983: "Is it acceptable for a member of the society to hold a view of [a] biblical author's intent which disagrees with the Founding Fathers and even the majority of the society, and still remain a member in good standing?" The society never said no. And the subsequent vote to retain Pinnock reveals that a large percent of the members do not believe it is necessary to hold to unlimited inerrancy as the ETS and ICBI framers meant it.

Now in the morning of the twenty-first century, evangelicalism is faced with a new challenge to the traditional view of inerrancy as expressed by ETS and ICBI. In fact, some are openly challenging the adequacy and even the correctness of the ICBI statement (see chaps. 4–11). Has the "Erosion of Inerrancy" (see Beale, *Erosion of Inerrancy*) been so strong that it cannot be rehabilitated? This leads us to pose the question for this book: Can this view of total inerrancy be reaffirmed for the twenty-first century? Does the ICBI statement need to be revised or even discarded? Is it possible to be a biblical scholar and still believe in unlimited inerrancy?

Before trying to answer these questions, we need to look at the background of this issue (chaps. 1–3) and examine the charges of those who challenge total inerrancy (chaps. 4–11). Then we can fully discuss the issues involved (chaps. 12–16) and finally respond to the challenge posed by the new evangelical and other scholars of this new era. In brief, our quest is whether we can reaffirm "Inerrancy for the New Generation" (which we answer in chap. 17 and the epilogue).

Sources

Beale, *Erosion of Inerrancy*

Geisler, *Inerrancy*

Hannah, *Inerrancy and the Church*

Hodge, A., and Warfield, *Inspiration*

Lindsell, *Battle for the Bible*

Pinnock, *Scripture Principle*

Warfield, *Inspiration and Authority*

———, *Limited Inspiration*

PART ONE

HISTORY
OF THE INERRANCY
CONTROVERSY

1

Background of the ICBI Chicago Statement on Inerrancy

Introduction

There has always been a battle for the Bible. Church history is plagued with deviant views on the topic. Origen (AD 185–254) denied the historicity of parts of Genesis and allegorized other passages as well. The biblical views of Theodore of Mopsuestia (AD 350–423) were challenged in the Middle Ages and afterward. During the Reformation, Calvin charged Servetus (AD 1511–53) with denying the factual inerrancy of parts of the Bible. Until modern times, however, none of the deviant views on Scripture became mainstream. This was true right up to the late 1800s, when the B. B. Warfield and Charles A. Briggs controversy broke out. Indeed, it was not until the early 1900s that unorthodox views of Scripture became widely accepted in mainline churches.

The Great Teachers of the Church

As has been demonstrated elsewhere (see Hannah, *Inerrancy and the Church,* 1984; Geisler, *Systematic Theology,* vol. 1; Woodbridge, *Biblical Authority,* 1982), *total* inerrancy has been the standard orthodox view throughout the history of the Christian church. This is true from the earliest times. The view of *limited* inerrancy (that only spiritual or redemptive matters are without error) is a late view in church history, arising as a result of accommodating the doctrine of inerrancy to modern science and biblical criticism (see below).

The Early Church Fathers

Justin Martyr (d. 165) spoke of the Gospels as the "Voice of God" (*Apology* 65). He stated, "We must not suppose that the language proceeds from men who were inspired, but from the Divine Word which moves them" (1.36). Irenaeus (d. 202) added that the Bible is "above all falsehood" (*Against Heresies* 3.5.1) and we are "most properly assured that the Scriptures are indeed perfect, since they are spoken by the Word of God and His Spirit" (2.28.2; 2:35).

Medieval Church Fathers

Summing up the early church, Augustine of Hippo declares: "I have learned to yield respect and honour only to the canonical books of Scripture: of these alone do I most firmly believe that the authors were completely free from error" (*Letters* 82.3). So "if we are perplexed by any apparent contradiction in Scripture, it is not allowable to say, the author of this book is mistaken: but either the manuscript is faulty, or the translation is wrong, or you have misunderstood" (*Reply to Faustus* 11.5).

Likewise, in the later Middle Ages Thomas Aquinas insisted that "it is heretical to say that any falsehood whatsoever is contained either in the gospels or in any canonical Scripture" (*Exposition on Job* 13, Lect. 1). For "A true prophet is always inspired by the spirit of truth in whom there is no trace of falsehood, and he never utters untruths" (*Summa* 2a2ae, 172, 6 ad 2).

The Reformation Period

The great reformer Martin Luther affirms that "the Scriptures, although written by men, are neither of men nor from men but from God" (*Luther's Works* 35:153). So "God's Word is God's Word.... When one blasphemously gives the lie to God in a single word, or says it is a minor matter, ... one blasphemes the entire God and makes light of all blasphemy" (37:26). Indeed, "whoever is so bold that he ventures to accuse God of fraud and deception in a single word ... likewise certainly ventures to accuse God of fraud and deception in all His words. Therefore it is true, absolutely and without exception, that everything is believed or nothing is believed" (Reu, *Luther and the Scriptures*, 33).

Likewise, John Calvin agrees, insisting that "the Bible has come down to us from the mouth of God" (*Institutes* 1.18.4). Thus "we owe to Scripture the same reverence which we owe to God; because it has proceeded from Him alone.... The Law and the Prophets are ... dictated by the Holy Spirit" (Urquhart, *Inspiration and Accuracy*, 129–30). Scripture is "the certain and unerring rule" (*Calvin's Commentaries*, Ps. 5:11).

> For when we reflect how prone the human mind is to lapse into forgetfulness of God, how readily inclined to every kind of error, ... it will be easy to understand how necessary it was to make such a depository of doctrine as would secure it from either perishing by the neglect, vanishing away amid the errors, or being corrupted by the presumptuous audacity of men. (*Institutes* 1.6.3)

Nor is it sufficient to believe that God is true, and cannot lie or deceive, unless you feel firmly persuaded that every word which proceeds from him is sacred, inviolable truth. (3.2.6)

The Post-Reformation Period

The same is true of the post-Reformation creeds. The Lutheran Book of Concord (1580) adds, "Therefore, as a whole and in all its details the Word of God [is] without contradiction and error." Indeed, H. D. McDonald has demonstrated (in *Theories of Revelation*) that the standard orthodox view of Scripture dominated Christendom up to the post-Darwinian end of the nineteenth century. It was then that the battle broke out in America.

The American battle was initiated by the Warfield/Briggs debate when Charles A. Briggs, a professor at Union Seminary in New York, denied inerrancy. B. B. Warfield and A. A. Hodge responded strongly with both books and articles. A. A. Hodge and B. B. Warfield wrote *Inspiration* (1881). Warfield penned "The Inspiration of the Bible" (1894) and "Smith on Inspiration" (1894), reprinted as *Limited Inspiration* (1961). Their views formed what has come to be known as the Old Princeton view, summed up in the following citations: "The New Testament continually asserts of the Scriptures of the Old Testament, and of the several books which constitute it, that they are the Word of God. What their writers said, God said" (*Inspiration*, 29). Thus "every element of Scripture, whether doctrine or history, of which God has guaranteed the infallibility, must be infallible in its verbal expression" (21–23). This is true because "throughout the whole of his work the Holy Spirit was present . . . everywhere securing the errorless expression in language and thought designed by God" (16).

Harold Ockenga summarizes this period well in his foreword to Harold Lindsell's bombshell book *The Battle for the Bible* (1976). Inerrancy dominated the fundamentalist-modernist controversy in the 1920s and 1930s. It was centered in the Presbyterian Church in the USA over the Auburn affirmation and was expressed in some withdrawing from Princeton Theological Seminary in 1929. That year a group of students followed J. Gresham Machen, Robert Dick Wilson, Oswald T. Allis, Cornelius Van Til, and Ned Stonehouse in forming Westminster Theological Seminary. By 1942 effects of denying the inerrancy of Scripture in the Protestant denominations organized under the Federal Council of Churches prompted the founding of the National Association of Evangelicals in St. Louis on the basis of inerrancy. During the summers of 1944 and 1945, Ockenga convened a group of evangelical scholars in Manomet Point, Massachusetts, to encourage evangelical writing based upon inerrant Scripture, and not dependent upon literature from a previous generation.

The Wenham Inerrancy Conference

As a result of the conferences of the World Evangelical Fellowship, it became evident that there were two views of Scripture held by evangelicals. To discuss the issue, Ockenga convened a conference at Gordon College in June 1966, which was attended by more than fifty men from various parts of the world. No unanimity emerged. The two opposing views of inerrantist and noninerrantist remained. In 1955, at the suggestion of Billy Graham, a group gathered first at Bass Rock, Massachusetts, and then in New York City to discuss the formation of *Christianity Today*, to be based on the inerrancy of Scripture.

However, the rift over inerrancy remained simmering on the back burner. Two important factors gave impetus to the limited inerrancy movement (that inerrancy was limited to only redemptive matters). First, neoevangelicalism arose originally from a sermon by Ockenga in 1948 at the Civic Auditorium in Pasadena. It was a call to repudiate separationism and involve evangelicals in social action while retaining a commitment to fundamental doctrines like inerrancy. It was not initially designed as a movement, but the name caught on as it was used by Edward Carnell and Harold Lindsell, and also by Carl Henry (who had already written *The Uneasy Conscience of Modern Fundamentalism*, 1947); Gleason Archer also began to support it. Soon after this, younger evangelicals started to join the movement, and the doctrinal emphasis was downplayed until inerrancy was no longer a characteristic of the group. The next significant move away from inerrancy was the action that occurred during the 1960s when Fuller Seminary faculty removed inerrancy from their doctrinal statement.

Fuller Seminary and the Battle for the Bible

According to Harold Lindsell (*Battle for the Bible*, chap. 6), in 1947 Charles Fuller invited Ockenga to join him in founding a School of Missions and Evangelism. "Biblical inerrancy" was part of the doctrinal statement. Harold Lindsell was the first dean and with Wilbur Smith, Everett F. Harrison, and Carl Henry formed the first faculty. The doctrinal statement of Scripture read: "The books which form the canon of the Old and New Testaments as originally given are plenarily inspired and free from all error in the whole and in the part. These books constitute the written Word of God, the only infallible rule of faith and practice." Such a statement meant that the Bible is free from errors in matters of fact, science, history, and chronology, as well as in matters having to do with salvation.

Within the ensuing years, doubts began to arise on the Fuller board and faculty about the inerrancy of Scripture. First, Fuller staff member Bela Vassady said his honesty kept him from signing the inerrancy part of the doctrinal statement, and he voluntarily left the school. By 1962 it became apparent that others at Fuller no longer believed in inerrancy. One wealthy and influential board member, C. David Weyerhaeuser, came to the conviction that the Bible was not inerrant. Two other faculty members came to the same conclusion, but neither was asked to leave the school. The founder's son, Daniel Fuller (after studying under Karl Barth in Basel), soon followed suit. Calvin Schoonhoven admitted that he did not believe in inerrancy when he was hired. Finally, David Hubbard was hired as president in spite of the fact that the syllabus on the Old Testament he had coauthored with

Robert Laurin stated that Adam was not historical, Moses had not written the whole Pentateuch, and Daniel was written after the great world kingdom events that are recorded as prophecies in his book (though Hubbard maintained that his own views were orthodox).

In December 1962, "Black Saturday" occurred at a faculty-trustee meeting in Pasadena. Here a number of faculty and board members expressed that they did not believe in the inerrancy of Scripture. Edward Johnson declared his belief that inerrancy was a "benchmark" belief and resigned because the board failed to take its stand on inerrancy (which was still in the doctrinal statement from its beginning).

The 1963–64 seminary catalogs still retained the usual statement that faculty members must have "concurrence" to the doctrinal statement including inerrancy "without mental reservation, and any who cannot assent agrees to withdraw from the institution." In the 1965–66 catalog this statement disappeared. So the school continued under the dark cloud of faculty and staff who signed the doctrinal statement with mental reservations. As time went by, faculty began to resign. First, Charles Woodbridge resigned (even before Black Saturday). Wilbur Smith was next to resign by spring of 1963. Harold Lindsell left in 1964, and Gleason Archer departed a couple years later.

In 1967 at the ETS meeting in Toronto, Daniel Fuller presented a paper in which he denied the factual inerrancy of the Bible, claiming that the Scriptures were only inspired and inerrant on revelational matters, not on nonrevelational matters such as science. This was followed by George Ladd's book *The New Testament and Criticism* (1967), in which he denies the factual inerrancy of Scripture. As the next decade rolled by, the influence of Fuller Seminary and its decision to scrap inerrancy became more pervasive. The full story is told in George Marsden's work *Reforming Fundamentalism: Fuller Seminary and the New Evangelicalism* (1987).

Even before the battle for the Bible began, which led up to the ICBI summit on inerrancy (1978), the Lausanne Covenant was formed by evangelists and missionaries in 1974. Its statement on Scripture reads in part as follows: "2. The Authority and Power of the Bible: We affirm the divine inspiration, truthfulness and authority of both Old and New Testament Scriptures in their entirety as the only written word of God, without error in all that it affirms, and the only infallible rule of faith and practice . . . (2 Tim. 3:16; 2 Pet. 1:21; John 10:35; Isa. 55:11; 1 Cor. 1:21; Rom. 1:16; Matt. 5:17, 18; Jude 3; Eph. 1:17, 18; 3:10, 18)."

This statement served as an indicator of evangelical unity on inerrancy even before the Chicago Summit. It clearly affirmed both the infallibility and inerrancy of Scripture when it declares: "We affirm *the divine inspiration, truthfulness and authority* of both Old and New Testament Scriptures *in their entirety* as the only written word of God, *without error in all that it affirms.*"

The Battle for the Bible Begins

In 1976 Harold Lindsell's book *The Battle for the Bible* blew the lid off the Fuller situation and labeled inerrancy a "watershed" issue. Foreseeing the problem for the broader evangelical church, in 1975 Francis Schaeffer wrote *No Final Conflict*, in which he says, "It is my conviction that the crucial area of discussion for evangelicalism in the next few years will be the Scripture. At stake is whether evangelicalism will remain evangelical." He met privately with a few of the ICBI leaders in Chicago and there pledged his support for the inerrancy movement, which he fulfilled later by signing the Chicago Statement on Biblical Inerrancy (1978), though he expressed his preference for the term "without error."

The anti-inerrancy movement became more aggressive by 1977 with the publication of the book *Biblical Authority* by Fuller Professor Jack Rogers. Gradually the inerrantists realized the need to respond. The first effort to produce a response to Rogers was the book *The Foundation of Biblical Authority* (1978), edited by James M. Boice. Meanwhile, plans were moving forward toward the inerrancy conference in Chicago in 1978.

The Origin of the International Council on Biblical Inerrancy (ICBI)

According to the official *ICBI Update* (December 1987), ICBI was birthed as follows: "In February 1977 God laid upon the hearts of a small band of His people a tremendous burden—the erosion of the authority and accuracy of Scripture. Having observed the preaching in many churches, the teaching in some seminaries and much of the popular Christian literature, there was great concern that many evangelicals were turning away from the Bible as the final authority in matters of Christian doctrine and living." Thus "the initial corps who gathered for prayer, discussion and planning were: Greg Bahnsen, John Gerstner, Norman Geisler, Jay Grimstead, Karen Hoyt, A. Wetherell Johnson, James Packer and R. C. Sproul. From this corps developed the formation of the ICBI Council and Advisory Board" (*ICBI Update*, 3). All agreed that something needed to be done to support the traditional, historic view on inerrancy. Plans were laid for the big 1978 summit in Chicago, which would produce the Chicago Statement on Biblical Inerrancy (see chap. 2).

Shortly after the ICBI summit, Jack Rogers and Roger McKim published a massive, historical 484-page defense of the noninerrancy or limited inerrancy view called *The Authority and Interpretation of the Bible* (1979). Then ICBI responded by producing and inspiring a raft of books defining and defending inerrancy—biblically, theologically, historically, philosophically, and hermeneutically. In order of publication, this included *Inerrancy* (Geisler, 1979); *Biblical Errancy: Its Philosophical Roots* (ed. Geisler, 1981); *Inerrancy and the Church* (ed. Hannah, 1984); *Hermeneutics, Inerrancy, and the Bible* (ed. Radmacher and Preus, 1984); *Applying the Scriptures* (ed. Kantzer, 1987). Another very important book, not under ICBI sponsorship, was the masterful refutation of Rogers's book by Trinity Evangelical Divinity School professor John Woodbridge, *Biblical Authority: A Critique of the Rogers/McKim Proposal* (1982). So thorough and incisive was this critique that Rogers chose not to respond to it. Also worthy of mention is H. D. McDonald on *Theories of Revelation* (1979) and *Inerrancy and Common Sense*, edited by Roger Nicole and J. Ramsey Michaels (1980). Since the ICBI movement helped spawn the Southern Baptist inerrancy resurgence, the book by the late Russ Bush and Tom Nettles, *Baptists and the Bible* (1980), should be noted as well. Another influential non-ICBI book was *God's Inerrant Word* (1974), edited by John Warwick Montgomery.

Summary and Conclusion

The inerrancy issue broke on the American scene in the late 1800s with the works of A. A. Hodge and B. B. Warfield. It continued in the fundamentalist-modernist controversy (of the 1920s and 1930s), but never became a dominant issue within evangelicalism until Fuller Seminary broke rank in the 1960s. The events leading to calling for the ICBI inerrancy movement began with the failure of the Wenham Conference to reach a consensus on the topic in 1966. It was given impetus by the Fuller Seminary decision to eliminate the requirement to hold to inerrancy, deleting it from the seminary's doctrinal statement during the same period. But the bombshell dropped with the publication of *The Battle for the Bible* (1976), when Harold Lindsell blew the lid off the Fuller situation. By this time the influence of Fuller on the broader evangelical community, along with the growing neoevangelical tendency away from inerrancy, made the situation ripe for an evangelical reaction to the drift away from this historic doctrine. In the atmosphere of Lindsell's warning and Francis Schaeffer's exhortation that this was a watershed issue that could change the very nature of evangelicalism, the International Council on Biblical Inerrancy was born.

In its ten-year plan (1977–1987), ICBI produced three summits and numerous books in defense of the doctrine of inerrancy. The first summit was on defining inerrancy (1978), the second on interpreting inerrancy (1984), and the last on applying inerrancy (1987).

In the wake of the ICBI effort, numerous denominations and schools were strengthened in their stand on Scripture, many adding inerrancy to their doctrinal position. One of the largest Protestant denominations—the Southern Baptist Convention—reversed their liberal direction and adopted the ICBI statement. Others joined the bandwagon, and the Chicago Summit's declaration and definition of inerrancy became the standard evangelical position again. It has remained that way for almost a generation now.

However, a new generation has arisen that knows not Lindsell, Henry, Archer, Schaeffer, Gerstner, Nicole, or Boice—all of whom have passed on to their reward—and once again inerrancy is being challenged. Part 2 of this book addresses the response to unlimited inerrancy by men like Clark Pinnock (chap. 4), Bart Erhman (chap. 5), Peter Enns (chap. 6), Kenton Sparks (chap. 7), Kevin Vanhoozer (chap. 8), Andrew McGowan (chap. 9), Stanley Grenz and Brian McLaren (chap. 10), and Darrell Bock and Robert Webb (chap. 11).

So now we face crucial questions: Can inerrancy be reaffirmed for this new generation? Or will it go the way of all flesh? More precisely, has the ICBI Chicago

Statement and commentaries on inerrancy become outdated? Does it need to be revised or discarded? Can it withstand the current attacks? As a founder and framer (Norman Geisler) of the ICBI position and as a young scholar of this new generation (Bill Roach), we wish to face this challenge head-on (chaps. 12–17) and respond to these questions. The readers will have to decide whether or not our efforts are successful.

Sources

Augustine, *Reply to Faustus*

Boice, *Foundation for Biblical Authority*

Bush and Nettles, *Baptists and the Bible*

Calvin, *Institutes*

———, *Commentaries*

Geisler, *Biblical Errancy*

———, ed., *Inerrancy*

———, *Systematic Theology*, vol. 1

Hannah, *Inerrancy and the Church*

Henry, *Uneasy Conscience*

Hodge, A., and Warfield, *Inspiration*

Irenaeus, *Against Heresies*

Justin Martyr, *Apology*

Kantzer, ed., *Applying the Scriptures*

Ladd, *New Testament and Criticism*

Lindsell, *Battle for the Bible*

Luther, *Luther's Works*

Marsden, *Reforming Fundamentalism*

McDonald, *Theories of Revelation*

Radmacher and Preus, eds., *Hermeneutics, Inerrancy*

Reu, *Luther and the Scriptures*

Rogers, *Biblical Authority*

Rogers and McKim, *Authority and Interpretation*

Schaeffer, *No Final Conflict*

Thomas Aquinas, *Exposition on Job*

———, *Summa*

Warfield, *Inspiration and Authority*

———, *Limited Inspiration*

Woodbridge, *Biblical Authority*

2

Formation of the ICBI Chicago Statement on Inerrancy

During October 26–28, 1978, the International Council on Biblical Inerrancy (ICBI) held a summit near O'Hare airport. The result was the famous Chicago Statement on Biblical Inerrancy. These nineteen articles, along with the Preamble and Short Statement and an official commentary, *Explaining Inerrancy* by R. C. Sproul, were produced. Over the next ten years, two other major conferences were held, one on hermeneutics and inerrancy (1984), and one on applying inerrancy to the issues of our day (1987). During this same time several scholarly volumes were produced under the auspices of ICBI, defending inerrancy. These include *Inerrancy* (ed. Geisler); *Hermeneutics, Inerrancy, and the Bible* (ed. Radmacher and Preus); *Biblical Errancy: Its Philosophical Roots* (ed. Geisler); and *The Church and Inerrancy* (ed. Hannah).

The Chicago Statement was produced by the summit scholars based on an initial draft by R. C. Sproul. It was later revised to its final form in light of the comments by the attendees and put in form by the Draft Committee composed of Edmund Clowney, Norman Geisler, Harold Hoehner, Donald Hoke, Roger Nicole, James Packer, Earl Radmacher, and R. C. Sproul. After considerable discussion, the final draft was presented to the participants and overwhelmingly approved by 240 of the 268 delegates (see appendix 1). Signers included noted evangelical leaders of the last part of the twentieth century, including James Boice, John Gerstner, Carl F. H. Henry, Kenneth Kantzer, Harold Lindsell, John Warwick Montgomery, Robert Preus, Francis Schaeffer, R. C. Sproul, John Wenham, Charles Colson, and numerous others. An official commentary on these articles was written by R. C. Sproul (*Explaining Inerrancy*), and a book covering the major addresses was published (*Inerrancy*, ed. Geisler), as were other books covering the history of inerrancy (*Inerrancy and the Church*, ed. Hannah) and philosophical presuppositions of the anti-inerrancy view (*Biblical Errancy: Its Philosophical Roots*, ed. Geisler).

For clarity, this Chicago Statement was formulated with both affirmations and denials. After the Drafting Committee agreed on the content, J. I. Packer was most helpful in putting it into succinct statements. The following is the Preamble, a Short Statement, and the nineteen articles:[1]

PREAMBLE

The authority of Scripture is a key issue for the Christian church in this and every age. Those who profess faith in Jesus Christ as Lord and Savior are called to show the reality of their discipleship by humbly and faithfully obeying God's written Word. To stray from Scripture in faith or conduct is disloyalty to our Master. Recognition of the total truth and trustworthiness of Holy Scripture is essential to a full grasp and adequate confession of its authority.

The following statement affirms this inerrancy of Scripture afresh, making clear our understanding of it and warning against its denial. We are persuaded that to deny it is to set aside the witness of Jesus Christ and of the Holy Spirit and to refuse that submission to the claims of God's own Word which marks true Christian faith. We see it as our timely duty to make this affirmation in the face of current lapses from the truth of inerrancy among our fellow Christians and misunderstanding of this doctrine in the world at large.

This statement consists of three parts: a summary statement, articles of affirmation and denial, and an accompanying exposition. It has been prepared in the course of a three-day consultation in Chicago. Those who have signed the summary statement and the articles wish to affirm their own conviction as to the inerrancy of Scripture and to encourage and challenge one another and all Christians to growing appreciation and understanding of this doctrine. We acknowledge the limitations of a document prepared in a brief, intensive conference and do not propose that this statement be given creedal weight. Yet we rejoice in the deepening of our own convictions through our discussions together, and we pray that the statement we have signed may be used to the glory of our God toward a new reformation of the church in its faith, life and mission.

We offer this statement in a spirit, not of contention, but of humility and love, which we purpose by God's grace to maintain in any future dialogue arising out of what we have said. We gladly acknowledge that many who deny the inerrancy of Scripture do not display the consequences of this denial in the rest of their belief and behavior, and we are conscious that we who confess this doctrine often deny it in life by failing to bring our thoughts and deeds, our traditions and habits, into true subjection to the divine Word.

We invite response to this statement from any who see reason to amend its affirmations about Scripture by the light of Scripture itself, under whose infallible authority we stand as we speak. We claim no personal infallibility for the witness we bear, and for any help which enables us to strengthen this testimony to God's Word we shall be grateful.

A SHORT STATEMENT

1. God, who is Himself truth and speaks truth only, has inspired Holy Scripture in order thereby to reveal Himself to lost mankind through Jesus Christ as Creator and Lord, Redeemer and Judge. Holy Scripture is God's witness to Himself.

2. Holy Scripture, being God's own Word, written by men prepared and super-intended by His Spirit, is of infallible divine authority in all matters upon which it touches: it is to be believed, as God's instruction, in all that it affirms; obeyed, as God's command, in all that it requires; embraced, as God's pledge, in all that it promises.

3. The Holy Spirit, Scripture's divine author, both authenticates it to us by His inward witness and opens our minds to understand its meaning.

4. Being wholly and verbally God-given, Scripture is without error or fault in all its teaching, no less in what it states about God's acts in creation, about the events of world history, and about its own literary origins under God, than in its witness to God's saving grace in individual lives.

5. The authority of Scripture is inescapably impaired if this total divine inerrancy is in any way limited or disregarded, or made relative to a view of truth contrary to the Bible's own; and such lapses bring serious loss to both the individual and the Church.

THE CHICAGO STATEMENT ON BIBLICAL INERRANCY (1978)
ARTICLES OF AFFIRMATION AND DENIAL

Article 1

We affirm that the Holy Scriptures are to be received as the authoritative Word of God.

We deny that the Scriptures receive their authority from the Church, tradition, or any other human source.

Article 2

We affirm that the Scriptures are the supreme written norm by which God binds the conscience, and that the authority of the Church is subordinate to that of Scripture.

We deny that Church creeds, councils, or declarations have authority greater than or equal to the authority of the Bible.

Article 3

We affirm that the written Word in its entirety is revelation given by God.

We deny that the Bible is merely a witness to revelation, or only becomes revelation in encounter, or depends on the responses of men for its validity.

Article 4

We affirm that God who made mankind in His image has used language as a means of revelation.

We deny that human language is so limited by our creatureliness that it is rendered inadequate as a vehicle for divine revelation. We further deny that the corruption of human culture and language through sin has thwarted God's work of inspiration.

Article 5

We affirm that God's revelation in the Holy Scriptures was progressive.

We deny that later revelation, which may fulfill earlier revelation, ever corrects or contradicts it. We further deny that any normative revelation has been given since the completion of the New Testament writings.

Article 6

We affirm that the whole of Scripture and all its parts, down to the very words of the original, were given by divine inspiration.

We deny that the inspiration of Scripture can rightly be affirmed of the whole without the parts, or of some parts but not the whole.

Article 7

We affirm that inspiration was the work in which God by His Spirit, through human writers, gave us His Word. The origin of Scripture is divine. The mode of divine inspiration remains largely a mystery to us.

We deny that inspiration can be reduced to human insight, or to heightened states of consciousness of any kind.

Article 8

We affirm that God in His Work of inspiration utilized the distinctive personalities and literary styles of the writers whom He had chosen and prepared.

We deny that God, in causing these writers to use the very words that He chose, overrode their personalities.

Article 9

We affirm that inspiration, though not conferring omniscience, guaranteed true and trustworthy utterance on all matters of which the Biblical authors were moved to speak and write.

We deny that the finitude or fallenness of these writers, by necessity or otherwise, introduced distortion or falsehood into God's Word.

Article 10

We affirm that inspiration, strictly speaking, applies only to the autographic text of Scripture, which in the providence of God can be ascertained from available manuscripts with great accuracy. We further affirm that copies and translations of Scripture are the Word of God to the extent that they faithfully represent the original.

We deny that any essential element of the Christian faith is affected by the absence of the autographs. We further deny that this absence renders the assertions of Biblical inerrancy invalid or irrelevant.

Article 11

We affirm that Scripture, having been given by divine inspiration, is infallible, so that, far from misleading us, it is true and reliable in all the matters it addresses.

We deny that it is possible for the Bible to be at the same time infallible and errant in its assertions. Infallibility and inerrancy may be distinguished, but not separated.

Article 12

We affirm that Scripture in its entirety is inerrant, being free from all falsehood, fraud, or deceit.

We deny that Biblical infallibility and inerrancy are limited to spiritual, religious, or redemptive themes, exclusive of assertions in the fields of history and science. We further deny that scientific hypotheses about earth history may properly be used to overturn the teaching of Scripture on creation and the flood.

Article 13

We affirm the propriety of using inerrancy as a theological term with reference to the complete truthfulness of Scripture.

We deny that it is proper to evaluate Scripture according to standards of truth and error that are alien to its usage or purpose. We further deny that inerrancy is negated by Biblical phenomena such as a lack of modern technical precision, irregularities of grammar or spelling, observational descriptions of nature, the reporting of falsehoods, the use of hyperbole and round numbers, the topical arrangement of material, variant selections of material in parallel accounts, or the use of free citations.

Article 14

We affirm the unity and internal consistency of Scripture.

We deny that alleged errors and discrepancies that have not yet been resolved vitiate the truth claims of the Bible.

Article 15

We affirm that the doctrine of inerrancy is grounded in the teaching of the Bible about inspiration.

We deny that Jesus' teaching about Scripture may be dismissed by appeals to accommodation or to any natural limitation of His humanity.

Article 16

We affirm that the doctrine of inerrancy has been integral to the Church's faith throughout its history.

We deny that inerrancy is a doctrine invented by Scholastic Protestantism, or is a reactionary position postulated in response to negative higher criticism.

Article 17

We affirm that the Holy Spirit bears witness to the Scriptures, assuring believers of the truthfulness of God's written Word.

We deny that this witness of the Holy Spirit operates in isolation from or against Scripture.

Article 18

We affirm that the text of Scripture is to be interpreted by grammatico-historical exegesis, taking account of its literary forms and devices, and that Scripture is to interpret Scripture.

We deny the legitimacy of any treatment of the text or quest for sources lying behind it that leads to relativizing, dehistoricizing, or discounting its teaching, or rejecting its claims to authorship.

Article 19

We affirm that a confession of the full authority, infallibility, and inerrancy of Scripture is vital to a sound understanding of the whole of the Christian faith.

We further affirm that such confession should lead to increasing conformity to the image of Christ.

We deny that such confession is necessary for salvation. However, we further deny that inerrancy can be rejected without grave consequences, both to the individual and to the Church.

The Official ICBI Commentary on the Chicago Statement

Foreseeing possible disputes on what the ICBI inerrancy statement meant, the ICBI wrote a commentary on its Chicago Statement, *Explaining Inerrancy*. It was prepared by R. C. Sproul, and the full text is available through Ligonier Ministries, Orlando, Florida. Unfortunately, it has been largely overlooked in subsequent discussion on inerrancy, particularly on disputed areas of discussion on inerrancy.

The following are important excerpts from the official ICBI commentary on the Chicago Statement on Biblical Inerrancy (1978). They speak to controversial areas of the Chicago Statement by some who have misinterpreted it to accommodate their own deviant views. For example, Clark Pinnock says, "I supported the 1978 Chicago Statement of the International Council on Biblical Inerrancy," noting that article 13 "made room for nearly every well-intentioned Baptist" (*Scripture Principle*[2], 266). But this is clearly contrary to what the ICBI framers meant by inerrancy, as is revealed in its official commentary on that article cited below:

ICBI Commentary on Article 12

It has been fashionable in certain quarters to maintain that the Bible is not normal history, but redemptive history with an accent on redemption. Theories have been established that would limit inspiration to the redemptive theme of redemptive history, allowing the historical dimension of redemptive history to be errant. (Sproul, *Explaining Inerrancy*, 36)

Though the Bible is indeed *redemptive* history, it is also redemptive *history*, and this means that the acts of salvation wrought by God actually occurred in the space-time world. (37)

The denial [in art. 12] explicitly rejects the tendency of some to limit infallibility and inerrancy to specific segments of the biblical message. (36)

ICBI Commentary on Article 13

When we say that the truthfulness of Scripture ought to be evaluated according to its own standards, that means that . . . all the claims of the Bible must correspond with reality, whether that reality is historical, factual or spiritual. (41)

"By biblical standards of truth and error" is meant the view used both in the Bible and in everyday life, viz., a correspondence view of truth. This part of the article is directed toward those who would redefine truth to relate merely to redemptive intent, the purely personal, or the like, rather than to mean that which corresponds with reality. (43–44)

ICBI Commentary on Article 18

When the quest for sources produces a dehistoricizing of the Bible, a rejection of its teaching or a rejection of the Bible's own claims of authorship, [then] it has trespassed beyond its proper limits. . . . It is never legitimate, however, to run counter to express biblical affirmations. (55)

"By biblical standards of truth and error" is meant the view used both in the Bible and in everyday life, viz., a correspondence view of truth. This part of the article is directed toward those [like Pinnock] who would redefine truth to relate merely to redemptive intent, the purely personal, or the like, rather than to mean that which corresponds with reality. (43–44)

Thus, what Scripture says, God says; its authority is His authority, for He is the ultimate author. (Packer, "Exposition," 69)

ICBI Commentary on Hermeneutics

Also, an official commentary on the ICBI Hermeneutics Statement (1982) was composed: Geisler, "Explaining Hermeneutics" (EH). The following are some relevant excerpts from it:

EH on Article 6: "We further affirm that a statement is true if it represents matters as they actually are, but is an error if it misrepresents the facts." The commentary on this adds, "The denial makes it evident that views which redefine error to mean what 'misleads,' rather than what is a mistake, must be rejected."

EH on Article 13: "We deny that generic categories which negate historicity may rightly be imposed on biblical narratives which present themselves as factual." Some, for instance, take Adam to be a myth, whereas in Scripture he is presented as a real person. Others take Jonah to be an allegory when he is presented as a historical person and [is] so referred to by Christ.

EH on Article 14: "We deny that any event, discourse or saying reported in Scripture was invented by the biblical writers or by the traditions they incorporated."

EH on Article 22: It "affirms that Genesis 1–11 is factual, as is the rest of the book." And, "The denial makes it evident that views which redefine error to mean what 'misleads,' rather than what is a mistake, must be rejected" (892).

Thus, what Scripture says, God says; its authority is His authority, for He is the ultimate author. (Packer, "Exposition," 69)

Influence of ICBI Statements on Other Scholarly Societies

After a long debate on the meaning of inerrancy in the Clark Pinnock case (2003), the largest group of evangelical scholars in the United States (the Evangelical Theological Society) adopted the ICBI statement as their definition of inerrancy (in 2003). This they believed would help them in future disputes over the meaning of its brief statement on inerrancy: "The Bible alone and the Bible in its entirety is the Word of God written, and therefore inerrant in the autographs."

Another scholarly group, ISCA—the International Society of Christian Apologetics (www.isca-apologetics.org)—has adopted the ICBI statement as its official interpretation of their doctrinal statement on inerrancy. And since some have injected their own meaning into the ICBI statement in order to claim agreement with it, ISCA added: "This doctrine is understood as the one expressed by the Framers of the International Council on Biblical Inerrancy in its 'Chicago Statement' and as interpreted by the official ICBI Commentary on it" (Sproul, *Explaining Inerrancy*).

Conclusion

We have just listed the primary sources on the ICBI inerrancy position. The two main statements are (1) the Chicago Statement on Biblical Inerrancy (1978) and (2) the Chicago Statement on Hermeneutics (1984). Two official commentaries on these statements are called, respectively, (3) *Explaining Inerrancy*, by R. C. Sproul, of which selections are included above; and (4) "Explaining Hermeneutics," by N. L. Geisler, which is appendix B in (5) *Hermeneutics, Inerrancy, and the Bible*, edited by Radmacher and Preus. This is the ICBI book with the conference papers on defining hermeneutics (1984). The other book, (6) *Inerrancy*, is on defining inerrancy (1978), includes papers from the first ICBI conference, and was edited by N. L. Geisler. These six works are the primary sources for ICBI's official understanding of inerrancy.

A careful reading of the first four pieces of literature listed above, as will be seen from their use in this book, is crucial to understanding the official ICBI understanding of what they meant by "inerrancy." Throughout this book this position will be referred to variously as the "historic," "classical," or "orthodox" view of inerrancy. It is also sometimes called "full," "factual," or "unlimited" inerrancy as opposed to "limited inerrancy," "inerrancy of purpose," "inerrancy of intent," or "inerrancy of redemptive statements only."

Sources

Geisler, ed., *Biblical Errancy*

————, "Explaining Hermeneutics"

————, ed., *Inerrancy*

Hannah, *Church and Inerrancy*

Packer, "Exposition"

Pinnock, *Scripture Principle*, 2nd ed.

Radmacher and Preus, eds., *Hermeneutics, Inerrancy*

Sproul, *Explaining Inerrancy*

3

Influence of the ICBI Chicago Statement on Inerrancy

Introduction

The influence of the ICBI stand on inerrancy has been extensive. Foremost among these influences is that it helped reverse decades of the drift from inerrancy in one of the largest Protestant denominations in the United States—the Southern Baptist Convention. Other crucial schools and denominations that were drifting in the wrong direction were also influenced to change course. This included Bethel Seminary in Minneapolis, Gordon Conwell Seminary, Wheaton College, and a number of smaller groups. With the exception of Fuller Seminary (which by this time had hardened its limited inerrancy view), the ICBI inerrancy has become the banner view of evangelicalism. Even the Evangelical Theological Society, the largest group of evangelical scholars in the country, adopted the ICBI Chicago Statement on inerrancy in 2003. So influential was the ICBI movement that, one may safely say, it made inerrancy the standard view of American evangelicals.

The Influence of ICBI

Space does not permit elaborating in full the many groups and movements influenced by the ICBI. Two movements call for further comment because of their size and influence. The first is the Southern Baptist Convention.

The ICBI Influence on Southern Baptists

What happened in the Southern Baptist Convention (SBC) is, so far as we know, unprecedented in history. Certainly it is unprecedented in American history. Never before has a major denomination reversed course in its doctrinal decline toward liberalism. Water simply does not flow back up after the water falls. However, as a result of the success of the Chicago Summit on inerrancy, this is exactly what did happen both theologically and denominationally in the SBC.

The Beginnings

Although a small group of SBC leaders had gathered earlier in an Atlanta hotel to discuss the issue, a major thrust of the inerrancy movement began in a small room in a hotel near O'Hare airport in Chicago. A small group of influential Southern Baptist leaders, inspired by the success of the ICBI conference on inerrancy, huddled together to strategize on how they could regain control of their seminaries, which had for decades been drifting away from inerrancy toward a more neo-Barthian view of the Scripture. The group included Paige Patterson, Judge Pressler, and W. A. Criswell. More than any other single person, Patterson deserves the credit for courageous leadership in putting this plan into operation.

The Game Plan

The SBC came up with a game plan to win back their seminaries and denomination from its drift away from this fundamental pillar of the Christian faith. It was not easy, and the road was long, but the result has proved the wisdom of their plan. The plan included recruiting delegates from the churches to vote for inerrancy-believing presidents who were prominent pastors in the SBC (including Adrian Rogers, Charles Stanley, Jimmy Draper, Bailey Smith, and Ed Young). Once these men were elected presidents by a vote of the delegates, they in turn appointed persons to crucial positions in the denomination, who in turn appointed board members in the seminaries. Once they had a majority on the boards, they could hire inerrantist presidents and deans, who were then able to hire inerrantist faculty and turn the schools around. This has since occurred at every major SBC seminary, including Southern, Southwestern, Southeastern, New Orleans, Golden Gate, and Midwestern. Liberty Baptist Seminary was already an inerrancy seminary when they later joined the fold, as was Luther Rice.

Within a few decades the inerrantists were able to control their seminaries again and build a foundation on inerrant Scripture. Today every major SBC seminary is committed to inerrancy. They have presidents and deans who are inerrantist. Their faculty are inerrantists, and their boards are governed by inerrantists. The result is that the top SBC seminaries now have more students than all the major liberal seminaries in the country combined! This indeed is one of the greatest doctrinal turnarounds in history. And a major impetus for it was provided at the Hyatt

Regency O'Hare in Chicago, inspired by the International Council on Biblical Inerrancy, which produced the Chicago Statement (see chap. 2 above). Given the thousands of graduates from these schools and the firm basis formed by inerrancy, there is no telling how enduring the legacy in souls, churches, and missions will result from this before our Lord returns.

In fact, the success of the ICBI movement spawned a similar summit among the Southern Baptists at Ridgecrest called "The Conference on Biblical Inerrancy." The papers from this conference were published as *The Proceedings of the Conference on Biblical Inerrancy* (Nashville: Broadman, 1987). Even before that, Russ Bush and Tom Nettles, professors at Southeastern Baptist Seminary, produced a scholarly tome on *Baptists and the Bible* (Chicago: Moody, 1980), demonstrating that the inerrancy tradition is deeply rooted in Baptist history.

Doctrinally, this movement resulted in the adoption of the Chicago Statement on inerrancy as the official view of the SBC. It is called the Baptist Faith and Message, which was adopted on June 14, 2000. Its stand on Scripture reads as follows (emphasis added):

> *The Holy Bible was written by men divinely inspired and is God's revelation of Himself to man. It is a perfect treasure of divine instruction. It has God for its author, salvation for its end, and truth, without any mixture of error, for its matter. Therefore, all Scripture is totally true and trustworthy.* It reveals the principles by which God judges us, and therefore is, and will remain to the end of the world, the true center of Christian union, and the supreme standard by which all human conduct, creeds, and religious opinions should be tried. All Scripture is a testimony to Christ, who is Himself the focus of divine revelation.
>
> Exodus 24:4; Deuteronomy 4:1–2; 17:19; Joshua 8:34; Psalms 19:7–10; 119:11, 89, 105, 140; Isaiah 34:16; 40:8; Jeremiah 15:16; 36:1–32; Matthew 5:17–18; 22:29; Luke 21:33; 24:44–46; John 5:39; 16:13–15; 17:17; Acts 2:16ff.; 17:11; Romans 15:4; 16:25–26; 2 Timothy 3:15–17; Hebrews 1:1–2; 4:12; 1 Peter 1:25; 2 Peter 1:19–21.

The crucial lines regarding the inerrancy of Scripture are put in italics. God is the author of Scripture, and it is expressed in "truth, without any mixture of error," and is "totally true and trustworthy."

ICBI Influence on the Evangelical Theological Society's Amazing Growth

Meanwhile, the other most important movement influenced by the ICBI-spawned inerrancy enthusiasm is the Evangelical Theological Society. Although it began earlier (in 1949), nonetheless, the ICBI has been used to strengthen and grow the movement. Indeed, its greatest growth has occurred since the 1978 ICBI inerrancy summit. Up to that time it had grown to about one thousand two hundred members. Today it is the largest group of evangelical scholars in the world, with over four thousand members.

When Success Becomes Failure

However, in one sense the success of ETS has been its downfall. Inerrancy was made popular through ICBI—so popular that ETS became the place to go and the society to join. This attracted many scholars to ETS who did not hold to inerrancy as the ETS and ICBI founders understood it. Thus, when it came time for a crucial vote on the Pinnock issue in 2003, there were not enough votes to expel him. Nonetheless, later there were enough votes to adopt the ICBI statement as the official ETS understanding of inerrancy. Unfortunately, as we shall see, there are no real teeth in the society to enforce it. For one thing, belief in the ICBI statement is not a condition for membership in ETS, and even people like Pinnock said he could agree with the ICBI statement as he interpreted it. Finally, to date ETS has no mechanism in place that requires ETS members to understand inerrancy in accordance with the meaning of the framers of the ICBI statement. So the adoption of the ICBI statement by ETS does not really have binding significance on what members must believe to join or vote in the organization.

A Lesson in History

A reading of all the ETS minutes on this matter is revelatory. It shows that the society, which once demanded agreement with what the framers meant by its statement on inerrancy, eventually allowed members to interpret the doctrinal statement as they wished. Herein resides the eventual downfall of the organization. For no organization, even the Flat Earth Society, can retain its integrity if people can interpret their founding statement the way they desire.

In 1965 the *Journal of the ETS*'s policy demanded a disclaimer and rebuttal of Dan Fuller's article denying factual inerrancy, published in the *ETS Bulletin*. They insisted "that an article by Dr. Kantzer be published simultaneously with the article by Dr. Fuller and that Dr. Schultz include in that issue of the *Bulletin* a brief explanation regarding the appearance of *a viewpoint different from that of the Society*" (1965).

By 2003 the favorable vote on retaining Pinnock's and Sanders's membership in ETS officially approved views similar to and even more radical than Dan Fuller's denial of factual inerrancy.

The 1970 minutes of ETS record that "Dr. R. H. Bube . . . has for three years signed his membership form with a note on his own interpretation of infallibility. The secretary was instructed to point out that it is impossible for the Society to allow each member an idiosyncratic interpretation of inerrancy, and hence Dr. Bube is to be requested to *sign his form without any qualifications*, his own integrity in the matter being entirely respected" (emphasis added).

This makes it clear that members could not give their own meaning to the statement but were bound by what the framers meant by it. Yet by 1976 ETS was knowingly allowing people to join who did not really agree with the ETS doctrinal statement.

In 1976 the ETS Executive Committee confessed that "some of the members of the Society have expressed the feeling that a measure of intellectual dishonesty prevails among members who do not take the signing of the doctrinal statement seriously." Other members of the society have come to the realization that they are not in agreement with the creedal statement and have voluntarily withdrawn. That is, "*in good conscience* they could not sign the statement" (1976 minutes, emphasis added).

By 1976 the society was aware that "*intellectual dishonesty prevails* among members who do not take the signing of the doctrinal statement seriously" (emphasis added). Yet they did nothing about it. The failure to do so encouraged others to join who did not really believe it either. Eventually (by 2003), they were able to get more than one-third of the society (37 percent) to vote successfully to retain a member (Clark Pinnock) who did not agree with what the framers meant by the statement.

In 1983, an ETS Ad Hoc Committee recognized the problem when it posed the question "Is it acceptable for a member of the society to hold a view of [a] biblical author's intent which disagrees with the Founding Fathers and even the majority of the society, and still remain a member in good standing?"

The society never said no to this crucial question. And later 37 percent of the society in effect gave a resounding yes when they refused in 2003 to expel a member (Clark Pinnock) who denied what the founders meant by inerrancy.

In 1983, speaking of some who held "Barthian" views of Scripture, the minutes of the ETS Executive Committee read: "President Gordon Clark *invited them to leave the society.*" But Clark Pinnock, holding an unrecanted Barthian view of Scripture, said flatly, "Barth was right to speak about *a distance between the Word of God and the text of the Bible*" (Pinnock, *Scripture Principle*, 99, emphasis added).

Even the minority of the ETS Executive Committee who refused to vote to expel either Pinnock or Sanders from the society admitted that a Barthian view of Scriptures would be grounds for dismissal (October 23 report, p. 6). Yet Pinnock expressed this unrecanted written view, and they refused to expel him (in 2003).

In November 2000, all the living founding fathers signed a statement that "the denial of God's foreknowledge of the decisions of free agents is incompatible with the inerrancy of Scripture."

No action was taken on this unanimous consent of the founders to expel open theists (like Pinnock) who held this view. Yet when the question as to whether a Roman Catholic who sincerely believed in inerrancy could belong to ETS (in 1998) on the basis of a verbal statement by one founding father (Roger Nicole), the ETS Executive Committee (without a vote of the membership) ruled unilaterally to exclude Roman Catholic inerrantists from the society. This was particularly strange since there was nothing in the ETS statement to define what is meant by "Bible." If it had said "Protestant Bible" or "sixty-six books of the Bible" (knowing that Roman Catholics add eleven more known as the Apocrypha), there would have been no question about what the framers meant. Or to put it another way, if one verbal statement by one founding father is sufficient to determine that the framers mean Protestant "Bible" and excludes Roman Catholic inerrantists from membership, then why would not the unanimous consent of all living framers be sufficient to exclude open theists like Clark Pinnock?

In November 2003, on a fateful day in Atlanta, the ETS membership voted 388 to 231 to expel Pinnock from ETS, several percent short (63 percent) of the two-thirds vote necessary to expel him. Or to put it another way, just over a third of the membership (37 percent) were able to resist the will of a strong majority who believed Pinnock's views were contrary to the ETS statement.

See chapter 4 for numerous statements by Pinnock that are clearly in opposition to the ETS and ICBI statements on inerrancy. This not only reversed the long-standing policy of ETS to enforce its stand on inerrancy; it also placed a stamp of approval on the policy to accept people into the organization whose views were contrary to what the founders meant by inerrancy. In effect, the ETS statement became a wax nose. The decision was clearly wrong for several reasons: (1) It was contrary to the unanimous written statement and request of all the living ETS framers. (2) It was contrary to ETS precedent, which expelled other members whose views were less deviant than Pinnock's. (3) It was contrary to a strong majority of ETS members (63 percent) who voted to expel Pinnock. (4) It is contrary to the ICBI standards now used by ETS to define inerrancy, which, if they had been applied to Pinnock, would have eliminated him from the society. (5) It stripped ETS of its doctrinal integrity since it admitted that the doctrinal statement had no fixed meaning but could mean what any member desired it to mean to him. (6) It left ETS under the tyranny of a small minority (37 percent) who could restrain the organization from putting teeth into a stronger doctrinal stand on the issue, since they could prevent any two-thirds majority vote necessary to change the situation.

In November 2003, after the Pinnock decision, the ETS membership voted to accept the ICBI statement on inerrancy as the proper definition of inerrancy. It was approved by 80 percent of the voters present. Bylaw 12 essentially refers ETS members to the ICBI Chicago Statement for advice "regarding the intent and meaning of the reference to biblical inerrancy in the ETS Doctrinal Basis." However, many felt that this was admirable but futile. It seemed to them that it was too little, too late. The horse was already out of the barn. They noted that the statement had no teeth since members need not accept it. They could still make the doctrinal statement mean what they wanted it to mean, and there was no way to expel them if they didn't—except by the arduous process of a two-thirds majority vote, which was not achieved to expel Pinnock. Now a mere minority 37 percent of the members could veto the effectiveness of the doctrinal statement.

And so it was that the inerrancy "frog" was gradually boiled to death in slowly warming water. Most good organizations, like ETS, do not go astray overnight. There are two unmistakable lessons here. First, don't stray from what the framers meant by their fundamental principles—whether it is the US Constitution or the ETS Doctrinal Statement. Second, monitor the membership and insist on consistency with what the framers meant.

ISCA—a More Excellent Way

We have learned from history and experience that there are no foolproof doctrinal statements. There always seems to be some way to get around them. Nonetheless, some statements and procedures seem to be better than others and hence have a chance for more longevity.

The founders of the International Society for Christian Apologetics (www.isca -apologetics.org) have embraced a stronger way to preserve its inerrancy heritage. The ISCA not only states its doctrinal position; it also names the way it is to be understood, as follows:

Statement of Inerrancy

Bible: "The sixty-six books of the Bible alone are the infallible and inerrant Word of God in the autographic text." It is worth noting that this automatically eliminates Roman Catholic members who believe there are eleven more inspired books in the Old Testament, called Apocrypha (by Protestants) and Deuterocanonical books (by Roman Catholics).

Also, to avoid misunderstanding (or persons having their own understanding), the ISCA statement adds: "This doctrine is understood as the one expressed by the Framers of the International Council on Biblical Inerrancy in its Chicago Statement and as interpreted by the official ICBI Commentary on it" (Sproul, *Explaining Inerrancy*).

This eliminates deviations on what is meant by inerrancy, not only through a longer and more detailed ICBI statement but also through the official ICBI commentary on it.

The same is true of another doctrinal statement of ISCA, the one on the Trinity, which gives the early creeds as the official definition of what is meant by the Trinity. It reads: "*Trinity*: God is a triunity of three Persons (Father, Son, and Holy Spirit) in one infinite, eternal, and uncreated essence, having infallible foreknowledge of all future events." It then adds, "The Trinity is understood here as it was expressed in the historic orthodox Nicene, Chalcedonian, and Athanasian Creeds." Of course, it remains to be seen whether a way to monitor and enforce these more explicit statements can be put in place that will help preserve the integrity of its membership longer. At any rate, what it has is a strong step in the right direction—one that ETS has not followed and hence is less likely to retain its founders' understanding of inerrancy.

The Current Turn of Events

Unfortunately, few movements—at least doctrinal ones—have permanent results. The ICBI inerrancy influence has lasted now for nearly a generation, but sadly there are signs of a turning tide. Books like *The Erosion of Inerrancy in Evangelicalism*, by G. K. Beale, have heralded the turn. Beale poses the real problem in the mouth of "Progressive Pat": "The doctrine of inerrancy, including the formulation of it in the Chicago Statement, is really a part of evangelicalism's past. It is now an outdated statement of twentieth-century evangelicalism" (13). Indeed, new books challenging the ICBI statement on inerrancy are emerging, some even making explicit attacks on it. Others are more subtle but nonetheless effective.

These attacks on inerrancy include Clark Pinnock and a bestselling former Moody-and-Wheaton-trained Bart Ehrman, who has moved from evangelical to agnostic and biblical critic. His book *Misquoting Jesus* reportedly sold over a hundred thousand copies in the first three months. It began with his failed attempt to reconcile in his mind an alleged error in the Gospels (see chap. 5 below).

Another book is by former president of the eastern region ETS meeting and former Westminster Seminary faculty member Peter Enns, who resigned from his teaching position in the wake of his book *Inspiration and Incarnation* (see chap. 6 below). It offers an "incarnational model" for both Christ and Scripture, which allows for error in both.

In addition, Kenton Sparks, professor at Eastern University and a self-proclaimed evangelical, also attacks inerrancy (see chap. 7). Wheaton College professor Kevin Vanhoozer has offered a more subtle approach, which undermines total inerrancy by way of contemporary linguistics (see chap. 8) without explicitly denying it. Andrew McGowan, Visiting Professor of Theology at Reformed Seminary in Jackson, Mississippi, makes no bones about his rejection of the ICBI statement on inerrancy in favor of the European model of James Orr, which allowed for errors in the Bible (see chap. 9). Most recently, Emergent Church voices, such as Stanley Grenz and Brian McLaren, have adopted a postmodern attack on inerrancy (chap. 10). Finally, we see how adoption of the methods of biblical critics, such as those by Darrell Bock and Robert Webb, can undermine the inerrancy of Scripture (chap. 11).

In the wake of this, the question before us is clear: Can inerrancy be reaffirmed by the new generation? Can the traditional claim to inerrancy, as expressed in the ICBI statement, be intelligently embraced and articulated for this new generation, to meet the challenges to inerrancy? In order to do so, we must be ready and able to answer questions about the nature of God (chap. 12), the nature of truth and error (chap. 13), the nature of language (chap. 14), and the nature of hermeneutics (chap. 15). We must respond to the "incarnational model" (chap. 16) as well as to a host of other objections (chap. 17). If we cannot answer these questions satisfactorily, then a new model must be sought. If we can answer them, then we can reaffirm inerrancy for a new generation.

Conclusion

The ICBI statement on inerrancy has had a wide influence in American evangelicalism. It literally turned the tide that was flowing, largely through the influence of

Fuller Seminary, in the wrong direction. Its role in the Southern Baptist Convention is virtually unprecedented in history. And its adoption by the Evangelical Theological Society (ETS) offers guidance to the largest group of evangelical scholars in the world. This is to say nothing of the numerous Christian denominations, organizations, and missions that have been inspired and reinforced in their conviction about the complete trustworthiness of Scripture.

Unfortunately, ETS lost the battle on Clark Pinnock's denial of total inerrancy. And evangelical thinkers of a new generation are raising serious questions about whether the ICBI stand is outdated. These voices of the new generation call for an answer, which the rest of this volume is dedicated to addressing.

Sources

Baptist Faith and Message, 2000

Beale, Erosion of Inerrancy

Bush and Nettles, Baptists and the Bible

Ehrman, Misquoting Jesus

Enns, Inspiration and Incarnation

Pinnock, Scripture Principle, 2nd ed.

Proceedings of the Conference on Biblical Inerrancy

PART TWO

RECENT CHALLENGES TO INERRANCY

4

Clark Pinnock on Inerrancy

Introduction

The late Clark Pinnock was a pivotal figure in the shifting view among some evangelicals regarding inerrancy. On this topic, he stands between the old generation and a new one. In his first major work on the topic, *A Defense of Biblical Infallibility* (1967), he was thought to be a champion of the orthodox view. He followed this with a more extensive defense in *Biblical Revelation: The Foundation of Christian Theology* (1971). Pinnock was a key early figure in the move to the right among Southern Baptists. One of his students at New Orleans Baptist Seminary was Paige Patterson, who later became the most courageous and active leader in the Southern Baptist Convention on the topic. Patterson not only led in the move back to inerrancy in the SBC; he has also been the president in the turnaround at two major Southern Baptist seminaries: Southeastern Baptist Theological Seminary (in Wake Forest) and Southwestern Baptist Theological Seminary (in Fort Worth). His brother-in-law, Charles Kelley, is president of New Orleans Baptist Theological Seminary. And Danny Akin, who was mentored by Paige Patterson, served as dean of the Southern Baptist Theological Seminary and is the current president of Southeastern Baptist Theological Seminary. Patterson is the single most influential figure in the resurgence of inerrancy in the largest Protestant denomination in North America.

Clark Pinnock went on to teach at another major inerrancy seminary, Trinity Evangelical Divinity School (TEDS) in Deerfield, Illinois, whose faculty consisted of many inerrantists who fled Fuller Seminary in Pasadena when Fuller made its fateful move of removing inerrancy from its doctrinal statement. During Pinnock's later years at TEDS, Pinnock began his move away from the traditional inerrancy position, which came to fruition as he moved to Canada and a more liberal environment. It was here that he wrote a book articulating his more *"dynamic personal model"* (*Scripture Principle* [1984], 103) views on inerrancy as well as those of open theism; as we will see, these go hand in hand and led to his trial and near expulsion from the Evangelical Theological Society.

Pinnock's Views on Inerrancy

Unless otherwise noted, the following list of citations was presented to ETS leaders and members as evidence of his denial of inerrancy at the Pinnock hearing and vote in November 2003. No detailed response was given to them. Request to speak to these points was cut off by the chairman. Pinnock made only a general statement about these citations, which amounted to him saying he would word some things differently if he were to revise *Scripture Principle*. In point of fact, Pinnock did later put out a second edition (2006), but he made no significant changes in the vast number of these controversial statements.

Pinnock's Last Statement on Inerrancy

Before his unexpected death in 2010, however, Pinnock did include a new summary chapter 10 and add an appendix titled "Inspiration and Authority of the Bible: Thoughts since 1984." However, it reflects no substantial change in his view from the first edition. But it does document his permanent departure from the unlimited inerrancy view of the Old Princetonians like Warfield and A. A. Hodge, the framers of the Evangelical Theological Society (ETS), and the founders of the International Council on Biblical Inerrancy (ICBI). In his departure from the historic orthodox view on inerrancy, noteworthy are the following admissions in Pinnock's last will and testament (*Scripture Principle*):

1. Pinnock continues to reject what he calls "the strict views of inerrancy" (254).
2. He continues to identify this strict view with the "Princeton position" of A. A. Hodge and Warfield (254).
3. Pinnock admits making his new view public after leaving Trinity Evangelical Divinity School and taking a position at the more liberal McMaster Divinity College in Canada in 1977 (260).
4. He acknowledges being "impacted" by Stephen Davis's book *The Debate about the Bible*, which clearly denied the factual inerrancy of the Bible (257).
5. Pinnock praises Stanley Grenz for his denial of foundationalism as a basis for inerrancy (254).
6. He reaffirms his Barthian-like view that the Bible itself is not a revelation of God but only "a witness to the life-giving message of our Lord Jesus Christ" (255).

7. Pinnock admits holding what he calls a "neo-evangelical" view of inerrancy (258).

8. He rejects Francis Schaeffer's view (which is that of the ICBI statement that Schaeffer signed) as a form of "rationalism" in favor of what he calls the F. F. Bruce's broader and more "bottom-up irenic" position (258), which "actively opposes" strict and "unqualified biblical inerrancy" (260).

9. Pinnock acknowledges that his view involves a "broadening use of the term 'inerrancy'" (259).

10. He claims that the view of "the perfect errorlessness of non-existent autographs was an abstraction that had died a death by a thousand qualifications. More importantly, it failed to prove the dynamic authority of the present text" (259).

11. Also, Pinnock claims that "there was a growing realization that for many believers strict adherence to the inerrancy doctrine endangers rather than protects evangelical faith" (259–69).

12. Pinnock says, "I commended the 1977 anti-inerrancy polemic of Stephen Davis for its 'pastoral service' to those who are troubled with marginal difficulties in the Bible" (260).

13. He describes his own view as changed from the traditional unlimited-inerrancy position to a limited-inerrancy view, saying, "By 1978 [it] had become my own" (260). Pinnock claims to still prefer the term "inerrancy" (at least in North America), though it is a limited inerrancy, not the unlimited and factual inerrancy held by Warfield and the ETS and ICBI framers. He calls his view a "more nuanced form of inerrancy" (261). He says, "The word 'inerrancy' can be retained legitimately, I concluded, when defined as 'a metaphor or the determination to trust God's word completely'" (261).

14. Pinnock affirms the typical limited inerrancy view, claiming, "Inerrancy had come to mean that the Bible can be trusted in what it teaches and intentionally affirms. A key passage like 2 Timothy 3:15–16 authorizes sturdy belief in the instructional significance of the Bible in matters relating to human salvation, but not necessarily [in] marginal matters unrelated to the need for, basis of, and practice of new life in Jesus Christ" (262). That is, "those portions of the Bible that intend to teach the will of God constitute the core of authoritative Scripture" (262). He clearly says, "I thus place myself today in an 'inerrancy of purpose' category" (262). He adds, "In other words, the Bible may contain errors of incidental kinds, but it teaches none" (264).

15. In spite of Pinnock's admittedly changed view, he continued to sign the ETS inerrancy statement (263), which according to the framers rejects that limited view of inerrancy for a total and factual inerrancy position (see chap. 2 above).

16. Pinnock rejects the view of Augustine (and all other orthodox inerrantists) that "what the Bible says, God says" (264).

17. He says, "I supported the 1978 Chicago Statement of the International Council on Biblical Inerrancy," noting that its famous article 13 "made room for nearly every well-intentioned Baptist" (266). (This clearly was a misunderstanding of what the ICBI framers meant by inerrancy, as revealed in its official commentary on the matter by R. C. Sproul, *Explaining Inerrancy*. See chap. 2 above.)

18. Pinnock rejects the Warfield view of inerrancy, claiming that "for us, the Bible seldom addresses its authority and says nothing about its inerrancy. The rationalistic (Eastern) model of biblical authority that I learned early from B. B. Warfield and others had exaggerated these concepts to fit a theological system that had been adopted in advance. I was learning 'not to force the Bible onto a Procrustean bed of extra-scriptural assumptions about authority and perfection'" (266).

19. He says, "I now know that Karl Barth had good reason for rejecting the concept of revelation as primarily information," though Pinnock does not deny some content to biblical revelation (267).

20. He concludes that "my core conviction had become one of certainty of truth arising more from the work of the Spirit through the biblical text than from a tight rationalism rooted in the supposed human theory of biblical errorlessness for the text per se" (267).

21. Pinnock acknowledges the influence of the charismatic movement in what he calls his move "from the scholastic to the pietistic approach" (268): in the 1970s, he says, "I came to soften my negative critique of Pentecostalism" (269), and he makes "A Truth Proposal for the Tongues Controversy" (269).

22. He describes the Bible as a "(slightly) imperfect document," adding, "the Christian agenda should be preoccupied less with the theory of precise inerrancy and more with a healthy concern for a spiritual power enabled by the Spirit of God, who both speaks through ancient Scripture and illuminates the contemporary reader for real life and mission" (270). Pinnock denies that his view is a liberal experientially based position, claiming only that he now sees "more importance in experience" (271).

23. Pinnock claims that "inerrancy . . . is not our preferred term for rendering the concept of biblical trustworthiness" because it "begs clear definition," which he ironically says is why he continues to use it! (272). He prefers terms like "infallibility" and "trustworthiness" and uses the Barthian illustration of the Bible's being like a scratched record through which comes "the Master's voice" in spite of the imperfections in the record (272). He then adds another Barthian belief that the living Word, Christ, is "adequately witnessed to by this sacred text" (272).

Despite Pinnock's rejection of the traditional view on inerrancy, he persists in using the term "inerrancy" to describe his new view and to claim that inerrancy is still a "badge" of evangelical authenticity and a "watershed" issue (256). However, as we shall see, Pinnock understands inerrancy in a significantly different sense than that meant by church fathers, the Reformers, the Old Princetonians, and the framers of the ETS and ICBI statements.

Pinnock's Unrecanted Views on Inerrancy

Clearly Pinnock's views are incompatible with the ICBI statement (which he said he could affirm), which was later adopted (in 2003) by ETS as its understanding of inerrancy. A careful reading of the following statements by Pinnock reveals their pivotal importance in the shift by some evangelicals to a more liberal "dynamic" view of inspiration. The quotes identified as *SP* are from the original 1984 edition of his book *The Scripture Principle*, which expresses his unrevised and unrecanted views before his ETS trial in 2003. Those listed as *SP²* are from the revised edition (2006) and reflect his reworded views from the earlier edition. But as will be seen, there is no substantial change in the objectionable and unorthodox aspects of Pinnock's view up to his recent unexpected death (in 2010). The minor grammatical and literary changes that do not reflect a substantial change in view are generally omitted. The headings for the quotations and the emphasis therein are ours:

THE BIBLE NOT COMPLETELY INERRANT

"This leaves us with the question, Does the New Testament, did Jesus, teach the perfect errorlessness of the Scriptures? No, not in plain terms" (*SP*, 57).

"Although *the New Testament does not teach a strict doctrine of inerrancy*, it might be said to encourage a trusting attitude, which inerrancy in a more lenient definition does signify. *The fact is that inerrancy is a very flexible term in and of itself*" (*SP*, 77).

"Once we recall how complex a hypothesis inerrancy is, it is obvious that *the Bible teaches no such thing explicitly. What it claims, as we have seen, is divine inspiration and a general reliability*" (*SP*, 58).

"Why, then, do scholars insist that the Bible does claim total inerrancy? I can only answer for myself, *as one who argued in this way a few years ago*. I claimed that the Bible taught total inerrancy because I hoped that it did—I wanted it to" (*SP*, 58).

Pinnock does not really make any substantial change in the revised versions here, but he does soften it and make it less explicit. It reads: "Why, then, do some scholars insist that the Bible does claim total inerrancy for itself? Some argue for inerrancy sincerely, hoping that it is true. They find reassurance in this hope" (*SP²*, 84).

"*For my part, to go beyond the biblical requirements to a strict position of total errorlessness only brings to the forefront the perplexing features of the Bible that no one can completely explain* and overshadows those wonderful certainties of salvation in Christ that ought to be front and center" (*SP*, 59). Here Pinnock admits that he rejects the traditional view of "total errorlessness" for the view of limited inerrancy.

Inerrancy of Intent, Not Fact

"*Inerrancy is relative to the intent of the Scriptures,* and this has to be hermeneutically determined" (*SP*, 225). Interestingly, this exact statement is omitted (though not recanted) in the revised edition. He still holds the same view but puts it in different words.

"All this means is that *inerrancy is relative to the intention of the text. If it could be shown that the Chronicler inflates some of the numbers he uses for his didactic purpose,* he would be completely within his rights and not at variance with inerrancy" (*SP*, 78).

> We will not have to panic when we meet some intractable difficulty. *The Bible will seem reliable enough in terms of its soteric [saving] purpose....* In the end this is what the mass of evangelical believers need—not the rationalistic ideal of a perfect Book that is no more, but the trustworthiness of a Bible with truth where it counts, *truth that is not so easily threatened by scholarly problems.* (*SP*, 104–5)

The Bible Not the Word of God

"Barth was right to speak about *a distance between the Word of God and the text of the Bible*" (*SP*, 99). The only change to this in the second edition is the addition of Barth's first name, Karl! (*SP²*, 126).

"*The Bible does not attempt to give the impression that it is flawless in historical or scientific ways.* God uses writers with weaknesses and still teaches the truth of revelation through them" (*SP*, 99).

"*What God aims to do through inspiration is to stir up faith in the gospel through the word of Scripture, which remains a human text beset by normal weaknesses* [*which includes errors*]" (*SP*, 100).

"*A text that is word for word what God wanted in the first place might as well have been dictated, for all the room it leaves for human agency.* This is the kind of thinking behind the militant inerrancy position. God is taken to be the Author of the Bible in such a way that he controlled the writers and every detail of what they wrote" (*SP*, 101).

The Bible Not Completely Infallible

"*The Bible is not a book like the Koran, consisting of nothing but perfectly infallible propositions....* The Bible did not fall from heaven. *... We place our trust ultimately in Jesus Christ, not in the Bible....* What the Scriptures do is to present *a sound and reliable* [*but not inerrant*] *testimony* to who he is and what God has done for us" (*SP*, 100).

Rejecting Warfield's View of Inerrancy

"*Inerrancy as Warfield understood it was a good deal more precise than the sort of reliability the Bible proposes. The Bible's emphasis tends to be upon the saving truth* of its message and its supreme profitability in the life of faith and discipleship" (*SP*, 75).

Rejecting ICBI's View of Total Inerrancy

There are a large number of evangelicals in North America appearing to defend the total inerrancy of the Bible. The language they use seems absolute and uncompromising: "The authority of Scripture is inescapably impaired if this total divine inerrancy is in any way limited or disregarded, or made relative to a view of truth contrary to the Bible's own" (Chicago Statement, preamble). *It sounds as if the slightest slip or flaw would bring down the whole house of authority. It seems as though we ought to defend the errorlessness of the Bible down to the last jot and tittle* in order for it to be a viable religious authority. (*SP*, 127)

Again, in his own words, Pinnock rejects the "total inerrancy" of the Bible held by the ETS and ICBI framers.

Dynamic Inspiration, Not Plenary Inspiration

"In relation to Scripture, we want to avoid both the idea that the Bible is the product of mere human genius and the idea it came about through mechanical dictation. *The* via media *lies in the direction of a dynamic personal model* that upholds both the divine initiative and the human response" (*SP*, 103).

"*Inspiration should be seen as a dynamic work of God. In it, God does not decide every word that is used,* one by one, but works in the writers in such a way that they make full use of their own skills and vocabulary while giving expression to the divinely inspired message being communicated to them and through them" (*SP*, 105). This is a denial of the traditional view of plenary (full) inspiration of the written text in all of its parts.

Redefining Inerrancy, Rejecting the Prophetic Model

"The wisest course to take would be to get on with *defining inerrancy in relation to the purpose of the Bible* and the phenomena it displays. When we do that, *we will be surprised how open and permissive a term it is*" (*SP*, 225). This view of limited inerrancy is known as the "inerrancy of purpose" or the "inerrancy of intent" view as opposed to the inerrancy of fact.

Pinnock eliminates the frank phrase "When we do that, *we will be surprised how open and permissive a term it is*" (*SP*, 225). However, he still affirms that "the ancient text must be allowed to remain pliable in the hands of the ministering Spirit of God" (*SP²*, 250). This softens but does not really change his view.

> At times I have felt like rejecting biblical inerrancy because of the narrowness of definition and the crudity of polemics that have accompanied the term. But in the end, I have had to bow to the wisdom that says we need to be unmistakably clear in our convictions about biblical authority, and in the North American context, at least, that means to employ strong language. (*SP*, 225)

Interestingly, this is omitted in *SP²*. Indeed, it seems to be inconsistent with his claim that "inerrancy" should be retained because it is a broad term that can include many views.

"Paul J. Achtemeier has called attention to the *inadequacy of the prophetic model* for representing the biblical category of inspiration in its fullness—[in his work] *The Inspiration of Scripture*" (*SP*, 232n8).

ADMITTING MINOR ERRORS IN THE BIBLE

"*The authority of the Bible in faith and practice does not rule out the possibility of an occasionally uncertain text, differences in details as between the Gospels, a lack of precision in the chronology of events recorded in the Books of Kings and Chronicles, a prescientific description of the world, and the like*" (*SP*, 104). This too is a denial of total inerrancy, which includes the inerrancy of fact, not merely the inerrancy of intent.

> What could truly falsify the Bible would have to be something that could falsify the gospel and Christianity as well. It would have to be a difficulty that would radically call into question the truth of Jesus and His message of good news. Discovering some point of chronology in Matthew that could not be reconciled with a parallel in Luke would certainly not be any such thing. (SP, 129)
>
> I recognize that the Bible does not make a technical inerrancy claim or go into the kind of detail associated with the term in the contemporary discussion. But I also see a solid basis for trusting the Scriptures in a more general sense in all that they teach and affirm, and I see real danger in giving the impression that the Bible errs in a significant way. Inerrancy is a metaphor for the determination to trust God's Word completely. (SP, 224–25)

Here one sees the very weak "general" sense in which the word "inerrancy" is employed by Pinnock. It would have been more forthright simply to deny the term.

HOLDING THAT THE BIBLE CONTAINS MYTH AND LEGEND

"*In the narrative of the fall of Adam, there are numerous symbolic features* (God molding man from dirt, the talking snake, God molding woman from Adam's rib, symbolic trees, four major rivers from one garden, etc.), so that it is natural to ask whether this is not *a meaningful narration that does not stick only to factual matters*" (*SP*, 119). This is a denial of the historicity of Adam, which the NT clearly affirms (cf. Rom. 5:12–14; Matt. 19:4–5; 1 Tim. 2:13). It also denies clear statements by the ICBI, which Pinnock claims he can accept.

The change here is interesting. He speaks rather of "God molding humans from dirt" (*SP*[2], 146). However, in an attempt at more gender-neutral language, he actually contradicts his original statement in the story that Eve was made from Adam's rib, not from dust as Adam was!

"On the one hand, *we cannot rule legend out a priori*. It is, after all, a perfectly valid literary form, and *we have to admit that it turns up in the Bible in at least some form*. We referred already to Job's reference to Leviathan and can mention also Jotham's fable" (*SP*, 121–22).

"Thus we are in a bind. *Legends are possible in theory—there are apparent legends in the Bible*—but we fear actually naming them as such lest we seem to deny the miraculous" (*SP*, 122).

"When we look at the Bible, it is clear that it is not radically mythical. *The influence of myth is there in the Old Testament. The stories of creation and fall, of flood and the tower of Babel, are there in pagan texts and are worked over in Genesis from the angle of Israel's knowledge of God,* but the framework is no longer mythical" (*SP*, 123).

"We read of a coin turning up in a fish's mouth and of the origin of the different languages of humankind. We hear about the magnificent exploits of Samson and Elisha. We even see evidence of the duplication of miracle stories in the Gospels. *All of them are things that if we read them in some other book, we would surely identify* [*them*] *as legends*" (*SP*, 123).

In the foregoing citations, Pinnock clearly denies the ICBI statements on inerrancy that he claims he could have accepted. For contrary to Pinnock's view, the ICBI framers clearly affirmed that Genesis 1–11 was history, not mythology. In contrast to Pinnock's views, consider the following ICBI statements via Geisler, "Explaining Hermeneutics" (EH):

EH on article 13: "We deny that generic categories which negate historicity may rightly be imposed on biblical narratives which present *themselves* as factual." Again, "Some, for instance, take Adam to be a myth, whereas in Scripture he is presented as a real person. Others take Jonah to be an allegory when he is presented as a historical person and [is] so referred to by Christ."

EH on article 14: "We deny that any event, discourse, or saying reported in Scripture was invented by the biblical writers or by the traditions they incorporated."

EH on article 22: emphatically declares that "Genesis 1–11 is factual, as is the rest of the book."

HOLDING ROBERT GUNDRY'S VIEW OF MIDRASH IN MATTHEW

"There is no mythology to speak of in the New Testament. *At most, there are fragments and suggestions of myth:* for example, *the strange allusion to the bodies of the saints being raised on Good Friday* (Matt. 27:52) and the sick being healed through contact with pieces of cloth that had touched Paul's body (Acts 19:11–12)" (*SP*, 124). This is noteworthy since Robert Gundry was expelled from the Evangelical Theological Society (ETS) in 1983 for his midrashic views, which denied the historicity of whole sections of the Gospel of Matthew. Yet Pinnock was later (in 2003) retained by ETS in spite of holding these more liberal views on inerrancy. He writes, "*There are cases in which the possibility of legend seems quite real.* I mentioned the incident of the coin in the fish's mouth (Matt. 17:24–27). . . . *The event is recorded only by Matthew and has the feel of a legendary feature*" (*SP*, 125).

Pinnock's Views on God

Since one's view on inerrancy and one's view of God are directly and logically related (see chap. 12), it is important to explore Pinnock's so-called "Openness" view of God as well. For if God can err, then to say the Bible is the Word of God is to allow for errors in it as well. Indeed, this is precisely the area wherein Pinnock's view led to his examination and near expulsion from ETS.

The Bible Has Predictions That Were Not Fulfilled

Pinnock holds that "some prophecies are conditional, leaving the future open, and, presumably, God's knowledge of it" (Most Moved Mover [MMM], 50; our emphasis here and below). He added, "There are imprecise prophetic forecasts based on present situations, as when Jesus predicts the fall of Jerusalem" (50). Further, "Despite Ezekiel, Nebuchadnezzar did not conquer the city of Tyre; despite the Baptist, Jesus did not cast the wicked into the fire; contrary to Paul, the second coming was not just around the corner (1 Thess. 4:17)" (51n66).

Jesus Even Made a False Prophecy

Pinnock declares that *"despite Jesus, in the destruction of the temple, some stones were left one on the other"* (Mt. 24:2)" (*MMM*, 51n66). He had to revise this particularly troublesome statement in order to save his scalp at the hands of the ETS committee that examined him for his alleged denial of inerrancy. One ETS member suggested to Pinnock that this could be a figure of speech meaning total destruction. Hence it was unnecessary to take it as a false prediction by Jesus. The truth is that archaeologists have discovered the stones to which Jesus referred, and there was literally not one left upon another. I (Norm) saw them on a recent trip to Jerusalem.

God Is Not Bound to His Own Word

According to Pinnock, "God is free in the manner of fulfilling prophecy and is not bound to a script, even his own" (MMM, 51n66). "We may not want to admit it but prophecies often go unfulfilled" (51n66).

God Is Limited and Corporeal

"In a sense," says Pinnock, *"creation was also an act of self-limitation. . . .* Creating human beings who have true freedom is a self-restraining, self-humbling, and self-sacrificing act on God's part" (*MMM*, 31). "As regards space, *the Bible speaks of God having living space in the heavens:* . . . Let's not tilt overly to transcendence lest we miss the truth that God is with us in space" (32). "If he is with us in the world, if we are to take biblical metaphors seriously, *is God in some way embodied?* Critics will be quick to say that, although there are expressions of this idea in the Bible, they are not to be taken literally. But *I do not believe that the idea is as foreign to the Bible's view of God* as we have assumed" (33). "The only persons we encounter are embodied persons and, *if God is not embodied, it may prove difficult to understand*

how God is a person. . . . Perhaps *God uses the created order as a kind of body and exercises top-down causation upon it*" (34–35).

God's Foreknowledge Is Limited

Pinnock declares, "*It is unsound to think of exhaustive foreknowledge, implying that every detail of the future is already decided*" (MMM, 8). "Though God knows all there is to know about the world, *there are aspects about the future that even God does not know*" (32). "Scripture makes a distinction with respect to the future; God is certain about some aspects of it and *uncertain about other aspects*" (47). "*But no being, not even God, can know in advance precisely what free agents will do, even though he may predict it with great accuracy*" (100). "*God, in order to be omniscient, need not know the future in complete detail*" (100).

God Changes His Mind

"*Divine repentance is an important biblical theme*," claims Pinnock (MMM, 43). "*Nevertheless, it appears that God is willing to change course*" (43). "Prayer is an activity that brings *new possibilities into existence for God and us*" (46).

God Is Dependent on Creatures

"According to the open view," says Pinnock, "*God freely decided to be, in some respects, affected and conditioned by creatures*" (MMM, 5). "In a sense *God needs our love* because he has freely chosen to be a lover and needs us because he has chosen to have reciprocal love" (30). "*The world is dependent on God* but God has also, voluntarily, made himself dependent on it. . . . God is also affected by the world" (31).

God Is Not in Complete Control of the World

Pinnock explains, "*This means that God is not now in complete control of the world. . . . Things happen which God has not willed. . . . God's plans at this point in history are not always fulfilled*" (MMM, 36). "Not everything that happens in the world happens for some reason; . . . [there are] things that should not have happened, *things that God did not want to happen*. They occur because God goes in for real relationships and real partnerships" (47). "As Boyd puts it: 'Only if God is the God of what *might be* and not only the God of what *will be* can we trust him to steer us'" (Pinnock's affirming the view of open theist Greg Boyd; 103, his emphasis here). "Though God can bring good out of evil, it does not make evil itself good and *does not even ensure that God will succeed in every case to bring good out of it*" (176). "*It does seem possible to read the text to be saying that God is an all-controlling absolute Being. . . .* But how does the Spirit want us to read it? Which interpretation is right for the present circumstance? *Which interpretation is timely? Only time will tell*" (64).

God Undergoes Change

According to Pinnock, "Even though *the Bible says repeatedly that God changes his mind and alters his course of action,* conventional theists reject the metaphor and deny that such things are possible for God" (*MMM,* 63). "I would say that God is *unchangeable in changeable ways*" (85–86). "On the other hand, being a person and not an abstraction, *God changes in relation to creatures. . . . God changed when he became creator of the world*" (86). "Accepting possibility [ability to suffer] may require the kind of doctrinal revisions which the open view is engaged in. If God is passible, then he is not, for example, *unconditioned, immutable,* and atemporal" (59n82).

Pinnock Admits Affinity with Process Theology

"*The conventional package of attributes is tightly drawn. Tinkering with one or two of them will not help much*" (MMM, 78). "*Candidly, I believe that conventional theists are more influenced by Plato, who was a pagan, than I am by Whitehead, who was a Christian*" (143). This is ironic, because Whitehead still denied virtually all of the attributes of the God of orthodox theology, biblical inerrancy, and all the fundamentals of the faith! Plato, by contrast, held many views consistent with evangelical belief, such as (1) Truth is absolute; (2) Meaning is absolute; (3) Values are absolute; (4) Man has an immortal spiritual dimension; (5) An eternal spiritual realm exists.

A Critique of Pinnock's View on Inerrancy

Despite Pinnock's claim to be able to affirm the ETS and ICBI statements on inerrancy, his views are clearly opposed to what the framers meant by those statements. He was willing to accept them only as reinterpreted through his lenses, which were contrary to what was intended by the ICBI framers and expressed in their official commentary on it, particularly on the nature of truth (art. 13). Pinnock did sign the more brief and less specific ETS statement, but even here he did so contrary to the framers' meaning and contrary to a majority of ETS members who voted on the issue in November 2003 in Atlanta. Interestingly, a friend of mine (Norman) who saw his signed doctrinal statement said that it was in pencil! Several things make it evident that his views on inerrancy were not in accord with either the original ETS statement or with the ICBI:

1. *A previous ETS member had been expelled from the society for holding Barthian views on Scripture.* In 1983 ETS President Gordon Clark asked a member to leave the society because of his views. The ICBI statement is more specific in denying Barthianism. Article 3 reads in part: "We deny that the Bible is merely a witness to revelation, or only becomes revelation in encounter, or depends on the responses

of men for its validity." The official ICBI commentary singles out Barth by name and declares: "For Barth it is fundamental to our humanity that we are liable to error" (Sproul, *Explaining Inerrancy*, 31). Therefore, since the Bible was written by men, then it too must err.

Pinnock remained unrepentant, even in his second edition, claiming that "Karl Barth was right to speak about a distance between the Word of God and the text of the Bible" (*SP²*, 126). And, "The Bible does not attempt to give the impression that it is flawless in historical or scientific ways. God uses writers with weaknesses and still teaches the truth of revelation through them" (*SP*, 99). Further, "What God aims to do through inspiration is to stir up faith in the gospel through the word of Scripture, which remains a human text beset by normal weaknesses [which includes errors]" (100). These are clearly unorthodox and Barthian views of Scripture, which ETS has rejected from its very beginning.

2. *Robert Gundry was expelled from ETS in 1983 for holding to a midrashic view of Matthew, which denied the historicity of whole sections of Matthew. Yet Pinnock holds the same basic view,* claiming that "there are fragments and suggestions of myth: for example, the strange allusion to the bodies of the saints being raised on Good Friday (Matt. 27:52) and the sick being healed through contact with pieces of cloth that had touched Paul's body (Acts 19:11–12)" (*SP*, 124). Pinnock also denies the historicity of sections of the Bible that are affirmed as true by Jesus or other biblical writers. The ICBI statement clearly affirms that this is contrary to inerrancy. Pinnock says, for example, "There are cases in which the possibility of legend seems quite real. I mentioned the incident of the coin in the fish's mouth (Matt. 17:24–27). . . . The event is recorded only by Matthew and has the feel of a legendary feature" (125). "In the narrative of the fall of Adam, there are numerous symbolic features (God molding man from dirt, the talking snake, God molding woman from Adam's rib, symbolic trees, four major rivers from one garden, etc.), so that it is natural to ask whether this is not a meaningful narration that does not stick only to factual matters" (119). He added, "On the one hand, we cannot rule legend out a priori. It is, after all, a perfectly valid literary form, and we have to admit that it turns up in the Bible in at least some form. We referred already to Job's reference to Leviathan and can mention also Jotham's fable" (121–22). And he says, "We read of a coin turning up in a fish's mouth and of the origin of the different languages of humankind. We hear about the magnificent exploits of Samson and Elisha. We even see evidence of the duplication of miracle stories in the Gospels. All of them are things that if we read them in some other book, we would surely identify as legends" (123).

However, the ICBI statement clearly rejects such beliefs as incompatible with inerrancy, affirming in article 18: "We deny the legitimacy of any treatment of the text or quest for sources behind it that leads to relativizing, dehistoricizing, or discounting its teaching, or its rejecting its claims to authorship." The official ICBI commentary on this adds, "When the quest for sources produces a historicizing of the Bible, a rejection of its teaching, or a rejection of the Bible's own claims of authorship, it has trespassed beyond its proper limits. . . . It is never legitimate, however, to run counter to express biblical affirmations" (Sproul, *Explaining Inerrancy*, 55). But this is precisely what Pinnock does. Indeed, in some cases he goes against what Jesus himself affirmed about Scripture by claiming that Jonah and the flood were legendary and not historical. But article 12 of the ICBI statement said clearly, "We further deny that scientific hypotheses about earth history may properly be used to overturn the teaching of Scripture on creation and the flood."

3. *Pinnock limited inerrancy to the redemptive intent of the Bible.* He declares: "All this means is that inerrancy is relative to the [redemptive] intention of the text." But in article 12, ICBI affirms, "We deny that biblical infallibility and inerrancy are limited to spiritual, religious, or redemptive themes, exclusive of assertions in the fields of history and science." The official ICBI commentary adds, "Though the Bible is indeed *redemptive* history, it is also redemptive *history*, and this means that the acts of salvation wrought by God actually occurred in the space-time world" (Sproul, *Explaining Inerrancy*, 37).

However, Pinnock at times places a wedge between these two. He declares: "All this means is that inerrancy is relative to the [redemptive] intention of the text. If it could be shown that the chronicler inflates some of the numbers he uses for his didactic [redemptive] purpose, he would be completely within his rights and not at variance with inerrancy" (*SP*, 78). He adds,

> We will not have to panic when we meet some intractable difficulty. The Bible will seem reliable enough in terms of its soteric [saving] purpose. . . . In the end this is what the mass of evangelical believers need—not the rationalistic ideal of a perfect Book that is no more, but the trustworthiness of a Bible with truth where it counts [namely, on redemptive matters], truth that is not so easily threatened by scholarly problems. (*SP*, 104–5)

4. *Pinnock's view of truth is contrary to the traditional view on inerrancy as expressed by the ICBI framers.* Pinnock held that truth is to be defined in terms of what the author purposed or intended to say, not in terms of whether or not it corresponds to the facts. He insisted, "All this means is that inerrancy is relative to the *intention* of the text. If it could be shown that the chronicler inflates some of the numbers he uses for his didactic *purpose*, he would be completely within his rights and not at variance with inerrancy" (*SP*, 78). As noted above, he claims that "The Bible will seem reliable enough in terms of its soteric [saving] *purpose*" (104).

Indeed, Pinnock was willing to accept the ICBI statement *if* everything was understood in terms of the framers' redefinition of "truth" in article 13, which affirms, "We deny that it is proper to evaluate Scripture according to standards of truth and error that are alien to its usage or purpose."

However, the framers of the ICBI statement saw this possible evasion and headed it off at the pass by asserting in the official ICBI commentary on it that truth is not to be defined in terms of its intention but in terms of its correspondence to the facts. It asserts, "When we say that the truthfulness of Scripture ought to be evaluated according to its own standards, that means that . . . *all the claims of the Bible must correspond with reality, whether that reality is historical, factual or spiritual"* (Sproul, *Explaining Inerrancy*, 41). It adds, "*By biblical standards truth and error is meant the view used both in the Bible and in everyday life, viz., a correspondence view of truth.* This part of the article is directed toward those [like Pinnock] who would redefine truth to relate merely to redemptive intent, the purely personal, or the like, rather than to mean that which corresponds with reality" (43–44, emphasis added). So, then, it is clear that the intentionalist view of truth used by those like Pinnock and others to make their views sound orthodox is emphatically contrary to the ICBI understanding of inerrancy.

5. *Pinnock's view of fallible prophecy is also incompatible with belief in an infallible and inerrant Bible.* He affirms: "Some prophecies are conditional, leaving the future open, and, presumably, God's knowledge of it" (*MMM*, 50). Also, "there are imprecise prophetic forecasts based on present situations, as when Jesus predicts the fall of Jerusalem" (*MMM*, 50). Other prophecies failed, for "despite Ezekiel, Nebuchadnezzar did not conquer the city of Tyre; despite the Baptist, Jesus did not cast the wicked into the fire; contrary to Paul, the second coming was not just around the corner (1 Thess. 4:17)" (*MMM*, 51n66). He even said that Jesus made a false prophecy: "Despite Jesus, in the destruction of the temple, some stones were left one on the other" (Matt. 24:2; *MMM*, 51n66). As stated, this was a serious charge by Pinnock, attributing an error to Christ himself. Pinnock was forced to change his view on this before the ETS examining committee in order to escape the charge that he had denied inerrancy. However, it was never revised in a reprint of the book.

Nonetheless, Pinnock never changed his mind that the Bible made fallible forecasts that did not come to pass. It is this that is incompatible with inerrancy for two reasons. First, if the Bible contains fallible forecasts, then it cannot be the infallible Word of God. No fallible assertions can be part of a totally infallible Word. Second, the open theists' claim that Bible predictions were not infallible but were simply fallible forecasts (like a weatherperson makes) is contrary to the biblical test for a false prophet. Deuteronomy 18:22 commanded that a prophet be stoned for making a prediction that "does not come to pass." Indeed, on this test for a false prophet, God himself would be subject to stoning—something not totally out of the question physically on Pinnock's view that God has a body!

6. *Pinnock clearly rejected the view of inerrancy of B. B. Warfield, which was held by the ICBI framers.* He writes, "Inerrancy as Warfield understood it was a good deal more precise than the sort of reliability the Bible proposes. The Bible's emphasis tends to be upon the saving truth of its message and its supreme profitability in the life of faith and discipleship" (*SP*, 75). But the Warfieldian view on inerrancy was the view of both the ETS framers and the ICBI framers. Indeed, the view of Warfield (and ETS and ICBI) was that whatever the Bible affirms, God affirms. In the official commentary on the ICBI Chicago Statement, *Explaining Inerrancy*,

by Sproul (69), we read: "Thus, what Scripture says, God says; its authority is His authority, for He is the ultimate author." In his classic book on the inspiration of Scripture, Warfield devotes a whole chapter to demonstrating this point. Clearly, Pinnock does not agree with this point that Warfield and his ETS and ICBI followers held. Hence, Pinnock's view is a denial of what the framers of the ETS and ICBI statements meant.

End of the Pinnock Story as the Slide from Inerrancy Begins

The Pinnock case was presented to the ETS leadership. A committee was appointed to examine him. When the committee presented the case to the membership in 2003, a strong majority of 63 percent voted to expel him, but this fell short of the two-thirds majority needed to expel him. And this was the end of the Pinnock story. However, there is more to the story of evangelicalism's fall from the historical traditional view on inerrancy. The rest of the story is told in the remaining chapters of this book. It includes the fall of former Moody-and-Wheaton-trained Bart Ehrman from evangelicalism to agnosticism, spawned by his inability to explain an alleged error in the Gospels. It included the departure of a professor (Peter Enns) from a historically strong stand on inerrancy as well as a Wheaton professor (Kevin Vanhoozer) whose subtle hermeneutical views challenge traditional inerrancy, as well as a professor (Andrew McGowan) from Reformed Seminary in Jackson, Mississippi, who opposes the ICBI statement on inerrancy directly and by name, and others. It also includes the undermining of inerrancy by the adoption of redaction criticism methods by Darrell Bock of Dallas Theological Seminary. And this no doubt is only the tip of the iceberg.

In the wake of this, the question before us is a challenge: Can inerrancy be reaffirmed by the new generation? As we move on in the twenty-first century, can the new challenges to inerrancy be answered? Has the ICBI statement become obsolete? Can it be defended? The authors of this book—who together span these two generations—will carefully examine these questions to see if an affirmative answer is possible.

Sources

Pinnock, *Biblical Revelation*   ——, *Scripture Principle*, 2nd ed.
——, *Defense of Biblical Infallibility*   ——, *Most Moved Mover*
——, *Scripture Principle*   Sproul, *Explaining Inerrancy*

5

Bart Ehrman on Inerrancy

Introduction

Bart D. Ehrman is a professor at the University of North Carolina at Chapel Hill. He is a leading expert on textual criticism and author of over twenty books on the topic. His recent works include *Jesus Interrupted: Revealing the Hidden Contradictions in the Bible (and Why We Don't Know about Them)*; *Lost Scriptures: Books That Did Not Make It into the New Testament*; the *New York Times* bestseller *Misquoting Jesus: Who Changed the Bible and Why* (2005); and his latest, *Forged: Writing in the Name of God—Why the Bible's Authors Are Not Who We Think They Are* (2011).

Currently, Ehrman is also one of the strongest academic voices speaking against the inerrancy of Scripture. He is a former evangelical turned agnostic (see the introduction to his book *Misquoting Jesus*). Ehrman attended Moody Bible Institute, where his doubts began, and Wheaton College, where his doubts grew. At Princeton Theological Seminary, he gave up his belief in the inerrancy of the Bible after struggling with an alleged contradiction in the Gospels (see chap. 17).

Ehrman's beliefs collide with inerrantists at several points. Not only does he believe there are errors in the Bible; he also denies the reliability of the biblical manuscripts. A subsidiary belief of the innerrantist is the view that the copies of the originals are reliable. Article 10 of the ICBI statement reads:

> We affirm that inspiration, strictly speaking, applies only to the autographic text of Scripture, which in the providence of God can be ascertained from available manuscripts with great accuracy. We further affirm that copies and translations of Scripture are the Word of God to the extent that they faithfully represent the

original. We deny that any essential element of the Christian faith is affected by the absence of the autographs. We further deny that this absence renders the assertions of biblical inerrancy invalid or irrelevant.

Ehrman's book *Misquoting Jesus* is a strong challenge to everything emphasized in the above ICBI statement. In fact, he denies the claim that the manuscript copies "faithfully represent the original" or that the autographs "can be ascertained from available manuscripts with great accuracy."

An Exposition of Ehrman's Views on Inerrancy

Ehrman speaks against the inerrantist position by giving reasons he opposes the historicity of both the original text and the transmission of the text. He says:

> I came to realize that it would have been no more difficult for God to preserve the words of scripture than it would have been for him to inspire them in the first place. If he wanted his people to have his words, surely he would have given them to them (and possibly even given them the words in a language they would understand, rather than Greek and Hebrew). The fact that we don't have the words surely must show, I reasoned, that he did not preserve them for us. And if he didn't perform that miracle, there seems to be no reason to think that he performed the earlier miracle of inspiring those words. (*Misquoting Jesus* [*MJ*], 11)

Ehrman's Overall Argument against Inerrancy

Ehrman argues against the inerrancy position by claiming that God did not preserve the original text. His argument is as follows (*MJ*, 260–61):

1. We do not have the original manuscripts of any of the books of the New Testament, but only copies—over five thousand copies, just in the Greek language in which these books were originally written.
2. Most of these copies are centuries removed from the originals.
3. All of these copies contain mistakes both great and small, as scribes either inadvertently or intentionally altered the text.
4. The vast majority of these changes are insignificant, immaterial, and of no importance for the meaning of the passages in which they are found.
5. Others, however, are quite significant. Sometimes the meaning of a verse, a passage, or an entire book depends on which textual variants the scholar decides are "original."
6. These decisions are sometimes relatively simple to make; but in other instances they are exceedingly difficult, even for scholars who have spent years working on the problem.

7. As a result, there are many passages of the New Testament where scholars continue to debate the original wording. And there are some in which we will probably never know what the authors originally wrote.

The arguments of Ehrman can be summarized into four premises: (1) The original manuscripts were not reliable and are nonexistent. (2) The transmission of manuscripts was unreliable. (3) There have been significant changes in the manuscripts. (4) These changes undermine the doctrine of inerrancy.

Ehrman's Four Basic Issues with Inerrancy Explained

Issue 1: The Original Manuscripts Were Not Reliable and Are Nonexistent

Ehrman believes that the original manuscripts of the Bible were a result of Jesus's interpretation of the Old Testament, and that method was continued by his followers. These manuscripts were written years later, by unqualified authors and/or scribes, and the collection of the canon of Scripture was much later and driven by theological motives that may or may not reflect the actual life and teachings of Jesus. Here are some of the arguments Ehrman offers in favor of his position:

1. JESUS WAS THE FOUNDER AND FIRST INTERPRETER OF THE CHRISTIAN CANON

Ehrman contends that Jesus was the founder of the Christian canon. He states, "In some sense Christians *started* with a canon in that the founder of their religion was himself a Jewish teacher who accepted the Torah as authoritative scripture from God, and who taught his followers his interpretation of it" (*MJ*, 30).

2. JESUS'S INTERPRETATION OF SCRIPTURE WAS EQUAL WITH SCRIPTURE

Ehrman holds that the early Christians added to the Old Testament canon: "Christians began accepting other writings as standing on par with the Jewish Scriptures. This acceptance may have had its roots in the authoritative teaching of Jesus himself, as his followers took his *interpretation* of scripture to be equal in authority to the words of scripture itself" (*MJ*, 30).

3. THE WRITINGS OF THE APOSTLES WERE CONSIDERED SCRIPTURE

The writings of the apostles were considered to be on par with Scripture. This is garnered from the fact that in the New Testament there is a reference to the writing of Paul as Scripture. When talking about the writings of Paul, 2 Peter 3:16 says, "There are some things in them that are hard to understand, which the ignorant and unstable twist to their own destruction, as they do the other Scriptures." Furthermore, it is clear that the writings of the apostles were considered Scripture because of their acceptance by the early Christians and patristic fathers.

4. The Canon of Scripture Is Only One of Many Competing Interpretations of the Life of Jesus

Ehrman claims that the received canon of Scripture represents only one of many competing Christianities. In fact, "Jesus's life, as we have seen, was interpreted by Paul and others in light of the Jewish scriptures" (*MJ*, 24). But there were other groups (whom Ehrman believes were equal in authority as the formers of the canon) that interpreted the life and teachings of Jesus differently. He says, "Already the apostle Paul rails against 'false teachers'—for example, in his letter to the Galatians. Reading the surviving accounts, we can see clearly that these opponents were not outsiders. They were Christians who understood the religion in a fundamentally different way" (28).

5. Many of the Books in the New Testament Were Not Written by the Assigned Authors

Many liberal textual critics argue that the books of the Bible were not written by their assigned authors. If the books were not written by the assigned author, then they were written by a later author(s). These later authors assigned authorship to the apostles because they carried enough authority to advance their theological motives and expression of Christianity (*MJ*, 23–29).

6. The Biases of the Authors Undermine Inspiration

If the biblical authors included any of their own biases, perspectives, beliefs, and so forth, then the Bible cannot be inspired. "Many of these authors no doubt felt they were inspired by God to say what they did, but they had their own perspectives, their own beliefs, their own views, their own needs, their own desires, their own understandings, their own theologies; and these perspectives, beliefs, views, needs, desires, understandings, and theologies informed everything they said. In all these ways they differed from one another" (*MJ*, 11). These differences among the writers create irreconcilable internal contradictions in the Bible—hence it cannot be inspired.

7. The Biases of the Interpreters Prompted Changes in the Text

The early Christian communities differed about the essential doctrines of Scripture. One example of this is the Gnostic Marcion. Ehrman believes, "Marcion's attempt to make his sacred texts conform more closely to his teaching by actually changing them was not unprecedented. Both before and after him, copyists of the early Christian literature occasionally changed their texts to make them say what they were already thought to mean" (*MJ*, 34). So many different Christian communities participated in this act of changing the text that we cannot be certain that the manuscripts we have today accurately reflect the originals.[1]

8. We Do Not Have the Original Manuscripts

Ehrman argues that either we believe in inerrancy and have the original manuscripts or accurate copies, or we do not believe in inerrancy because we do not have the originals or accurate copies. His position is that one should hold to the latter because the former is false. The former is false because

> the reality is that we don't have the originals—so saying they were inspired doesn't help much, unless I can reconstruct the originals. Moreover, the vast majority of Christians for the entire history of the church have not had access to the originals, making their inspiration a moot point. Not only do we not have the originals, we don't have the first copies of the originals, or copies of the copies of the copies of the original. (*MJ*, 10)

9. Late Copies of the Originals Are Filled with Too Many Errors to Know the Originals

The reason the original manuscripts cannot be known is because "What we have are copies made much later—much later. In most instances, they are copies made many *centuries* later. And these copies all differ from one another, in many thousands of places. As we will see later in this book, these copies differ from one another in so many places that we don't even know how many differences there are. Possibly it is easiest to put it in comparative terms: there are more differences among our manuscripts than there are words in the New Testament" (*MJ*, 10).

10. The Humanity of the Bible Argues against Its Inspiration

It is claimed that the humanity of the Bible removes the divine inspiration of the Scriptures. Ehrman believes that "just as human scribes had copied, and changed, the text of scripture, so too had human authors originally *written* the texts of scripture. This was a human book from beginning to end. It was written by different human authors at different times and in different places to address different needs" (*MJ*, 11).

11. The Biblical Authors Were Illiterate and Unable to Write Inerrant Books

Ehrman believes that because the accepted authors of Scripture were considered to be illiterate (Acts 4:13), then it would have been impossible for them to accurately record inerrant texts (*MJ*, 39).

12. Scribes Were Illiterate and Not Trustworthy in Ancient Times

Ehrman elaborates upon the fact that it was a common practice of former cultures to use a scribe to record letters, books, and so forth. But he believes that many of these scribes were illiterate and unable to accurately record the message. He offers an example from a professional scribe named Petaus, who was thought to have been unable to accurately record a message (*MJ*, 38–39, 71). If a professional scribe used by the government was unable to accurately record the message, then can we with any certainty believe that an unprofessional common scribe would be able to accurately record a book of the New Testament? Ehrman believes that these early scribes were so prone to error that we can be almost certain that the originals and copies contain errors (43, 46, 50–51, 59, 210).

13. MUCH OF EARLY CHRISTIAN DOCTRINE WAS BASED UPON FALLIBLE HUMAN ORAL TRADITION

Early centuries were known for using oral tradition to communicate messages. Not all oral traditions can be preserved because people tend to elaborate upon the original sayings or events of an individual. There was a time period between the life and teachings of Jesus. So there clearly was a chance for the message of Jesus to have been changed and adapted by the different Christian communities. Ehrman believes that the variants found in the manuscripts are due to the theological interpretations of each competing Christian community (*MJ*, 97–98).

14. THE FORMATION OF THE CANON WAS VERY LATE

It is believed that because the canon was formed much later than the penning of the original books, we cannot know with certainty which books were considered to reflect the actual life and teachings of Jesus. Ehrman says,

> The decisions about which books should finally be considered canonical were not automatic or problem-free; the debates were long and drawn out, and sometimes harsh. . . . The books we call the New Testament were not gathered together into one canon and considered scripture, finally and ultimately, until hundreds of years after the books themselves had first been produced. (*MJ*, 35–36, 153)

Finally, the books that are included in the canon were chosen by the group that won the battle for orthodoxy (153–54).

Issue 2: *The Transmission of Manuscripts Was Unreliable*

Ehrman also believes that the Bible is filled with transmissional or copyist errors. At one point he says,

> Scholars differ significantly in their estimates—some say there are 200,000 variants known, some say 300,000, some say 400,000 or more! We do not know for sure because, despite impressive developments in computer technology, no one has yet been able to count them all. . . . There are more variations among our manuscripts than there are words in the New Testament. (*MJ*, 89–90)

However, he admits that most of these errors don't affect the overall message of the text (207–8).

With this in mind, Ehrman still believes that the Bible has errors due to the transmission of the text. Here are the arguments he offers in support of his position:

1. No Manuscript from the Ancient World Is Trustworthy

In the ancient world no person was completely sure that any manuscript one was reading was what the author penned. There is always a chance that the scribe altered the text in some fashion. In fact, some of the scribes could have altered large portions of the text, and no one would have ever known (*MJ*, 46).

2. Most of the Errors Occurred in the First Two Hundred Years

Ehrman claims that most of the errors in the text of the Scripture occurred in the first two hundred years. The reason for this is because most of the early scribes were amateurs (*MJ*, 57). And it was not until the third and fourth century, after Constantine made Christianity the official religion, that professional scribes were used to transmit the text (55, 71–74). Therefore, "the texts that are closest in form to the original are, perhaps unexpectedly, the more variable and amateurish copies of early times, not the more standardized professional copies of later times"[2] (74).

3. Scribes Made Errors Because They Grew Inattentive

Scribes were human beings, and human beings grow tired and weary. Sometimes "scribes grew inattentive; sometimes they were hungry or sleepy; sometimes they just couldn't be bothered to give their best effort" (*MJ*, 55). Because of these human qualities, we can expect the manuscripts to be filled with copyist errors.

4. Scribal Notes Proves That There Were Changes in the Text

In some of the manuscripts are scribal notes on the side of the text to tell the reader there is a variant or there was a correction in the new manuscript. The point is that the scribes did intentionally change the text. And if they intentionally changed the text, how can we know which ones were driven by pure motives and which ones were driven by theological motives (*MJ*, 55–56)? Furthermore, there is no guarantee that the changes the scribes made in the text were changes toward the original. There is a chance the scribe was changing the text in a way that does not represent the original (57).

5. Early Opponents of Orthodox Christianity Recognize the Manuscript Changes

An early opponent named Celsus believed that the manuscripts of Scripture were changed in so many places as to render the originals unknowable. An early apologist named Origen tried to respond to these charges. But the point is that even an early opponent of Christianity clearly recognized the poor copyist practices among Christians. But ironically, it was Origen and the orthodox who claimed that Celsus and his heretical group changed the text (*MJ*, 52).

6. Some Copyist Errors Were Due to the Lack
of Punctuation in Greek Manuscripts

Early Greek manuscripts did not have punctuation marks. These marks are used to help the reader understand different words, where sentences end and begin, and to allow the reader to understand the authors' writings. But the scribes were not always able to understand the writings of the manuscripts because they were unable to read the text (*MJ*, 48–49). For instance, in the phrase "GODISNOWHERE," does it read "God is now here" or "God is nowhere"? Clearly the inability to read these types of words had to have created errors in the transmission of the manuscripts.

7. Once There Is an Error, It Could Affect
the Entire Textual Tradition

If an error enters into a manuscript, it could affect that entire textual tradition. This error could in fact become more predominant than the errorless original (*MJ*, 57). Since most of the texts were copied locally, it is not a surprise that different regions had different textual readings (72). The identity of the reading in a manuscript would seem to imply the identity of the origin (124). Therefore, there could be entire textual traditions filled with hundreds of errors, yet with no way to know which tradition is correct.

8. All Contemporary English Translations Are Based
upon Faulty Documents

Based upon all of these assumptions about the transmission of the text, Ehrman concludes,

> Even the translation you hold in your hands is affected by these textual problems we have been discussing, whether you are a reader of the New International Version, the Revised Standard Version, the New Revised Standard Version, the New American Standard Version, the New King James, the Jerusalem Bible, the Good News Bible, or something else. They are *all* based on texts that have been changed in places. (*MJ*, 209)

Issue 3: Many Changes in the Manuscripts Are Significant

Ehrman believes that there are two types of changes found in the manuscripts of the New Testament: (1) accidental and (2) by design (*MJ*, 46). He argues that the accidental changes could have occurred because the scribes were reading the wrong line or because certain words looked alike (25, 91). Changes by design, Ehrman contends, were intentional efforts by early scribes to preserve their theological convictions (152, 215). The reasons behind these changes were to (1) fix known errors in the text, (2) prevent errors of interpretation, (3) circumvent mistakes, (4) combat theological heretics, (5) emphasize certain doctrines, and (6) provide euphonic liturgical wording (94–97). He concludes that the only reason "orthodoxy" was able to decide upon the canon was because they simply won the theological battle, not necessarily because their views represented the original manuscripts—because the scribes had changed them in so many places that we do not know which ones were the original (153–54).

Ehrman offers multiple examples of what he considers to be changes in a single text that affect the interpretation of an entire book by investigating three christological heresies: (1) Adoptionist; (2) Docetic, and the (3) Separationist (132, 155, 162, 170). Furthermore, the scribes made later social changes in order to accommodate the changing social scene concerning women in the early church and conflicts with both Jews and pagans (177–205).

Thus Ehrman believes that the scribes intentionally changed the text to suit their theological and social beliefs. Some of these may have been harmless attempts to correct a text, but others were intentional changes to portray Christianity in a different light. Although it is outside of the limits of this work to offer a sufficient defense of each doctrine, it will be pointed out later that the historicity of the New Testament and the teaching of the early church disproves Ehrman's claim that the theological heretics were equally justified in their interpretations as orthodox Christianity.

Issue 4: These Changes Have an Effect on the Doctrine of Inerrancy

Ehrman believes that his conclusions about the transmission of the biblical text prevent it from being inerrant. As he says, "I realized already in graduate school, even if God had inspired the original words, we don't have the original words. So the doctrine of inspiration had been changed and, in some cases, lost. Moreover, I came to think that my earlier views of inspiration were not only irrelevant, they were probably wrong" (MJ, 211).

According to Ehrman, inerrancy is a new doctrine created by nonintellectual fundamentalists (4, 8, 13, 110, 249). He says, "I realized that most Christians throughout history—in fact the vast majority of Christians—have never thought any such thing about the Bible. And most Christian thinkers today do not think so" (251). He explains that the reason people believe in inerrancy is because they are pressured into believing it through institutional fundamentalist "brainwashing" (4). And through that brainwashing, people accept the literal interpretation of the Bible and write foolish books pertaining to end-time prophecy (12–13, 110).

Ehrman seems to have more respect for the Barthian view of Scripture. In fact, this was the view he held to after he gave up the inerrancy position (251). When talking about the issue of whether the Bible *is* the Word of God or the Word of men, he says, "Actually, I don't think it does have to be one or the other. In fact, most Christian thinkers I know think that the Bible is *both*: a book containing the Word of God and a book shaped by human hands" (250). "The Bible is understood in many, many ways (by many, many different Christians); but for most Christians it in some sense contains or conveys the Word of God, even though this word comes through the human words of the text, written by human authors" (251).

Finally, he even believes the Barthian position gives too much credence to the text of the Bible. The Bible is inspired (like any other book) insofar as it is inspiring, not because it is the Word of God or contains the Word of God. Rather, it is a human book, with its own biases, perspectives, opinions, ideas, and errors (251).

An Evaluation of Bart Ehrman's Views on Scripture

In responding to Ehrman's challenges to inerrancy, it is important to distinguish between the *evidence* and the best *explanation* of that evidence. Most biblical scholars agree about the basic historical facts concerning the New Testament, but they disagree about the interpretation of those facts. Further, the way one interprets the facts will depend on their presuppositions. As we shall see, this is certainly the case concerning Bart Ehrman.

Response to Ehrman's Philosophical Presuppositions

Bart Ehrman believes that people should approach the Bible without any presuppositions. They should not read the text through the eyes of faith but as neutral scientific observers. The difficulty with this claim is that even Ehrman does not approach the text as a neutral scientific observer but as one with presuppositions that are contrary to inerrancy. Thus it is no surprise that his conclusions oppose inerrancy.

RELATIVISM AND AGNOSTICISM

It is a fact that in the early centuries there was a battle between orthodox and heretical expressions of Christianity. But Ehrman contends that the modern reader cannot know which of these expressions represent the real Christianity—since orthodoxy only expresses the view of those who "won" the theological and political battle. And it was the task of their scribes to change the manuscripts to accommodate their theological convictions.

While the claim about theological orthodoxy merely "winning" the battle will be dealt with later, there seems to be a deeper philosophical presupposition undergirding the claim. Ehrman believes that because there were diverse expressions among the early Christians, each expression was equally valid. Andreas J. Kostenberger and Michael J. Kruger explain the significance of such a claim:

> Put differently, the sheer *existence* of disagreement among early Christians requires that we declare no one view to be right. Thus, from Ehrman's perspective, one must merely demonstrate that some group during the New Testament era disagreed with "orthodox" Christians about any given topic—and instead thought they were "orthodox" themselves—and then we all are obligated to agree that distinctions between heresy and orthodoxy are meaningless. (*Heresy of Orthodoxy* [*HO*], 163)

Kostenberger and Kruger elaborate upon Ehrman's relativistic presupposition:

Moreover, if the existence of disagreement amongst two groups (that are both sincere) means that no one position can be considered true, then, on Ehrman's reasoning, we could never affirm any historical truth unless there was virtually *zero* disagreement about it. And it seems this is precisely the way Ehrman wants it to be. If he can slip such an unattainable standard into the debate without anyone realizing it, then he can prove his case just by trotting out example after example of divergent Christian groups. However, such an exercise only proves compelling to those already committed to the "no-one-view-is-the-right-view" principle from the outset. (*HO*, 163).

The inconsistency of Ehrman's view becomes apparent when he deviates from his philosophical presupposition and claims to have the correct view. The many examples he offers are red herrings to the fact that he is a philosophical relativist. Hence, even his conclusions are tenuous at best. Practically, his work discourages true scholarship because even the most devout orthodox and critical scholarship is viewed as inadequate because it fails to accord with Ehrman's agnostic presuppositions.[3]

SKEPTICISM AND ANTISUPERNATURALISM

Ehrman also approaches the Bible with an antisupernatural presupposition. He discredits the validity of miracles by appealing to David Hume's argument against miracles (Geisler and Turek, *I Don't Have Enough Faith* [*IDHEF*], 205), which can be stated as follows:

1. Natural law is by definition a description of a regular occurrence.
2. A miracle is by definition a rare occurrence.
3. The evidence for the regular is always greater than that for the rare.
4. A wise person always bases one's beliefs on the greater evidence.
5. Therefore, a wise person should never believe in miracles.

If the four premises of Hume's argument are true, then it necessarily entails that a wise person should not believe in miracles. And if it is true that inspiration and inerrancy are both miracles, then it necessarily follows that no wise person should believe in these rare events.

The difficulty with Hume's argument is that it proves more than he desires. If true, it would not only discredit miracles; it would also discredit all unusual and extraordinary events—even ones for which there is good evidence. This makes any deviation from uniform repetition unbelievable. Unfortunately for Hume, premise 3 is not true because the evidence for the regular is not always greater than the rare (*IDHEF*, 206).

There are many counterexamples within the naturalistic worldview held by Ehrman that are contrary to Hume's claim. Scientists believe in many naturalistic singular events for which there are unrepeated singularities. For example, they believe in (1) the single origin of the universe through big-bang cosmology;

(2) the single origin of life when life-forms emerge spontaneously from non–life-forms; (3) the origin of new life-forms through macroevolution. None of these events were observed, and none have been repeated. Yet these are widely believed to have occurred (*IDHEF*, 206). Furthermore, in order to be consistent, people should discredit the plausibility of all singular events—even the singular event of one's birth.

Hume's theory also discredits the notion of a repetition of events. John Gerstner and R. C. Sproul have some added insight: "Uniformity itself rests upon repetition, a series or sequence of same or similar events. But the series can never be established because before there can be two such similar events there must first be one. The first, however, would be unique and therefore incredible. Its repetition cannot resurrect it because repetition becomes impossible by definition" (Sproul, Gerstner, and Lindsley, *Classical Apologetics*, 151).

Ehrman consistently appeals to Hume's argument to discredit the idea of an inerrant original and trustworthy copies. The problem with such a claim is that by the same argument he should discredit the validity of any singular or repetitious event in all of human history too. The many counterexamples to Ehrman's claim make it both logically inconsistent and practically self-defeating.

Deconstructionism and Hermeneutical Subjectivity

Ehrman goes beyond the historical claims about changes in the text through his embrace of postmodern deconstructionism. This hermeneutic teaches that through the act of reading a text, the reader deconstructs the author's meaning and reconstructs their own. It does not advocate that the reader annihilates the text; rather, they create a new text. It advocates that each time a person approaches a text, they should reread it with the intention of creating a new meaning.

Ehrman embraces this view: "And so to read a text is, necessarily, to change a text. That's what the scribes of the New Testament did. They read the texts available to them and they put them in *other* words. Sometimes, however, they *literally* put them in other words." On the one hand,

> when they did this, they did what all of us do every time we read a text, but on the other, they did something very different from the rest of us. For when we put a text in other words in our minds, we don't actually change the physical words on the page, whereas the scribes did precisely that, changing the words so that the words later readers would have before them were different words, which then had to be put into yet other words to be understood. (*MJ*, 217–18)

The implication of Ehrman's view is that the process of changing the text still occurs today. Every time a person reads the Bible, they are changing the meaning of the text to suit their own cultural and theological agenda. The implications of this view are disastrous. For no one can ever arrive at an accurate copy of anything because each time the text is read, it is inherently changed. Furthermore, the search for an original biblical autograph is rendered futile because even the original author changed the God-given text through the mere act of writing.

Such a view is only credible if one accepts that all language and truth are culturally relative, which they are not (see chaps. 13 and 14 below). There are many counterexamples against such deconstructionism:

1. If all meaning is rendered futile because it is limited by language, then the works of all deconstructionists are also futile because they are limited by language.
2. They embrace Wittgenstein's conventionalism, contending that all meaning is relative to the situation. But if that were the case, then even that statement would be culturally relative. If it is not culturally relative, then there are statements that are not culturally relative—hence it would be self-defeating (see chap. 14 below).
3. Deconstructionism is an attempt not to be dogmatic about language. But they are dogmatic when they claim that individuals cannot be sure about anything.
4. Practically, this view is self-defeating for even the deconstructionist expects the reader to interpret the text according to the meaning the deconstructionist has given it, not the meanings the readers give to it.

So, the deconstructionist is hanged on his own gallows. His view is contrary to his own practice and expectation. For he would not tolerate anyone deconstructing his claim for deconstructionism. He embraces the self-defeating position that he is sure that there is nothing you can be sure about. He assumes a fixed meaning to his statements that there is no fixed meaning in statements (see Geisler, *Systematic*, 1:167–68).

Therefore, it should be clear that Ehrman is reading the text of Scripture not as a neutral observer. There are clear philosophical presuppositions undergirding his claims, and they are the main factors driving his denial of the inspiration and inerrancy of the Bible.

Response to Erhman's Methodological Presuppositions

BAUER-EHRMAN THESIS THAT HERESY PRECEDED ORTHODOXY

In their book *The Heresy of Orthodoxy*, Kostenberger and Kruger attempt to disprove what they have labeled as the Bauer-Ehrman thesis. The thesis has its origin in the work of Walter Bauer, titled *Orthodoxy and Heresy in Earliest Christianity*. But it has also had profound impact upon the Jesus Seminar, Rudolf Bultmann, James Dunn, and now Bart Ehrman. Kostenberger and Kruger explain the origin and define the thesis by claiming that

prior to the publication of this volume [by Bauer], it was widely held that Christianity was rooted in the unified preaching of Jesus' apostles and that it was only later that this orthodoxy (right belief) was corrupted by various forms of heresy (or heterodoxy, "other" teaching that deviated from the orthodox standard or norm). Simply put, orthodoxy preceded heresy. In his seminal work, however, Bauer *reversed* this notion by proposing that *heresy*—that is, a variety of beliefs each of which could legitimately be authentically "Christian"—*preceded the notion of orthodoxy* as a standard set of Christian doctrinal beliefs. (*HO*, 24, emphasis added)

Bauer argued that what is considered orthodox Christian doctrine is merely the view that was imposed by the ecclesiastical hierarchy (*HO*, 24). The diversity in early Christianity proves that there was no single normative expression, and definitely no orthodoxy. What is considered to be "orthodoxy" stems from the Roman churches' ability to rewrite both history and the text of Scripture, hence eradicating traces of earlier diversity (24). Kostenberger and Kruger summarize the view by saying, "Thus what later became known as orthodoxy does not organically flow from the teaching of Jesus and the apostles but reflects the predominant viewpoint of the Roman church as it came into full bloom between the fourth and sixth centuries AD" (25).[4]

Bauer's thesis was accepted and used as a basis for reexamining early Christianity. There were early critiques of Bauer's view, but he ultimately laid the foundation for subsequent critical scholarship. Bart Ehrman is the mainstream expression of Bauer's thesis. He goes beyond Bauer by claiming that the orthodox not only won, but they also determined which books were to be included in the canon. In short, Ehrman contends that the "winners" were able to secure their expression of Christianity and eradicate all opposing views by choosing the books of the Bible, and hiding the other books and expressions from subsequent church history (*MJ*, 30–32).

There are many flaws with this view.[5] Here are a few of them:

1. Just because there is diversity among different groups claiming to be Christian does not necessarily entail that each group has an equal authority to base their claim. Undergirding this thesis is a relativistic understanding of truth (See "Relativism and Agnosticism" above).
2. Bauer selectively disregards the testimony of the New Testament and focuses entirely upon works of the second century through the fourth century. He repeatedly claims to have chosen his work from the earliest sources, but failure to deal with the text of the New Testament is a failure to investigate documents written by the eyewitnesses and contemporaries of the life and teachings of Jesus.
3. The text of the New Testament offers writings from eyewitnesses (e.g., John, Peter, Paul) making clear distinctions between orthodoxy and heresy. Other works were based on eyewitness testimony (Luke 1:1–4). Indeed, recent New Testament scholars (cf. Bauckham, *Jesus and the Eyewitnesses*) have defended the eyewitness testimony of the New Testament. In fact,

in the book of Galatians, one of Paul's earliest epistles, which even critics accept, he recognizes the Judaizers' heresy to be "another" gospel and says, "If anyone is preaching to you a gospel contrary to the one you received, let him be accursed" (Gal. 1:6–9).

4. The writings of the New Testament opposed heresy. Paul repeatedly spoke against the seed forms of Gnosticism (Col. 2); the Pastoral Epistles are works to refute heresy; Jude spoke against false teachers; Peter spoke against eschatological heretics (2 Pet. 3); John spoke against docetists and other false teachers (1 John 4) and against heresy to the churches in Revelation. Clearly, it is simply untrue to claim that there was not an early expression of orthodoxy prior to heresy.

5. The early Christians were dedicated to following the "apostles' teaching" (Acts 2:42; cf. Eph. 2:20), not creating new forms and expressions of Christianity. In the spread of the early church to Gentiles, they were routinely making sure that they were in accordance with the message and expression found at Pentecost and with the apostles' teaching.

6. There are early creeds and confessional statements that precede the text of Scripture. While many of these are included in Scripture (Matt. 16:16; Mark 8:29; John 11:27; Acts 2:36; Phil. 2:6–11; Col. 1:15–20; Heb. 10:29; 1 Pet. 1:3; Jude 17), it is clear that Christians prior to the books of the New Testament had orthodox confessions about Christ and his teachings (cf. 1 Tim. 3:16; 1 Cor. 15:3–7).

7. The New Testament hope in the Messiah is grounded in the Old Testament. The Gospel writers were intentional to include references concerning the lineage of Christ (Matt. 1:1–17; Luke 3:23–38). The writings portrayed Christ to be in accordance with the Old Testament prophecies of the coming Messiah (Matt. 1:1; Rom. 1:1–4). Peter (Acts 2) and Paul (Acts 13) both cited OT texts in support of their belief that Jesus is the Messiah.

8. The works of the early Christian apologists continue the unbroken line of orthodoxy. Irenaeus, who knew Polycarp (a disciple of John the apostle), is a classic case in point (see *Against Heresies*). In their works they are repeatedly combating false ideas in defense of the "faith that was once for all delivered to the saints" (Jude 3).

9. All of these arguments and declarations were made prior to the formations of the classic creeds of the third and fourth century.

So the Bauer-Ehrman thesis fails because it is a historical fact that orthodoxy preceded heresy. Only special pleading with the facts can avoid this conclusion.

Brief Response to Ehrman's Conclusions

Since methodology determines theology, it is no surprise that Ehrman's conclusions about Scripture are not orthodox. He has four basic charges: (1) The original manuscripts were not reliable and are nonexistent. (2) The transmission of manuscripts was unreliable. (3) There have been significant changes in the manuscripts. (4) These changes undermine the doctrine of inerrancy. It is granted that if his premises are correct, then so would his conclusion be correct. However, as we will see, these premises are open to serious challenge. Let's examine them briefly and then take a look at the positive defense for the historicity of the New Testament:

1. THE ORIGINAL MANUSCRIPTS WERE NOT RELIABLE AND ARE NONEXISTENT

Ehrman believes that the original manuscripts of the Bible were a result of Jesus's misinterpretation of the Old Testament, and that this method was continued by his followers. His first premises are that (1) Jesus was the founder and first interpreter of the Christian canon, (2) Jesus's interpretation of Scripture was considered equal with Scripture, and (3) the writings of Jesus's apostles were considered Scripture. With the exception in premise 1 that Jesus and the apostles misinterpreted the Old Testament,[6] these three premises are correct, and there is no reason for an orthodox theologian to challenge them.

Ehrman's claim that "the canon of Scripture is only one of many competing interpretations of the life of Jesus" is true but misleading. It was one interpretation, but it was also the only *correct* one since it was made based on multiple eyewitnesses and contemporaries of the events. Certainly there were early heresies. Even the New Testament records some of them (e.g., 1 Tim. 4; 2 Tim. 2; Col. 2; 1 John 4). However, there is no reason to accept Ehrman's claim that these other views were *equally valid claims* to be Christian.

First of all, the only authentic first-century record we have of apostolic teaching is in the New Testament, and it condemns these other views as false interpretations of Christianity. Even most critics like Ehrman agree that the twenty-seven books of the New Testament were written in the first century. If so, then they alone have the claim to be apostolic writings.

Second, we have no other contemporary writings from the first century even claiming to come from an apostle or his associate. And the ones we have from close to the end of first century (like Ignatius, Polycarp, and Clement of Rome) do not contradict the apostolic writings but support them.

Third, the immediate successors of the first-century apostolic writers (like Irenaeus) strongly insisted that only the apostolic interpretation based on four and only four Gospels is the correct interpretation of Christ and his teaching. For example, Irenaeus (AD 120–200) knew Polycarp, who was a disciple of the apostle John. And Irenaeus wrote *Against Heresies*, in which he declares: "It is not possible that the Gospels can be more or fewer in number than [the four] they are. For there are four zones of the world in which we live, four principal winds, while the Church is scattered throughout all the world, and the 'pillar and ground' of the Church is the Gospel and the spirit of life; it is fitting that she should have four pillars" (3.11.8). In short, Irenaeus believed that there were four and only four Gospels and that they were written by the people whose names they bore: two were apostles (Matthew and John), and the other two were associates of two apostles, Mark with Peter, and Luke with Paul.

As for Ehrman's claim that many of the books in the New Testament were not written by the assigned authors, two points are sufficient. First, some of them were written by the assigned authors. Even the critics accept that Paul wrote at least four books (1 and 2 Corinthians, Romans, and Galatians). It is widely accepted that Luke wrote Acts and the Gospel of Luke, and that Luke was closely associated with the apostle Paul (Col. 4:14). And many scholars believe that John either wrote or directed the writing of his Gospel (cf. John 19:35; 21:24). Second, other writings were based on eyewitness testimony (see Bauckham, *Jesus and the Eyewitnesses*). Further, there is sufficient evidence to believe that the traditional writers of most, if not all, of the New Testament were actually the writers of those texts (see Carson and Moo, *Introduction to the New Testament*). If so, then all the authors of the New Testament were either apostles or associates of an apostle. This would include

Matthew—*an apostle of Jesus*
Mark—*an associate of the apostle Peter*
Luke—*an associate of the apostle Paul*
John—*an apostle of Jesus*
Paul—*an apostle of Jesus*
James—*the brother of Jesus*
Peter—*an apostle of Jesus*
Jude—*the brother of James*
Hebrews—*an associate of the apostles* (2:3; 13:23)

For our purposes here, it doesn't matter if all these were the actual authors or not since even most critics agree that some were and most (if not all) of the others were based on eyewitnesses—which is sufficient to show the reliability of the New Testament.

Interestingly, a former Bultmannian critic of the New Testament, Eta Linnemann, who studied under both Bultmann and Dibelius, has recanted her view and now accepts the early dates and traditional authors of all the New Testament books. She reveals her reasons in two books: *Is There a Synoptic Problem?* and *Historical Criticism*. Even an unrecantant "Death of God" New Testament scholar, Bishop John Robinson, revised his critical view of the New Testament before he died and concluded that the dates should be: Matthew—AD 40–60+; Mark—AD 45–60+; Luke—AD 57–60+; John—AD 40–65+ (*Redating the New Testament*, 352–54). On these earlier dates, they would have been written either by the traditional authors or under their supervision. Noted biblical archaeologist William F. Albright concluded, contrary to his earlier more liberal views, that every book in the New

Testament was written "very probably sometime between about 50 and 75 AD" ("More Conservative View").

The other claims by Ehrman are not supported by the evidence either:

The biases of the authors undermine inspiration. In response, the following evidence favors their reliability: (a) There were multiple authors. (b) They were eyewitnesses or based on eyewitness accounts. (c) They accepted the Epistles of Paul (1 and 2 Corinthians, Romans, and Galatians), which are sufficient testimony to the basic fact about Jesus as recorded in the Gospels. (d) The internal evidence supports the trustworthiness of the accounts. (e) Legal scholars have supported the reliability of the New Testament witness. (f) Roman historians of that period confirm the reliability of the records. (g) Most of the books of the New Testament were written by or under the direction of educated persons (e.g., Luke the doctor; Saul/Paul of Tarsus, rabbinic scholar). (h) Biases (which everyone has) do not necessarily negate truthfulness. Holocaust witnesses are biased against it but are the best witnesses about it. Even the critics have biases that would, by their own criterion, eliminate their view on these matters. These and other evidences are developed below under "The Historicity of the New Testament."

The biases of the interpreters prompted change in the text. As we show below, the autographic text of Scripture can be reproduced with a very high percentage of accuracy—so much so that no basic teaching of Jesus or doctrine of the Christian church is undermined by these minor variations in the manuscripts. This is true for a couple basic reasons. First, despite the thousands of variants, they are not in thousands of places. Second, most of them are not significant variants. Finally, none of them affect any basic doctrine of Scripture, for what may be in doubt in one text is clearly taught in other texts.

2. The Transmission of Manuscripts Was Unreliable

This point is supported by Ehrman with the following claims: (1) We do not have the original manuscripts or good copies. (2) Late copies of the originals are filled with too many errors to know the original.

These are both contrary to fact, as just indicated. They will be addressed more completely below. This section offers cumulative evidence so great that there is no basis for any reasonable doubt, unless one is willing to reject the authenticity of all documents from antiquity, the legal processes used in courts, and everyday common sense. At that point, one should become critical of the critics and skeptical of the skeptics.

As for Ehrman's claim that the humanity of the Bible argues against its inspiration, we offer the following points. First, this is based on the fallible premise that "humans always err" (from the popular saying "To err is human"). But humans do not *always* err. There are some inerrant phone books where all the numbers are correct. Second, it begs the question by denying that there is a theistic God who can supernaturally intervene and keep the biblical authors from erring, as the Scriptures say he did. For Jesus said to his disciples, "The Holy Spirit . . . will teach you all things and bring to your remembrance all that I have said to you" (John 14:26). He added, "When the Spirit of truth comes, he will guide you into all the truth" (16:13). Peter described the process by which God does this: "No prophecy ever had its origin in the human will, but prophets, though human, spoke from God as they were carried along by the Holy Spirit" (2 Pet. 1:21). Only if one has, like Ehrman, antitheistic and antisupernatural presuppositions could he conclude that those who wrote the New Testament necessarily erred.

As for Ehrman's claim that the biblical authors were unable to write inerrant books because they were illiterate, two points should be made. First of all, not all biblical writers were "illiterate." The apostle Paul was not, and he is the traditional author of either thirteen or fourteen books (if he wrote Hebrews) of the New Testament. Even ardent critics admit that Paul wrote four books, which, as we will see below, are sufficient to support the historicity of Jesus, his basic teachings, and his death and resurrection—the very core of Christian teaching. Further, Luke the physician and first-rate historian wrote two more crucial books of the New Testament: the Gospel of Luke and the book of Acts. So with the widely accepted books of Paul, one Gospel, and Acts all written by highly educated men, Ehrman's criticism rings hollow.

Second, even the books by the other New Testament writers (e.g., James, Peter, John, and Jude) do not preclude their writing reliable history. Indeed, ordinary people do not ordinarily have the extraordinary presuppositional baggage that some educated people (like Ehrman) have. A jury is made up of ordinary people, and as a whole they do a good job in determining the truth. Further, this criticism is again begging the question. For it denies that a supernatural God was involved in the process, as the New Testament says he was (John 14:26; 16:13; 2 Tim. 3:16; 2 Pet. 1:2–21). As for imperfect humans producing a perfect book, Ehrman neglects the fact that God can draw a straight line with a crooked stick!

Third, as for the charge that the scribes were a lower-class illiterate people, this has been proved to be false (Kostenberger and Kruger, *Heresy of Orthodoxy*, 183–86). It is true that many of the early Christians were illiterate, but the literacy rate of the entire Roman Empire was only about 10–15 percent of the population. But just because they were illiterate does not prove that they did not place high value upon the biblical text. What is more, the social makeup of the Christian community was not substantially different than the surrounding communities. This is evidenced by the fact that some owned houses, had slaves, and possessed resources to travel. These people were definitely wealthy, and according to Ehrman they would have been literate. Furthermore, the leaders of the churches were able to read and write, which is evidenced by the Gospels themselves and the works of the early church fathers and letters among the churches. Finally, claiming from Acts 4:13 that Peter and John were illiterate is unfounded. The text claims that they were "uneducated," and in the context of the day this means that they were not formally trained in the rabbinical teachings. An appeal to Celsus to show that the Christians were an illiterate and perverse people is unfounded. There is evidence that Celsus was overstating his case. Origen acknowledged this and showed that this did not constitute all of the Christian movement.

Ehrman also wrongly asserts that scribes were illiterate and not trustworthy in ancient times. This premise is supposed to undermine the accuracy of many copies of the original text. But this process is crucial to the inerrancy position for, as shown above (in the introduction to this chapter), inerrantists claim that we do not need the inerrant original text because we have good copies of it. First of all, evangelicals believe that God "providentially" guided the copying process so as to produce a reliable, adequate, and even highly accurate copy of the autographic text. Second, even on a purely human plane, with no supernatural help, the copies of Homer, Plato, Aristotle, and others from the ancient world have produced adequate copies for us to know what they taught. And as shown below, we have a more accurate copy of the original New Testament than they do of their original texts. Third, regardless of what prompted scribal errors, the science of textual criticism is able to weed out the variant readings and produce a reliable text. Even Ehrman admits that the vast majority of the variants are not significant and do not affect the central teaching of the biblical text. Here again, Ehrman's antitheistic and antisupernatural presuppositions hinder him from coming to the correct conclusion.

Finally, this claim is clearly false for many reasons: (1) While there are changes in the text of Scripture, not all changes are equal in significance. Most of them were trivial, not changing the meaning of the text. (2) The presence of scribal notes proves that the copyists knew where the changes were made and that they wanted the reader to be aware of these changes. (3) Though it is true that the scribes were real people, who grew tired and weary, it is not true to claim that these copyist errors occurred often enough to make the overall manuscripts historically unreliable. These kinds of errors are known, but they do not discredit any theological doctrine. Hence, these kinds of scribal changes do not affect the reliability of the New Testament manuscripts in conveying the original message.

Ehrman also contends that much of early Christian doctrine was based upon fallible human oral tradition. But this conclusion is wrong for several reasons. First of all, as we shall show, the accepted early dates of some New Testament books of Paul (AD 55–57) rule this out. This is only 22 to 24 years after AD 33, when Jesus was crucified (see Hoehner, *Chronological Aspects*). Even noted archaeologist William F. Albright and "Death of God" theologian Bishop John Robinson date some Gospels as early as AD 40–50. This is much too early for Ehrman's fallible "traditions" to develop. Ehrman's thesis here is contrary to the well-established arguments from a noted Roman historian that Luke wrote Acts by about AD 61 (Hemer, *Book of Acts*). And his Gospel was written prior to that (cf. Luke 1:1; Acts 1:1).

Further, it is wrong to claim that all oral tradition is equal to a game of telephone. The reason the preservation of oral teachings seems impossible to a modern reader is because modern culture is not based on oral tradition. In like manner, it would seem odd to an oral tradition that the modern world does not function according to oral teachings. New Testament scholar William Lane Craig points out that "in an oral culture like that of first-century Palestine the ability to memorize and retain large tracts of oral tradition was a highly prized and highly developed skill. From the earliest age children in the home, elementary school, and the synagogue were taught to memorize faithfully sacred tradition. The disciples would have exercised similar care with the teachings of Jesus" ("Evidence for Jesus").

Finally, it is known that first-century persons kept written records. Archaeologists have found holders of their tablets. Writing things down was not uncommon, even a couple thousand years before the time of Christ, as has been demonstrated by the discovery of the Mari Letters and the Ebla Tablets. Since Matthew, the traditional author of the first Gospel, was a tax collector, he no doubt was used to keeping records. It should be no surprise, then, if he would record the long discourses of Christ (Matt. 10; 13; 23:2–35). Luke was an educated person and speaks of many who set out to "compile a narrative" about the life of Christ (Luke 1:1) before him (i.e., before AD 61) and of his desire "to write an orderly account" of the same (1:3). So there is no reason why there could not also have been written records by eyewitnesses and even apostles of the word and works of Christ.

Ehrman also argues that (14) the formation of the canon was very late, but this misses the point. The question here is the reliability of the New Testament, not its final canonicity (that is, its later acceptance by the church at large). What we do know and what does bear on the reliability of the original New Testament manuscripts is that they were cited early and often, starting from the late first century. Also, within the first century after Christ, every book in the New Testament (except 3 John, a tiny one-chapter book) were cited during the century immediately following Christ. So it is not a question as to when everyone in the church eventually recognized the New Testament. Rather, they are authentic as first-century books during eyewitness and apostolic times, as supported by their immediate use as inspired books.

Most of the other faulty premises of Ehrman can be lumped together: (1) No manuscript from the ancient world is trustworthy. (2) Most of the errors occurred in the first two hundred years. (3) Scribes made errors because they grew inattentive. (4) Scribal notes proves that there were changes in the text. (5) Early opponents to orthodox Christianity recognized the manuscript changes. (6) Some copyist errors were due to the lack of punctuation in Greek manuscripts. (7) Once there is an error, it could affect the entire textual tradition.

First of all, (1) is clearly an overstatement. If true, we would have to wipe out most of ancient and medieval history. And the fact that (2) most of the errors occurred in the first two hundred years is not a definitive argument for the accuracy of the copy we have because (a) it would wipe out virtually all books from the ancient historians since almost none have manuscripts that are that early. (b) It overlooks the multitude of manuscripts in other languages (some 19,000). (c) More important, it overlooks the 5,700-plus Greek manuscripts we have and the likelihood that the original readings were preserved in them. (d) Most important, it overlooks the providence of God. Surely, a theistic God has both the desire and ability to preserve his basic truths for humankind.

Further, the fact that (3) scribes made errors because they grew inattentive is logically true and would carry weight if textual criticism were unable to recognize such errors. But the science of textual criticism has been able to recognize errors of this type and many others. Hence, this type of reasoning does not affect the validity of the text of Scripture. The presence of scribal notes (4) demonstrates that the scribes knew where they were changing the text, not that they were trying to hide it from readers. If a scribe were trying to hide such changes, they surely would not include a large side note pointing out the change! The fact that non-Christians were able to spot errors (5) does not disprove the text of Scripture and should be seen as bettering the precision of the text. They allow subsequent textual critics to validate the exact place where the changes were made and then make corrections to later copies.

Ehrman frequently appeals to the lack of punctuation in the manuscripts as evidence that the scribes must have changed the text (6). This type of reasoning, while dealt with briefly above, fails because the scribes were trained in the copyist techniques of their day. As noted, the GODISNOWHERE illustration is a false analogy. It wrongly compares modern English with the Koine Greek of the New Testament. First, it misuses proper English grammar, which would say, "God does not exist." Second, during that time period, Greek was one of many languages that did not use punctuation. While it seems foreign to a modern reader, it would have been customary for a native speaker and copyist of this language to encounter this type of literature. Also, in cases where it was difficult to understand each word, the copyist copied letter for letter. Finally, it fails to take note that the context would readily indicate how to separate the letters into words. No such illustration exists in the New Testament.

Further, the claim that all contemporary English translations are based upon faulty documents is not true because the word "faulty" assumes that they are inadequate and inaccurate in conveying the essential truth of the originals. Thus we disagree with his claim that many changes in the manuscripts are significant. As will be shown below, no changes affect the essential teachings of Christianity: as even Ehrman admits, most errors are minor and do not affect the message of the text (MJ, 55).

To review, Ehrman argues that (1) the original manuscripts were not reliable and are nonexistent; (2) the transmission of manuscripts was unreliable; (3) there have been significant changes in the manuscripts; (4) these changes undermine the doctrine of inerrancy. But as we have shown, the first three premises are not supported by the evidence. And if they are not true, then the conclusion does not follow. So he has not succeeded in undermining the doctrine of inerrancy. To do that he would have to find an original text with an error in it (which all agree we have not found), or else to show that we cannot adequately reconstruct the original text from the copies we have. And if the manuscripts are reliable, then we do have the claims and credentials of Christ to be the Son of God and to be confirmed by miracles (see Geisler and Turek, *I Don't Have Enough Faith*, chaps. 8–15). And since miracles are possible (ibid., chaps. 1–4), Ehrman has also failed to disprove them and inerrancy. Indeed, to turn the tables, Erhman's view bears the heavy burden of disproving God. For even if it is possible for God to exist, then miracles are possible. And if miracles are possible and the New Testament documents are reliable, then we have a reliable account of Jesus's claim to be God and to be offering unprecedented miracles to support his claim. Once the possibility of God's existence has been granted, which only hard-core atheism even argues against, albeit unsuccessfully (see Geisler, "God, Alleged Disproofs of"), then it remains only to show the cumulative evidence for the reliability of the New Testament documents.

The Historicity of the New Testament

Not only has Ehrman failed to overturn inerrancy with his unjustified skepticism; he has overlooked the overwhelming cumulative case for the reliability of New Testament manuscripts and of the strong case for the historicity of the New Testament based on them. There are several lines of evidence supporting the historicity of the New Testament. Combined together, they make a formidable case. This includes both external and internal evidence.

The External Evidence for the Historicity of the New Testament

More external evidence exists for the New Testament than for any book from the ancient world. There are more manuscripts, earlier manuscripts, better-copied manuscripts, based on more multiple eyewitness testimony, and confirmed by more other early sources than for any other book of its time.

1. THE NUMBER OF THE NEW TESTAMENT MANUSCRIPTS

The number of New Testament manuscripts is greater than for any other book from ancient history. There are roughly 5,700 Greek manuscripts in existence compared to many other books from antiquity that only have seven to ten manuscripts. Yet few scholars of antiquity dismiss the general reliability of manuscripts on Plato, Aristotle, and others as not substantially reliable. The most for any other book is Homer's *Iliad*, with 643 manuscripts. But the New Testament has nearly ten times as many manuscripts. Therefore, by contrast the New Testament has the most textual support of any book from antiquity.

Ehrman's argument that the original has been lost due to the high number of errors fails. For what he fails to tell his readers is that with the greater number of manuscripts, there is also a greater number of sources to confirm the essential original message. And with the greater number of manuscripts, there is greater chance that the original text is preserved in those manuscripts. On the contrary, while having few manuscripts does decrease the number of changes, it also decreases the ability to know where the text has been changed and, hence, the ability to reconstruct the original text.

What is more, in addition to Greek manuscripts are numerous copies of the New Testament in other languages. In fact, there are over 19,000 early translations in Old Syriac, Old Latin, Coptic, Latin Vulgate, and other languages. With nearly 6,000 Greek manuscripts, this totals some 25,000 copies of the New Testament (in whole or in part). Nothing else in the ancient world even comes close to this. So, to conclude that we do not have a reliable record in the New Testament is to wipe out the textual basis for all of ancient history!

2. The Early Date of the New Testament Manuscripts

New Testament textual critics desire to have manuscripts as close as possible to the original. No other book from antiquity has a smaller gap between the time of the original and the first existing manuscript. The earliest undisputed manuscript is a fragment from the Gospel of John called the John Rylands Papyrus ($\mathfrak{P}^{52}$), dated AD 117–38. Many scholars believe this was written within a generation of its original composition (ca. AD 95). The nature of circulation in the ancient cultures and the fact that it was written in Asia Minor and found in Egypt demands that it must have been written in the first century. Whole New Testament books, including a Gospel and some Epistles, are found in the Bodmer Papyri (ca. AD 200). This is only one century from when the eyewitnesses died. Most of the entire New Testament, including the Gospels, is available in the Chester Beatty Papyri from 150 years after the composition of the New Testament (AD 250).

In view of the evidence, noted British manuscript scholar Sir Frederic Kenyon concluded that "the interval then between the dates of original composition and the earliest extant evidence becomes so small as to be in fact negligible, and the last foundation for any doubt that the Scriptures have come down to us substantially as they were written has now been removed. [Thus] both the *authenticity* and the general *integrity* of the books of the New Testament may be regarded as finally established" (*Bible and Archaeology*, 288–89).

The next closest books are the works of Homer, which have 643 manuscripts with a 500-year time gap; Demosthenes, with 200 manuscripts and a 1,400-year time gap; Herodotus, with 8 manuscripts and a 1,400-year time gap; and Plato, with 7 manuscripts and a 1,200-year time gap (Geisler and Turek, *I Don't Have Enough Faith* [*IDHEF*], 226). Clearly the New Testament is the most well-attested book from all of ancient history. *If one denies the reliability of the New Testament based upon the number of manuscripts and the interval of time between its original composition and nearest copy, then they would have to thereby discredit the reliability of every work from ancient history!*

3. The Accuracy of the New Testament Manuscripts

Further, the New Testament is more accurately copied than any other book from ancient history. Ehrman's mentor at Princeton, Professor Bruce Metzger, conducted a research project comparing the accuracy of the copies of the New Testament to other ancient works. He concluded that the Hindu *Mahabharata* was copied with about 90 percent accuracy, and Homer's *Iliad* with 95 percent accuracy (*IDHEF*, 229). This is a more than sufficient degree of accuracy to provide the essential teaching of the originals. However, by contrast, scholars have shown that the New Testament was estimated to have been copied with up to 99 percent of accuracy. Manuscript experts Westcott and Hort estimated that only about one-sixteenth of errors rise above "trivialities." That would make copies 98.33 percent accurate (Westcott and Hort, *New Testament*, 2:2). Ezra Abbot's figures yield a text that is 99.75 percent pure (see Warfield, *Introduction*, 13–14). The great New Testament Greek scholar A. T. Robertson declared that "the real concern is with a 'thousandth part of the entire text.'" That would be 99.9 percent accuracy on anything of real concern (ibid., 22).

What is more, even Ehrman himself admits that the manuscript variants themselves do not affect the central message of the New Testament. He wrote: "It would be a mistake, however, to assume that the only changes being made were by copyists with a personal stake in the wording of the text. In fact, *most of the changes found in our early Christian manuscripts have nothing to do with theology or ideology*. Far and away the most changes are results of mistakes, pure and simple—slips of the pen, accidental omissions, inadvertent additions, misspelled words, blunders of one sort or another" (*MJ*, 55, emphasis added).

Kostenberger and Kruger make a good point when they note that

> significant variants would be a problem *if* we could assume that every one of them was as equally viable as every other. The problem with such an assumption, however, is that it stands in direct contradiction to the entire history of textual criticism—indeed, to the very *existence* of the field itself—which has consistently maintained that not all textual variants are equally viable and that our methodology can determine (with a reasonable degree of certainty) which is the original text. If that is the case, then these few "significant" textual variants do not materially affect the integrity of the New Testament because, put simply, we can usually spot them when they occur. (*Heresy of Orthodoxy*, 209–10, 218)

Textual criticism allows for the reconstruction of the text even if errors were made during the transmission process. Suppose that there were four different manuscripts with errors in the same verse. Romans 8:1, "There is therefore now no condemnation for those who are in Christ Jesus," could look like this:

1. There is th#erefore now no condemnation for those who are in Christ Jesus.
2. There is th#refore now no condemnation for those who are in Christ Jesus.
3. There is the#efore now no condemnation for those who are in Christ Jesus.
4. There is ther#fore now no condemnation for those who are in Christ Jesus.

The message of the original text can clearly be found in these manuscripts. Even in one manuscript (with an error), 100 percent of the message comes through. And the more errors (with more manuscripts) we have, we become more sure of the message since we have multiple confirmation of every other letter each time there is a new manuscript with another error. Percentage-wise, there are actually fewer errors in the New Testament than are represented by this example.

Further, Ehrman's stress on the multiplicity of manuscript variants is seriously misleading. For if one word is misspelled in 3,000 manuscripts, this is counted as 3,000 errors. But this is the equivalent of zero errors that affect the message of the New Testament. Mariano Grinbank discovered 16 errors in Ehrman's book *Misquoting Jesus*.[7] Since this first edition is reported to have sold 100,000 copies in the first three months, this would mean (the way Ehrman counts errors in the Bible manuscripts) that there are 1.6 million errors in Ehrman's books! Yet no reasonable person would argue that because of this we cannot trust the copies to convey Ehrman's original thoughts on the matter.

Further, Ehrman's argument that there are political and cultural influences on the variant readings in the New Testament is also misleading. Suppose three manuscripts with such biases existed that read:

1. YOU HAVE WON TEN MILLION DOLLARS
2. THOU **HAST WON** TEN MILLION DOLLARS [with a King James bias here]
3. Y'ALL **HAVE WON** $10,000,000 [with a Southern bias here!]

Notice that of the 28 letters in line 2, only 5 of them [in bold] are the same in line 3. That is, only about 18.5 percent are the same. Yet the message is 100 percent identical. They are different in form but not in content. Likewise, even with the many differences in the New Testament variants, 100 percent of the message comes through.

4. THE CONFIRMATION OF THE NEW TESTAMENT MANUSCRIPTS BY EARLY CHURCH FATHERS

The church fathers who lived in the first few centuries of the Christian church provided some 19,368 citations of the text of the Gospels alone. This includes 268 by Justin Martyr, 1,038 by Irenaeus, 1,017 by Clement of Alexandria, 9,231 by Origen, 3,822 by Tertullian, 734 by Hippolytus, and 3,258 by Eusebius (Geisler and Nix, *General Introduction*, 431). Even before these authors, we find earlier citations: Pseudo-Barnabas (AD 70–130) cited Matthew, Mark, and Luke; Clement of Rome (ca. AD 95–97) cited Matthew, John, and 1 Corinthians; Ignatius (ca. AD 110) referred to six of Paul's epistles; Shepherd of Hermas (AD 115–140) cited Matthew, Mark, Acts, 1 Corinthians, and other books; the *Didache* (ca. AD 120–150) referred to Matthew, Luke, 1 Corinthians, and other books; and Papias, companion of Polycarp, who was a disciple of the apostle John, quotes John's Gospel (Geisler, *Systematic Theology*, 1:463–64).

The significance of these citations is that they argue that the Gospels were in existence before they were cited, which places them within the first century, while some of the eyewitnesses (such as John) were still alive. Second, it also argues for an early date for the orthodox message of the life and teachings of Jesus Christ. If this be the case, it virtually eliminates any time gap between the completion of the New Testament and the proclamation of orthodoxy.

Ehrman has repeatedly made a big deal out of the fact that we still do not have the originals. But there are two problems here. First, there is a difference between the original *manuscripts* and original *text* (i.e., the autographic text). We agree that we do not have the original manuscripts, but we do not agree that we do not have the autographic text preserved in the manuscripts. The great manuscript expert of the last century, Sir Frederic Kenyon, wrote:

> The number of mss. of the New Testament, of early translations from it, and of quotations from it in the oldest writers of the Church, is so large that it is practically certain that the true reading of every doubtful passage is preserved in some one or the other of these ancient authorities. This can be said of no other book in the world. (*Our Bible*, 55, emphasis added)

Second, another problem with Ehrman's argument is that he has incorrectly contended that we either have *all* or *nothing*, that we can either be fully assured or we can have no assurance of the text. This false dichotomy has allowed him to draw false conclusions about the trustworthiness of the Bible. But this is beside the issue since everyone, including Ehrman, agrees that we do possess accurate copies of a large portion of original autographs (Kostenberger and Kruger, *Heresy of Orthodoxy*, 228–29).

Third, we not only have the autographic text (perhaps in its entirety) preserved in the manuscript copies somewhere, but we know where with 99-plus percent accuracy. This means that we can identify almost the complete autographic text in the manuscripts we have. Where is it found? It is found in the Nestle-Aland Greek New Testament, with its critical apparatus, which Ehrman himself and virtually all other New Testament scholars use.

Fourth, with regard to the essential message of the autographic text, we have 100 percent of it. No major New Testament teaching is affected by any of the variant readings in the manuscripts. As Philip Schaff noted of the variant readings known in his day, only fifty were of real significance, and there is "[no] *article of faith or a precept of duty which is not abundantly sustained by other and undoubted passages, or by the whole tenor of Scripture teaching*" (*Companion to the Greek Testament*, 177, emphasis added).

5. THE EXISTENCE OF MULTIPLE ACCOUNTS ABOUT JESUS IN THE NEW TESTAMENT

It is a well-established rule of law that "only on the evidence of two witnesses or of three witnesses shall a charge be established" (Deut. 19:15). But in the case of the New Testament, there are eight or nine writers (depending on whether Paul wrote Hebrews). There was Matthew, Mark, Luke, John, Paul, Peter, James, Jude, and the writer of Hebrews. Even if all the traditional authors are not the actual authors (and even the critics admit that some were), nonetheless, by the critics' own (late) dates for the New Testament (viz., AD 70–100), they were still written during the time of contemporaries and eyewitnesses of the events. To have twenty-seven pieces of literature written by eight or nine contemporary authors, all of whom were giving the same basic message about Christ, is unprecedented. Nothing like it exists for any other book from antiquity. This alone should be sufficient evidence for the reliability of the New Testament documents.

By contrast, the life of Alexander the Great, the basics of which are widely accepted as true, is based on no contemporary writers and only several histories some three to five hundred years later. *A fortiori* (with the greater force), considering that we have twenty-seven documents from contemporaries of the events, one should have no hesitation in accepting their general reliability, particularly on the core events on which their testimony overlaps.

6. THE EYEWITNESS NATURE OF THE NEW TESTAMENT

Not only are there earlier, more multiple, more accurate, and more numerous contemporary documents for the basic New Testament events; these documents were also based on eyewitness testimony. This is indeed what the Gospel of Luke claims: "Many have undertaken to compile a narrative of the things that have been accomplished among us, just as those who were *eyewitnesses and ministers of the word have delivered them to us*" (Luke 1:1–2, emphasis added). One eyewitness was the apostle Paul, who studied at the feet of the great Jewish scholar Gamaliel (Acts 22:3). And Luke the physician was not only an educated eyewitness; his writing has also been confirmed in numerous details by archaeological and literary sources (see below).

One thing is clear: the New Testament repeatedly claims to be based on eyewitness testimony. And given the character of the early Christians, who often sealed their testimony by death, there is no good reason to reject this claim. Consider the following quotations (with added emphasis): "*He who saw it* [the crucifixion] *has borne witness—his testimony is true*" (John 19:35). "*This is the disciple who is bearing witness about these things, and who has written these things*, and we know that his testimony is true" (21:24). "That which was from the beginning, which *we have heard, which we have seen with our eyes, which we have looked upon and have touched with our hands*, concerning the Word of life— . . . we . . . proclaim" (1 John 1:1–2). "This Jesus God raised up, and of this *we all are witnesses*" (Acts 2:32). "Peter and John answered them, '. . . We cannot but speak of *what we have seen and heard'"* (4:19–20). *"We are witnesses of all that he did* both in the country of the Jews and in Jerusalem. They put him to death by hanging him on a tree, but God raised him on the third day and *made him to appear"* (10:39–40). "I delivered to you . . . what I also received: that Christ . . . was buried, that he was raised on the third day in accordance with the Scriptures, and that *he appeared to Cephas, then to the twelve. Then he appeared to more than five hundred brothers at one time, most of whom are still alive,* though some have fallen asleep. Then *he appeared to James, then to all the apostles. Last of all, . . . he appeared also to me"* (1 Cor. 15:3–8). "How shall we escape if we neglect such a great salvation? It was declared at first by the Lord, and *it was attested to us by those who heard,* while God also bore witness by signs and wonders and various miracles and by gifts of the Holy Spirit distributed according to his will" (Heb. 2:3–4). Peter records: "We did not follow cleverly devised myths when we made known to you the power and coming of our Lord Jesus Christ, but *we were eyewitnesses of his majesty"* (2 Pet. 1:16). "So I exhort the elders among you, as a fellow elder and *a witness of the sufferings of Christ,* as well as a partaker in the glory that is going to be revealed" (1 Pet. 5:1).

A recent book by Richard Bauckham (*Jesus and the Eyewitnesses*) argues convincingly that the New Testament is based on eyewitness testimony. He concluded that "reading the Gospels as eyewitness testimony . . . honors the form of historiography they are. From its historical perspective, radical suspicion of testimony is a kind of epistemological suicide. It is no more practical in history than it is in ordinary life" (506). Bauckham is not alone in his conclusion. Numerous scholars have come to the same conclusion, including Craig Blomberg (*The Historical Reliability of the Gospels* and *The Historical Reliability of John's Gospel*), F. F. Bruce (*The New Testament Documents: Are They Reliable?* and *Jesus and Christian Origins*), D. A. Carson and Douglas Moo (*Introduction to the New Testament*), William Lane Craig (*Knowing the Truth*), C. H. Dodd (*History and the Gospels*), Donald Guthrie (*New Testament Introduction*), Gary Habermas (*The Historical Jesus*), Colin Hemer (*Book of Acts*), John Montgomery (*History and Christianity*), Eta Linnemann (*Is There a Synoptic Problem?*), Bruce M. Metzger (*The Text of the New Testament*), Nigel Scotland (*Can We Trust the Gospels?*). In fact, there are several thousand biblical scholars in the Evangelical Theological Society, virtually all of whom accept the reliability of the New Testament documents as based in eyewitness testimony!

Therefore, given that there are multiple documents based on numerous eyewitness testimonies of honest men, the burden of proof falls on the skeptic and critic, not on those who accept the reliability of the New Testament. Bart Ehrman is not only swimming upstream; he is also drowning in evidence against his view.

7. THE CONFIRMATION OF THE HISTORICAL ACCURACY OF LUKE, THE AUTHOR OF THE THIRD GOSPEL

One of the Gospel writers, Luke the physician, is known to have been the writer of a highly accurate New Testament narrative, the book of Acts. The earlier work of Sir William Ramsay (*St. Paul the Traveler and the Roman Citizen*) and the more recent word of the noted Roman historian Colin Hemer (*Book of Acts*) have demonstrated the minute historical accuracy of the book of Acts.

Four points are important in this confirmation of the Gospel record: First, the author of the book of Acts, known as Dr. Luke, the companion of the apostle Paul, was an accurate historian. Second, he was also the writer of the Gospel of Luke. Third, he wrote Acts before AD 62 (only three decades after Jesus died), while numerous eyewitnesses were still alive. Fourth, he wrote the Gospel of Luke before he wrote Acts. Hence, the Gospel of Luke was written by an accurate historian by about AD 60–61, during the lifetime of numerous eyewitnesses (Luke 1:1–4).

The first point is demonstrated by Colin Hemer, who shows that the writer of Acts has detailed, specific, and firsthand knowledge of numerous things about which he wrote. These include (1) a natural crossing between correctly named ports (Acts 13:4–5); (2) the proper river port, Perga, for a ship passing from Cyprus (13:13); (3) the proper location of Lycaonia (14:6); (4) the unusual but correct declension of the name Lystra, the correct language spoken there, and two gods associated with the city, Zeus and Hermes (14:8, 12); (5) a conspicuous sailors' landmark at Samothrace (16:11); (6) the association of Thyatira with cloth dyeing (16:14); (7) the proper locations where travelers would spend the nights on this journey (17:1); (8) the correct designation of Gallio as proconsul (18:12); (9) the name Tyrannus attested on a first-century inscription (19:9); (10) the appropriate route for passing across the open sea from Cyprus, favored by persistent northwest winds (21:3); (11) the correct identification of Ananias as high priest (23:2) and Felix as governor (23:26, 34); (12) agreement with Josephus for the name Porcius Festus (24:27); (13) the proper description of a *Gregale* as a south wind suddenly becomes a violent nor'easter, called *Eurakylōn* (27:13–14); (14) correct identifications for stopping places along the Appian Way (28:15). In over eighty such things, the author of Acts did not make a single mistake! He is known to be a first-rate first-century historian.

Further, the same author, known as "Luke the beloved physician" (Col. 4:14), the companion of the apostle Paul (2 Tim. 4:11), also wrote the Gospel of Luke, to which he refers in Acts 1:1 as "the first book" (ESV) or "former book" (NIV) of "all that Jesus began to do and teach, until the day when he was taken up" (1:2). Not only did (1) Luke refer to the Gospel bearing his name; also, (2) both books were written to the same person, "Theophilus" (Luke 1:1; Acts 1:3), and (3) in the same style of an educated Greek. This is supported by other lines of internal and external evidence (see Geisler, *Popular Survey*, 85–86), including his medical interest, traveling companions, and the testimony of early church fathers such as Irenaeus, Tertullian, Clement, Origen, and Jerome.

What is more, Colin Hemer lists fifteen lines of evidence supporting a date prior to AD 62 for the book of Acts. Just a few are sufficient to make the point: (1) There is no mention of the destruction of Jerusalem in AD 70. For a historical record of this time and place not to mention this most crucial historical event in the life of the first-century Jews (if it had already occurred) is akin to writing the life of

President John F. Kennedy after his death without mentioning his assassination in Dallas in 1963. (2) Likewise, there is no mention of the Jewish War that broke out in AD 66. (3) The apostle Paul is still alive (Acts 28), so it must have been before his death around AD 65. (4) There is no hint of the death of James the brother of Jesus, at the hands of the Sanhedrin, which Josephus (*Jewish Antiquities* 20.9.1) says occurred in AD 62. This and almost a dozen more things support a date for Acts before AD 62 (*Book of Acts*, 376–82).

Therefore, we have good evidence to conclude that the Gospel of Luke was written by an accurate first-century historian within three decades of the death of Christ, while numerous eyewitnesses were still alive to confirm it. Indeed, this is exactly what Luke says in his prologue: "just as those who from the beginning were eyewitnesses and ministers of the word have delivered them to us, it seemed good to me also, having followed all things closely for some time past, to write an orderly account for you, most excellent Theophilus, that you may have certainty concerning the things you have been taught" (Luke 1:2–4).

Given that the vast majority of scholars, liberal and conservative, agree that Matthew and Mark were written prior to Luke (cf. Luke 1:1) and convey the same basic view that Mark does (the three "Synoptic" [same view] Gospels), then it follows that we have here three credible historical records of the life, teaching, death, and resurrection of Christ.

8. The Confirmation by the Accepted Epistles of Paul

An oft-overlooked but powerful argument for the basic reliability of the Gospel record about Jesus's life and teaching is found in the accepted epistles of the apostle Paul.

Placing late dates on the Gospels and trying to cast doubt on their reports fails to undermine their historical reliability for many reasons. One is that it is widely accepted by critics that Romans, 1 and 2 Corinthians, and Galatians are genuine epistles of the apostle Paul and that they were written between AD 55 and 57. But these four epistles confirm the basic historicity of the Gospels for the life, teachings, death, and resurrection of Christ.

In fact, there are twenty-seven such facts about Jesus in these accepted epistles of Paul, including (1) Jewish ancestry of Jesus (Gal. 3:16); (2) his Davidic descent (Rom. 1:3); (3) his virgin birth (Gal. 4:4) and (4) his life under Jewish law (4:4); (5) his brothers (1 Cor. 9:5); (6) his twelve apostles (1 Cor. 15:7); (7) one disciple was named James (1 Cor. 15:7); (8) some apostles married (1 Cor. 9:5); (9) Paul's knowing Peter and James (Gal. 1:18–2:16); (10) Jesus's poverty (2 Cor. 8:9); (11) his meekness and gentleness (2 Cor. 10:1); (12) his abuse by others (Rom. 15:3); (13) his teachings on divorce and remarriage (1 Cor. 7:10–11) and (14) his view on paying wages to ministers (1 Cor. 9:14); (15) his view on paying taxes (Rom. 13:6–7); (16) his command to love one's neighbors (Rom. 13:9); and (17) his views on Jewish ceremonial uncleanness (Rom. 14:14); (18) Jesus's titles of deity (Rom. 1:3–4; 10:9); (19) his institution of the Lord's Supper (1 Cor.

11:23–25); (20) his sinless life (2 Cor. 5:21); (21) his death on the cross (Rom. 4:25; 5:8; Gal. 3:13), (22) to pay for our sins (1 Cor. 15:3; 2 Cor. 5:21; cf. Mark 10:45); (23) his burial (1 Cor. 15:4); (24) his resurrection on the "third day" (1 Cor. 15:4) and (25) his postresurrection appearances to the apostles (1 Cor. 15:5–8); (26) his postresurrection appearances to others, including five hundred people, most of whom were still alive when Paul wrote 1 Corinthians (1 Cor. 15:6); and (27) Jesus's present position at God's right hand (Rom. 8:34).

These facts not only confirm the general reliability of the Gospels, but even apart from the Gospels they also provide the essential core of teachings about Christ on which Christianity is based. To put it another way, if there were no Gospels such as we have, Christianity would not crumble.

9. Legal Testimony Supporting the Gospel Witnesses

Simon Greenleaf was professor of law at Harvard University. He was challenged to apply the rules of legal evidence from the book he authored (*A Treatise on the Law of Evidences*, 1853) to the New Testament witnesses and documents. His conclusions are found in his book *The Testimony of the Evangelists* (*TE*, 1847 ed.). He wrote: "The narratives of the evangelists are now submitted to the reader's perusal and examination, upon the principles and by the rules already stated. . . ." He set out to "ascertain whether, if they had thus testified on oath, in a court of justice, they would be entitled to credit; and whether their narratives, as we now have them, would be received as ancient documents, coming from the proper custody. If so, then it is believed that every honest and impartial man will act consistently with that result, by receiving their testimony in all the extent of its import" (53–54).

Greenleaf added,

> All that Christianity asks of men on this subject, is, that they would be consistent with themselves; that they would treat its evidences as they treat the evidence of other things; and that they would try and judge its actors and witnesses, as they deal with their fellow men, when testifying to human affairs and actions, in human tribunals. Let the witnesses be compared with themselves, with each other, and with surrounding facts and circumstances; and let their testimony be sifted, as if it were given in a court of justice, on the side of the adverse party, the witness being subjected to rigorous cross-examination. The result, it is confidently believed, will be an undoubting conviction of their integrity, ability, and truth. (*TE*, 46)

Other attorneys have come to the same conclusion. Thomas Sherlock was the first to use the legal motif in his book, *The Tryal of the Witnesses of the Resurrection* (1729). Attorney Frank Morrison wrote *Who Moved the Stone?* (1930). Attorney and theologian John Montgomery published *History and Christianity* (1964). And more recently, Lee Strobel penned *The Case for Christ* (1998). All agree that from a legal standpoint, using the normal rules of legal evidence, the New Testament witnesses would have stood up in a court of law.

10. Archaeological Confirmation of the New Testament

No book from ancient times has more archaeological confirmation than the Bible. Noted biblical scholar Nelson Glueck declares: "As a matter of fact, however, it may be stated categorically that no archaeological discovery has ever controverted a biblical reference. Scores of archaeological findings have been made which confirm in clear outline or exact detail historical statements in the Bible" (*Rivers in the Desert*, 31). After surveying the evidence, even the secular magazine *U.S. News & World Report* concluded: "In extraordinary ways, modern archaeology has affirmed the historical core of the Old and New Testaments—corroborating key portions of the stories of Israel's patriarchs, the Exodus, the Davidic monarchy, and the life and times of Jesus" (Sheler, "Is the Bible True?" 52). Onetime critical biblical scholar W. F. Albright, known as the "Dean of Archaeologists," not only came to accept the general historical reliability of the Bible, but also concluded of the New Testament in particular that "in my opinion, every book of the New Testament was written by a baptized Jew between the forties and the eighties of the first century AD (very probably sometime between about 50 and 75 AD)" ("More Conservative View").

Just to mention a few of the finds related to Jesus, one could mention: (1) the city of his birth (Bethlehem); (2) inscription on a coin of the caesar (Augustus) under whom he was born; (3) the tomb of King Herod who tried to kill him; (4) the city of Nazareth, where Jesus was reared; (5) the synagogue in Capernaum, where he ministered; (6) the Sea of Galilee, where he ministered; (7) the Mount of Olives, where he prayed; (8) the temple steps, where he ministered; (9) the stones of the temple that he predicted would be torn down; (10) the Arch of Titus, who destroyed Jerusalem as Jesus predicted; (11) inscription of Pilate as Prefect of Judea, who tried him; (12) inscription of the high priest Caiaphas, who condemned Jesus to death; (13) the city of Jerusalem, where he died; (14) Johanan, a first-century crucifixion victim, who was nailed to a cross as Jesus was; (15) an empty tomb with stones like the one in which Jesus was buried. This does not even mention numerous other places where Jesus walked and visited that have been unearthed—the sum total of which provide amazing archaeological confirmation of the New Testament picture of the life, death, and resurrection of Christ.

11. Non-Christian Sources Confirm Basics of the Gospel Record

Noted New Testament scholar F. F. Bruce wrote the major work on *Jesus and Christian Origins outside the New Testament.* Summarizing the evidence, Gary Habermas shows that these extrabiblical sources contain the basic outline of the Gospel record about the life and teachings of Jesus (*Historical Jesus*). Sources include Tacitus, Suetonius, Thallus, the Jewish Talmuds, and Josephus. From his work he ascertained twelve facts universally from twenty to one hundred fifty years after the death of Jesus. He showed that early Christians, Jews, and Roman sources confirm some universal understandings about the life and teaching of Jesus and his followers:

(1) Jesus was from Nazareth.
(2) He lived a virtuous life.
(3) He performed unusual feats.
(4) He introduced new teaching contrary to Judaism.
(5) He was crucified under Pontius Pilate.
(6) His disciples believed he rose from the dead.
(7) His disciples denied polytheism.
(8) His disciples worshiped him.
(9) His teachings and disciples spread rapidly.
(10) His followers believed they were immortal.
(11) His followers had contempt for death.
(12) His followers renounced material goods.

Considering that these non-Christian sources were all rather "adversarial witnesses" and that they nonetheless confirmed these major events about Jesus and his early followers—this is good supplementary substantiation of the basic truths of the Gospel record.

The Internal Evidence for the Historicity of the New Testament

In addition to the strong external evidence for the reliability of the Gospels, there is also very good internal evidence. In fact, if one knew nothing about the Bible or Christianity but discovered a New Testament in an antique book sale, he could just by reading it get a strong sense of its credibility. Here is why.

1. THE NEW TESTAMENT WRITERS DID NOT TRY TO HARMONIZE THEIR ACCOUNTS

Even though the Gospel stories are unanimous on the central facts about the life, death, and resurrection of Christ, nonetheless there are many conflicting accounts. These divergent accounts demonstrate that the writers did not try to harmonize their stories, even though they were aware that previous accounts differed (cf. Luke 1:1–2). For example, in Matthew 28:2 it says there was one angel at the tomb and in John 20:12 it says there were two angels. Matthew 27:5 says that Judas hanged himself, but Acts 1:18 claims that he fell down and his bowels burst out. Surely no writers trying to harmonize their accounts would allow these conflicts if they were real contradictions. Although it has never been demonstrated that these are real contradictions,[8] there is still enough evidence to be certain that the writers were not conspiring to create a false story. That these and other accounts are different but not contradictory is further demonstrated in more detail later (chap. 17).

In actuality, the apparent conflicts support the multiple but independent authenticity of the record. For no judge would accept the testimony of several witnesses who gave identical, word-for-word testimony about a crime. The differences and independence of the witnesses speaks to their reliability.

2. THE NEW TESTAMENT WRITERS WROTE PASSAGES THAT PLACED JESUS IN A BAD LIGHT

If the New Testament writers were trying to fabricate a story about the life of Jesus, they surely would not include passages that place him in a bad light. But the fact that they did include such passages is evidence to the internal authenticity of the Gospel records. Among some of these facts include Jesus's being called "a drunkard" (Matt. 11:19), "insane" (John 10:20), one who "[has] a demon" (John 8:48), that his brothers did not believe in him (John 7:5), and that his relatives thought he had lost his mind (Mark 3:21). Surely anyone creating a story years later to put Jesus in a good light or deify him would not have included events like these.

3. THE NEW TESTAMENT WRITERS LEFT DIFFICULT PASSAGES IN THE TEXT

It is not likely that anyone trying to create a story about a perfect man, let alone the God-man, would have included these stories in the text. Those passages include Jesus's claiming to be God (Mark 14:61–62; John 5:23; 8:58; 10:30; 17:5). Nor would they have left in the text statements by Jesus that seem to contradict that, saying, "The Father is greater than I" (John 14:28), and "Concerning that day and hour no one knows, not even the angels of heaven, nor the Son" (Matt. 24:36).

Nor would they let stand the demanding teachings of Jesus, as found in the Sermon on the Mount, such as: "Everyone who looks at a woman with lustful intent has already committed adultery with her in his heart" (Matt. 5:28); "Everyone who divorces his wife, except on the ground of sexual immorality, makes her commit adultery, and whoever marries a divorced woman commits adultery" (5:32); "Love your enemies and pray for those who persecute you, so that you may be sons of your Father who is in heaven" (5:44–45).

Neither would they have put in the record such demanding statements as "Unless you eat the flesh of the Son of Man and drink his blood, you have no life in you" (John 6:53). Or, "If anyone comes to me and does not hate his own father and mother and wife and children and brothers and sisters, yes, and even his own life, he cannot be my disciple" (Luke 14:26).

Each of these commands is difficult and goes against the natural interests of every human being. These are clearly commands that people would not impose upon themselves. Therefore the evidence points against their being fabrications.

4. THE NEW TESTAMENT WRITERS WROTE SELF-INCRIMINATING STORIES

If one or more of the apostles wrote a Gospel or had a strong influence upon the writing of a Gospel (as probably was the case of Peter on Mark or Paul on Luke), then why would they leave self-incriminating stories in the record? Even if later disciples wrote them, why would they leave such incriminating stories in them against their mentors or heroes in the faith? These include the following stories:

1. All the disciples fall asleep after Jesus asks them to pray (Mark 14:32–41).
2. Jesus calls Peter "Satan" (Matt. 16:23).
3. Peter denies the Lord three times (Luke 22:34).
4. The disciples flee persecution (at the crucifixion, Mark 14:50).
5. Peter cuts off the ear of the high priest's servant (Mark 14:47).
6. The disciples doubt that Jesus rose from the dead (Luke 24:21–25; John 20:24–25) even though Jesus repeatedly taught that he would rise from the dead (Matt. 12:39–41; 17:9, 22–23; Mark 8:31; 9:31; 10:34; John 2:19–22; 3:14–18).

Clearly, the best explanation for these self-incriminating stories being included in the Gospel record points to the fact that they were reporting the truth of the events. People don't make up incriminating stories about themselves or those they admire.

5. The New Testament Writers Distinguished Jesus's Words from Their Own

Redaction critics believe that the Gospel writers were *creating* the words of Jesus, not *reporting* them. But the evidence points in favor of their reporting Jesus's words. Why? Because they clearly distinguish the words of Jesus from their own. This is evident from the fact that red-letter editions of the Gospels can be produced, even though there were no quotation marks in the originals. In fact, any normal teenager could, with a red marker, make a red-letter edition of the Gospels with little problem.

The apostle Paul clearly distinguished Jesus's words from his in writing 1 Corinthians (7:10, 12). So did Luke in writing Acts (9:4–5, 10; 12:15; 20:35). Matthew was clear in distinguishing the words of Old Testament teachers and traditions alongside the words of Jesus: "You have heard that it was said" (Matt. 5:21, 27, 31, 33, 38, 43), "but I say to you" (5:22, 28, 32, 34, 39, 44).

This is not to say that we have the exact words (*ipsissima verba*) of Jesus in the Greek New Testament but only the same voice or sense (*ipsissima vox*). For Jesus probably spoke in Aramaic (cf. Matt. 27:46), and the New Testament text is in Greek. Further, some of Jesus's words may be abbreviated or paraphrased. It is only to say that the Gospel writers are not creating what Jesus taught; they are reporting it, even if sometimes abbreviating, paraphrasing, or summarizing it. This is evident from the clear way in which they distinguish Jesus's words from their own.

6. The New Testament Writers Did Not Deny Their Testimony under Persecution or the Threat of Death

If a person were fabricating a story, one of the easiest ways to challenge their views is to persecute or threaten to kill that person unless they change their views. It is well attested in both the text of Scripture (Acts 4–8; 2 Cor. 11:24–28) and examples throughout early church history that the Gospel writers and early Christians still did not deny their testimony even under the threat of death. It is also a psychological fact if any person is willing to endure such hardships, then they believe the testimony to be true. This is clear from the earliest record in Acts. When threatened, Peter says, "Whether it is right in the sight of God to listen to you rather than to God, you must judge, for we cannot but speak of what we have seen and heard" (4:19–20).

Later the first Christian martyr, Stephen, spoke with such boldness in the face of death and made no retractions, but "falling to his knees he cried out with a loud voice, 'Lord, do not hold this sin against them.' And when he had said this, he fell asleep" (Acts 7:60). History records that perhaps eleven of the twelve apostles were martyred, without any retracting their testimony. But it is a psychological fact that people do not die for what they believe to be false (even Muslim terrorists believe what they are dying for). And neither the character, the moral teaching, nor the manner of their death gives evidence that the New Testament witnesses were bearing false witness.

The cumulative case for the historicity of the New Testament is overwhelming. Nothing like it exists for any book from antiquity. Only antitheistic or antisupernatural biases could keep one from coming to this conclusion. There are more, earlier, and better eyewitness contemporary documents for the New Testament than for any other book from that period. If one rejects its reliability, then on the same grounds one would have to wipe out virtually all history based on documents.

Brief Comments on Two Other Issues

In his debate on this issue, Ehrman brings up two objections to accepting the historicity of the New Testament: (1) the incredibility of miracles (answered above), and (2) the unknowability of history. Space does not permit an extended response to this here, and it is treated completely elsewhere (see Geisler, *Systematic Theology*, vol. 1, chap. 11). It will suffice to make two comments. First, it is self-defeating to claim that no one can have an objective view of the past, since one cannot know bad history without knowing good history. Second, if—with all the manuscripts, writers, witnesses, and supporting evidence we have for the New Testament—we are still left with no objective truth about the distant past, then *a fortiori* (with the greater force) we do not have any objective knowledge about anything else in the distant past (all of which are based on much less evidence). If, on the contrary, we can know anything about the past, then we can certainly know that the New Testament is a reliable source for the life, teachings, death, and resurrection of Christ.

Conclusion

Bart Ehrman's denial of the inspiration and inerrancy of Scripture has many driving factors. Some of those include his reaction to his training as a youth and the appeal of academic sophistication to him. Others relate to his struggle with the problem of evil.[9] But clearly the reason he accepts many of his conclusions are because of his philosophical presuppositions and methodological ideology. Yet all of these have been shown to be faulty. This faulty methodology has led to his faulty theology. Thus his presuppositions, methodology, and historical claims are unjustified, as well as his denial of the inspiration and inerrancy of the Bible, which flows from these presuppositions. So to the degree that belief in the inerrancy of the autographic text is dependent on there being reliable copies, inerrancy can withstand the attacks by Ehrman.

The truth is that no book from antiquity can boast the cumulative evidence for its reliability that the New Testament possesses. For there are more, earlier, and better manuscripts than for any other book of its time. Further, there are more, earlier, and more eyewitness-based accounts than any other text from ancient times. What is more, Roman historians, non-Christian sources, legal experts, and archaeological finds provide further evidence of its authenticity. Considering the multiple, cumulative, and independent nature of the testimony, there is no reasonable basis for doubting the reliability of the New Testament.

As the noted Harvard legal expert Simon Greenleaf says, "All that Christianity asks of men on this subject, is, that they would be consistent with themselves; that they would treat its evidences as they treat the evidence of other things." If they did this, "then it is believed that every honest and impartial man will act consistently with that result, by receiving their testimony in all the extent of its import" (cited above).

Sources

Albright, "More Conservative View"

Bauckham, *Jesus and the Eyewitnesses*

Craig, "Evidence for Jesus"

Ehrman, *Misquoting Jesus*

Geisler, *Baker Encyclopedia*

———, *Systematic Theology*, vol. 1

Geisler and Nix, *General Introduction to the Bible*

Geisler and Turek, *I Don't Have Enough Faith*

Glueck, *Rivers in the Desert*

Grinbank, "Bart Ehrman's Millions and Millions of Variants, Part 1 of 2"

Habermas, *The Historical Jesus*

Hoehner, *Chronological Aspects of the Life of Christ*

Johnson, S. L., *The Old Testament in the New*

Jones, *Misquoting Truth*

Kaiser, *Uses of the Old Testament in the New*

Kenyon, *The Bible and Archaeology*

———, *Our Bible and the Ancient Manuscripts*

Kostenberger and Kruger, *The Heresy of Orthodoxy*

Linnemann, *Historical Criticism*

———, *Is There a Synoptic Problem?*

Rawlings, *Trial by Fire*

Robertson, *Textual Criticism*

Schaff, *Companion to the Greek Testament*

Sheler, "Is the Bible True?"

Sproul, Gerstner, and Lindsley, *Classical Apologetics*

Warfield, *Introduction*

Westcott and Hort, *New Testament*

6

Peter Enns on Inerrancy

Introduction

Peter Enns is a former professor at Westminster Theological Seminary, which is a longtime institutional friend of inerrancy. In the wake of the controversy over his views on Scripture, Enns resigned from Westminster and took a position at Princeton—the very school from which Westminster split in 1929 over this same issue. He is writing now for BioLogos (see Appendix 2). As we shall see, Enns's views are typical of the new generation of evangelicals, which does not fit into the traditional mold. In fact, as the following discussion will reveal, his views are a serious challenge to inerrancy as it has been embraced by orthodox Christians down through the centuries and as it has been expressed by the Evangelical Theological Society (ETS) and the International Council on Biblical Inerrancy (ICBI).

The Inspiration and Incarnation Model

In his book *Inspiration and Incarnation* (2005), Enns employs the model of Christ's incarnation—long used to defend inerrancy—to undermine it. In short, he argues that if Christ, the living Word, partook of full humanity with its accompanying limitations and imperfections, then why should God's written Word be any different. As such, this book has done exactly what the author intended—it provoked a scholarly "conversation" (*Inspiration and Incarnation* [*II*], 167) on a very important evangelical topic. Like most books of its kind, there is much with which one can agree and some things on which there is disagreement. Let's begin with some points of agreement.

Points of Agreement with Enns's Incarnational Model of Scripture

Professor Enns confesses that the "Bible is God's word" (*II*, 15, 108, 161). Likewise, he asserts that the Bible is a unique book in the "coming together" of divine and human elements (168). Furthermore, he claims that "for God to reveal himself means that he accommodates himself" (109). Also, he contends that the "incarnational model" (of comparing the Bible and Christ) is a helpful one (20). He also acknowledges the "full humanity" (20) of the Bible, an important part of which is the diversity in Scripture (77). Like most other evangelicals, he holds that the "canon is closed" (67). He properly claims to reject a "cultural relativism" (168) where the Bible is not held to be a "standard for faith" (169).

As for the relation of external evidence to the Bible, we agree with Professor Enns that our assumptions determine how we understand evidence (*II*, 48). We also concur that Genesis does not borrow from Babylonian origin stories because the similarities are only conceptual, not textual (55). Enns also points out that there are similar truths in other religions known from general revelation (58). He correctly notes that the similarity of Genesis with other ancient texts does not diminish the inspiration of the Bible (39). Nor is the Bible directly dependent on their creation and flood stories (29). Enns acknowledges that archaeology supports the historicity of Israel's monarchy (43) and that our problems with the Bible are largely due to our misconceptions (15). He rightly acknowledges that conflicting passages are sometimes not addressing the same situation (90). Thus, there is often no "fundamental contradiction" between apparently different texts (96). Even conflicting proverbs are both correct in their specific situations (76). He also affirms that one cannot properly apply the law without recognizing the different situations that are addressed (94–95).

As for his view of God, Enns is correct in asserting that God does not need creation to be complete in himself (*II*, 103). Also, God knows far more about what the Bible teaches than the human writers did (161). God transcends the world; nonetheless, he can and does interact with the world (104–5).

On the matter of biblical interpretation, there are several points of agreement as well. Enns rightly observes that the Old Testament should be understood in light of the climax of Israel's history, which is Christ (*II*, 120). Likewise, Christ is both the beginning and the end of Bible interpretation (163). There is Christ-related "coherence" in the Bible (170). Further, the Bible is clear on the central matters of our faith (170). Of course, this list is not exhaustive. However, it does suggest that his view significantly overlaps with the historic evangelical view of Scripture.

Points of Disagreement with Enns

In spite of the many good things that Enns affirms, there are many troubling things to ponder. First we will list some of them, and then we will engage the most important ones. The standard of comparison will be the view of inerrancy held by the founders of the Evangelical Theological Society (ETS), the framers of the Chicago Statement on inerrancy (1978) by the International Council on Biblical Inerrancy (ICBI). This is in accord with our overall purpose here to determine whether the traditional view of total inerrancy can be reaffirmed for this new generation, or whether the ETS and ICBI understanding of inerrancy must be seriously changed or discarded.

Disagreement about the Nature of the Bible

Enns claims that the non-Christian worldview of their day influenced what the biblical authors wrote (*II*, 14). He also holds that it is a misconception to think the Bible has a unique and unified outlook (16). He says myth is a proper way to describe Genesis, even though he claims that it also contains history (41, 49). Enns believes that "the Bible seems to be relativized" by the culture of its day (43). He claims that we cannot reason back from the evidence for the historicity of later Old Testament books to that of earlier ones (43–44). There is no objective and unbiased view of history (45). Enns believes it is a fallacious assumption that the Bible is accurate in all details (47). He holds that all attempts to state the nature of the Bible are open to examination (48). On top of this, he holds that Genesis was not recorded until the first millennium BC (52) and that God adopted the mythical categories within which Abraham thought (53). Enns also asserts that God transformed the ancient myths to focus on himself (54). Likewise, he believes that the Bible does not say the flood was universal (55). He affirms that Israel's laws were not new in content but were unique in that they were connected to a monotheistic community—Israel (57). Enns also believes that Old Testament history is not false because it isn't objective (62). He holds the critical view that Samuel and Kings were not written until the fourth or fifth centuries BC (63). Enns thinks there was only one cleansing of the temple by Jesus (65), even though the Gospels have two accounts at different times. He asserts that the Old Testament laws are culturally relative and not normative (67). Some moral laws of the OT are not binding on us today (67). Likewise, the Bible is not a timeless how-to book that applies today (67). Holding diverse factual content is not incompatible with accepting its theological message (73). He declares that there are contradictions in Ecclesiastes (77–78). Enns claims that Ecclesiastes does not teach the notion of an afterlife (79). According to Enns, there are inconsistencies in the moral law in the Old Testament (85). Even the Mosaic law is inconsistent; Exodus conflicts with Deuteronomy (87). God allows the law to be "adjusted over time" (87). He chides the NIV for assuming inerrancy as a basis of its translation (92). Enns also believes that the Bible was written during five hundred to one thousand years, which is five hundred years less than most evangelical scholars hold.

Disagreement about God and Theology

Enns appears to diverge from the classical view of God, which undergirds the traditional view on inerrancy. We also disagree with the position of Enns that God learned through his interaction with Abraham (*II*, 103). He also claims that God reacts to man's actions (104) and that Moses could get God to actually change his plans (105). Enns rejects the view that God does not really change (105). He does not accept any behind-the-scene view in favor of taking the Bible as it is (106). Enns thinks our prayers do have an effect on God and his declarative plans (107). He speaks against an apologetic stance that defends the Bible against the charge of error (108). Enns is opposed to apologetics that defend the perfection of the Bible (109). He claims that we must accept the Bible as the Word of God by faith (66, 169), not by reason or evidence.

Disagreement about Interpreting the Bible

Professor Enns believes that New Testament writers used a so-called Second Temple hermeneutics (*II*, 117). The traditional historical-grammatical method is generally a good approach, but "original context" means not only grammar and history but also the hermeneutics of the time (117). Daniel was given a deeper meaning of Jeremiah's words about the seventy years (119). The biblical writers dig for deeper "mysteries" in the text (131). There is a "superfulfillment" in Christ of Old Testament texts that were not speaking of him (136). Abraham's "seed" had double and deeper meaning (137). Paul changed an Old Testament text, adding a word (and changing the meaning; 140–42). Nonhistorical tradition is part of the New Testament interpretation of the Old Testament (143). The apostles did not come to the view that Jesus is Lord from an objective interpretation of the Old Testament (153). The New Testament takes the Old Testament out of context and puts it in another context, the context of Christ (153). Israel is replaced by the church (God's higher, deeper meaning; 154). The historical-grammatical interpretation should not be the normative method (159). God intended more than the human authors of the Bible did (160). The Bible is [merely] a written witness to Christ (161). Christian interpretation is well beyond scientific markers (objective criteria; 162). Proper interpretation is a community activity, combining both the historic community and the family of God. The proper interpretation of the Bible is not a fortress to defend but a pilgrimage to take (162). The categories "inerrancy" and "infallible" can never be fully understood (168). We have no absolute point of reference to interpret the Bible stripped of our own cultural context. The incarnational model helps us to see the multidimensional gospel (169). The Bible is not a timeless rule book or owner's manual (169). Hence, the available evidence transcends the labels of conservative or liberal (171).

Interacting with Central Issues

Now that we have set forth many of the areas of agreement and disagreement with Professor Enns, we will interact with several issues relating to the nature and understanding of Scripture. First we will look at his understanding of God.

Understanding of the Nature of God

It is axiomatic that the statement "The Bible is the Word of God" (which Enns endorses; II, 21, 108) is no stronger than what is meant by "God." As the founding statement of the Evangelical Theological Society puts it, "The Bible alone, and the Bible in its entirety, is the Word of God written and is therefore inerrant in the autographs." There is a clear logical connection ("therefore") made here with "the Word of God" and "inerrant" autographs of the Bible. It is implied that since God cannot err, then neither can his Word.

Relation of Biblical and Systematic Theology

Despite the fact that Enns *claims* his view does not lend support to the Openness View of God (see chap. 4 above), which holds that God has no infallible foreknowledge of future human free acts (II, 106), the evidence is to the contrary. All the following points affirmed by Enns clearly support the Openness View of God; he declares: (1) God actually learned through his interaction with Abraham (103). (2) God reacts to man's actions (104). (3) Moses was able to get God to change his plans (105). (4) He rejects the view that says God does not really change (105). (5) He rejects any behind-the-scene view in favor of taking the Bible as it is (106). (6) He also holds that our prayers do have an effect on God (107). Since we have addressed open theism in details elsewhere (Geisler, House, and Herrera, *Battle for God*), we will only note here that these conclusions are both contrary to Scripture, which affirms that God does not change (1 Sam. 15:29; Heb. 6:18; Titus 1:2: James 1:17), and sound reason, which demands that there be an ultimate unchanging Being by which all change is measured. As for infallible foreknowledge, the God of the Bible knows "the end from the beginning" (Isa. 46:10). Hence, he was able to predict the cross of Christ before the foundations of the world (Rev. 13:8; Acts 2:22–23), predetermine the elect (Eph. 1:4; Rom. 8:29), predict Judas would betray Christ (John 13:26; 17:12; Acts 1:16), and make numerous other infallible predictions, including whole kingdoms of the world (Dan. 2; 7) and the birth (Mic. 5:2), death (Isa. 53), and the resurrection of Christ (Pss. 2; 16; cf. Acts 2:24–30). Indeed, God's test for a false prophet (namely, if he gives a false prophecy) assumes that only God can make infallible predictions of the future (Deut. 13:2–3; 18:22).

Enns also claims, contrary to traditional inerrantists, that there is no evidence that God providentially guided the customs of the day (II, 57) so as to be a fitting vehicle of his Word through the human authors. But the Bible speaks of God's providential knowledge and care extending to details like the death of a sparrow or the number of hairs on our head (Matt. 6:25–30). Indeed, the International Council on Biblical Inerrancy (ICBI) Chicago Statement (1978) declares in article 8: "We affirm that God in His work of inspiration utilized the distinctive personalities and literary styles of the writers whom *He had chosen and prepared*" (emphasis added). The official ICBI commentary on this article (Sproul, *Explaining Inerrancy*, 28) adds, "The writers of Scripture were [*providentially*] *chosen and prepared by God* for their sacred task" (emphasis added).

Enns also opposes any apologetics that defends the perfection of the Bible (*II*, 109). He claims that we accept the Bible as the Word of God by faith (66, 169), not by reason or evidence. Yet, as we shall see next, he accepts extrabiblical evidence as being all but determinative in deciding the meaning of the biblical text. But if this kind of extrabiblical evidence can be used so strongly, then why cannot other archaeological evidence be used to support the historicity of the Bible? Indeed, Enns admits that such evidence supports the historicity of Israel's monarchy (43), though he denies that the Nuzi material supports the historicity of the patriarchs (30). Other than an antisupernatural bias, there is no reason why similar evidence cannot be used to support the historicity of New Testament books like Acts and Luke. But once one admits this, he is already doing evidential apologetics, which Enns rejects.

Ironically, Enns is implicitly rejecting his own incarnational model by positing a deeper, mystical, allegorical meaning to the biblical text than the historical-grammatical method reveals. For in the incarnation there was a union of the divine and human so that what Jesus said was one with what God said. So we must conclude that there was a divine concurrence in the adaptation to human finitude (not to human error) in what God said and what Jesus said. If so, then both were affirming one and the same meaning and truth. There was no separation. To deny this is to employ a heretical view of the union of the divine and human natures in Christ. Likewise, by analogy, in the incarnational model of Scripture, God and the human authors affirm one and the same thing in one and the same text. The fact that God knows more about the topic than the human author—or that more is affirmed elsewhere—is irrelevant. The truth is that in the union of the divine and human natures in Scripture, they both are affirming one and the same thing.

Relation of Extrabiblical Data to Interpretation

Many of the novel and questionable views expressed by Enns seem to be related to his misunderstanding of the relation of extrabiblical data to the Bible. He declares that the Genesis story is "firmly rooted in the worldview of its time" (*II*, 27). He even acknowledges that this extrabiblical data is sometimes highly influential in determining the meaning of the Bible (48).

In this connection, Enns is clearly overly enamored with the alleged Second Temple interpretation (which we discuss in chap. 15 below) that he feels the New Testament writers are making of the Old Testament (*II*, 155). In these New

Testament texts he sees the authors using a midrash-like nonfactual spiritual embellishment of certain Old Testament passages, such as Paul's making the rock that followed Israel into a midrash-like story to emphasize his Christotelic interpretation of the Old Testament. Space only permits a brief response to this mistaken interpretation.

First, even Enns admits that this is a minority view among evangelicals. Indeed it is and rightly so since it yields results that are incompatible with evangelical beliefs (see chap. 15 below).

Second, he also acknowledges that there are no clear rules to prevent one from taking his "Christotelic" view too far (*II*, 162). But if there are no objective criteria on which to determine the truth of Scripture, then in the final analysis the decisions will be made subjectively. Indeed, he admits that his view involves developing "deep intuitions" (102) in order to come to these conclusions.

Third, he acknowledges that one must reject the traditional historical-grammatical method of interpretation and that to do this one must discover multiple layers of meaning (*II*, 161). But this is both dangerous and self-defeating, as we argue below (in chap. 15).

Fourth, there is no uniformity to Second Temple hermeneutics. It ranges from good and sophisticated interpretation to some wild and crazy views (see Beale, *Erosion of Inerrancy*, 92). Midrashic, allegorical, or mythological views were only one strain. Others took a more literal approach, as indeed the Qumran community did in its belief in a literal messianic fulfillment of Old Testament prophecy.

Fifth, even C. H. Dodd, no evangelical, contended that the greatest influence on the apostles was Jesus, whom he believed had a very contextual approach to the Old Testament (Beale, *Erosion of Inerrancy*, 99).

Sixth, other evangelical scholars have offered alternative interpretations without jettisoning an objective hermeneutic to do so. See the helpful book by Thomas A. Howe, *Objectivity in Biblical Interpretation*. Other evangelicals, like Walter Kaiser, have long defended a literal hermeneutic of the Old Testament by the New Testament.

Finally, Enns's view of the New Testament interpretation of the Old Testament is clearly contrary to the ICBI view on inerrancy, which has been adopted as the official view of the ETS. As is clear from the above citations, Enns violates at least four of the ICBI articles, including the following:

Article 12

We affirm that Scripture in its entirety is inerrant, being free from all falsehood, fraud, or deceit.

We deny that Biblical infallibility and inerrancy are limited to spiritual, religious, or redemptive themes, exclusive of assertions in the fields of history and science. We further deny that scientific hypotheses about earth history may properly be used to overturn the teaching of Scripture on creation and the flood.

Article 14

We affirm the unity and internal consistency of Scripture.

We deny that alleged errors and discrepancies that have not yet been resolved vitiate the truth claims of the Bible.

Article 15

We affirm that the doctrine of inerrancy is grounded in the teaching of the Bible about inspiration.

We deny that Jesus' teaching about Scripture may be dismissed by appeals to accommodation or to any natural limitation of His humanity.

Article 18

We affirm that the text of Scripture is to be interpreted by grammatico-historical exegesis, taking account of its literary forms and devices, and that Scripture is to interpret Scripture.

We deny the legitimacy of any treatment of the text or quest for sources lying behind it that leads to relativizing, dehistoricizing, or discounting its teaching, or rejecting its claims to authorship.

Likewise, views like those of Enns are criticized by official ICBI commentaries on the Chicago Statement in its articles on hermeneutics and inerrancy. Consider the following:

ICBI Commentary on Article 12

"It has been fashionable in certain quarters to maintain that the Bible is not normal history, but redemptive history with an accent on redemption. Theories have been established that would limit inspiration to the redemptive theme of redemptive history, allowing the historical dimension of redemptive history to be errant" (Sproul, *Explaining Inerrancy* [*EI*], 36). Further, "Though the Bible is indeed *redemptive* history, it is also redemptive *history*, and this means that the acts of salvation wrought by God actually occurred in the space-time world" (37). Also, "The denial [in article 12] explicitly rejects the tendency of some to limit infallibility and inerrancy to specific segments of the biblical message" (36).

ICBI Commentary on Article 13

"When we say that the truthfulness of Scripture ought to be evaluated according to its own standards that means that . . . all the claims of the Bible must correspond with reality, whether that reality is historical, factual or spiritual" (Sproul, *EI*, 41). He adds, "By biblical standards of truth and error is meant the view used both in the Bible and in everyday life, viz., a correspondence view of truth. This part of the article is directed toward those who would redefine truth to relate merely to redemptive intent, the purely personal, or the like, rather than to mean that which corresponds with reality" (43–44).

ICBI Commentary on Article 18

"When the quest for sources produces a dehistoricizing of the Bible, a rejection of its teaching or a rejection of the Bible's own claims of authorship, [then] it has trespassed beyond its proper limits. . . . It is never legitimate, however, to run counter to express biblical affirmations" (Sproul, *EI*, 55).

ICBI Commentary on Hermeneutics

Also, an official commentary on the ICBI Hermeneutics Statement was composed: Geisler, "Explaining Hermeneutics" (EH). The following are some relevant excerpts from it.

EH on article 6: "We further affirm that a statement is true if it represents matters as they actually are, but is an error if it misrepresents the facts." The EH commentary on this adds, "The denial makes it evident that views which redefine error to mean what 'misleads,' rather than what is a mistake, must be rejected."

EH on article 13: "We deny that generic categories which negate historicity may rightly be imposed on biblical narratives which present themselves as factual." Also, "Some, for instance, take Adam to be a myth, whereas in Scripture he is presented as a real person. Others take Jonah to be an allegory when he is presented as a historical person and [is] so referred to by Christ."

EH on article 14: "We deny that any event, discourse or saying reported in Scripture was invented by the biblical writers or by the traditions they incorporated."

EH on article 22: It "affirms that Genesis 1–11 is factual, as is the rest of the book." And, "The denial makes it evident that views which redefine error to mean what 'misleads,' rather than what is a mistake, must be rejected" (892).

One thing is evident in view of all these ICBI statements: Professor Enns's views are incompatible with those of the framers of the ETS and ICBI statements. And since these statements affirm the total inerrancy of the Bible, then it follows that Enns has denied the historic doctrine of the inerrancy of the Scriptures.

Objectivity and Interpretation

As will be shown later (in chap. 15), inerrancy and the historical-grammatical method of interpreting the Bible are closely linked. However, Enns rejects this as such and embraces a postmodern form of subjectivism in interpreting Scripture (discussed in more detail in chap. 15 below). He contends that the traditional historical-grammatical method is generally a good approach, but it is insufficient (*II*, 159). It must be augmented with a so-called Second Temple midrash-like view that adds spiritual embellishment to the text (117). He believes Daniel was given a deeper meaning of Jeremiah's words about the seventy years (119). He claims that the biblical writers dig for deeper "mysteries" in the text (131). In Christ there is a "superfulfillment" of Old Testament texts that were not speaking of him (136). Abraham's "seed" had double and deeper meaning (137). He sees nonhistorical tradition as part of New Testament interpretation of the Old Testament (143).

Further, Enns affirms that the apostles' view on the deity of Christ did not result from an objective interpretation of the Old Testament (*II*, 153). He claims that Christian interpretation went beyond any objective criteria (162). Hence, biblical interpretation is not a fortress to defend but a pilgrimage to take (162). He affirms that the categories "inerrancy" and "infallible" can never be fully understood (168). We have no absolute point of reference to interpret the Bible stripped of our own cultural context. The Bible is not a timeless rule book or owner's manual (169). New Testament writers use Second Temple hermeneutics (117). The traditional historical-grammatical method is generally a good approach, but "original context" means not only grammar and history but also hermeneutics of the time (117). Daniel was given a deeper meaning of Jeremiah's words about the seventy years (119). The biblical writers went deeper, digging for "mysteries" in the text (131). In Christ there is a "superfulfillment" of Old Testament texts that were not speaking of him (136). Abraham's "seed" had double and deeper meaning (137). Paul changed the passage, adding a word (and changing the meaning; 140–42). Nonhistorical tradition is part of New Testament interpretation of the Old Testament (143). The New Testament takes the Old Testament out of context and puts it in another context, the context of Christ (153). Israel is replaced by the church (God's higher, deeper meaning; 154).

According to Enns, the historical-grammatical method is not the normative method (*II*, 159). God intended more than the human author of the Bible did (160). Christian interpretation is well beyond scientific markers or objective criteria (162). Proper interpretation is a community activity, a historic community, the family of God down through the centuries. Bible interpretation is not a fortress to defend but a pilgrimage to take (162). The categories "inerrancy" and "infallible" can never be fully understood (168). We have no absolute point of reference to interpret the Bible stripped of our own cultural context. An incarnational model helps us to see a multidimensional gospel (169). The Bible is not a timeless rule book or owner's manual (169). Thus, Enns is unwilling to call his view either liberal or conservative (171). As a matter of fact, it should be called neo-Barthian.

However, ICBI inerrantists insist on the historical-grammatical hermeneutic in their famous Chicago Statement (1978), declaring: "We affirm that the text of Scripture is to be interpreted by grammatical-historical exegesis, taking account of its literary forms and devices, and that Scripture is to interpret Scripture. We deny the legitimacy of any treatment of the text or quest for sources lying behind it that leads to relativizing, dehistoricizing, or discounting its teaching, or rejecting its claims to authorship."

Further, ICBI held a whole conference defending the historical-grammatical hermeneutic (1982) in a series of articles (see Radmacher and Preus, eds., *Hermeneutics, Inerrancy, and the Bible*) and in a commentary on the articles (Geisler, "Explaining Hermeneutics"). As we shall see, Enns's view falls far short of these standards.

An Evaluation of the Position of Peter Enns on Scripture

In view of later discussion (in chap. 15), the evaluation can be brief here. One cannot deny that objective meaning can be derived from the text without having an objective understanding of the text. Nor can one say that all interpretation is progressive without standing outside the process to make this pronouncement. Further, there is no way to know that God intended a deeper meaning for a given text when all we have is the written text to inform us what God means. To use other texts to obtain this alleged "deeper" meaning does not avoid the problem for two reasons. First, even here all we have is the written text to go by. Second, what the biblical text says elsewhere does not add to what another text says; it simply gives us more on this topic. A given text cannot affirm (or deny) any more than that given test affirms (or denies). To claim any more for it is to attempt to read beneath, behind, or beyond the lines, rather than reading the lines. In the final analysis, Enns is not augmenting the historical-grammatical method of interpretation: he is negating it.

The Incarnational Model

Professor Enns is correct in positing an incarnational model that includes two important factors: (1) the "full humanity" of Scripture; (2) the unity of the divine and human elements of the Bible. However, he seems to be seriously lacking in his understanding that these elements involve factually and historically incorrect materials (*II*, 168). Likewise, he contends that his model handles diversity better (73). Also, it aids us in seeing a multidimensional gospel (169). But this does not escape the charge of hermeneutical relativity, which is self-defeating.

On closer examination it becomes apparent that by "incarnational model" Enns does not mean what is traditionally meant by orthodox theologians who make this comparison between Christ and Scripture. For they argue that just as Christ was fully human without sin, even so the Bible is fully human but without error. After all, both the Savior and Scripture are called "the Word of God." But God can neither sin nor err. Hence, God's Word (living or written) cannot sin or error. Indeed, both are called perfect (flawless) in the Bible. The living Word of God is said to be "without sin" (Heb. 4:15); "without blemish or spot" (1 Pet. 1:19); one who "committed no sin, neither was deceit found in his mouth" (2:22); "righteous" (3:18); "pure" (1 John 3:3); one "who knew no sin" (2 Cor. 5:21); "holy, innocent, unstained, separated from sinners" (Heb. 7:26). Using the biblical incarnational analogy, it is difficult to see how the written Word of God could be imperfect and errant. Indeed, the Bible is said to be "perfect" (flawless; Ps. 19:7), "truth" (John 17:17), "breathed out by God" (2 Tim. 3:16), unbreakable ("cannot be broken"; John 10:35), imperishable (Matt. 5:17–18), Spirit-uttered words (2 Sam. 23:2; John 14:26; 16:13), and comprised of "every word that proceedeth out of the mouth of God" (Matt. 4:4 KJV). Clearly, the incarnational analogy as presented in the Bible favors the inerrancy of all that the Bible affirms (see chap. 16 for a fuller discussion).

The Accommodationist View

Although it is acknowledged that historically orthodox theologians have held that a divine adaptation is necessary for God's communication with human beings, there has nonetheless been a serious shift in the meaning of the category "accommodation" in more recent times. So serious is the shift that we have, for some time, advocated that evangelicals discard the term "accommodation" for the word "adaptation." This will not be the first time that it becomes necessary to use a new term to describe something previously thought to be good (the word "gay" once had different connotations than it now has). Certainly, when God revealed himself in Holy Scripture, there was an adaptation to human finitude. But there was no accommodation to human error. For God cannot err (Titus 1:2; Heb. 6:18). Unfortunately, Enns seems to believe that God can accommodate himself to factually incorrect affirmations (i.e., errors). But this is a denial of the inerrancy of Scripture, a denial manifested in several things he said.

First, he uses some ambiguous terms for the Bible, such as that the Bible is "messy" (*II*, 109) and Jesus "completely assumed" cultural trappings of the world around him (17). Hence, the Bible cannot be kept from the "rough and tumble drama of human history" (109). But he nowhere clearly disassociates this from implying that there are affirmations in the Bible that entail factual mistakes or misrepresentations. Indeed, at times Enns seems to admit that there are these kinds of errors in the Bible. For example, he holds that the biblical authors really believed there were other gods (i.e., polytheism) (98).

Second, by using a true incarnational model, words and phrases like "messy" (*II*, 109), "completely assumed" cultural trappings of the world around him (17), and entering the "rough and tumble drama of human history" (109)—at best these are ambiguous and at worst they veil a denial of the inerrancy of the written Word of God and, by comparison, the sinlessness of the Son of God.

Third, Enns speaks against an apologetic stance that defends the Bible against the charge of error (*II*, 108). If he believes the Bible is inerrant, he should have no hesitation in trying to defend it against false charges that it is not.

Finally, Enns believes there are inconsistencies in the moral law in the Old Testament (*II*, 85). He believes that Exodus conflicts with Deuteronomy (87). He says that God allows the law to be "adjusted over time" (87). Also, he holds that the NIV translation is wrong for assuming inerrancy as a basis of its translation (92). But what is this but an implied denial of inerrancy?

In view of this, it is apparent why Enns prefers to move beyond the "battle for the Bible" that is being fought over whether or not the Bible affirms any errors—statements that are factually incorrect. It is because he does not believe in inerrancy. Indeed, Enns seems to favor a neo-Barthian view of Scripture wherein the Bible is merely "the written witness to Christ" (*II*, 161). Or, the book wherein

God "speaks to the church" (46). These statements are true as far as they go, but they do not go far enough. Indeed, they seem to be a cover for a neo-Barthian view denying the historic orthodox view that the Bible is the infallible and inerrant written Word of God.

Conclusion

When the true view of Enns is unveiled, it is easier to understand the kind of theological paranoia Enns reveals about his view when he exhorts others not to speak of views like his with "judgmental suspicions" (*II*, 172) or "predispositions against new ideas," or to consider such views to be "on a slippery slope." Likewise, he warns against "power plays" and tries to "vilify persons holding" such views, or warns against those who "go on the attack" against it and "jump to conclusions" about one's motives and engage in "build[ing] our own kingdoms," all of which he calls the "angry evangelical syndrome" (173). Of course, the net effect of ad hominem phrases like these is to build a protective wall around his admittedly minority and clearly unorthodox views. By so doing, he hopes to ward off any critical analysis that would consider them unbiblical and/or unorthodox.

There is always a danger when one sets out, as Enns does, to reconcile his view of the Bible with "modern biblical scholarship" (*II*, 13). Often when this takes place, one trades orthodoxy for academic respectability. This criticism should come as no surprise to Enns since he recognizes that one's worldview influences how he interprets the Bible (14). He writes: "The assumptions we have about the nature of God (which includes notions of revelation and inspiration . . .), and so on, will largely determine how we understand the evidence" (48). Why then should we expect that most of "modern biblical scholarship" (which he wishes to accommodate), based as it is on antisupernatural biases, is reconcilable with the Bible? An attempt to reconcile a supernatural God who performed supernatural events recorded in a supernaturally inspired book with naturalistically based scholarship that denies all of the above is doomed to failure.

Sources

Beale, *Erosion of Inerrancy*

Enns, *Inspiration and Incarnation*

Geisler, House, and Herrera, *Battle for God*

Howe, *Objectivity in Biblical Interpretation*

Johnson, S. L., *Old Testament in the New*

Kaiser, *Uses of the Old Testament in the New*

Radmacher and Preus, eds., *Hermeneutics, Inerrancy*

Sproul, *Explaining Inerrancy*

7

Kenton Sparks on Inerrancy

Introduction

In his book *God's Word in Human Words* (2008), the theologian Kenton L. Sparks provides a thought-provoking evaluation of the traditional evangelical view of Scripture in relation to higher criticism. From an inerrantist point of view, there are both positive and negative dimensions to Sparks's position. Let's begin with the positive ones.

Some Positive Features of Sparks's View of Scripture

Of the many things in this book worth commending, Sparks adequately presents the various evangelical and nonevangelical approaches to higher criticism (*God's Word* [*GW*], 18–23). Though he was critical of Gleason Archer, he did commend him for studying the Bible historically (137–38). Sparks also believes that fideistic approaches by some evangelicals are an unwarranted response to higher criticism (137–39). He is clearly aware of the evangelical arguments used to defend inerrancy (248–51), such as the incarnational analogy used by conservatives (252), the appeals to the claims of Christ (164–65), deductive arguments from God's perfection (139), and different approaches to divine accommodation (231–56). He also offers an overview of the history of biblical criticism (57–204), incorporating views of major theologians such as Augustine, Aquinas, Calvin, and Barth (28–30, 125, 172–78, 235–42, 309–10). He even claims that inerrancy is a theologically important concept, implied by the nature and concept of God (256).

112

Sparks offers a succinct summary of the various evangelical and nonevangelical hermeneutics and their effects upon inerrancy (*GW*, 171–203). He recognizes that secular philosophy affects the understanding of epistemology, language, and inerrancy (33–55). Sparks understands that the Bible is both a divine and human book (76, 373). He correctly claims that God is perfect and cannot err (55, 139), and that the Bible is God's revelation to humanity (73). Sparks also acknowledges that the Bible is a very human book in human language (55–58, 76–77, 121, 193, 206). He is aware of the need for the Holy Spirit to illuminate human minds (31, 203). Sparks sees the need for Christian theology to be rooted in the Bible and holds that it is best summarized in the historic creeds (21–22). He recognizes that the church, academia, publishers, and all individuals must wrestle with the doctrine of inerrancy and its implications (165–67, 357–74). It is clear that Sparks has a broad knowledge of the topic and its implications, and that much of what he suggests overlaps with the historic evangelical view of Scripture.

An Evaluation of Sparks's Basic Proposals

In spite of these commendable features, Sparks's proposal forms a serious problem for the traditional inerrancy position held by evangelical Christians (*GW*, 21–22, 134) and as expressed by the framers of the statement adopted by the Evangelical Theological Society (ETS) and the International Council on Biblical Inerrancy (ICBI).[1] As such, Sparks's proposals demand attention.

Ad Hominem Rhetoric in Sparks

Much of Sparks's work consists of enhanced rhetoric against the traditional inerrancy position. He claims that inerrantists are "naïve fundamentalists" (*GW*, 362), equivalent to believing in a flat earth (373), and they are not real academics (13). Further, he labels the inerrantist position as outdated and considers critical scholars to be the Copernicus and Galileo of the modern era (17–18). He contends that evangelicals want to do away with contemporary science and that it is the higher critics who suffer at their hands (275).

It should be clear that these and other similar statements are little more than ad hominem attacks, rather than biblical or rational arguments against inerrancy. Nonetheless, he tries to paint himself as the true scholar suffering at the hands of traditionalists.

An Antisupernatural Bias

Scattered throughout Sparks's work is an antisupernatural bias. He realizes that evangelicals recognize this bias and therefore devotes a considerable section supporting Ernst Troeltsch's argument against the historicity of miracles (*GW*, 313–22). This critique uses historiography and appeals to the principle of analogy to argue for an implicit form of naturalism. His argument can be summarized as follows (Geisler, *Systematic Theology*, 1:216–17):[2]

1. The past can only be reconstructed based on the analogy of events known to us in the present.
2. Present historical events do not provide us with any miraculous events.
3. Hence, miraculous events cannot be part of any reconstruction (history) of past events.

In response, we point out that Troeltsch's understanding of the principle of historical analogy is a form of historical uniformitarianism. It assumes that all history must be understood without miraculous events. Like David Hume's view, historical uniformitarianism reduces to the position that miracles should be disbelieved even if they occur. C. S. Lewis rejects this view, stating, "If we admit God, must we admit a miracle? Indeed, indeed, you have no security against it. That is the bargain. Theology says to you in effect, 'Admit God and with Him the risk of a few miracles, and I in return will ratify your faith in uniformity as regard the overwhelming majority of events'" (*Miracles*, 109). This being the case, then to deny miracles altogether, one must disprove God. For as long as it is possible for God to exist, then it is possible for miracles to exist. Thus historical uniformitarianism is reducible to atheistic naturalism. In short, miracles are special acts of God. If God exists, then acts of God are possible; therefore, any alleged historical procedure that eliminates miracles and wishes to preserve God is logically flawed.

Appeal to a More "Flexible" Solution concerning Contradictions

Sparks believes that contemporary hermeneutics should have flexibility in interpreting the text to allow for reconciliation of apparent contradictions within the text. He appeals to interpreters throughout church history who, he believes, were sensitive with their interpretations of the text before non-Christian audiences, especially in matters pertaining to science ("After Inerrancy" [AI], 5). After quoting Aquinas and Augustine, he says, "They also believed that where the scientific evidence seemed clear and convincing, our interpretations of Scripture would have to be adjusted accordingly" (5).[3]

Sparks is in favor of moving away from a literal reading of Genesis to a more allegorical interpretation. He says, "Christians have long maintained that the Bible includes several mysterious levels of meaning and have turned to these when the so-called literal meaning seemed wrong" (AI, 6). "The other common strategy for 'adjusting' the Bible's discourse actually admits the errors but pins the blame on the human audience of Scripture" (6). These interpreters overcome these contradictions by appealing to the idea that the writers of these texts accommodated their writings to the confused viewpoints of the ancient audience (6). God allowed inferior and errant practices to enter Scripture because "humanity was not prepared to manage their sudden elimination" (6). These "fallen elements of biblical religion are gradually eliminated in the course of the redemptive process" (7).

Response to Ancient Solutions

While God's special revelation in Scripture and his general revelation in nature cannot conflict, there is sometimes a conflict between the interpretations of Scripture by theologians and the interpretations of scientists about general revelation. Sometimes theologians have been wrong, such as the Roman Catholic Church in condemning Galileo for rejecting a geocentric solar system. Likewise, some biblical interpreters have taken the phrase "the four corners of the earth" (Rev. 7:1) to mean that the earth is square. At other times scientists have been wrong in assuming the polygenetic origin of mankind and in positing macroevolution. However, this is not an argument against the infallibility of the Bible but an argument for the fallibility of biblical interpreters.

Postmodern Practical Realism

Sparks believes that postmodernism provides a valuable resource for theological reflections on Scripture (AI, 8). He argues that humans do not find reality but create reality and truth. Instead, he argues for practical realism. He says, "Unlike Antirealism, it holds that tradition does not blind us to the truth but rather turns out to be the practical, adequate and useful way that human beings grasp it" (8). This is never a perfect grasp of reality. This grasp is "not like a toggle switch that is either right or wrong. . . . It can be very good or very bad, but never perfect. In the best cases, human knowledge is *wholly adequate* for the needs of the situation" (8). But Sparks rejects either univocal or analogical knowledge of God (see chap. 14 below), which leaves us with equivocal language: it leaves us in skepticism.

Practical realism, unlike modern realism, is opposed to the one-for-one correspondence between interpretation and fact (AI, 8). "Our understanding of reality is 'right' when our model or concept of reality is 'close enough' to the facts to give us success in what we are trying to do. The result is never 'the brute truth.' It is at best partial and useful, though always warped in some way or the other" (8). Because human beings are finite and fallen creatures, they can never have a perfect, God's-eye viewpoint; they are always partial and warped (8). Hence, "good theology will not be content with any single text of Scripture. It will realize that all of Scripture's voices, taken together, give us the fullest understanding of God and his voice" (9).

Response to Practical Realism

As we show elsewhere (in chap. 14 below), our knowledge of ultimate reality (e.g., God) is real but analogical. We apprehend God but cannot completely comprehend him. Total agnosticism is self-defeating since it involves the contradiction that we know we cannot know anything about God. On the other hand, total dogmatism is equally wrong. God knows infinitely, and we can only know finitely. But what we know we know truly, even if it is only partially. As the apostle Paul says, "Now I know in part; then I shall know fully" (1 Cor. 13:12). This is not just practical realism; it is also actual realism. We can know reality truly, even though we do not know it exhaustively.

Theological Hermeneutics

This approach to hermeneutics seeks to interpret the Bible through its creedal, ecumenical, biblical, and theological character. It is creedal in that its participants embrace the Christian creedal traditions. It is ecumenical because the creeds allow for a variety of legitimate expressions of the Christian faith. It is biblical because Scripture is taken seriously and is essential to inform the theology of the church. Finally, says Sparks, it is theological because it is committed to the Chalcedonian principle that Scripture is "both divine and human and that, because of this, it presents theology through the limited perspectives of the human horizon. As a result, one cannot simply read off of the Bible's pages; one must read the text and then reflect theologically on how it relates to other biblical texts and to God's voice as it speaks through tradition, cosmos and Spirit" (AI, 9–10).

For Sparks, theological hermeneutics seeks to find the "divine discourse" in Scripture rather than the human discourse (AI, 10). It strives to know what God is saying through the text (10). God cannot err, but humans can err. And since God spoke through a diversity of human authors, that creates an occasion for contradictions and errors to arise. Theological hermeneutics overcomes these apparent contradictions by ignoring the "human meanings in favor of better and more useful 'divine meanings' that are provided via allegories and the 'spiritual sense' of Scripture" (10).

Response to Theological Hermeneutics

The Bible is both divine and human; it is a coauthored set of books. So what the Bible says, God says. Hence, to claim that the Bible has erred is to claim that God has erred. We do have to go beyond the mere statements in the Bible to do theology, but we must not go against the Bible. Neither can one statement in the Bible contradict another, for it is God's Word as well as man's. Hence nothing in the Bible is contradictory for God cannot contradict himself. And nothing in our theology about the Bible should be contradictory for we are made in the image of God and told to "avoid . . . contradictions" (1 Tim. 6:20). The law of noncontradiction is literally undeniable for every attempt to deny this law actually affirms it in the very denial.

Genre Determines Meaning

Sparks embraces Hans-Georg Gadamer's horizons of meaning (GW, 43, 53, 212). He claims that people need to embrace the hermeneutical spiral to reconcile the divine and human discourses (206). Hermeneutics is a process equivalent to Hegel's dialectic going from the particular to the whole, to create the meaning of the text (261, 279, 328). Genre establishes the ground rules for communication and dialogue between the reader and the author because it allows for the horizons of meaning to merge (207). Misunderstanding occurs because people fail to understand the genre of the text (208–9). Good interpretation must go beyond the words of the text's *locutionary act* (what is spoken or written) to the *illocutionary* act (what the author or speaker was trying to accomplish) (208). Because words grasp only small parts of reality, the interpreter should ask questions beyond and behind the text to encompass the whole of the literary event (209–10). In this respect, Sparks echoes the view of Kevin Vanhoozer (see chap. 8 below).

Response: Genre Does Not Determine Meaning

The essence of what Sparks is arguing is that genre determines meaning and that meaning is obtained through a process of fusing the horizons of meaning through the hermeneutical spiral (*GW*, 30, 38, 177, 209–12, 246, 262). However, the nature of the objectivist position is not that objectivity can be indubitably demonstrated but that it cannot be avoided. The self-defeating nature of the subjectivist position is that one cannot deny that objective meaning can be derived from the text without having an objective understanding of the text. When people look for deeper meaning through illocutions, they are projecting ideas that go beyond the text. There is no way to know if God or the authors intended a deeper meaning when all we have to go by is the text.

The second difficulty with the idea that genre "gives meaning" is that the interpreter must read the text and attempt to discern the patterns that would indicate conformity to the characteristics of a particular genre (Howe, "Does Genre Determine Meaning?" [DGDM?] 3). This requires that the person have at least a rudimentary knowledge of the text prior to classifying the genre. This rudimentary knowledge occurs when a person approaches the text according to the historical-grammatical interpretive methodology, which goes from the particulars to the whole (6). Thus Sparks cannot avoid the necessity of the historical-grammatical interpretation of Scripture.

The Hermeneutical Circle Is Not Vicious

There is a hermeneutical circle in the relationship of the genre to the elements arranged into their particular form, but it is not a vicious circle. Genre classification enhances the understanding of meaning, or it may qualify initial readings, but it does not determine meaning (DGDM? 8). The following chart by Professor Howe summarizes the relationship between genre and the material that forms the literary work (8):

Genre	Words and Sentences
The Whole	The Parts
Enhances Meaning	Determines Meaning
Form of the Text	Material of the Text
Arises from the Text	Constitutes the Text
Secondary Consideration	Primary Consideration

Furthermore, the idea that genre determines meaning suffers from another logical mistake. In order to discover the genre of a particular text, one must already have a developed genre theory. But as Howe notes:

> A genre theory comes from studying and comparing individual texts, and this is done prior to and apart from genre classification. If this is so, then it must be the case that there is some meaning communicated to the interpreter apart from whether the interpreter has recognized any given genre classification. But, if genre determines meaning, then this scenario is impossible. The interpreter must know the genre before he knows the text. But this is tantamount to imposing genre expectations upon the text. (DGDM? 10–11)

Many critical scholars use genre classification to excuse and authorize a particular treatment of the biblical text. They employ this method because they do not accept the historical accounts of much of Scripture, so they simply classify it as poetry, fiction, midrash, and so forth. The difficulty with such an approach is that if a person cannot trust the Bible about things of earth and can classify them in such a way as to remove their historical validity, then how can a person trust the Bible when it comes to the things of heaven? Why do they not also classify heavenly truths in such a way as to remove their eternal validity? The truth is that many of them do.

The Appeal to Language Games Fails

Sparks appeals to Wittgenstein's language games to clarify the relationship between genre and meaning (GW, 29). Wittgenstein illustrates the notion of language games by comparing them to real games. When a person investigates real games, it is clear that there is no one common characteristic of every game to define the essence of all games. Rather, as a person looks at all the games, they will conclude that while there is not a single characteristic or essence, all games overlap to some degree, with differences in detail. The point appears that there is no single essence to the nature of language.

But this is a false appeal used by critical hermeneutics because language games are not like genres. They employ a Fregean confusion between meaning and referent to divert the conversation. As Professor Howe observes:

> If the speaker and hearer were playing two games, then communication would not have occurred on any level, and the hearer would not be able to move from his own language game to the game being played by the speaker since there is no nature or essence that could make such a transition possible. Also, if the hearer is merely confused about the referent, then this indicates that some communication has occurred even though the two are employing different genres. It is the single essence or nature of language that makes the transition from one genre to another possible. (DGDM? 16)

Genre classification is possible only because there is a basis in reality for meaning. As will be shown later (in chap. 14), this similarity is found in the similarity in being between the Creator and the creatures made in his image (Gen. 1:27). Once this similarity is established, the identification of objective meaning (see chap. 14 below) can be identified by means of the normal historical-grammatical method of interpretation (DGDM? 16–17).

Multiple Meanings Deny Inerrancy

Not only does Sparks hold that there are multiple meanings in a given text of Scripture; he also believes these meanings are sometimes contradictory. This is a clear denial of inerrancy. He labels these different voices as different trajectories in Scripture that move beyond the text (*GW*, 295, 299, 326). Some of these would include differences in theology and ethics between the Old and New Testaments (295–97), differences between the text of Scripture and contemporary science (296), or for the people of today to listen to the living voice of Christ to bring new trajectories (299). But, as will be argued later (in chap. 14), there is only one meaning for a text (*sensus unum*), though it may have many implications. Here Sparks confuses meaning and significance.

Further, the implications that Sparks draws from these trajectories is that the many installments of the living voice can contradict the written Word. He says, "As a result, God's Word has not been passed to us as a single, univocal voice but as a series of disparate and sometimes contradictory installments, whose final significance must be spiritually discerned by listening—with the Spirit's help—to that full range of God's discourses" (*GW*, 327). Finally, "By reason and spiritual wisdom, the church is able to discover from these diverse voices the unique voice of God for us today. Theological interpretation is a process that hears God's univocal *Word* by listening to his many *words*" (327).

Sparks's methodology is clearly contrary to the claims of Scripture because it undermines its divine authority. He uses the term "trajectories" to argue that God is moving the church in a new direction. Yet clearly by "trajectories" Sparks recognizes that the new direction contradicts God's previous statements in the Word of God. But this method is contrary to the nature of God, who "never lies" (Titus 1:2; cf. Heb. 6:18) and is not a "God of confusion" (1 Cor. 14:33) and warns us to "avoid ... contradictions" (1 Tim. 6:20).

There is no reason to believe that God is speaking new normative revelation today. The Scriptures are clear on this issue: "Long ago, at many times and in many ways, God spoke to our fathers by the prophets, but in these last days he has spoken to us by his Son" (Heb. 1:1–2). Now that the canon of Scripture is closed, believers are to find the message and will of God in the written Word of God. As the Chicago Statement on Biblical Inerrancy put it (in art. 5), "We deny that later revelation, which may fulfill earlier revelation, ever corrects or contradicts it. We further deny that any normative revelation has been given since the completion of the New Testament Writings."

The Charge of a Purely Deductive Approach

Sparks is opposed to what he considers the traditional deductive approach, which argues from the nature of God and the claims of Scripture to contend for inerrancy (see chap. 12 below). He believes that individuals such as B. B. Warfield and Carl F. H. Henry are using a Cartesian form of reasoning (*GW*, 138). He claims that Henry "desires indubitable religious knowledge and fully believes that he can get it from an inerrant Bible" (138–39). Sparks goes on to state,

> Once we deductively recognize that Scripture claims or implies its own inerrancy, says Henry, we may safely assume that any circular conclusions that inductively imply error in Scripture are quite mistaken, either because of poor reasoning or because we do not have all of the data that we need to reach the correct conclusion. So much for biblical criticism. (139)

Instead, Sparks argues for an inductive approach to the study of Scripture. He believes this method recognizes the validity of the critical scholars and the humanity of the Bible. He says, "It is one thing to argue that God does not err in Scripture; it is quite another thing to argue that the human authors of Scripture did not err" (*GW*, 139).

Furthermore, in reference to Calvin, he says:

> On this score [that God does not err but accommodates to errant human viewpoints] I quite agree with Calvin and could sign my name to the list of those who argue, in a similar way, that inerrancy is a theologically important—and indeed, ancient—concept implied by the nature and concept of God. On the other hand, fundamentalist notions of inerrancy that deny the influence of flawed human perspectives in the text are bound to be found wanting, not only because of theological and philosophical necessity (finite human perspectives are never inerrant) but also because theological diversity of Scripture is so transparent. To attribute error to God is surely heresy, but to deny the errant human elements in Scripture may verge on a kind of Docetism. (*GW*, 256)

Finally, Sparks says:

> I will strongly support a doctrine of inerrancy when it comes to Scripture; but I will further suggest that this doctrine, as traditionally understood, differs significantly from the doctrine as it has come to be understood by those evangelicals who stand more or less firmly within the Cartesian tradition. In my opinion, this tradition leads one into an epistemological cul-de-sac, which demands of the Bible something that it is not so that our human interpretations of Scripture can be turned into "verbal idols." (*GW*, 55)[4]

Response to Sparks's Cartesian Argument

In response to Sparks, several observations are worth making. First, it is important to recognize that Cartesian rationalism has had some negative effects upon theology. But it is false to claim that the whole of the modern inerrancy position is driven by Cartesian ideals. The ICBI commentary on biblical inerrancy (Sproul, *Explaining Inerrancy*) recognizes the negative effects of false philosophical ideas upon inerrancy and specifically mentions rationalism to be one of them (*GW*, 72). In light of these false presuppositions, it says, "When these un- and antibiblical principles seep into men's theologies at a presuppositional level, as today they frequently do, faithful interpretation of Holy Scripture becomes impossible" (72–73).

Second, the inerrantists' argument is by no means purely deductive. It is based first on a complete induction of all Scripture, which yields two premises: (1) God cannot err, and (2) the Bible is the Word of God. Once a complete inductive study of all Scripture is made and it yields these two premises, then and only then is there a legitimate deductive inference with its claim: (3) Therefore the Bible cannot err. Even so, before one can know exactly what is meant by an error, all the data (phenomena) of Scripture must be taken into full consideration so that one can know precisely what is meant by an error. This too is a thoroughly inductive procedure. A more comprehensive step-by-step procedure of how this works is treated elsewhere (see Geisler, *Systematic Theology*, vol. 1, chap. 12). It is sufficient to note here that an adequate biblical and theological method yielding a sophisticated doctrine of inerrancy is based thoroughly in a complete inductive study of Scripture both for its basic premises and for a nuanced understanding of what an error would mean. The ICBI framers recognized this and incorporated it into article 13 of the Chicago Statement on inerrancy. It reads in part: "We further deny that inerrancy is negated by Biblical phenomena such as a lack of modern technical precision, irregularities of grammar or spelling, observational descriptions of nature, the reporting of falsehoods, the use of hyperbole and round numbers, the topical arrangement of material, variant selections of material in parallel accounts, or the use of free citations."

Third, for the inerrantist position to succumb to circular reasoning as charged, it would have to claim that the Bible is inerrant because it claims to be inerrant.[5] Rather, the inerrancy position is grounded in a deductive argument that is grounded in the essential nature of a perfect God, who cannot communicate error.[6] Christianity, unlike the ancient philosophies, recognized that it was of the nature of the Divine Being to be perfect.[7] Likeness is based upon agreement or communication of form. And if God is perfect, then what he produces must be perfect. Thus, when God "breathed out" the Word of God (2 Tim. 3:16), then it too must be perfect. The concept of formal equivalency is what Warfield pointed to with the motto "As Scripture says, God says; and as God says, Scripture says." Or, as God is perfect, so are the Scriptures perfect; and as the Scriptures are perfect, so is God perfect.[8]

Fourth, the purely inductive method of Sparks fails because it leads to the belief that errors exist in the original autographs. His approach appeals to the humanity of the Bible to account for supposed errors and contradictions. Proponents of that approach live by the motto *Errare humanum est* (To err is human). In response, inerrantists do not deny the humanity of the Bible, but they deny that it is *necessary* for humans to err. Everyday life confirms that humans are able to not err. There are inerrant exams, phone books, and letters. When it comes to the Scriptures, God is the primary cause, and the human authors are secondary causes. And it is impossible for a secondary cause to rise above a primary cause. The theological implication is that even though humans are imperfect and have a tendency to err, it does not bleed through to the text of Scripture. Peter affirmed this when he says, "For no prophecy was ever produced by the will of man, but men spoke from God as they were carried along by the Holy Spirit" (2 Pet. 1:21). Practically speaking, even God can draw a straight line with a crooked stick!

Fifth, it is false to claim that the inerrantist position is a form of doceticism that treats the text like "verbal idols" and disregards higher critical studies. Rather, as article 14 of the Chicago Statement says, "We affirm the unity and internal consistency of Scripture. We deny that alleged errors and discrepancies that have not yet been resolved vitiate the truth claims of the Bible." Because God is Truth and the Word of God flows from the nature of God, it would follow that even with the diversity and scope of interest, there is an internal unity and consistency. God's truthful nature brings unity out of diversity. God is a God of order, and it would be contrary to his nature that his Word be incoherent and filled with contradictions.

This article recognizes the problems of harmonization and what appear to be contradictions pointed out by critics. They usually claim that the Bible is *full* of contradictions. But the evidence reveals this to be an overstatement of the case. Defenders of the inerrancy position have labored to show that these supposed contradictions can be resolved and over time many already have been resolved. Hence, there is reasonable expectation that the rest can be resolved too. There is a parallel in the presence of anomalies in the scientific world. They cause scientists to rethink their theories about biology, geology, and the like. The field of science does not disregard a well-attested theory because scientists have not been able to resolve an anomaly. In the same respect, every student of Scripture can apply the same scientific method to the study of Scripture and claim that the well-attested doctrine of inerrancy should not be disregarded because of supposed contradictions.

This is not special pleading since as knowledge and scholarly work progress, one is able to harmonize what once seemed to be explicit contradictions. And today scholars can approach the text of Scripture with the same confidence in order to allow the Scriptures to have a fair hearing. The inerrancy position has forced academics to dig deeper into the text of Scripture, which is exactly what a person would expect with a book of its size and scope. This is not unparalleled in other disciplines since as science progresses it is able to explain many things that it could not in previous generations.

Jesus's Accommodation to Human Fallenness

Sparks makes the serious claim that Jesus accommodated his teachings to human fallenness: when commenting on Matthew 19:1–9, he claims that Jesus attributed Moses's permission of divorce to accommodation. In this case God has accommodated his revealed law to the cultural and ideological perspectives of the ancient Near East, which permitted divorce and which reflected the fallenness and hardness of the human heart (*GW*, 241–42). Sparks states:

> In the language of our modern discussion, *I would argue that Jesus not only allowed for, but explicitly testified to, Scripture's theological and ethical accommodation to fallen humanity.* So if we were at first surprised by the accommodationist theology of the church fathers, we need be no longer; indeed, their accommodationist theology was apparently in some measure derived from this Gospel text. (241–42, emphasis added)

Sparks recognizes the christological implications of this claim: "If the critical evidence against the traditional authorial attributions in the Old Testament is as strong as it seems to be, then it is perhaps evangelical Christology—and not critical scholarship—that needs to be carefully reconsidered" (*GW*, 164–65). Implications arise from Sparks's view:

> If Jesus was fully human, as orthodoxy demands, then it is likely that he learned— along with other ancient Jews—that Moses, Isaiah, and Daniel wrote their books, irrespective of factual and historical realities. Moreover, even if Jesus knew the critical fact that Moses did not pen the Pentateuch, it is hardly reasonable to assume that he would have revealed this information to his ancient audience. To the extent that Jesus drew upon his omniscience in everyday life and conversation, it would have been constantly necessary for him to pass up opportunities to tell those around him what he knew. (165)

Response to Sparks's Accommodationist View

Sparks's accommodationist view creates a christological crisis. His argument that to err is human is based upon a kind of Gnostic idea that any contact with human fallenness makes error unavoidable. This argument should be rejected for what it is, namely, neo-Gnosticism. Although Sparks argues for the sinlessness of Christ and claims to hold to theological orthodoxy, the logical implications of this view are that Jesus accommodated himself to err and could have accommodated to sin as well. However, this is clearly against the basic New Testament teaching that Jesus did not sin (Heb. 4:15; 2 Cor. 5:21; 1 Pet. 2:22–23; 1 John 3:2–3).

Further, it was not a matter of Jesus's knowing who the true author of a text was and passing up the opportunity to say so (as Sparks suggests), but of Jesus's affirming that the author of a text was Moses, David, or Isaiah (as he did on various occasions)[9] when he knew this was false. This would be divine deception. So in either alternative Sparks suggests (God's knowing or not knowing who the true authors were), the divine "accommodation" proposed by Sparks would involve a divine error or sin, as the case may be. But this is wholly unacceptable for any orthodox theologian. So, either the Bible is inerrant or else Christ was not.

The theological implications of Sparks's view are serious as well. For if true, then the very teachings of Jesus in human language are tainted with error. Orthodox Christology has never held that the Second Person of the Godhead erred in his human words—but the logic of Sparks's position requires this conclusion. The implications are that the Son of God himself is not the "lamb without blemish or spot" (1 Pet. 1:19); instead, he partook of sin and error, and thus the saints in heaven will not be freed from their sin and error—though the Scriptures teach that they will be freed (1 Cor. 13:10; 1 John 3:2; Rev. 21:4). For they will still be human in heaven. And if being human necessarily involves being in error, then the saints in heaven will also be sinful and errant.

However, there is no reason to contend that Christ adhered to this extreme accommodationist position. Rather, orthodoxy has always taught that God has adapted his revelation to human *finitude* and never accommodated it to human *fallenness*. The reason is because it would be contrary to the very nature of God as truth to accommodate to error. Actually, there are two views that must be distinguished: (1) First, God does adapt himself to human finitude, but (2) God does not accommodate himself to human error. Sparks confuses these two.

Classical orthodoxy recognizes that God is transcendent. Because of this, God must "stoop down" to speak with humanity. However, this adaptation to finitude is never an accommodation to myths, error, or sin—for God to adapt to error would cause God to lie, which is "impossible" (Heb. 6:18). God uses anthropomorphisms through the medium of analogical language to speak to humanity, but he does not accommodate to error and sin. A partial knowledge of God and truth is not a complete lack of knowledge or errant knowledge (1 Cor. 13:12). God may not tell us everything, but all that he does tell us is true (see Geisler, "Accommodation," in *Baker Encyclopedia*, 1).

There are many reasons to contend that Jesus never accommodated to human sin. First, it would be contrary to the life and actions of Jesus to claim that he accommodated to sin or error. Jesus repeatedly stood against the traditions of his day (Matt. 15:3), and corrected false views of the Bible (Matt. 5:21–48). Jesus rebuked religious teachers for holding false views of the Bible (Matt. 22:29; 23:16–33; John 2:15–16; 3:12). Second, accommodation to error and sin would be contrary to Jesus's nature. Jesus's closest friends recognized his high moral character (2 Cor. 5:21; Heb. 4:15; 1 Pet. 1:19; 1 John 3:3; 4:17). The crowds were amazed with his teaching (Matt. 7:29). The Roman leaders and soldiers declared him to be innocent of the charges against him and a righteous man (Luke 23:4, 47). Finally, if we believe that Jesus is God, as all orthodox theologians do, he could not lie or deceive people. For it is "impossible for God to lie" (Heb. 6:18; cf. Titus 1:2), and Jesus is the Son of God (Matt. 16:16–18; John 1:2, 14; 8:58). Further, God's "word is truth" (John 17:17) and "Let God be true though every one were a liar" (Rom. 3:4). Whatever limitations Jesus had while a human being were necessary in order for redemption and communication to occur. Nevertheless, there is no error involved for Jesus is God, and God cannot err. It is contrary to his very nature.

Sparks appeals to the fact that Jesus learned like any other human being and grew in wisdom (*GW*, 164), as Luke says (2:52), and he did not know the day of his return (Matt. 24:36). From this he reasons that Jesus might not have known about the authorship of certain books of the Bible or that Moses did not write the Pentateuch but that four authors (J,E,P, and D) did (77–78). Hence, when speaking of Moses as the author, Jesus accommodated to error. However, it is one thing to affirm that Jesus did not know the date of his return or about the modern elaboration of JEPD. It is quite another thing to affirm that Jesus was wrong and affirmed error. Jesus's limitations as a man did not hinder him from affirming truth. Whatever Jesus taught came with divine authority (Matt. 28:18–20). Furthermore, Jesus also taught only what the Father told him to teach (John 5:30; 8:28). To charge Jesus with error is to charge God the Father with error, since he only spoke what the Father told him to speak (John 8:26).

Accommodation and the Incarnational Analogy

The inerrancy position is grounded in the nature of God and in the Bible's being the Word of God. The traditional argument can be stated this way:

1. God cannot err.
2. The original Bible is God's Word.
3. Therefore, the original Bible cannot err.

Upon examination, Sparks accepts premise 1 but rejects premise 2, and necessarily the conclusion. He argues that the Bible is a divine book accommodated to finite and fallen humanity. He extends this argument to reject the whole orthodox incarnational analogy. Sparks says:

> The Christological argument fails because, though Jesus was indeed sinless, he was also human and finite. He would have erred in the usual way that other people err because of their finite perspectives. He misremembered this event or that, and mistook this person for someone else, and thought—like everyone else—that the sun was literally rising. To err in these ways simply goes with the territory of being human. These errors are not sins, not even black marks against our humanity. They stem from the design of God, which God has declared to be very good. As a result, the Christological analogy cited in the Chicago Statement seems to be a good one, but it sends us in a direction opposite to what the statement's framers supposed. The finite, human form of Jesus tells us that Scripture's authors and their discourse will be finite and human. (*GW*, 252–53)

Sparks further argues against the parallel between the incarnation and inerrancy, calling it a confusion of theological categories (*GW*, 253). He argues that while theologians throughout church history have used the analogy, it is not perfect. He writes:

Nevertheless, the parallel is not precise in all respects. The joining of humanity and divinity in Scripture is of a different sort than the hypostatic union of deity and humanity in Christ. The Son incarnate brings humanity and divinity together into one person, whereas the Scriptures speak divine revelation through finite and fallen human authors. (253)

Scripture's humanity is perhaps better illustrated through an adoptionistic metaphor (God has adopted the human author's words as his own) than through a christological metaphor (where the human Word *is* God). Such a distinction would theoretically highlight the substantive difference between God's *written Word* and the *incarnate Word* to which the written Word testifies (see John 5:39). (253)

At any rate, Sparks insists that "if there is going to be an argument that frees the personalities, ideas, and temperaments of Scripture's human authors from fallenness and finitude, it will need to take a very different path. The christological analogy ends before it can serve as an objection to the implications of accommodation" (253).

There are many reasons for rejecting Sparks's conclusions about accommodation and his rejection of the incarnational analogy in favor of an adoptionistic analogy.

First, he has misstated the incarnational analogy by claiming, "The Son incarnate brings human and divinity together into one person, whereas the Scriptures speak divine revelation through finite and human authors" (*GW*, 253). The incarnational analogy teaches that just as the divine and human came together into one *person*, even so the divine and human came together in one set of *propositions* (or sentences). If the verbal form of Scripture is "breathed out" by God (2 Tim. 3:16), then there is a propositional unity that combines both the divine and human elements in one and the same verbal structure.

The reasoning of the incarnational analogy can be stated as follows:

1. God's living Word and his written Word are similar:
   a. They both have a divine and human dimension.
   b. These two dimensions are combined in one unity.
   c. Thus, both are without flaw.
2. Hence, both God's living Word and his written Word are without flaw morally:
   a. God's living Word is without sin.
   b. God's written Word is without error.

This argument contends that Jesus as God could not have erred and Jesus as man could have erred but did not. In the same way the Bible in its divine nature could not have erred and in its human nature it could have erred but did not.

Sparks's adoptionist analogy has serious flaws. Adoptionism is a false doctrine teaching that Jesus was only a man but was adopted by God because of his divine powers. This is said to have occurred when God declared from heaven, "This is my beloved Son" (Matt. 3:17). Sparks's argument fails for numerous reasons. First, the adoptionist analogy fails because it would have to argue that logically the Bible was a human book that became a divine book. Yet even Sparks does not argue for this position but that the Scripture had its origin in God.

Second, if he is going to argue that an adoptionist analogy is correct, then by comparison he would have a heretical adoptionist Christology too. However, Scripture clearly affirms that Jesus was not a man who was adopted into divine sonship. Rather, he was the eternal Son of God (John 1:1, 3; 8:58; Col. 1:16–17; Heb. 1:3).[10] Likewise, Scripture repeatedly affirms that it is the very Word of God (2 Tim. 3:16; John 10:35; 2 Pet. 1:20–21). It was not merely adopted as the Word of God when it was really only the words of man. For the very words of Scripture were "breathed out" by God (2 Tim. 3:16). Indeed, David says, "The Spirit of the LORD speaks by me; his word is on my tongue" (2 Sam. 23:2).

Third, for the adoptionist analogy to hold, it would have to argue that the Bible was adopted because of its special divine powers just as Christ was adopted because of his special divine powers. The analogy falls apart because if the Bible contains as many errors and accommodations to human finitude as Sparks claims, then there are no special divine powers manifest in the text of Scripture. Indeed, he claims that the moral contradictions in Scripture make it "downright sinister or evil" ("After Inerrancy" [AI], 3).

Fourth, the analogy fails because it would imply that the Bible changes from being a human book to being a divine book. According to the adoptionist analogy, for Jesus to go from not being God to being God would imply a change. But it is not possible for the divine nature to undergo change or for a human nature to become a divine nature. Therefore the analogy fails. In fact, it leads to heresy.

Sinister, Evil, and Contradictory Ethics

As examples that make the Bible "downright sinister or evil" (AI, 3), he appeals to Deuteronomy 20:16–18 and Matthew 5:43–45. In the former text, God commands the nation of Israel to commit genocide. In the latter text, Jesus commands the people, "Love your enemies." This, he believes, is an obvious contradiction between the law of Moses and the words of Jesus. Furthermore, in the exodus account, God is portrayed as killing innocent children. Later, in the book of Joshua, God commands Israel to kill men, women, children, and animals (Josh. 6:20–21).

Sparks believes that the existence of these telltale signs of contradictions arise because the text of Scripture was written by finite, fallen human beings, who erred in the ways that human beings usually err (AI, 5). Quoting with approval James Orr's work in *The Fundamentals*, he believes that inerrancy is an intellectual disaster: "One may plead, indeed, for 'a supernatural providential guidance' which has for its aim to exclude all, even the least, error or discrepancy in statement, . . . but this is a violent assumption which there is nothing in the Bible really to support. It is perilous, therefore, to seek to pin down faith to it as a matter of vital importance" (5). Therefore, appeal to these types of accounts are straightforward evidence that inerrancy is "intellectual disaster" (5).

Response to Sinister, Evil Accounts

As noted earlier, the Bible cannot contradict itself because it is God's Word and God cannot contradict himself. Hence, the error is not in the Bible; it is in the interpreter of the Bible who thinks he sees contradictions there. As Augustine aptly says, "If we are perplexed by any apparent contradiction in Scripture, it is not allowable to say, The author of this book is mistaken; but either [1] the manuscript is faulty, or [2] the translation is wrong, or [3] you have not understood" (Augustine, *Reply to Faustus* 11.5). In Sparks's case, it is the interpretation that is wrong. God is the author of life; God gives life, and he can take it or command another to take it.

For example, the command to wipe out the wicked Canaanites was a divine command. He had justification for it (see Lev. 18), and it was his war. As the psalmist says, "For not by their own sword did they win the land, nor did their own arm save them, but your [God's] right hand and your arm" (Ps. 44:3). As Job put it, "The LORD gave, and the LORD has taken away" (Job 1:21). God himself says, "See now that I, even I, am he, and there is no god beside me; I kill and I make alive" (Deut. 32:39). God is sovereign over life and has the right to take what he gives. Indeed, he does it to every human being—it is called death. Hence, if he commands the death of another, whether in self-defense (Exod. 22:2), in capital punishment (Gen. 9:6), or in cutting out the cancer of a guilty Canaanite civilization, it is his right to do so (cf. Lev. 18). The reason it is wrong for us to intentionally kill an innocent human being is because it is "murder" (Exod. 20:13) to take the life of an innocent person, made in the image of God (Gen. 1:27; 9:6). Hence, it is not the Bible that errs here but Sparks who errs.

Theistic Evolution

Sparks and the BioLogos website (see appendix 2 below) have a clear agenda—to move evangelicals to embrace evolutionary theory. They recognize that an affirmation of biblical inerrancy presents an obstacle to evolutionary theory. Theologians should move beyond the "simpleminded" understanding of Genesis and evolution (*GW*, 360). The "evidential threshold" has been crossed, and the biblical text can no longer be reconciled with science. The biblical writers believed these accounts were true because they were trapped in the limits of their ancient cosmology and observations. "The Bible says human beings were created on day 6 of a six-day creation process, and science tells us that human beings were created through a complex evolutionary process that took millions of years" (AI, 3). Theologians and pastors should take the advice of men like Augustine and Calvin and quit using Genesis as a science book (*GW*, 361). And if they do so, "perhaps, in a few decades or so, evangelical Christians will be no more troubled by the apparent 'conflict' between Genesis and evolution than by the conflict between Genesis and Copernicus. The result will not be an unbiblical liberalism so much as a Christian movement that has come to grips with scientific reality" (361).

Theistic Evolution and Biblical Inerrancy

There are so many flaws in Sparks's argument that it is difficult to know where to begin. First, it is based on a false accommodationist theory (addressed in chap. 16 below). The God of truth cannot accommodate to our errors; God merely adapts himself to our finitude. Second, evolution is not a fact; it is an unproved hypothesis. Hence, there is no real factual conflict with Genesis. The conflict is between an unproved hypothesis and the clear teaching of Scripture that God created matter, life, new kinds of life, and human beings in his own image (Gen. 1:1, 21, 27).[11] Third, it is not a "simpleminded" view to believe in creation. Some of the great minds in history and in contemporary thought have held the view. Fourth, the age of the earth is not a settled view for either science or theologians. So it is not a fact that contradicts anything. Here again, it is a conflict between theories about God's revelations, not a conflict between his revelations in Scripture and in nature. Fifth, a historical-grammatical reading of Genesis 1 and 2, which is both biblically called for and hermeneutically necessary (see chap. 15 below), demands a literal understanding of creation as opposed to any form of macroevolution. This is clear from (1) the use of the word "create" (*bārā'*) in this context; (2) the affirmation that each created thing developed after "its kind"; (3) the manner in which man was created from the dust; (4) the manner in which Eve was created from Adam; and (5) the return of man to the dust from which he came (not to animals from which he came). Only an unacceptable, unbiblical, and self-defeating rejection of the historical-grammatical interpretation of Scripture can make room for macroevolution. And the application of this kind of nonliteral hermeneutic to the Gospels will undermine other orthodox fundamentals (like the virgin birth, death, and resurrection of Christ). In short, logically macroevolution and an evangelical view of Scripture and other essential doctrines are incompatible.

Finally, the biblical writers were not trapped in a false cosmology. Inerrancy allows for observational statements that are factually correct. The Bible is a prescientific book, but it is not unscientific. Whenever it makes a statement about the space-time world, it is correct since it is God's Word, and God cannot make a mistake about anything. Again, the mistakes are in our interpretation, not in his revelation. And as a matter of fact, there is no contradiction between the facts, whether historical or scientific, and what the Bible teaches (see Geisler and Howe, *Big Book*).

Biblical Contradictions

Sparks appeals to what he considers to be many problems with the Scriptures (AI, 2–3; GW, 57–132). He points to tension between the statements about Judas's death in Matthew 27:3–8 and Acts 1:18–19. He cites other contradictions: God has a body and that God is a Spirit (John 4:24). Israel's forebears foreknew God's name, Yahweh (Amos 9:1), yet other texts explicitly claim that they did not (Gen. 28:16; Exod. 6:2–3). God's people should divorce unbelieving spouses, yet other texts say they should not divorce them (Ezra 9–10; 1 Cor. 7:10–16). One text of Scripture portrays David as an adulterer and murder, and another portrays him as righteous and innocent (2 Sam. 11–12; 1 Chron.). The Bible claims that there was a worldwide flood, but geological and biological evidence prove this never happened (AI, 30).

Numerous objections have been leveled against inerrancy. Most of them have been answered elsewhere in more extensive works (see Archer, *Bible Difficulties*; Geisler and Howe, *Big Book*). Many of the major ones are answered below (in chap. 17). None of them seem any more difficult than the one shared by the late Kenneth Kantzer, dean of Trinity Evangelical Divinity School. He told of two reliable friends who gave seemingly contradictory reports of the death of another friend. An eyewitness report said she was hit by a bus, injured but not killed. She died sometime later. Another eyewitness report said the same person was riding in a car, hit broadside, thrown from the car, and died instantly. Kantzer believed both reports because the eyewitnesses were reliable, but he had no way to reconcile them. His trust was later vindicated when he received the whole story: Just as one witness said, she was hit by a bus, injured, but not killed. Further, a good Samaritan picked her up and drove her toward the hospital. However, on the way, just as the second witness said, the car was hit, she was thrown from it, and she died instantly. I know of nothing in the Bible that seems more contradictory than what the two original witnesses said. What resolved this conflict? It was the added information that she was picked up by a good Samaritan and killed on the way to the hospital. What is the moral of the story? It is that those who think there are contradictions in the Bible do not know too much: they know too little. Likewise, if we collect more information on remaining unresolved difficulties in the Bible, it is reasonable to believe that they can be resolved too.

Conclusion

Sparks offers many positive insights into the nature of Scripture and the history of interpretation. Though we cannot deal with all of his individual claims in a short chapter, it should be clear that his attempt to explain "God's Word in human words" falls into serious errors. If individuals were to accept his view of Scripture, they would have to adopt antisupernaturalism, believe that God can act contrary to his nature, accept a christological adoptionist heresy, embrace that the Bible accommodates fallenness and error, and embrace a radical hermeneutics and neo-Barthianism.

Historical evangelicalism should be aware of these new-generation scholars like Sparks who embrace critical hermeneutics and historical criticism. Sparks was trained in an American evangelical seminary and once served on the pastoral staff at a large evangelical church. But he represents the face of the new liberalism on the American scene. Although he claims to be an evangelical in his doctrine of

Scripture, that claim should be rejected. In fact, the philosophical and theological implications of his views of Scripture have serious consequences for the nature of God and for Christology.

Albert Mohler alluded to Sparks as one of the new faces on the American scene speaking against the inerrancy position. He has said, in the title and introduction of his article "Inerrancy of Scripture": "We are entering a new phase in the battle over the Bible's truthfulness and authority. We should at least be thankful for undisguised arguments coming from the opponents of biblical inerrancy, even as we are ready, once again, to make clear where their arguments lead."[12]

Sources

Calvin, *Institutes*

Geisler, *Baker Encyclopedia*

———, *Systematic Theology*

Howe, "Does Genre Determine Meaning?"

Lewis, *Miracles*

Mohler, "Inerrancy of Scripture"

Sparks, "After Inerrancy"

———, *God's Word*

Thomas Aquinas, *Summa*

Vanhoozer, *Is There Meaning?*

Warfield, "Inspiration"

Wittgenstein, *Tractatus*

8

Kevin Vanhoozer on Inerrancy

Introduction

Some authors we are considering, like Bart Ehrman (chap. 5), explicitly deny any kind of biblical inerrancy. Others, like Clark Pinnock (chap. 4) and Andrew McGowan (chap. 9), deny unlimited inerrancy. But some, like Kevin Vanhoozer, claim to affirm inerrancy but adopt philosophical positions that undermine it. This view is more difficult to analyze.

Vanhoozer, a professor at Wheaton College, is particularly hard to evaluate because his views are not always explicitly stated. Often they are hidden beneath philosophical terminology, in illustrations, or in favorable quotations of other authors. The subtlety of his view makes it all the more necessary to analyze and evaluate in light of the traditional stand on inerrancy taken by the Evangelical Theological Society (ETS) and the International Council on Biblical Inerrancy (ICBI) statement on inerrancy, which was adopted by ETS (see chap. 3 above).

Points of Agreement with Vanhoozer on Scripture

There are many views on Scripture held by Vanhoozer with which a traditional inerrantist could agree. These fall into several areas. The first areas of agreement deal with the nature of inerrancy itself.

Agreement on Inerrancy

Vanhoozer believes that "inerrancy is most appropriate as a description of biblical assertions" ("Lost in Interpretation?" [LI?], 113). He even declares that the Bible is "infallible" (92). He rejects Karl Barth's view of Scripture (99). Vanhoozer also accepts propositional revelation (LI? 110; *Drama of Doctrine* [DD], 268). He speaks of the "cognitive content of Scripture" (LI? 100). Vanhoozer embraces the objectivity of truth (*Is There Meaning in This Text?* [MT?], 215) and the correspondence view of truth (LI? 102). He holds that the Bible contains more than propositional truth (*MT?* 209; LI? 103). He also accepts the coauthorship of the Bible by both God and the human authors (*MT?* 265). He even roots inerrancy in the nature of God and in the Bible's own teaching about itself ("Inerrancy of Scripture" [IS], 1).

Inerrancy Defined

To put it in Vanhoozer's own words, "Whereas inspiration concerns the origin of the Bible's authority, inerrancy describes its nature. By inerrancy we refer not only to the Bible's being 'without error' but also to its inability to err. . . . Inerrancy, positively defined, refers to a central and crucial property of the Bible, namely, its utter truthfulness" (IS, 1). We also agree with Vanhoozer that

> the basis for the doctrine of biblical inerrancy is located both in the nature of God and in the Bible's teaching about itself. First, if God is perfect—all-knowing, all-wise, all-good—it follows that God speaks the truth. God does not tell lies; God is not ignorant. God's Word is thus free from all error arising either from conscious deceit or unconscious ignorance. Such is the unanimous confession of the Psalmist, the prophets, the Lord Jesus and the apostles. Second, the Bible presents itself as the Word of God written. (IS, 1)
>
> The inerrancy of Scripture means that Scripture, in the original manuscripts and when interpreted according to the intended sense, speaks truly in all that it affirms. (IS, 3)

We also concur that both infallibility and inerrancy should be used of Scripture and that they are related. Vanhoozer says:

> The older term to express biblical authority—infallibility—remains useful. Infallibility means that Scripture never fails in its purpose. . . . Inerrancy, then, is a subset of infallibility; when the Bible's purpose is to make true statements, it does this too without fail. Yet the Bible's other speech acts—warnings, promises, questions—are infallible too. (IS, 6)

Agreement on Hermeneutics

As for his view on the interpretation of Scripture, he claims to hold to the "literal" interpretation of the text (*MT?* 302–3). Vanhoozer even believes there is "fixed" meaning in the text (215). He also opposes "hermeneutical relativism" (LI? 92). Vanhoozer praises Carl Henry for stressing the cognitive content of Scripture (94–95). He sees the difference between what the text affirms and why it affirms it. Vanhoozer understands the close relationship between inerrancy and hermeneutics (96–97). He recognizes the use of phenomenal language in the Bible such as "the sun raising or setting" (107), and he rightly sees that language is the common medium that an author and the reader share. So language and understanding are a community affair. Likewise, Vanhoozer is to be commended for seeing that letters and words as such do not have meaning. At best, they have only potential meaning. Rather, the smallest unit of meaning is a sentence that forms the words in such a way that they can convey meaning (*MT?* 312). The author's intention is crucial to meaning (*First Theology* [*FT*], 169). The meaning of words and sentences is found in their context (LI? 91). He also affirms the Protestant principle of interpretation that the Bible is the best interpreter of the Bible.

In Vanhoozer's own words, we agree that "the question of meaning should precede the question of truth. We must first determine what kind of claim is being made before we can rule on its truthfulness. . . . We must, therefore, say that the literal sense of Scripture is its literary sense," the sense the author intended to convey in and through a particular literary form (IS, 5). "Inerrancy means that every sense, when interpreted correctly (i.e., in accordance with its literary genre and its literary sense), is wholly reliable" (6). Indeed, the ICBI statement on inerrancy (art. 13) declares,

> We deny that it is proper to evaluate Scripture according to standards of truth and error that are alien to its usage or purpose. We further deny that inerrancy is negated by Biblical phenomena such as a lack of modern technical precision, irregularities of grammar or spelling, observational descriptions of nature, the reporting of falsehoods, the use of hyperbole and round numbers, the topical arrangement of material, variant selections of material in parallel accounts, or the use of free citations.

Other Areas of Agreement

One of the original insights of J. L. Austin, on whom Vanhoozer depends for his philosophy of meaning and language, is that not all language is propositional truth. This is also true of biblical language, which includes confessions, yearnings, promises, predictions, commands, and exclamations. We also agree that there is great value in stories, parables, and figures of speech. Indeed, much of the Bible is in these forms. Also, we concur that in the Bible's literary forms there is great personal, persuasive, and evocative value. Certainly, God intended it that way.

On the practical level, Vanhoozer rightly insists that God's Word is transformational, not merely informational (LI? 110). The Bible calls for obedience, not just understanding (110). The Bible is not given to us merely for our consideration; it also calls on us for our commitment. These and other things not listed are all positive contributions to this topic by Vanhoozer.

Some Questions about Vanhoozer's Views on Scripture

Dr. Andreas Kostenberger has also raised some questions about Vanhoozer's theological method on his website in his review of Vanhoozer's *Drama of Doctrine*, to which Vanhoozer responded directly.[1] Unfortunately, when it comes to Scripture, Vanhoozer tends to take away with one hand what he has given with the other. This is evident in several areas. We will begin with his view of meaning.

Questions about Meaning

Some of Vanhoozer's statements raise serious questions. The first of these pertains to speech-act theory. Is it really an adequate way to explain meaning, truth, and inerrancy? Interestingly, even Vanhoozer raises some doubt on this issue when he writes: "It may be that speech-act philosophy is ultimately inadequate to the descriptive task" (*MT?* 326). Indeed, he admits revising it to fit his own purposes (177n40).

Speech-Act Theory

Nonetheless, Vanhoozer does adopt a version of speech-act theory of language originated a generation ago by J. L. Austin (the "Martin Luther" of the views) and advanced by John Searle (the "Melanchthon"), who systematized it. Austin observed (in his article "Other Minds," 1946) that not all statements are true or false, or even indicative. For instance, some are warnings, promises, exclamations, and so forth. Later (in 1962), Austin distinguished between locutionary act—an utterance with a definite sense and a reference (e.g., "The door is open"); illocutionary act—an act one may perform in making that utterance (e.g., a hint to close the door); and perlocutionary act—an act one may incite by making that illocution (inciting someone to close the door; see article on "Austin, John Langshaw," in *Encyclopedia of Philosophy*, ed. Edwards, 213).

Vanhoozer applies this to the meaning of the biblical text, saying,

> Austin distinguishes three different things we do with words, three kinds of linguistic acts: (1) the locutionary act: utter words (e.g., saying the word "Hello"); (2) the illocutionary act; what we do in saying something (e.g., greeting, promising, commanding, etc.); (3) the perlocutionary act—what we bring about by saying something (e.g., persuading, surprising)." (*MT?* 209)

He applies this to the Bible as follows: (1) locution—the text of Scripture itself; (2) illocution—what the author meant by these words—his intention; (3) perlocution—what the author wanted to accomplish by his intention.

As applied to Scripture, Vanhoozer writes: "My proposal, then, is to say both [that] the Bible is the Word of God (in the sense of its illocutionary acts) and to say that the Bible becomes the Word of God (in the sense of achieving its perlocutionary effect" (*FT,* 195). To focus on the text apart from its illocution is pure "letterism" or "locutionism" (*MT?* 312) since words have no meaning in and of themselves apart from their intended purpose. So the basic unit of meaning is the speech act, not the individual words (312).

In another place Vanhoozer explains it this way:

> Austin distinguishes three components of the total speech act: (a) *the locutionary act* "is roughly equivalent to 'meaning' in the traditional sense," (b) *the illocutionary act* is what we *do* in saying something, and (c) the perlocutionary act is "what we bring about or achieve by saying something, such as convincing, persuading." ("Semantics of Biblical Literature" [SBL], 86)

Vanhoozer calls his view "a Trinitarian theology of holy Scripture." For example,

> The Father's activity is locution. God the father is the utterer, the begetter, the sustainer of word.... The Logos corresponds to the speaker's act of illocution, to what one does in saying.... The Spirit's agency consists rather in bringing the illocutionary point home to the reader and so achieving the corresponding perlocutionary effect—whether belief, obedience, praise or some other. (*FT*, 154–55)

He believes that the real meaning, which he calls "thicker" meaning (*MT?* 284), is not in what is affirmed in the text (which he calls "thinner" meaning), but in the purpose the author had in using the text (LI? 106, 113). That is, the real meaning is not in the locution (the text) but in the illocution (what the author intended to do with the text). But as we will show later (in chaps. 14–15 below), this view has serious difficulties. So the real meaning of the text is not in the text but in the author's speaking through the text in an illocutionary act. Thus, for Vanhoozer, the author speaks through his text, but the text does not speak. He claims that only authors speak, not books (106). For example, the locution in Joshua 10 (which he mistakenly identifies as Joshua 9), which affirms that the sun stood still, is not what the passage is teaching. Indeed, it may involve a mistaken cosmology of the day. Rather, the real point of the text is the illocution or purpose of the text. So "what the author is *doing* in Joshua [10] is narrating history in order to display how God has made good on his promise to Israel to bestow the Promised Land" (106–7).

Response to Vanhoozer's Speech-Act View

Whatever merits speech-act theory may have in other contexts, as it is used by Vanhoozer on Scripture, it has serious drawbacks. In fact, as used to express an orthodox view of inerrancy, it is incapable for the task. This is not to say it is necessarily the cause of the wrong view, but it certainly is an instrumental impediment to expressing it. There are many reasons for this.

First, Vanhoozer claims that one cannot say, as the International Council on Biblical Inerrancy (ICBI) did in its widely accepted Chicago Statement, that "the Bible is true and reliable in all matters it addresses" (art. 11). Why? Because "strictly speaking, however, 'it' neither affirms nor addresses; authors do" (LI? 106).[2] But this is contrary to both Scripture and the nature of objective truth (see chap. 13 below). It is contrary to the Bible, which speaks of "the Scripture . . . saying" (Gal. 3:8). John writes, "Another Scripture says" (John 19:37) and "as the Scripture has said" (7:38).

We speak the same way today in phrases like "the Bible says" or the "Scriptures tell us." Further, it is contrary to the objective nature of truth to claim that books cannot speak. For if there is objective meaning in a piece of literature (e.g., "Eat more vegetables"), then the text speaks for itself. True, an author is needed to put this objective truth in the text. But once it is there, it is there for all to read what the text says.

Further, even though a government official caused the meaning to exist in a stop sign, nonetheless it is there in the sign for all to read. And when they read it correctly, they understand the meaning of its author(s). As will be shown later (in chaps. 14–15 below), meaning is not found in the author (the efficient cause), or the purpose of the author (the final cause), or in individual words, but in the form or structure those words take in a sentence in a given context. That is to say, meaning is not found behind the text, beyond the text, or beneath the text, but it is found *in* the text itself (the formal cause). So the central mistake of the speech-act theory is to misunderstand the role of language in communicating meaning. These theorists wrongly believe that language is only an instrumental cause, not the formal cause of meaning. They think that language is something *through which* we see the real meaning beyond it, rather than that *in which* we see the meaning in the very form and structure it takes as it resembles (participates) in the reality seen.

In the first line of Aristotle's famous work *On Interpretation* (*De interpretatione*), he gives his famous "semantic triangle," in which he asserts that the significance of words is subordinated to the understanding of things. This is how words, passion of the soul, and things are triangulated. Aristotle affirms that "letters are not the same for all, . . . but the passions of the soul are the same for all." In short, words are culturally relative, but meaning is not. Words are not naturally related to things, but passions of the soul are naturally related by likeness to things.[3]

According to a conventionalist view, meaning is culturally relative. But according to the inerrancy position, only symbols (e.g., words) are culturally relative; the meaning expressed in a formation of words (into a sentence) is not culturally relative. It resembles the reality of which it speaks. As we demonstrate later (in chap. 14), the very claim that meaning is culturally relative or purely subjective is offered as an objectively meaningful statement. Objective meaning is literally undeniable.

Second, in confusing purpose (why) and meaning (what), Vanhoozer turns attention away from the real locus of meaning (the formal cause—the text itself in its context), forsaking the only objective place where meaning is found (namely, in the objective truth of the text itself) and places it where one cannot identify objective meaning (in the intention or purpose of the author). Here there are no objective criteria, and there is a lot of supposition and guessing. For example, "The door is open" is a clear affirmation for which we can know the objective meaning and truth (by checking to see whether it is open or not). But it is simply a guess to suppose that the real meaning is in the illocutionary purpose of the author, which we suppose was a hint to close the door. How do we know the author did not mean, "Isn't it wonderful that we are getting all that fresh air?"? In this case, the implication would be just the opposite of the other supposition. If one responds by claiming we could eliminate the guessing by looking at other statements in the context, one should be reminded that we only know the meaning of these statements (locutions) and how they relate to the locution at hand by way of the locution (affirmation) itself, not because of any alleged hints (illocutions) in these statements.

Third, contrary to Vanhoozer, locutions (affirmations made in a text) are not "thin" or nearly vacuous of meaning. They have meaning. We know exactly what the statement "The door is open" means. And if we wish to know more, we can look at other locutions (affirmations) in the context of that text, that book, and the rest of Scripture that cast light on what it means. How do we know what a given affirmation means? Context, context, context. It is not by guessing intents or purposes of an author. How can we obtain a "thicker" meaning? By deriving other locutions (affirmations) from the immediate context and the remote contexts and piling them on until we achieve a meaning that is sufficiently "thick." We do not need to resort to guessing alleged intentions of authors. As a matter of fact, we only know an author's intention (illocutions) by what is found in his affirmations (locutions). So whatever illocutions we can induce, we do so only from studying other locutions.

Vanhoozer's illustration that the "sun stood still" (in Josh. 10:13) is ill chosen and reveals the subjectivity and danger of his view. He claims that the locution ("Stand still") is in error, but the illocution (what God wants to say to us through that statement) is inspired and without error. What was that? It was to affirm God's covenant relation with his people! What is this but another way to claim that only the guessed redemptive purpose of the author is inspired and without error, not what the author actually says (LI? 106)? This turns any attempt at an objective hermeneutic into a subjective guessing game. What is more, there is no need to resort to speech-act theory to explain the difficulty. Biblical authors, as people today, speak of the "sun rising" and "setting" in the everyday language of appearance because this is precisely what the sun is doing from an observational point of view. Even scientists (meteorologists) all over the country say things like "The sun will rise tomorrow at six." No one has to do an illocutionary maneuver on their statement to know what it means, nor for that matter, how they should respond to the information.

Fourth, by confusing *what* is said (meaning) and *why* it is said (purpose), Vanhoozer opens the linguistic door to deny inerrancy. For things affirmed in a text (locutions) that are not in accord with the author's purpose are not inspired and inerrant. As just noted in the Joshua illustration, it turns the affirmation of the author (his locution) into an erroneous statement through which he is conveying (by an illocution) why he is saying it. This is essentially the same as the inerrancy-of-purpose view or redemptive-purpose-only view of Jack Rogers and Clark Pinnock (see chap. 4). This error involves an intentionalist view of truth, that only what the author of Scripture intended to say is inerrant, not what he did say. But on this basis, then every well-intended statement, even ones that are incorrect, are true (see chap. 13). This leads us to our next point.

Questions about the Correspondence View of Truth

Although Vanhoozer claims to accept a correspondence view of truth, he redefines it and expands it to fit his own purposes. For example, he admits expanding it and broadening it to include "personal" truth and "relational" truth (LI? 93, 111). He claims that the word "truth" applies to areas of the Bible that are making no truth claims whatsoever. He wrote: "Inerrancy, then, is a subset of infallibility; when the Bible's purpose is to make true statements, it does this without fail. Yet the Bible's other speech acts—warnings, promises, questions—are infallible too" (IS, 6). Thus the traditional correspondence view of truth is inadequate.

Our comments on Vanhoozer's views on the correspondence view may be summarized here. As we shall see, his views are seriously lacking for many reasons.

First, all views of truth have an inherent correspondence to reality, because the proponents believe their view corresponds to reality. Most basic of all is the fact that the correspondence view of truth is literally undeniable for the very denial it purports to corresponds with reality. We have offered numerous arguments for the correspondence view of truth elsewhere (see chap. 13 below).

Second, without a correspondence view of truth, there is no basis for knowing an error. For in that case there is nothing out there (in reality) to which it must be made to correspond. Almost anything could be true on this view, as long as it was well intended.

Third, it is a misnomer to speak of "relational" or "personal" truth. There are truths about relationships and truths about persons in Scripture, but truth itself is not relational or personal. It is propositional, that is, it makes a statement that affirms or denies something about something.

Fourth, Vanhoozer appears to misunderstand the nature of truth as correspondence to reality. He seems to have been misled by Wittgenstein's criticism that correspondence is the "picture" theory wherein a statement corresponds to the facts if it mirrors them. But this is not what "correspondence" means (see chap. 13). Correspondence means a statement (or expression) must *match* reality, not necessarily *mirror* it. It must correctly *reflect* reality, but not necessarily *resemble* it. It must properly represent reality, not reproduce it. A statement corresponds to reality when it correctly signifies, conforms to, or agrees with reality, not when it is a mirror image of it.

Fifth, since Vanhoozer's understanding of the correspondence view of truth is inadequate, it is little wonder that he believes there must be an "enlarged" sense of truth (LI? 102), expanded to fit the biblical data. However, when it is so expanded, the correspondence view is actually negated. For instance, by understanding correspondence in terms of the redemptive "purpose" of the biblical authors (106, 113), Vanhoozer in effect undermines biblical inerrancy. For on this broader definition, many things affirmed in the Bible turn out to be incorrect and mistaken, but Vanhoozer will not consider these to be "errors" because they are not essential to the redemptive purpose of the text.

This is why Vanhoozer rejects Aristotle's classic definition of truth as inadequate (LI? 103). It is also why he redefines "reality" (to which truth corresponds) in a more "flexible" way (101n41). He also speaks of other kinds of correspondence like "cartographic" correspondence and "theodramatic correspondence," which embraces acts as well as words. Truth for Vanhoozer is depicted as an atlas with layers of maps used to understand reality (103). Truth is multilayered and perspectival. This affects his view of interpretation, to which we now turn.

Contrary to Vanhoozer, the ICBI statement on truth (in art. 13), affirms:

> By biblical standards of truth and error is meant the view used both in the Bible and in everyday life, viz., a correspondence view of truth. This part of the article is directed toward those who would redefine truth to relate merely to redemptive intent, the purely personal, or the like, rather than to mean that which corresponds with reality. (Sproul, *Explaining Inerrancy*, 43–44)

Questions about Propositional Truth

Though Vanhoozer does not deny that there is propositional revelation in the Bible, he definitely downplays and diminishes it (LI? 94). First, he downplays it by minimizing it. He does not acknowledge the vast amount of propositional truth implied in nonpropositional language, as noted above. Further, he diminishes the value of propositional revelation by claiming that it has little practical value in inducing a response of obedience to God (110). He also makes a false dichotomy, such as either God is personal or else he is reduced to an abstract "set of detached propositions" (108).

Vanhoozer admits that there are propositional truths. He even calls himself a "modified propositionalist" (LI? 107). However, he denies that all truth is propositional—a statement that itself is a propositional truth. He even defines his view as "postpropositional" ("Voice and the Actor," 75–76), but he insists that "the *post* in *postpropositional* does not mean *against* but *beyond*. There is *more*, not less, in the canon than propositional revelation" (*DD*, 276). While most propositionalists would agree with this, Vanhoozer leaves little doubt that he is not a fan of the traditional use of propositional revelation. He is particularly critical of the Princetonian view of A. A. Hodge and B. B. Warfield, a view that he carries all the way down to Carl Henry, calling it the "Hodge-Henry hypothesis." He claims that "in the final analysis, what was new about Princetonian's view of Scripture was not their understanding of the Bible's truthfulness but rather their particular view of language interpretation, in which the meaning of the biblical text was the fact-historical or doctrinal—to which it referred" (IS, 5). In short, he is rejecting both the adequacy of the correspondence-to-fact view of truth and the historical-grammatical method of interpretation that goes along with it.

Also, he believes that the propositional view is "small" and "reductionistic" (DD, 268), which tends to see all of Scripture in terms of revelation, to see the essence of information (e.g., truth content), and to see theology in terms of processing this information (e.g., *scientia*). He rejects the propositional view, which claims that "Scriptures contain a body of divinely given information actually expressed or capable of being expressed in propositions" (268). He claims that "propositionalism leaves something to be desired on both accounts; its notion of science and of the text alike are ultimately too narrow" (268). He proposes to replace this with what he calls "canonical-linguistical theology" (266). First, an evaluation of Vanhoozer's view of propositional revelation is necessary.

In response to Vanhoozer's attack on propositional revelation, several observations are relevant. We begin with comments on what Vanhoozer himself admits.

First of all, while Vanhoozer's basic intuitions and goals are admirable, the means of attaining it—by Christianizing speech-act theory—is highly questionable. There is nothing in the traditional propositional theology that does not allow for, or even call for, practical theology. Of course, propositional truth is not the ultimate goal of theology; practical theology is. God wants us to live the truth, not just to know the truth. But the truth can't be lived unless we first know the truth to be lived. And downplaying and diminishing propositional revelation is a misdirected way to accomplish this.

Second, as Vanhoozer's own description admits, he is diminishing much of the history of Christianity from the first century to our time. Even he acknowledges that "for large swaths of the Western tradition, the task of theology consisted in mining propositional nuggets from the biblical deposit of truth" (LI? 94). He admits that the roots of this go back to the New Testament where "the Pauline shaft in particular was thought to contain several rich doctrinal lodes" (94). He also correctly observes that this carried into the Middle Ages. He wrote: "According to Thomas Aquinas, Scripture contains the science of God: the unified teaching from God about God. . . . Doctrine is essentially sacred teaching, a divinely revealed informative proposition about an objective reality" (94). Following this, in "19th-century Princeton, A. A. Hodge and B. B. Warfield laid the groundwork for conservative evangelical theology by insisting on the importance of propositional truth" (94). In short, Vanhoozer's view is against the mainstream of Christianity for the last two thousand years!

Third, Vanhoozer is correct in claiming that not every statement in the Bible is in a propositional form. However, this does not mean that there are not other truths there that can be put into propositional form. Certainly, there are questions, commands, prayers, exclamations, and confessions that are not propositional in form. However, he is wrong in overlooking that many of these have implied propositional truth in them. For example, a prayer such as "God, forgive me of my sin" implies many propositional truths, including (1) There is a God; (2) I have sinned; (3) God is forgiving; (4) A person needs to confess one's sin in order to be forgiven. For example, a command such as "Go and preach the gospel to all the world" is an imperative, not a declarative, sentence. While it is not a proposition as such, it nonetheless contains many propositions by implication, such as (1) All persons are lost; (2) Only the gospel can save them; (3) God has the right to command us to preach the gospel; (4) The gospel is necessary for their salvation; and so forth.

So, though all the Bible is not in propositional form, nonetheless there is a lot more propositional truth in the Bible than what is in propositional form (of affirmation or denial). Though not all truth claims in the Bible are in propositional form (many are in stories and parables), nonetheless all truth in the Bible is propositionalizable. Vanhoozer obscures this fact by his deemphasis on propositional truth.

Fourth, even Vanhoozer's stress on God's redemptive actions (in addition to his words) overlooks an important point: we know about these redemptive actions because of God's propositional revelation. Without the propositional truths of the Bible, we would have no authoritative knowledge about these events of Vanhoozer's so-called "theodrama." As important as God's actions are to our redemption, we would have no inspired or authoritative record of them without the propositional truths of Scripture.

Fifth, in his zeal to deemphasize propositional truth, Vanhoozer includes things under the rubric of "truth" that do not belong there as such. As noted above, he expands and broadens truth to include "personal" and "relational" truth (LI? 93, 111). But, as will be shown below, there is no such thing as personal truth. There are truths about relationships, but no relational truths. Truth is a correspondence with reality, and only statements (or expressions) that correspond to reality can be said to be true. This is not to say that truth is not personal. No one who has ever carried on a romance by mail denies that propositional statements can both reveal a person to them and evoke a response to that person. The same is true of God's love letter to us called the Bible. And everyone who has stood at an altar and uttered the proposition "I do" to the pastor's factual questions about whether they would love their spouse in sickness and in health and forsake all others for them knows how personal and transformational propositional truth can be. Likewise, God's propositional love letter to us (the Bible)—with all of its propositional truth about God, about us, and about the love relationship between us—is eminently personal and life changing.

Typical of postmodern thinking is Vanhoozer's emphasis on "stories" over propositional revelation (LI? 100–101, 107). But this is misdirected for several reasons. First, even a story contains propositional truth. Second, he believes that biblical "stories" need not be actually (factually) true in their postmodern context. They only need to convey an important spiritual truth and elicit a proper response. They may in fact be myths. Indeed, Vanhoozer seems to believe that many things in the Old Testament are legendary and not historical (98–99). He accepts C. S. Lewis's unorthodox belief that the Old Testament contains myths that became real in the New Testament (*DD*, 80–81, 230, 284, 348; *LI?* 110). But total inerrantists deny this, as the above citations reveal, affirming that truth is what corresponds to reality.

The truth of the matter is that truth matters. Richard Weaver demonstrates this in his excellent book on the topic, *Ideas Have Consequences*. As the famous evangelical preacher A. W. Tozer said on the first page of his helpful book on the topic (*Knowledge of the Holy*), "What you think of God is the most important thing about you." Yes, what we "think" (ideas) and say (statements, propositions) can be and are important in our response to the God about whom we think and affirm these things.

Finally, Vanhoozer also diminishes logic along with propositional revelation. And along with this, he downplays the need for systematic theology. He stereotypes systematic theology, contending that the main defect of propositionalism is that it reduces the variety of speech actions in the canon to one type, the assertion. This "results in a monologic conception of theology and truth" (*DD*, 266). This, he says, is to "reduce theo-drama . . . to a mere theory" (266). But this is not only a stereotypical straw-man fallacy; it also involves a false dichotomy. For there is a third alternative to "theo-drama" and "mere theory." There is propositional *truth that transforms*, whether it is in discourse, dialogue, parable, or narrative form. Vanhoozer forgets that ideas have consequences; truth transforms, especially biblical truth. Jesus says, "You will know the truth, and the truth will set you free" (John 8:32).

Further, downplaying logic—which is so necessary to clear thinking—is demeaning of God, the source of reason, and is destructive of good thinking by God's people. Vanhoozer speaks against viewing theology as a "*scientia* of Scripture [and] depicting it as the process of abstracting revealed truths—propositions—from the biblical text and arranging them in logical order" (*DD*, 268). He concedes begrudgingly that this is "one way of conceiving canonical fittingness" (*DD*, 266), but he makes it very clear that this is neither an adequate nor preferred way. He rightly sees Thomas Aquinas as "the paradigmatic instance" of this "cognitive-propositional" approach, followed by Protestant scholastics of the sixteenth century, nineteenth-century Princetonians (like Charles Hodge), and twentieth-century evangelicals (like Carl Henry). Vanhoozer offers the noble thought that "nothing is gained by caricaturing, much less demonizing this group of theologians" (i.e, the main flow of theology from the early creeds through Augustine, Anselm, Aquinas, the Reformers, and on into the twentieth century!) (*DD*, 267). However, he has a difficult time of living up to his ideal. For he cannot resist stereotyping, diminishing, demeaning, and even undermining this propositional view of truth himself.

What is wrong, we ask, with viewing "theology as a *scientia* of Scripture" and "extracting propositions . . . from the biblical text and arranging them in logical order" (*DD*, 266)? Whatever is wrong with it is also wrong with modern science in doing the same thing with God's general revelation in nature. Sure, we are all refreshed by a walk in the woods, in nature as it is, but this does not forbid the same person from the systematic and logical scrutiny of the same data in a lab. Is this not an appropriate part of carrying out the mandate to "subdue [the earth] and have dominion over [it]" (Gen. 1:28)? By the same logic (really, antilogic) that Vanhoozer is using on God's special revelation in Scripture, we apparently would have to reject the value of a scientific approach to God's general revelation in nature.

In this connection, Vanhoozer makes some unfortunate statements about the use of logic in theology. He says, "It is important to remember that the theologian's trust should not be in logic but in God." He adds, "When both Scripture and logic are used in the elicitation of doctrine, does the doctrine rest solely upon Scripture, or has reason become the foundation of theological argumentation?" Finally, "theology ought never be content with logical rather than life or casual rather than covenantal relations" (DD, 268). We have dealt with this at greater length elsewhere (Systematic Theology [ST], vol. 1, chap. 5); a few comments are in order here.

First, again Vanhoozer presents a false dichotomy. It is not either logic or life, nor is it either logic or the Bible. It is a both/and situation, not an either/or one. The Bible calls on us to use our reason (Isa. 1:18; 1 Pet. 3:15). Indeed, the use of our minds is part of the great commandment, which includes loving God with all our "mind" as well as our heart (Matt. 22:37). Surely Vanhoozer would not want us to rid our thinking of the laws of logic. The apostle Paul admonishes us to "avoid . . . contradictions" (1 Tim. 6:20). Even the Westminster Confession of Faith (which is a classic creed in Vanhoozer's Reformed tradition) encourages the use of logic in theology and speaks (in chap. 1, sect. 6) of "the whole counsel of God, . . . either expressly set down in Scripture, *or by good and necessary consequence may be deduced from Scripture*." Using logic to deduce truths from Scripture (which is the basis for these truths) is not basing the truths on logic. Logic is only the rational instrument (coming from a rational God and inherent in rational creatures made in his image) that enables us to discover certain truths that are implied in Scripture.

Vanhoozer's distaste for logic becomes evident in his canonical and hermeneutical pluralism. Not only does he believe there is a pluralism in the truth expressions of Scripture (DD, 283–84); he also sees a pluralism of interpretations of Scripture (276). This leads to our next point.

Questions about Interpretation

Vanhoozer is correct in seeing a connection between hermeneutics and inerrancy. Ironically, his own view is an example of it. For by employing an alien hermeneutics, he undermines inerrancy. This can be seen in many areas. Consider the following:

He Holds to Multiple Meanings in a Text

Vanhoozer denies the *sensus unum* (one-meaning) understanding of Scripture (MT? 265, 301; LI? 90, 106). He claims that God means more by the same text than the human author does (*sensus plenior*). This is where forsaking the Hodge-Henry view leads to a hodgepodge view. For if both God and the human author affirm one and the same text, then how can God be affirming more in this same text by the same words than the human author does? One would have to read behind the text, beyond the text, or beneath the text to get this extra meaning. It cannot be in the text since the human author has affirmed in the text the very same words that the divine author has. Vanhoozer's error here is in confusing meaning and significance. There is only one meaning in the text, but there are multiple significances. There is only one interpretation but many applications.[4]

To say that God intends more than the human author is to miss the point that both God and the human author, as coauthors, affirm one and the same thing in one and the same text. Since even Vanhoozer admits that by "intention" of the author, he does not mean some unexpressed intention but the author's expressed intention in the text, then wherever the one and the same intention is expressed, there must be one and the same meaning. Only by confusing expressed intention (what is asserted) with purpose (why it is asserted) can one come up with more than one meaning (i.e., purpose) for a text. Of course, God has greater purposes than a human author does because God alone sees at once the whole canonical scope of revelation and all he wants to accomplish through it.

God certainly knows more about the topic discussed in the text than the human author does. Also, God sees more implications in the text than the human author does. Likewise, God sees more applications for the text than the human author does. But God does not affirm more in a given text than the human coauthor does. They both mean one and the same thing by one and the same text.

The multiple-meaning view of Vanhoozer confuses meaning and significance. There is only one meaning, but there are a multitude of significances in a given text. Meaning deals with *what* the text affirms, but significance deals with *how* one should relate the text to various situations. Vanhoozer's speech-act theory leads him astray in this regard. Since he limits the real meaning of the text to illocutions (what the author is doing with the text), not to the locutions (what is affirmed in the text), and since the author or authors (including God, the coauthor) may intend different uses for one and the same text, then it would follow (according to speech-act theory) that there are many meanings in the text. However, if the meaning in the text is found in its affirmations (locutions), as we show (see chaps. 14–15), then there is only one meaning in the text since there is only one set of affirmations (stated or implied) in one text.

Vanhoozer's satirical stereotyping of objective textual meaning is misdirected. He categorizes it with "the death of the author" view and "the worst sort of re-ductionism, where communicative acts and intentions are stripped away from the text, leaving an autonomous linguistic object" (*FT*, 170). This is wrongheaded for many reasons. First, there is no meaning in a text unless a meaner (author) puts it there. But once he puts it there, it is there in the text, even after the author physi-cally dies. Second, the author's intentions are not stripped away from the text; rather, they are found expressed *in* the text. Third, the text is not autonomous for whatever meaning was given to it by its author. The text is the author's child, not his master. And the child lives on after the father is gone.

He Denies the Historical-Grammatical Interpretation

Although Vanhoozer claims allegiance to the historical-grammatical interpretation, in point of fact he denies it by going beyond it. For he admits believing it is inadequate and admits the need to move beyond it. He writes, "Our understanding of infallibility is thus in profound agreement with the earlier statement of inerrancy . . . even while moving beyond them" (SBL, 103). But once one denies that there is only one objective meaning in one objective propositional revelation in the text, then meaning is up for grabs. It is no longer objectively knowable. In such a case the interpreter is swimming in a sea of hermeneutical subjectivity, for there are no objective criteria in a text by which one can eliminate false meanings being applied to the text. Indeed, he admits the subjectivity of the interpretative process, claiming that it is an illusion to think otherwise (*MT?* 150–51).

Vanhoozer insists that "the claim to see texts as they are is illusory. Every reader sees what one can see from one's position in society, space and time. . . . Reading, then, is no exception to relativity theory. . . . We are never not in a situation. . . . A set of interpretive assumptions is always in force" (*MT?* 151). Again, one wonders how he could make such statements if his claim is true. For the claim that all interpretations are subjective offers itself as an objective interpretation of the matter.

Although Vanhoozer claims that the basic meaning of the biblical text is "literal," yet he understands this as a "literary" meaning. And this meaning is determined by many factors outside the text, including tradition (*DD*, 164), the Christian community (LI? 112), and even "theodramatic" (LI? 101–2) and "cartographic" (LI? 103) considerations.

He Uses Up-front Genre Decisions to Determine the Meaning of a Text

Vanhoozer adopts the all-too-common current trend in hermeneutics to use up-front genre decisions about the kind of text that is being studied. He insists that this is necessary to avoid taking a passage in a "literalist" way when it is really not talking about literal, factual history as we understand it.

After giving with one hand that he believes in a "literal" (*MT?* 304) interpretation of the Bible, he takes this away with the other hand by defining "literal" as "literary" (304). That is, a reader must determine what kind of literature it is before one can understand it properly. This is done by determining its genre before one begins to interpret the text (LI? 101, 105).

Vanhoozer emphasizes the importance of genre by citing C. S. Lewis in support of his view: "He [Lewis] suggests that two biblical passages may not be inerrant in exactly the same way; that is, not every biblical statement must state historical truth. Inerrancy must be construed broadly enough to encompass the truth expressed in Scripture's poetry, romances, proverbs, parables—as well as histories" (SBL, 79).

Besides the fact that inerrant means completely true, and truth does not come in degrees, there are some serious difficulties with this approach.

A Critique of Up-front Genre Decisions

The use of up-front genre decisions about the biblical text is both misdirected and dangerous.[5] In fact, it leads to the denial of the historicity of long-held historical sections of Scripture, which undermines essential doctrines of the Christian faith.

First, there is an implicit danger in making up-front genre decisions. Take, for example, the genre category of "myth" or "legend," which contains, among other things, the performance of unusual feats. Just because we know from experience that some stories from antiquity contain unusual feats, this does not mean that a biblical story with unusual feats should be listed as a nonhistorical myth or legend. This is to load genre decision with an antisupernaturalist bias before one considers the evidence for the historicity of the event recorded in the text. But this procedure begs the question against the historical reliability of the text before one begins to examine the evidence.

Second, making up-front genre decisions is a question-begging procedure. It is based on questionable, predetermined classification from other literature that is then applied to biblical literature. For all the genre categories are made from the study of extrabiblical sources. These categories are then applied to the piece of biblical literature in question to see which one it fits into. The method as such does not allow for the possibility that the Bible may offer a new genre of its own that does not fit any of these categories, for example, redemptive history or (in the New Testament) Gospel history. But once these biblical genre categories are tacitly rejected (by taking the possible genre categories from nonbiblical genre sources), then it begs the question to insist that biblical (redemptive) history must be forced into one of these nonbiblical genres.

An example of the fallacy of this kind of question-begging procedure is the critical argument against the Pauline authorship of the Pastoral Epistles. Liberal scholars have often argued that Paul could not have written 1 and 2 Timothy and Titus because they differ from Paul's known style and vocabulary. But this begs the question since the "known style" did not include the way he wrote in these Pastoral Epistles. If the vocabulary and style of Paul in the Pastoral Epistles had been included in the overall "known style" of Paul, then there would have been no exclusion of them as Pauline. The same fallacy will occur if anyone tries to determine my (Norm's) style from our *Philosophy of Religion* and then applies that as "Geisler's style" to my book for teens, *Living Loud*. Yet I am indisputably an author of both books.

When the question-begging up-front genre approach is applied to the Gospels, the same fallacious results occur. For a set genre determined outside the New Testament that includes wonder-workers will have as one of its characteristics that it is legendary and nonhistorical. Thus, to nobody's surprise, when one looks at the Gospels and sees a wonder-worker there, one will be disposed to conclude that the miracle stories are nonhistorical legends. This is what Rudolf Bultmann and his followers have done to the New Testament. Consider the words of Bultmann himself:

> All this is the language of mythology. . . . To this extent the kerygma is incredible to modern man, for he is convinced that the mythical view of the world is obsolete. . . . There is nothing specifically Christian in the mythical view of the world as such. It is simply the cosmology of a pre-scientific age. . . . All our thinking today is shaped irrevocably by modern science. . . . It would involve a sacrifice of the intellect, . . . [for] man's knowledge and mastery of the world have advanced to such an extent through science and technology that it is no longer possible for anyone seriously to hold the New Testament view of the world—in fact, there is no one who does. (*Kerygma and Myth*, 3–4)

Clearly, his naturalistic genre categories do not allow him to consider a document with miracles in it as anything other than mythical.

Third, no genre decision can be made up front. Instead, one must study the whole document first in order to determine what genre category to put it in. But one cannot study the document in order to make this determination without using a method of interpreting the document. But either one uses the historical-grammatical method to do this or one does not. Whoever uses it has not made an up-front genre selection against it. If he does not use the historical-grammatical method, then he begs the question by rejecting that method before he begins. In effect, he is *legislating* the meaning of the text rather than *listening* to it. So one cannot avoid using the historical-grammatical method, which does not make up-front genre decisions against the historicity of a narrative. Rather, a wise reader looks at the text and listens to it to determine what the document is claiming. One is not cramming the text into a predetermined category into which it may or may not fit. When someone so looks and listens, Gospel literature may become a genre category of its own, in which one can have miraculous events that are also historical. When this is done objectively, we believe that only an unjustified anti-supernaturalist bias can hinder one from concluding that the Gospel literature is historically based (see Geisler, *ST*, vol. 1, chaps. 11, 26).

However, Vanhoozer makes some statements that reveal he has made this up-front genre decision and/or a category mistake about the some events in the Old Testament. For example, he denies the historicity of Genesis 1–11 (LI? 98–99). More seriously, he made an unorthodox statement about the resurrection that implies it was not a literal, physical bringing back to life of the dead body of Jesus, which lay in the tomb of Joseph of Arimathea. He writes, "Finally, Jesus' body was raised 'a spiritual body' (1 Cor. 15:44), though according to Paul, the spiritual body was just as real and historical as the physical body" (*MT*? 304). The wording here is important. The resurrection body is real, yet not a "physical body" but a "spiritual" one.

We have spoken elsewhere (see Geisler, *Battle for the Resurrection*) in defense of the biblical, orthodox, and creedal affirmations that Jesus rose from the dead in the very same physical body, now in glory, in which he died. This is evidenced by the empty tomb, the empty grave clothes, his crucifixion scars, his being physically touched, and his eating physical food—all after the resurrection. Indeed, John says that the body that was raised from the dead was the very same body that died. He recorded Jesus as saying, "'Destroy *this temple*, and in three days I will raise *it* up.'.... He was speaking about the temple of his body" (John 2:19, 21, emphasis added).

Jesus's resurrection body was not "spiritual" or immaterial by nature. The widely misused text in 1 Corinthians 15:44 does not affirm that his resurrection body was not physical for many reasons. (1) It is called a *sōma* (body) in this text, a term that always means a physical body when used of an individual human being in the New Testament (Robert Gundry, *Sōma in Biblical Theology*); (2) The term "spiritual" is an adjective (not a noun) describing what kind of physical body (a noun) it was, namely, one whose source of life was spiritual; (3) the same word "spiritual" is used by the same author (Paul) in the same book of other physical entities such as the physical rock, the physical water, the physical food (manna) that God gave to the children of Israel in the wilderness (10:2–4), and even of a godly believer in a physical body (2:15). What was "spiritual" about all these things is that they had a spiritual (i.e., supernatural) *source* (God), not a spiritual (immaterial) *substance*. The Bible is called a spiritual book, but this does not mean it is immaterial.

Unqualified as it is, Vanhoozer's statement about a "spiritual" resurrection is akin to the neo-orthodox (or neo-Gnostic) view that the physical body of Jesus simply inexplicably disappeared, vanished from the tomb. Even some evangelicals like John Stott have held this view. James Boice wrote: "If we had been present in the tomb at the moment of the resurrection, we should have noticed that all at once the body of Jesus seemed to disappear. John Stott says that the body was 'vaporized,' being transmuted into something new and different and wonderful" (*Foundations of the Christian Faith* [1986], 354–55). But vaporization or annihilation is not resurrection. In short, what dies (the body) must come back to life or there is no resurrection.

Finally, even Vanhoozer admits the subjectivity of the genre procedure. He claims that "the purpose of exegesis is not to excavate [the text] but to explore canonically embodied truth by becoming apprentices of the literary forms, and this involves more than mastering propositional content. By learning imaginatively to follow and indwell the biblical text, we see through them to reality as it actually is 'in Christ'" (LI? 109). Biblical truth is not discovered by exegeting the text but by a creative imagination that sees through the text to its literary forms and thus beyond the text.

He Claims That Purpose Determines Meaning

Another error of Vanhoozer is the belief that purpose determines meaning (LI? 113). As noted above, this is a confusion of *what* (meaning) the author affirms and *why* (purpose) the author affirms it. It also confuses meaning (what) and significance (how). Vanhoozer writes, "Interpretation remains incomplete without an appreciation of a text's significance, its meaningfulness. . . . Significance just is 'recontextualized meaning'" (*MT?* 422–23). How the author intends to *apply* the text to a specific situation in no way replaces or negates what he actually affirms in a text, nor the other ways the text may be legitimately applied. Every assertion in the Bible must be understood, however, in the light of its purpose. "What is this purpose? The ultimate purpose of Scripture is to draw us into the drama of redemption" (LI? 113).

However, purpose does not determine meaning. The meaning of *what* one says can be understood apart from knowing *why* (the purpose) the author said it. If a person says to another, "Here is one thousand dollars I am giving to you," it is perfectly clear what these words mean apart from knowing the purpose of the giver. If he later learns that the giver was trying to buy his support for a cause he did not believe in, then he understands the purpose (significance) of the words, but they do not get any new meaning. The meaning remains the same (see chap. 15 below).

He Claims There Is No Certainty in Interpreting Texts

Vanhoozer, like others in our postmodern climate, stresses the uncertainty of our interpretation of Scripture. He said clearly, "When it comes to interpreting texts, honesty forbids certainty. Human knowing, of books and of the Book of Nature, is mediate and approximate. Here Christians agree with chastened post-moderns" (*MT?* 207). Anyone who claims certainty has hermeneutical pride and needs to exercise a "hermeneutics of humility" (463). He writes, "It may therefore be the preeminent temptation of the fundamentalist, insofar as he craves for certainty" (463). No wonder, for Vanhoozer takes certainty as unattainable "absolute knowledge," which only God can have, and its opposite as "absolute agnosticism" (462).

Ironically, Vanhoozer seems quite sure of the subjectivity of the interpretative process: "The claim to see texts as they are is illusory. Every reader sees what one can see from one's position in society, space, and time" (*MT?* 150–51). He seems oblivious of the fact that he has hanged himself on his own gallows. For by his own standard, this very statement should be seen as "illusory"!

What is more, the Bible speaks of our having certainty about what God has revealed. Luke said he wrote so that his reader(s) could "have *certainty* concerning the things you have been taught" (Luke 1:3–4; emphasis added in this paragraph). Acts speaks of "many *convincing* proofs" of Christ's resurrection (Acts 1:3 NIV). John declares that he wrote so believers may "know" they "have eternal life" (1 John 5:13). Paul says, "I *know* whom I have believed, and I am *convinced* that he is able" (2 Tim. 1:12). Of course, our certitude is moral, not mathematical, but it is not suspended somewhere in the sphere of Vanhoozer's hermeneutical uncertainty.

He Misinterprets Article 13 of the ICBI Inerrancy Statement

Vanhoozer is not atypical of those who claim allegiance to inerrancy and would like to show some acceptance of the most definitive and widely accepted statement on the topic, which was made by the ICBI. Indeed, he admits "going beyond" the

ICBI statement: "Our understanding of infallibility is thus in profound agreement with the earlier statement of inerrancy . . . even while *moving beyond them*" (SBL, 103, emphasis added). As we shall see, "our understanding" really means Vanhoozer's *mis*understanding of it, particularly of article 13. And once it is properly understood in the light of the official ICBI interpretation of it by framers of the statement, there is no "profound" agreement at all. There is, in fact, profound disagreement.

The most often cited article 13 reads:

> We affirm the propriety of using inerrancy as a theological term with reference to the complete truthfulness of Scripture. We deny that it is proper to evaluate Scripture according to standards of truth and error that are alien to its usage or purpose. We further deny that inerrancy is negated by Biblical phenomena such as a lack of modern technical precision, irregularities of grammar or spelling, observational descriptions of nature, the reporting of falsehoods, the use of hyperbole and round numbers, the topical arrangement of material, variant selections of material in parallel accounts, or the use of free citations.

However, what Vanhoozer (and Pinnock; see chap. 4 above) fail to say is that they are taking the denial out of context and contrary to the stated meaning of the ICBI framers, of which I (Norm) was one. For the official ICBI commentary on this very statement supports the traditional correspondence view of truth that Vanhoozer rejects. It declares: "*When we say that the truthfulness of Scripture ought to be evaluated according to its own standards, that means that . . . all the claims of the Bible must correspond with reality, whether that reality is historical, factual or spiritual*" (Sproul, *Explaining Inerrancy* [*EI*], 41). It adds, "*By biblical standards of truth and error is meant the view used both in the Bible and in everyday life, viz., a correspondence view of truth. This part of the article is directed toward those who would redefine truth to relate merely to redemptive intent, the purely personal, or the like, rather than to mean that which corresponds with reality*" (43–44, emphasis added).

So it is only by twisting and distorting what the ICBI framers meant by "truth," namely, as being correspondence to reality, that Vanhoozer and others can claim some kind of agreement with a statement on total inerrancy that they reject. One has to assume either total ignorance by Vanhoozer on what the ICBI founders meant by truth or else total disregard. Once Vanhoozer has been made aware of this, honesty demands a retraction of his misuse of the ICBI statement.

He Rejects Articles 9 and 11 of the ICBI Inerrancy Statement

Vanhoozer could not sign the ICBI statement as meant (see appendix 1). There are reasons for this. For one, he admits to not believing articles 9 and 11. Article 9 reads: "We affirm that inspiration, though not conferring omniscience, *guaranteed true and trustworthy utterance on all matters of which the Biblical authors were moved to speak and write*. We deny that the finitude or fallenness of these writers, by necessity or otherwise, introduced distortion or falsehood into God's Word." Article 11 adds: "We affirm that Scripture, having been given by divine inspiration, is infallible, so that, far from misleading us, *it is true and reliable in all the matters it addresses.* We deny that it is possible for the Bible to be at the same time infallible and errant in its assertions. Infallibility and inerrancy may be distinguished, but not separated" (emphasis added above). Indeed, the official ICBI commentaries on the articles state the matter even more strongly. "When the quest for sources produces *a dehistoricizing of the Bible, a rejection of its teaching or a rejection of the Bible's own claims of authorship,* [then] it has trespassed beyond its proper limits. . . . It is never legitimate, however, to run counter to express biblical affirmations" (*EI*, 55).

Further, "By biblical standards truth and error is meant the view used both in the Bible and in everyday life, viz., *a correspondence view of truth.* This part of the article is directed toward those who would redefine truth to relate merely *to redemptive intent,* the *purely personal,* or the like, rather than to mean that *which corresponds with reality*" (*EI*, 43–44).

Also, an official commentary on the ICBI Hermeneutics Statement supports these same points ("Explaining Hermeneutics" [EH]). The following are some relevant excerpts from it (emphasis added).

EH on article 6: "We further affirm that a statement is true if *it represents matters as they actually are, but is an error if it misrepresents the facts.*" The commentary on this adds, "The denial makes it evident that *views which redefine error to mean what 'misleads,' rather than what is a mistake, must be rejected.*"

EH on article 13: "*We deny that generic categories which negate historicity may rightly be imposed on biblical narratives which present themselves as factual.*" "*Some, for instance, take Adam to be a myth, whereas in Scripture he is presented as a real person. Others take Jonah to be an allegory when he is presented as a historical person and [is] so referred to by Christ.*"

EH on article 14: "*We deny that any event, discourse or saying reported in Scripture was invented by the biblical writers or by the traditions they incorporated.*"

EH on article 22: It "affirms that Genesis 1–11 is factual, as is the rest of the book." "The denial makes it evident that *views which redefine error to mean what 'misleads,' rather than what is a mistake, must be rejected*" (EH, 892).

A careful reading of Vanhoozer reveals that he does not agree with these statements about total factual inerrancy and historicity of the biblical narratives. He writes: "Is mine an approach that assumes the truth of the Bible is a matter of its correspondence to historical fact? Not necessarily. On the contrary, I have argued that literary genres engage with reality in different ways, with other illocutionary forces besides the assertive. *This, to my mind, represents a decisive parting of the ways, for it means that not all parts of Scripture need be factually true*" (*MT?* 424–25, emphasis added).

Vanhoozer also charges that "in their zeal to uphold the truth of the Bible, fundamentalists tend to interpret all narratives as accurate historical or scientific records" (*MT?* 425). Unlike Clark Pinnock (see chap. 4 above), Vanhoozer does not identify these directly with events in the lives of Adam, Eve, Job, Elisha, Jonah, and even Jesus, but he no doubt has some of these same stories in mind. Indeed, he implies that Genesis 1–11 is myth, insisting that "Evangelicals must not let a particular theory of truth and factuality determine what the author of Genesis 1–11 is proposing for our consideration" (LI? 99).

However, this would deny the historicity of Adam, which the inspired New Testament emphatically affirms. Indeed, many orthodox teachings set forth in the New Testament are based on an understanding of the historicity of the Genesis account. These include (1) Jesus's teaching about marriage; (2) the role of women in the church (1 Tim. 2:12–14); (3) the relation of male and female in marriage (1 Cor. 11:3). More important, the doctrines of (4) human depravity and (5) salvation are based on a literal understanding of Genesis 1–3. Paul writes, "Therefore, just as sin came into the world through one man [Adam], and death through sin, and so death spread to all men because all sinned. . . . Yet death reigned from Adam to Moses" (Rom. 5:12–14). No fair reading of this passage can fail to see that Adam is viewed as a literal historical person through whom literal physical death came upon all men. In fact, Jesus himself referred to Adam as a literal person (Matt. 19:4–6), as did Luke (Luke 3:38).

Questions about His Interpretation of Thomas Aquinas on Truth

It is good to see Reformed theologians citing Thomas Aquinas since most have long neglected him (see Geisler, *Thomas Aquinas*, chap. 1). However, Vanhoozer misquotes Thomas when he claims that Thomas views faith as both personal and propositional. He says Thomas limits truth to propositions about reality, but Thomas says, "Truth is defined by the *conformity* of intellect and thing; and hence to know this *conformity* is to know truth" (Thomas, *Summa* 1.16.2). Elsewhere he adds, "For all understanding is achieved by way of some assimilation of the knower to the thing known, . . . a harmony we call the *matching* of understanding and thing" (Thomas, *On Truth* 1.1). Again, "For the meaning of truth consists in a *matching* of thing and understanding. . . . So the notion of truth is first found in understanding . . . which *corresponds* to the thing and can be expected to *match* it" (1.3, emphasis added).

Further, Thomas held that true statements could be made positively about God. This is what he meant by analogous God-talk (see chap. 14 below). Thus there is no dichotomy between propositions and persons for true propositions can be affirmed about God. These he called "names" and we call "attributes." So, unlike Vanhoozer, Thomas Aquinas saw no dichotomy between propositions and the person of God. Nor did he believe that the "personal" was part of truth that could be said of God. This truth for Thomas was the correspondence between a proposition about God and God himself.

Questions about His Dichotomy between Informational and Transformational Truth

Vanhoozer stresses, and rightly so, the transformational nature of the truth that the Bible presents to us. Surely the God of Scripture wants Scripture to change our lives. "You shall therefore be holy, for I am holy," says the Lord (Lev. 11:45). Jesus adds, "You therefore must be perfect, as your heavenly Father is perfect" (Matt. 5:48). Certainly God has presented truth that has transforming power in Scripture, for "the word of God is living and active" (Heb. 4:12). And God-breathed Scripture is "able to make" us "wise for salvation" (2 Tim. 3:15–16). It is "profitable" for "training in righteousness" and "every good work" (3:16–17).

However, there is an important distinction (which Vanhoozer neglects) between so-called transformational truth and informational truth that transforms. All truth as such is informational since it is propositional, but some information is explosive. Some ideas have serious consequences. Such are the ideas presented in the Bible about God, humanity, sin, and salvation. These informational truths are truths that truly transform.

Vanhoozer's goal is admirable and biblical: God wants to change our lives for the good. However, his statements about the nature of truth are not true. In Scripture, God presents transformational truths, but it is informational truth with the power to transform. Many winners of the lottery have discovered (mostly to their harm) that the simple objective propositional truth "You have won 50 million dollars" is a truth that transforms. It did change their lives for better or for worse. But what changed one's life was not a nonpropositional, nonobjective personal, relational truth. It was a factual, objective, propositional truth.

Questions about Biblical Infallibility

Vanhoozer claims that Scripture is "infallible." However, even here he takes with one hand what he gives with the other. For his definition of "infallible" is weak, meaning "not liable to fail" (LI? 113). He spells this out as meaning that the "Bible is wholly trustworthy and true because its direction is wholly reliable" (113). But one could drive a Mack truck full of errors through the opening in this statement. At best it is merely an inerrancy of intent, not an inerrancy of fact and statement. It is no different in kind from Pinnock's redemptive-purpose inerrancy (see chap. 4 above).

There is nothing wrong with the word "infallible." Rightly defined as applied to Scripture, it means what the *American Heritage College Dictionary* gives as its primary meaning: "incapable of erring." The same reference defines "inerrant" as "incapable of erring; infallible." Basically, the definitions are interchangeable. Unfortunately, the definition of "infallible" as "incapable of erring" has been considerably weakened today in common usage. Nonetheless, theologically, "infallibility" is a good word, and when used in conjunction with inerrancy, they describe well the position of total inerrancy, which Vanhoozer rejects.

Questions about His Incarnational Model and Inspiration

The incarnational model of Christ's assuming human nature has played a significant role in the debate about the inerrancy of the Bible (see chap. 16 below). Traditionally, conservative theologians have used it in support of inerrancy, arguing for a strong parallel between the perfection of both the living Word and written Word of God. They reason that just as Christ (the living Word) is both divine and human in one person and without sin, even so the Bible (the written Word) has a divine and human dimension cojoined in one set of propositions (sentences) without error.

The tables on this illustration have been turned by Barthians and neo-Barthians, who now argue that just as Christ was completely human and errant as a human being, even so the Bible is completely human and errant as a human book.

Although he does not develop the new incarnational model, Vanhoozer does inform us enough to know that he stands in the latter camp. First of all, he speaks of divine "accommodation" in order to be "intelligible to finite, historically-conditioned creatures. God stoops to speak and show" (LI? 107).

Second, Vanhoozer carries this divine accommodation even further. Though he rejects Kenton Sparks's view that God also accommodates to errors in the Bible but is not teaching them (LI? 107), yet he rejects Carl Henry's contention that inerrancy includes not only the theological teachings of the Bible but also scientific and historical matters "insofar as they are part of the express message of the inspired writings" (107). Already this leaves him with some form of limited inerrancy.

Third, Vanhoozer takes a step further when he tries to discern between "the authorial intention" in the text as distinct from what is affirmed in it (which may include errors).

He uses his speech-act distinction between locution (what the text affirms) and illocution (the purpose for which the author is using the text), namely, God's redemptive purposes (LI? 107). We saw earlier, in the case of Joshua and the sun, how far this can lead someone from what the text is actually saying.

Finally he takes the fatal step. Vanhoozer claims that in the incarnation of Jesus, "his body is considered 'sinful flesh' (Rom. 8:3 RSV) and was made a sin offering (Heb. 10:5–10)" (MT? 304). He adds, "Jesus' flesh, therefore, was physical, Jewish, sinful [in the incarnation] and spiritual [in the resurrection]" (305). Based on this (faulty) Christology, Vanhoozer develops his (faulty) incarnational analogy as follows: "the body of Jesus is to his meaning ('Christ') as the letter is to the meaning of the text." He continues:

> What is of interest, however, is the way in which the body of Jesus progressively acquires determinate meaning in a series of expanding contexts of descriptions. Such an approach allows me to resist reducing the significance of the body of Jesus to the physical level, just as I will later resist reducing the literal sense to its most primitive level, namely, the empirical objects named by individual words. (305)

So we move progressively from Jesus's body as physical, to his body as Jewish, to his body as sinful, and finally to his body as spiritual. Only in this way can we get "a thick description" of the body of Jesus. "Similarly, only when we consider the text as a literary act requiring a number of levels of description can we give an account of what the author is doing in the text, . . . [namely,] a sufficiently 'thick description' of the literal sense" (305). This Vanhoozer (mis)identifies with the Reformation insight that "the infallible rule of interpretation of Scripture is Scripture itself" (305). He believes we will know when it is sufficiently "thick" by the evidence in the text itself (305).

Clearly, if Jesus is sinful at one state (in the incarnation), then Vanhoozer has gone all the way with a Barthian view that Jesus's humanness (and by analogy, the Bible's humanness) involves assuming sinful human flesh (Barth, *Church Dogmatics I*, 2, 150ff)!

Questions about Sola Scriptura and Tradition

Although Vanhoozer's claims to hold to *sola scriptura* (the Bible only) and the Protestant principle of perspicuity (clarity), he undermines them by redefining them. Historically, these were the Protestant alternative to the Catholic insistence that tradition is needed to understand Scripture.

Sola Scriptura Denied

Vanhoozer contends that "it takes many interpreters and interpretive traditions fully to appreciate and understand the divine discourse" (LI? 111). To be sure, he sees tradition as ministerial and not magisterial (as Rome does). Nonetheless, his view angles more toward Anglicanism or Eastern Orthodoxy than the standard Reformed position. He argues clearly for the need of tradition in interpreting the Bible. He writes:

> The holy script, however, is both complete and incomplete. On the one hand, the story of God's word-acts in the history of Israel and in Jesus Christ is finished. . . . On the other hand, without a people to employ it, the script lacks something essential. . . . While tradition does not *compete* with Scripture, might tradition *complete* it? (*DD*, 164)

Vanhoozer believes that

> the formula "the Bible Alone" is, in the eyes of many, as good a recipe for fragmentation in the church as has ever been invented! Hence the concern, ancient and contemporary, for the guardrails of tradition. Twentieth-century hermeneutics seems to confirm the point: exegesis without tradition—apart from participation in the history of a text's reception—is impossible. On this view, there really is no choice between the Bible or tradition; rather, the only relevant question is, whose tradition? (*DD*, 113)

His answer is "Catholicity." For "truth is the daughter of time, it has been said, and this is a good argument for attending to catholicity, the tradition of interpretation passed on through the centuries" (LI? 112). So, while the Bible is the sole basis for our faith both formally and materially, nonetheless, our understanding of the Bible is formed by tradition.

Perspicuity Denied

Historic Protestantism has insisted that the Bible alone—interpreted in the normal, literal, historical-grammatical way—is sufficiently clear on all essential teachings. This is possible because of the perspicuity (clarity) of Scripture. By contrast, Vanhoozer says that meaning is a community affair. "Meaning, one might say, is no longer an affair of consciousness, but of community" (*MT*? 218). He speaks of the need to "constitute a community of interpreters sharing a primary concern of the book's verbal meaning" (303). Once one examines the complicated, multifaceted, traditional, and communal elements employed by Vanhoozer, it is not difficult to see why he rejects the historic Protestant views of perspicuity. For the traditional view affirms that a person of average understanding and intelligence can understand the main message of the Bible. By contrast, it would take a historian, theologian, and philosopher to understand the main message of the Bible according to Vanhoozer's method.

Catholicity and Tradition

In effect, Vanhoozer replaces the historical-grammatical method and *sola scriptura* with two other means of understanding Scripture: Catholicity and tradition. For if the ordinary, common, everyday way of understanding the Bible is not sufficient, then we must look elsewhere. He summarily dismisses Rome, though his view leaves him vulnerable to their claims. After all, if we cannot understand the main message of the Bible without ecclesiastical help, as Vanhoozer claims, and if all other help, as he admits, is fallible, then why not accept infallible ecclesiastical help? He spells out no reasons against this. In fact, he offers many reasons for accepting tradition (*DD*, 115–85).[6] However, Vanhoozer admits to the truth of some things that argue against the use of tradition to interpret Scripture.[7]

First, "truth is the daughter of time, . . . and this is a good argument for attending to catholicity, the tradition of interpretation passed on through the centuries" (*LI*? 112). But Rome claims to preserve the oldest tradition.

Second, there are conflicting traditions outside of the magisterial tradition of Rome (*LI*? 111). Of course, these same arguments are also good reasons for rejecting tradition and catholicity (East or West) and for accepting the even older biblical ground in *sola scriptura*, understood in its perspicuity by the literal, historical-grammatical interpretation.

Third, he notes that "there are multiple interpretive traditions" (*LI*? 111). However, he glosses over the fact that these interpretive traditions come up with contradictory doctrines in important and even crucial areas. To mention only a few, there are opposite views on: (1) the primacy of Rome; (2) the infallibility of the pope; (3) the canonicity of the Apocrypha; (4) the veneration of Mary; (5) the bodily assumption of Mary; (6) the worship of the consecrated host; (7) the venerations of images; (8) prayers to Mary; (9) the use of indulgences; (10) the necessity of works for salvation, and so on. Rome says yes to all of these, and most of the rest of Christendom say no to most of these. Which tradition is correct?

Fourth, Vanhoozer recognizes another good argument against accepting tradition. He quotes Augustine, saying, "If we are to look back to long custom or antiquity alone, then also murderers and adulterers, and similar persons can defend their crimes in this way because they are ancient" (LI? 111). In brief, antiquity is no proof of authenticity. It is better to rest our case on the only infallible and inerrant revelation from God—the Bible. As the ETS doctrinal statement put it, "*The Bible alone* and the Bible in its entirety is the Word of God written, and therefore inerrant in the autographs" (emphasis added).

Fifth, another reason can be given against using tradition to interpret Scripture. For there is a tradition, based on a misunderstanding of what Jesus said, that goes back to the time of the apostles and is false. John mentions it (in John 21:20–23). It is the false tradition that the apostle John would not die.

Sixth, even the venerable test for a true tradition mentioned by Vincent of Lérins (died ca. 445) fails. He offered the dictum that a true tradition is one that has been believed everywhere, always, and by everyone. Yet on this test even some essential orthodox and creedal doctrines fail the test, such as accepting the deity of Christ and the Trinity, to say nothing of the hypostatic union of the two natures of Christ in one person and a host of other doctrines.

Seventh, the test of "universal consent of the fathers" was pronounced by the allegedly infallible Council of Trent (1546–64) as a test for an apostolic tradition. But this too falls short of being a test for many of the infallibly pronounced doctrines of the Catholic Church, including the immaculate conception of Mary (which even Thomas Aquinas rejected), the bodily assumption of Mary, the veneration of Mary, purgatory, indulgences, the worship of the consecrated host, transubstantiation, and the infallibility of the pope.

Tradition in the sense of "good history" linking present teachings with teachings of the apostles as recorded in the New Testament—this has value (see Geisler, *Is Rome the True Church?* appendixes 1 and 3). For this is historical confirmation of what the New Testament teaches, not a hermeneutical principle to be used in interpreting Scripture.

Conclusion

Vanhoozer has many positive and commendable statements about Scripture and its interpretation. He is not a Barthian, and he is a confessed inerrantist, albeit of a modified variety. He teaches at a school (Wheaton College) that requires its faculty to affirm inerrancy. He also claims to affirm much of the ICBI inerrancy statement as he understands it. But that is precisely the problem since the way he understands it is not the way the framers meant it, as is demonstrated from the official commentaries on the ICBI statements.

So what we have set out to discover (whether Vanhoozer's view on inerrancy is in accord with the standard evangelical ICBI statements on inerrancy) has a decidedly negative answer. The reasons for this are not insincerity on his part but are philosophical. Vanhoozer buys into a certain theory of language (like the speak-act theory) and interpretation that undermine the very position he purports to accept.

It is not uncommon for an evangelical—and certainly for a so-called "post-conservative" such as he claims to be—to buy into alien philosophy of language and meaning that undermine the historic, orthodox view on inerrancy. The root problem is philosophical, not factual. Evidence for this is that as the evidence has mounted from manuscript and archaeological discoveries in favor of Scripture, the deviations from Scripture become more radical. We do well to heed Paul's warning: "See to it that no one takes you captive by philosophy" (Col. 2:8). Rather, it is our task as Christians to "destroy arguments and every lofty opinion raised against the knowledge of God, and take every thought captive to obey Christ" (2 Cor. 10:5).

Sources

Aristotle, *On Interpretation*

Austin, *Do Things with Words*

Boice, *Foundations of the Christian Faith*

Bultmann, *Kerygma and Myth*

Edwards, ed., *Encyclopedia of Philosophy*

Geisler, "Explaining Hermeneutics"

———, *Philosophy of Religion*

———, *Systematic Theology*, vol. 1

———, *Thomas Aquinas*

Geisler and Betancourt, *Is Rome the True Church?*

Geisler and Holden, *Living Loud*

Kaiser, *Toward an Exegetical Theology*

———, *Uses of the Old Testament in the New*

Kaiser and Silva, *Biblical Hermeneutics*

O'Callaghan, *Thomistic Realism*

Sparks, *After Inerrancy*

Sproul, *Explaining Inerrancy*

Tozer, *Knowledge of the Holy*

Vanhoozer, *Drama of Doctrine*

———, *First Theology*

———, "Inspiration of Scripture"

———, *Is There Meaning?*

———, "Lost in Interpretation?"

———, "Semantics of Biblical Literature"

———, "Voice and the Actor"

Weaver, *Ideas Have Consequences*

9

Andrew McGowan on Inerrancy

Introduction

In some ways Professor Andrew McGowan's challenge to inerrancy is one of the most dangerous because it is clear, direct, and comes from within evangelicalism. McGowan is a visiting professor at a major Reformed seminary in the United States in Jackson, Mississippi, which has had a long-standing commitment to inerrancy. Unlike some other evangelicals, McGowan attacks the ETS and IBCI stand head-on. In place of total inerrancy, he offers a view of limited inerrancy, following the European model of James Orr. Further, there are many positive and appealing things about his position, which makes it all the more difficult to detect its serious flaws. Let's consider some of these positive things first.[1]

The Positive Contributions of McGowan's Work

There are many commendable features of this book that are well worth listing. First of all, McGowan sees this matter to be a "watershed issue" (*Divine Spiration* [*DS*], 9). Further, he observes that *theopneustos* in 2 Timothy 3:16 should be translated as "spiration" or "breathing out." He declares that "God the Holy Spirit breathed out the Scriptures" (118). McGowan also affirms the value of the word "infallible" (39, 48) since the term "inerrancy" alone is insufficient. After all, there can be inerrant phone books with no errors that do not thereby have divine authority. He also sees the ICBI (International Council on Biblical Inerrancy) statement as "most significant" (104) and would choose it, if necessary, over the errancy view of Rogers and McKim (212). Likewise, McGowan would choose B. B Warfield over Jack Rogers of Fuller Seminary (*DS*, 161). He even cites favorably both John Woodbridge's critique of Rogers and McKim (*DS*, 99) as well as the critique of Donald Bloesch, who agrees with his choice (100, 125). Nor does McGowan deny that God can, if he chooses, produce an inerrant text (113–14).

He even holds that the Bible is a "co-authored" book by both God and human beings (148). McGowan says, "The instruments of this divine spiration were certain human beings" (*DS*, 118). Then, too, his definition of inspiration hits some important key notes of the doctrine when he affirms that "the Holy Spirit caused men to write books and his supervisory action was such that although these books are truly the work of human beings, they are also the Word of God" (43). And he is certainly right in denying the "mechanical dictation" of Scripture (163).

Further, the book is on track in rejecting the neo-orthodox view of Scripture that the Bible merely "becomes the Word of God" in a moment of encounter with God through the Bible (29). He also holds that it is not the Word of God subjectively but is God's Word objectively (73). Likewise, revelation is not merely an event, as many neo-orthodox claim (21). McGowan also correctly affirms that inspiration is verbal (136) and that there are not any degrees of inspiration (134). He observes that it is not the authors of Scripture that are inspired (39, 133) but the Scriptures they wrote. McGowan also makes an often overlooked but important distinction that it is not the Bible that needs illumination but only human minds (45–47). Another crucial point is that one should not claim for the Bible what it does not claim for itself (121). Nor does he reject the view that there are implicit or logically entailed claims in Scripture. Indeed, McGowan says the use of logic is "appropriate" (117), and "contradictions" should be avoided (212). More could be added, but these will suffice.

An Evaluation of McGowan's Basic Proposals on the Nature of Scripture

In spite of all these fine features, McGowan's proposal is a direct and serious proposal by an otherwise conservative Reformed scholar to the ICBI Chicago Statement since it came out (in 1978). As such, McGowan's proposals demand attention.

The Claim That the Word "Inerrancy" Should Be Discarded

McGowan argues that the term "inerrancy" should be discarded by evangelicals (*DS*, 13). He offers several reasons for this, one of the most often repeated of which is that the term "inerrancy" implies scientific precision (117). McGowan also believes it is recent in origin, not being found in early creeds but being a result of heated battle between early twentieth-century fundamentalists and liberals (121). Neither does he believe the term is biblical, but he calls it a "violent assumption" (135) of fundamentalist thinking. "Inerrancy," he believes, is an apologetic response to the Enlightenment (50, 115). He also argues that it does not have the weight of history behind it.

First of all in response, both sides of the debate can agree that there is nothing sacred about the word "inerrancy." Indeed, it is not the *term* so much as it is the *truth* of inerrancy that is important to preserve. The basic question is whether or not the Bible is completely without error in all that it affirms. This can be said in more than one way. But before we hasten to throw away the term "inerrancy," let us remind ourselves of the strength of the word and the weakness of the suggested alternative terms.

Second, as for the argument that the word "inerrancy" is not biblical, by that same logic, the word "Bible" is not biblical for it is nowhere used of the Bible in the Bible. Further, it too does not have the weight of early history behind it. So should we discard it also? Indeed, the word "Trinity" is not in the Bible and did not appear in the earliest ecumenical creeds such as the Apostles' Creed (second cent.), the Nicene Creed (325), or the Chalcedonian Creed (451). Does that mean we should discard it? The answer is negative, and the reasons are that though the term "Trinity" is not biblical, nonetheless the truth is biblical, and it is a good term to describe it. The same is true of the word "inerrancy."

Third, the term "inerrancy" need not mean "scientific precision," as is wrongly alleged by anti-inerrantists. Every term should be understood in its context and with the qualifications given to it by its users. Even McGowan agrees that the ICBI statement makes numerous qualifications on the meaning of the term (*DS*, 106). But these qualifications clearly deny the misimplications of modern "scientific precision." Article 13 of the ICBI Chicago Statement declares plainly: "We further deny that inerrancy is negated by Biblical phenomena such as a lack of *modern technical precision*" (emphasis added).

Fourth, it is well to remember that the term "inerrancy" also has some strong features in its favor. For one, it is negative, and negative terms are powerful. Consider the force of the Ten Commandments, many of which are stated in negative terms: "You shall not murder" or "You shall not bear false witness" or "You shall not commit adultery" (Exod. 20:13, 16, 14). Further, the sentence "The Bible is true" is not nearly as strong as "The Bible is without error." Even McGowan himself commends the ICBI statement for having "denials" as well as "affirmations" (106). But the denials are negative, which is the reason they help in clarifying the point at hand. "Inerrancy," as a negative term, does the same thing. It is readily apparent that the statement "The Bible is without error" is clearer and stronger than the statement "The Bible is true." For the latter does not make it clear whether the Bible is *completely* true.

Considering the Alternatives

We readily grant that no term, including "inerrancy," expresses all that the Bible claims about itself. Nonetheless, by comparison the term stands tall as compared to most of the alternatives offered.

The Term "Infallible"

McGowan favors the word "infallible" over the word "inerrant" (*DS*, 48, 123, 125, 162). He insists that the word "infallible" is "more dynamic (or organic) and is a less mechanical view of authority" (49). It carries with it the idea that "the Holy Spirit infallibly uses God's Word to achieve all he intends to achieve" (49). However, this use of the word "infallible" is precisely why the term "inerrant" is also needed. We acknowledge the strength of the term "infallible," if it is used in the sense of "unerring" in connection with the word "inerrant." However, the term "infallible" has been rendered fallible by the intentionalist sense in which it is used by limited inerrantists and noninerrantists. My *Webster's Ninth Collegiate Dictionary* gives the primary definition of "infallible" as "incapable of error; unerring." In this sense of the term, inerrantists have no problem since it is perfectly compatible with the term "inerrant." It is the secondary and weaker sense of the term that the inerrantists reject as inadequate: "not liable to mislead, deceive, or disappoint." Indeed, McGowan speaks of Scripture that "infallibly achieves God's purposes" (149). He quotes Bavinck's view with approval,[2] saying: "In his organic view, Bavinck focuses not on the text of Scripture as such but upon its meaning and *purpose*" (158, emphasis added). Likewise, he affirms "that *intention* [of Scripture] is no other than that it should make us 'wise unto salvation'" (159, emphasis added).

However, focusing on the intention or purpose of the Bible, rather than on its affirmations and denials, does not necessarily mean that the Bible is without all errors in all that it affirms. Many statements with good intentions, even those that achieve their intended results, contain errors (see chap. 13 below). So by that definition of "infallible," the Bible could have an infallibly correct error. But this is nonsense. Since the term "infallible" carries these connotations for many, it is necessary to add the word "inerrant" to make clear what the Bible teaches on the topic.

Of course, in the good sense of the term "infallible" (incapable of error), it is not an either/or situation. The Bible is both infallible and inerrant. But, unlike McGowan's implication, the Bible is not merely infallible in its *intentions* and achievements but also in its *affirmations* (and denials). Truth is not found in intentions because humans can, and often do, utter errors with good intentions. So defining either infallibility or inerrancy in terms of intentions, achieved or not, does not measure up to what the Bible claims for itself, which is that truth must be judged by its correspondence to the facts. Indeed, even McGowan seems to admit this elsewhere when he commends "modes of rationality that actually *correspond with the nature of its objectively given reality*" (*DS*, 73, emphasis added). Indeed, ICBI clarified the meaning of "truth" as correspondence in an official authorized commentary on the Chicago Statement, affirming that "by biblical standards of truth and error [in art. 13, on "Truth"] is meant the view used both in the Bible and in everyday life, viz., a correspondence view of truth."[3]

The correspondence view of truth (see chap. 13 below) is in fact the one that the Bible[4] embraces. For example: It is implied in the ninth commandment ("You shall not bear false witness" [Exod. 20:16]), meaning, "Don't misrepresent the facts." It is also entailed in Acts 24, which says you can "learn the truth" when you "verify [the facts]" (vv. 8, 11 NIV). Further, it is manifest in Genesis 42:16 when Joseph says they should look at the facts "so that your words may be tested to see if you are telling the truth" (NIV). In addition, it was employed in the test for a false prophet whose prophecy was considered false "if the word does not come to pass or come true" (Deut. 18:22). It is also utilized in everyday conversations when we consider something false if it misrepresents the facts (e.g., we say, "Check the facts" or "Check it out for yourself" and the like). Indeed, the correspondence view of truth is essential to a legal oath when one promises "to tell the truth, the whole truth, and nothing but the truth." To be sure, the biblical words for "truth" (Heb. 'ĕmet; Gk. alētheia) often imply more than mere correspondence, but never less than that. "Truth" often implies reliability or trustworthiness. But trustworthiness flows from the fact that it corresponds to reality. So the Bible is trustworthy because it corresponds to reality, not the reverse.

We can and do agree that the word "inerrancy" alone is insufficient to describe what the Bible is.[5] It also has sanctity, infallibility, indestructibility, indefatigability (can't be worn out), indefeasibility (can't be overcome). Indeed, it can save (1 Pet. 1:23), nourish (1 Pet. 2:2), wash (Ps. 119:9), purify (Jer. 23:29a), shatter (23:29b), cut deeply (Heb. 4:12), prevent sin (Ps. 119:11), illuminate (119:105), comfort (Rom. 15:4), and predict (2 Pet. 1:19). The truth is that no one word covers all that the Bible is, just as no one attribute exhausts all that God is. However, this is not to say that the Bible is not inerrant as well. Nor is this to say we can rob it of this characteristic any more than we can strip it of infallibility.

McGowan Prefers the Word "Authentic"

McGowan prefers the word "authentic" (DS, 213) to "inerrant." However, the term "authentic" as used of Scripture is theologically anemic. The Bible claims much more than this for itself. Jesus refers to the Bible as indestructible (Matt. 5:17–18), unbreakable (John 10:35), the "word of God" (John 10:35), and as coming "out of the mouth of God" (Matt. 4:4 KJV). Paul said, it is "God-breathed" (2 Tim. 3:16 NIV). These concepts are insufficiently described by the term "authentic." After all, one can have an authentic coin minted with mistakes on it or an authentic copy of the famous "Wicked Bible," which translated Exodus 20:14 as "Thou shalt commit adultery"! (mistake in KJV reprint, 1631). There is also "authentic" Confederate currency and persons with authenticity—all of which falls far short of what is perfect.

The same goes for terms like "trustworthy" and "reliable." The Bible is trustworthy like a good friend, but even trustworthy friends make mistakes. It is reliable like a good map, but even good maps can have errors on them. These terms are far too weak to describe what is meant by a God-breathed book that was jointly authored by God and humans. So, both of these terms fail to measure up to what the Bible claims for itself.

Having said all this, there are other good ways to describe what is meant by inerrancy. "Totally free from all error in everything it affirms" is a good phrase. But for a single word, it is difficult to beat the term "inerrancy." And as defined by the ICBI statement, it is clearly the best single word available in English. It would be unwise to discard it for words like "trustworthy," "reliable," "authentic," or even "infallible in purpose." The proper use of "infallible" and "inerrant in all it affirms" is a good and powerful way to express the biblical doctrine.

The term "inerrancy" is the correct term to use because it is strong enough to keep most opponents of the view from using the same term and redefining it to mean whatever they would like it to mean. McGowan is a clear example of an individual who understands the doctrine of inerrancy and will not subscribe to it because the term "inerrancy" demands too much. Clearly, unlike those in favor of using terms such as "authoritative," "inspired," "infallible," and the like and discarding of the term "inerrancy," by its etymological definition "inerrancy" demands that there be a separation between the inerrantist and errantist position (because both sides of the inerrancy debate would show no disregard for the terms authoritative, inspired, infallible, and the like). In the history of the church, and in the christological controversy in particular, orthodoxy and heresy have been distinguished from one another because of a single Greek term (*homoiousios* [similar] vs. *homoousios* [same]). In the same respect the term "inerrancy" is favorable because it is strong enough to separate orthodoxy from heresy. For Christ is of the same nature as God's nature, not just of a nature similar to God's.

The Claim That Inerrancy Does Not Follow from God's Nature

Typical of strong Calvinists, McGowan embraces a form of divine voluntarism. Ethical voluntarism declares that something is good because God wills it; God does not will it because it is good. However, this would make all the moral commands of God in Scripture arbitrary. For example, according to voluntarism, God could will that love is wrong and hate is right. But this is not only counterintuitive; it is also morally repugnant, to say nothing of being unbiblical since by nature "God is love" (1 John 4:16). Further, voluntarism would undermine unconditional election, a doctrine dear to the heart of a Reformed theologian. For if voluntarism were true, then God could change his mind about who the elect are or even whether the elect will ultimately be saved.

This same kind of voluntarism is evident in McGowan's argument against inerrancy. In one of the most important sections in the book, he writes: "Inerrantists make an unwarranted assumption about God. The assumption is that, given the nature and character of God, the only kind of Scripture he could 'breathe out' was Scripture that is textually inerrant. If there was even one mistake in the *autographa*, then God cannot have been the author, because he is incapable of error" (*DS*, 113). Thus, McGowan says inerrancy is not a legitimate inference from the Bible (115) but is merely an "a priori" argument (131). Yet this is precisely what both the Evangelical Theological Society (ETS) and the International Council on Biblical Inerrancy (ICBI) have affirmed (see chap. 12 below).

McGowan goes on to say that "the argument of the inerrantists is that God is *unable* to produce anything other than an inerrant autographic text. . . . I agree with the inerrantists that God *could* have brought into being inerrant autographic texts, had he chosen to do so, but I reject their argument that he *must* have acted in this way" (113–14). He concludes, "I think it is wrong to prejudge the nature of Scripture through some deductivist approach, based on what we believe inspiration must mean, given God's character" (136). We cannot "assume that they must be inerrant because God cannot lie" (137). This could hardly be more clear and, in my view, more faulty. Indeed, McGowan affirms that "having chosen, however, to use human beings, . . . God did not overrule their humanity" (118). And this humanity involved "discrepancies and apparent contradictions, because that is what God intended" (119). Several observations are in order in this regard.

First, McGowan is a voluntarist on what God could or could not do in producing a God-breathed book. That is, he affirms that God was free to make an original Bible with or without errors in it. God was under no necessity imposed upon him by his own nature to produce an errorless original. As incredible as this may sound, *McGowan's biblical voluntarism entails the claim that for God, speaking the truth is optional, not necessary!* If ever there was a misdirected and overstated view of God's sovereignty, this is it.

Indeed, this is precisely where inerrantists sharply disagree with people like McGowan. This disagreement is reflected in the basic statement on Scripture of the Evangelical Theological Society, to which McGowan refers. It reads, "The Bible alone, and the Bible in its entirety, is the Word of God written and is *therefore* inerrant in the autographs" (emphasis added). The word "therefore" logically connects the Word of "God" and "inerrant" to make it clear that neither God nor the Bible errs. This meaning of the word "therefore" has been confirmed by a living framer of the statement, namely, Reformed theologian Roger Nicole.

Further, and more important, the Bible makes it clear that God cannot choose, even if he desires to do so, to produce an imperfect original. Why? "Because it is *impossible* for God to lie" (Heb. 6:18). Paul speaks about "God, who *cannot* lie" (Titus 1:2 NKJV). He declares, "[God] cannot deny himself" (2 Tim. 2:13). Numerous other Scriptures speak of God's unchanging nature (Num. 23:19; 1 Sam. 15:29; Ps. 102:25–27; Heb. 1:10–12; Mal. 3:6; James 1:17). No serious examination of all these Scriptures in context can support a voluntarist interpretation that God can change his essential nature, even if he wanted to do so. If this is so, then McGowan's central thesis fails, and the inerrantist's argument stands firm: (1) God cannot err. (2) The original Bible is God's Word. (3) Therefore, the original Bible cannot err.

To deny this conclusion, as McGowan knows, one must deny at least one or the other of the two premises. His attempt to deny the first premise fails. It goes against the grain of God's very nature as truth to presume that such an unchangeably true Being can err, if he wishes to do so. God is truth (Deut. 32:4; Ps. 31:5) by his very unchangeable nature, and as such, he "*cannot* lie" (Titus 1:2 NKJV); "It is *impossible* for God to lie" (Heb. 6:18). To do so, would be to deny himself, and "he *cannot* deny himself" (2 Tim. 2:13; emphasis added in paragraph).

Further, the Holy Spirit is "the Spirit of truth" (John 15:26). And the Word of God is the utterance of the Spirit of truth. Jesus says, "When the Spirit of truth comes, he will guide you into all the truth" (John 16:13). Peter adds, "Knowing this first of all, that no prophecy of Scripture comes from someone's own interpretation. For no prophecy was ever produced by the will of man, but men spoke from God as they were carried along by the Holy Spirit" (2 Pet. 1:20–21). David confesses, "The Spirit of the LORD speaks by me; his word is on my tongue" (2 Sam. 23:2). Now by simple logical inference,

1. The original Bible is the utterance of the Spirit of truth.
2. The Spirit of truth cannot utter error.
3. Therefore, the original Bible cannot utter error.

Here again, to deny inerrancy one must deny at least one or more of the two premises. McGowan's attempt to deny the first premise fails. Truth is not an option with God: it is a necessity.

McGowan also believes that the copies of the Bible are inspired (*DS*, 159). Given that inspiration means "spirated" or "breathed out" (Gk. *theopneustos*) by God, and given that McGowan recognizes errors in the copies, he is left with explaining just how God can breathe out these errors. Indeed, according to this analysis, it is not only possible for there to be errors in what God breathes out; it may be actual as well. But this is contrary to the very nature of God as truth to breathe out error. God cannot overrule his unchangeable nature by his sovereignty any more than he can will himself out of existence!

An Implied Accommodation Theory

Upon closer analysis, McGowan also seems to reject the second premise of the argument for inerrancy as well, namely, that "the Bible is the Word of God." According to this view, God accommodates himself, not only to human finitude but also to human error in the production of Scripture. For he declared that even "the autographs (if we could view them) might very well look just like our existing manuscripts, including all the difficulties, synoptic issues, discrepancies and apparent contradictions" (*DS*, 119).

However, *nowhere does Scripture support the view that God accommodates himself to human error rather than merely adapts himself to human finitude.* In short, a truly human book, such as the Bible, can still avoid errors. If this were not so, then by the same logic, one must conclude that the divine accommodation in the incarnation means that Christ sinned. This is the way McGowan attacks the so-called incarnational model often used by evangelicals to illustrate their view (see chap. 16 below).

The error at the root of this view appears to be based on a Barthian and neo-Gnostic view of human fallenness, in which any contact with this fallen human world makes sin unavoidable. It is to argue that since the Bible was written by fallen human beings in fallen human language, it too must inevitably partake of errors as well.

There is another serious problem with this radical view of divine accommodation.[6] If contact with a fallen world makes error inevitable, then not only does this mean there can be (and probably are) errors in the original Bible; it also means that the incarnate Christ too must partake of both the same proneness to error and sin. But the New Testament makes it very clear that Jesus did not sin (Heb. 4:15; 2 Cor. 5:21; 1 Pet. 1:23; 1 John 3:2–3). Likewise, it would mean that the very teachings that came from Jesus's lips would have been tainted with error since he too was speaking in a fallen human language. But this belief would precipitate a christological crisis unacceptable to orthodoxy. Surely no one who believes in the union of two natures in the one person of Christ, the Second Person of the Godhead, thereby affirms error in his human words. Hence, McGowan's view of divine accommodation to error in the production of Scripture must be rejected. The fact is, however, that finitude does not necessitate fallenness. If it did, then not only would the Son himself have partaken in sin and error, but the beatified saints in heaven also would not be free from sin and error, as the Scriptures teach they will be (1 Cor. 13:10; 1 John 3:2; Rev. 21:4).

Rejecting the Traditional Incarnational Analogy

According to the orthodox inerrantists' reasoning, just as God in his living Word (the Savior) has united with the human nature of Christ without sin, even so God is united with his written Word (the Scripture) yet without error. McGowan objects to this analogy with two basic arguments (*DS*, 118–21).

First, he argues that unlike Christ, whose two natures are united in one person, there is no such union of the divine and human in Scripture. But McGowan misses the point, even on his own grounds. For elsewhere he speaks of a coauthorship of Scripture (118, 148). He cites with approval the following: "This enables Bavinck faithfully and clearly to emphasize both sides of any orthodox doctrine of Scripture, namely, that God is the author but yet the human beings are the authors" (148). This would mean that both the human and divine aspects of Scripture are united in one set of *propositions* (better, "sentences") or verbal expression in like manner to the divine and human being united in one *person* in Christ. This conclusion is borne out also by the fact that McGowan holds to "verbal" inspiration by affirming that "I disagree with him [James Orr] on [his denying] verbal inspiration. It seems to me that there is no good reason for arguing that the content but not the form of the Scriptures have come to us from God" (136). But if the verbal form of Scripture is "breathed-out" from God, as McGowan claims it is, then there is a propositional (better, "sentential") unity that combines both the divine and human elements of Scripture in one and the same verbal structure.

Even McGowan's own definition of Scripture supports this orthodox incarnational model, for he says, "The Holy Spirit caused men to write books and his supervisory action was such that although these books are truly the work of human beings, they are also the Word of God" (*DS*, 43). Again, there is a unity between the human and divine in God's written Word (the Scripture) that is analogous with the union of the divine and human in his living Word (the Savior).

Further, McGowan argues wrongly that the word "divine" does not apply to Scripture, as it does to the divine nature of Christ in the incarnation. He writes, "Only God is divine and therefore only God can have a divine nature" (*DS*, 120). But in a very important sense, this is not so. Even Peter affirms that in some real sense we are "partakers of the divine nature" (2 Pet. 1:4). Surely this is not in a metaphysical sense (e.g., we can't be infinite, uncreated, and immutable) but in a moral sense (we can be true, good, and holy). McGowan seems to unwittingly answer his own question when he admits, "I am not denying that the Scriptures (like human beings) can share some of the divine attributes" (120). But that is all that is necessary for the analogy to be a good one, namely, to have strong similarities, which it has.

As for the Bible not being God, of course it is not. That is why the incarnational model is an analogy (for things similar but not identical). No informed evangelical ever held that the Bible was God and should be worshiped. The Bible is like God in his moral attributes (like the need to be true and holy), not in his nonmoral (metaphysical) attributes (like infinite and eternal). In view of this, the incarnational reasoning can be stated as follows:

1. God's living Word (Christ) and his written Word (the Savior) are similar in that
   a. They have a divine and human dimension.
   b. These two dimensions are combined in one unity.
   c. Thus, both are without flaw.
2. Hence, both God's living Word and his written Word are without flaw morally in that
   a. God's living Word is without sin.
   b. His written Word is without error.[7]

The remaining question is this: How can the effect (an inerrant Bible) be greater than the cause (errant humans)? Of course, it cannot, but the ultimate Primary Cause is God; the human writers are only the secondary causes. Their imperfection and tendency to err does not bleed through to effect the Bible because God can draw a straight line with a crooked stick! Or in biblical terms: "No prophecy was ever produced by the will of man, but men spoke from God as they were carried along by the Holy Spirit" (2 Pet. 1:21). In theological terms, to cite McGowan himself, "the Holy Spirit caused men to write books and his supervisory action was such that although these books are truly the work of human beings, they are also the Word of God" (*DS*, 43). Since the Scriptures did not originate from "the will of man" but from the will of God, and since the superintending Spirit of truth "cannot lie," then what God uttered in these human words cannot err.

McGowan's Neo-Barthian Implication

Although McGowan rightly disowns some neo-orthodox beliefs such as a denial of objective propositional revelation and revelation coming only in acts and not words, nonetheless he is not without Barthian influence in this matter. In fact, I would call his view neo-Barthian in some significant respects. First, as already noted (and discussed more fully below), McGowan allows for the possibility of errors in the original text of the Bible—the breathed-out Word of God. Second, he speaks of the Bible as an instrument through which God speaks—rather than the Bible being the voice of God itself. As to the first he says, "The Scriptures are the record of the revelation that God has given to his church" (*DS*, 21). He adds, "Our knowledge of the love of God in Christ comes to us through the voice of God speaking in the Scriptures" (31). Again, "God's Word came to us in the form of human witness" (112). Finally, he cites James Orr with approval: "God has given a historical, supernatural revelation and, . . . the Scriptures are the 'record' of this revelation" (132). But what is this but a more euphemistic way to affirm Barth's scratched-record analogy of someone hearing the master's voice through an imperfect recording. This is contrary to Scripture, which describes itself as "perfect" (Ps. 19:7; Heb. *tāmîm*, "without flaw")—the same word used of the Passover lamb (Exod. 12:5), which was to be "without blemish." But the Bible speaks of itself as the true revelation of God himself (the very Word of God), not a faulty record of it.

This conclusion is also supported by McGowan's claim that the Bible has no authority in itself: only God has authority (*DS*, 45). But if the Bible is the Word of God written, then it has the authority of God in it since it is God's voice speaking in the words of Scripture. One would think that—with McGowan's emphasis on the "dynamic" nature of inspiration (49), to wit, that God is continually speaking through his Word (155)—he would not have fallen into the Barthian error of claiming that the Bible is not the revelation of God but merely a human record of it, through which God speaks to us. This is undoubtedly why McGowan also claims there is some truth in the Barthian claim that "the Bible becomes the Word of God" to us or is "a subjective revelation" to us (156).

Finally, this neo-Barthianism in McGowan is also supported by his contention that the Bible is only an instrumental revelation. He writes, "The purpose of Scripture is instrumental to the work of the Spirit" (*DS*, 24). Likewise, he speaks with approval of Barth's "arguing that our knowledge of the love of God in Christ comes to us through the voice of God speaking in the Scriptures" (31). Thus, God speaks "by His Spirit through His Word" (31). So the Bible is "the means" by which he communicates with us (31). In short, the Bible is not the revelation of God; it is the instrument through which God's revelation comes to us. But once this distinction is made and the wedge is driven between the words of the men who wrote the Scriptures and the voice of the God who speaks through these fallible human voices, then we cannot have a true revelation from God.

Faulty Logic in the McGowan Analysis

Part of the reason McGowan is able to come to these wrong conclusions about inerrancy is the faulty logic he employs. A few examples will suffice. Many of them are forms of the notorious straw-man fallacy. First, the false charge that inerrantists hold to mechanical dictation is rejected by even the fundamentalist John R. Rice, who nonetheless admits to crediting "verbal dictation."[8] However, no Calvinist, like McGowan, who believes in irresistible grace should have any problem with believing that God can work on different persons with their unique styles to produce exactly what God wants them to say without dictating it to them.

Second, he alleges a straw-man atomistic view "that every isolated word of Holy Scripture is inerrant" (DS, 65). This word-by-word revelation is found primarily in cultic dictation or in orthodox Muslims' beliefs about the origin of the Qur'an, but not in an evangelical view of inspiration that accepts holistic inspiration. That is, a word properly taken in the context of a whole sentence, and a sentence taken in the whole context of a literary unity (and ultimately that taken in the context of the whole Scripture)—that is inspired and inerrant. In brief, a whole sentence (with all of its parts) is an inerrant revelation from God if understood in its proper contexts. Paul stresses the importance of a singular "seed" in contrast to "seeds" (Gal. 3:16 NIV). The absence of a letter can change the whole meaning of a doctrine, as discovered with an early creed. The Greek word for "same" (homoousion) differed from the word for "similar" (homoiousion) by only one letter, the letter i (the letter iota in Greek). This one tiny letter was the difference between orthodoxy and heresy, on affirming whether Christ was the same or only similar to God. So in this sense, even letters are inspired, not in isolation from words, sentences, and the overall context, but as a crucial part of the whole, as the holistic meaning.

Another straw man created by McGowan is what he calls "inflexible literalism" (DS, 65, 103). He equates ICBI with fundamentalists (103, 123). However, the ICBI Chicago Statement on inerrancy goes to great lengths to deny this charge: so detailed were the statements that, strangely, McGowan criticized it for being so careful to define its meaning this precisely. Article 13 declares:

> We further deny that inerrancy is negated by Biblical phenomena such as a lack of modern technical precision, irregularities of grammar or spelling, observational descriptions of nature, the reporting of falsehoods, the use of hyperbole and round numbers, the topical arrangement of material, variant selections of material in parallel accounts, or the use of free citations.

Article 18 adds, "We affirm that the text of Scripture is to be interpreted by grammatical-historical exegesis; taking account of its literary forms and devices, and that Scripture is to interpret Scripture." Likewise, article 6 declares: "We affirm that the whole of Scripture and all its parts, down to the very words of the original, were given by divine inspiration. We deny that the inspiration of Scripture can rightly be affirmed of the *whole* without the parts, or of some parts but not the *whole*" (emphasis added). What is this but a holistic inspiration?

Third, McGowan also contends that God's revelation "can never become mere data to be processed by the theologian, rather than the means by which God confronts and communicates to us." But once again, whoever said that the Bible is "mere data" for us to process? The Word of God is not merely an object to be studied (*DS*, 73). It is also to be obeyed (James 1:22). The very ICBI statements (which McGowan rejects) states the contrary in the very first statement: "God, who is Himself Truth and speaks the truth only, has inspired Holy Scripture in order to reveal Himself to lost mankind through Jesus Christ. . . . Holy Scripture is God's witness to Himself" (no. 1, *Shorter Statement*). Article 3 declares: "We affirm that the written Word in its entirety is revelation given by God." How can one conclude from this, as McGowan does (117), that inerrantists believe the Bible is viewed merely as an object to be studied, rather than a revelation to be obeyed?

Fourth, it does not seem to concern McGowan that he admits to the logical fallacy of "circular reasoning" in his apologetic (*DS*, 32). This begs the question by saying in essence: "We know the Bible is the Word of God because the Bible (as the Word of God) tells us so." McGowan cites Bavinck with approval that "Holy Scripture is self-attested (*autopistos*) and therefore the final ground of faith. No deeper ground can be advanced. To the question 'Why do you believe Scripture?' The only answer is: 'Because it is the word of God.' But if the next question is 'Why do you believe that Holy Scripture is the word of God?' a Christian cannot answer" (31). Even Van Til, whom McGowan cites favorably (37), could offer a transcendental argument in response, namely, because nothing else in the world makes sense apart from positing that the Triune God is revealed in canonical Scripture. However, one can be sure that neither McGowan nor any other fideist would accept this reasoning when a Muslim says, "Why should we believe the Qur'an is the Word of God? The only answer is: Because the Qur'an says it is the Word of God." I am sure McGowan would want some good evidence and reasons before he accepted the Qur'an as the Word of God, regardless of what the Qur'an says about itself.

As for the claim that in such an answer "we are setting these things as a higher authority than the voice of God speaking in Scripture," we point out that besides confusing epistemology and ontology, he is overlooking the fact that the Bible itself commands us to use "reason" (1 Pet. 3:15) and evidence (Acts 1:3) to test truth claims. Moses gave tests for a false prophet (Deut. 13 and 18). John exhorted us to "test the spirits to see whether they are from God" (1 John 4:1), and Paul "reasoned" (Acts 17:2, 17) with Jews and Greeks to demonstrate that Jesus was the Messiah. Indeed, Jesus himself used reason and evidence to substantiate his claims to be God.[9] As Augustine says, "Who cannot see that thinking is prior to believing? For no one believes anything unless he has first thought that it is to be believed."[10]

Fifth, McGowan is also guilty of taking a text out of its context. He does this with a statement made by B. B. Warfield, the great Princetonian defender of inerrancy. Warfield is careful to stress the humanity of Scripture as well as its divine origin. In so defending the humanity of the biblical authors, Warfield and A. A. Hodge state that the authors of Scripture were dependent on human languages, which "bear everywhere indelible traces of error," and on human "sources and methods in themselves fallible" and personal knowledge that was "defective, or even wrong" (*DS*, 211). But using this to support McGowan's errant view of inerrancy is totally unjustified for two reasons. First, it omits the crucial point: God in his providence overrules these human weaknesses and produces an inerrant product through their human pens. To repeat, this only proves the point that God can draw a straight line with a crooked stick. Second, even in this quote McGowan overlooks the fact that Warfield is not saying that these human sources always err. Indeed, he qualifies it by the phrases "in large measure" and "in many matters." Finally, Hodge and Warfield (*Inspiration*) clearly say that they are referring to these human sources "in themselves," not as superintended by a God who cannot err.

Sixth, McGowan sometimes throws the baby out with the bathwater. For example, he lumps "propositional" revelation with the alleged necessity of "scientific precision" and rejects them both together. Thus propositional truth gets thrown out along with modern "scientific accuracy." But most inerrantists, indeed all who signed the ICBI or ETS statements as defined by ICBI, do not believe that one has to believe in "scientific accuracy" in order to believe in propositional revelation (*DS*, 117). This same unnecessary lumping occurs with "inerrancy" and "fundamentalism" (103, 123) as well as with "inerrancy" and "literalism." This association is made, in spite of the fact that inerrancy proponents explicitly deny such implications (see above).

Answering Other Objections to Inerrancy Raised by McGowan

McGowan raises many other objections to inerrancy (see also chap. 17 below). Several call for a brief response since they are held by many as significant obstacles to belief in inerrancy.

Death of Inerrancy by a Thousand Qualifications

Strangely enough, McGowan criticizes the ICBI and ETS inerrantists for stipulating so many qualifications to their view. This is odd in view of the fact that the noninerrantist holds the opposite on all these points, and yet they are not criticized for all their qualifications. Further, McGowan actually commends the ICBI statement for making things clearer by having "denials" as well as "affirmations." But these additional negative qualifications make the doctrine even clearer.

Basically, inerrancy does not die a death by "a thousand" qualifications for two reasons. First of all, the so-called qualifications do not kill it but enhance it and thus keep it alive. In short, they do not negate all meaning in the original claim; they clarify it by negating things from it that do not belong to it.

Second, there are not "a thousand" qualifications; there really are only two basic ones: (1) Only the original text is inerrant. (2) Only what is affirmed as true in the text is true, and not anything else. The rest of the so-called "qualifications" are not really qualifications by inerrantists but misunderstandings by noninerrantists. Hence, the rewording is necessary only because opponents have misunderstood or mischaracterized the doctrine. This calls for a denial by inerrantists that helps one to understand what was implied in the original affirmation that everything affirmed as true in the text, is true (and everything affirmed as false is false). Just as the early creeds had to grow in order to explain what they meant in earlier more simple forms because later heretics misunderstood, distorted, or challenged it, even so later inerrantists have had to add more "qualifications" to explicate the original meaning as opposed to the heretical challenges of their day.

For instance, it should have been sufficient to simply say: (1) The Bible is the Word of God, but because some have denied the obvious, it is necessary to add that (2) the Bible is the *inspired* Word of God. However, when some use inspired in a human sense, it is necessary to say that (3) the Bible is the *divinely* inspired Word of God. But since some deny such a book is infallibly true, it is necessary to add that (4) the Bible is the divinely inspired, *infallible* Word of God. Likewise, when some claim it is only infallible in intent but not in fact, then it is necessary to clarify that it means (5) the Bible is the divinely inspired, infallible, and *inerrant* Word of God. Even here some have argued that it is only inerrant in redemptive matters, hence it is necessary to add that (6) the Bible is the divinely inspired, infallible, and inerrant Word of God *in all that it affirms on any topic*. And so on. There is no apparent end to this process. Why? Because when someone denies the obvious, it is necessary to affirm the redundant. It is not the inerrantists' fault that they seem to be adding when they are simply explicating what the original statement meant. So the inerrantists cannot be blamed for the alleged "qualifications" (really, further clarifications of the original meaning in the light of later denials). It is the opponents of inerrancy who should be blamed for denying the obvious. If (1) "The Bible is the Word of God," then of course it is divinely inspired, infallible, inerrant, and so forth. But if one denies the obvious, then inerrantists must affirm the redundant to make our view clear.

No Mention of Inspiration and Inerrancy in the Early Creeds

In response to this charge, it is crucial to remember that the belief in a divinely authoritative Bible is everywhere presupposed by the creeds. Almost the entire Apostles' Creed (2nd cent.) is made up of phrases that are dependent on the Bible. Likewise, the Nicene Creed (325) uses many of the same phrases and explicitly states that these truths were "spoken through the prophets." The Chalcedonian Creed (451) uses many of the same phrases from the previous creeds and adds explicitly that "we have the prophets of old" (in the Old Testament) and what "the

Lord Jesus Christ himself taught" through the apostolic writings in the New Testament. The divinely authoritative basis for the teaching of the Christian church is evident both implicitly and explicitly in the earliest general creeds of the church.

Second, there was little need to mention the Bible more explicitly since it was not seriously challenged. The creeds grew out of needs. The needs of the day were centered more on the deity and humanity of Christ, the Trinity, and the resurrection. Hence, they were highlighted. Creeds grew out of controversy, and there was no serious controversy in the early church on the divine origin of Scripture.

Third, it is well established that the view of the early fathers was strongly in favor of inerrancy. Noted authority on the early fathers, J. N. D. Kelly, characterized the view of the early fathers when speaking of Tertullian's view that "Scripture has absolute authority; whatever it teaches is necessarily true, and woe betide him who accepts doctrines not discoverable in it."[11] Augustine summed up the early fathers well in declaring: "If we are perplexed by any apparent contradiction in Scripture, it is not allowable to say, The author of this book is mistaken; but either [1] the manuscript is faulty, or [2] the translation is wrong, or [3] you have not understood."[12] What is this but an affirmation of the inerrancy of the original text of the Bible?

Why Did God Not Preserve the Autographs?

McGowan asks: "If textual inerrancy is so vital to the doctrine of Scripture, why did God not preserve the autographs of precise copies of the same?" (DS, 109). He adds, "What was the point of God acting supernaturally to provide an inerrant text providentially if it ceased to be inerrant as soon as the first or second copy was made?" (109).

In response, evangelical scholars have long pointed out several things that McGowan nowhere addresses at any length or refutes. First, there are important reasons to have a perfect autograph, the foremost of which is that the God of absolute truth cannot utter error (see above). For "It is impossible for God to lie" (Heb. 6:18). The "Spirit of truth" (John 16:13) cannot utter untruths.

Second, since God did not breathe out the copies, it is possible for them to err. However, God has providentially preserved them as a whole from any substantial error. In short, we have good copies of the original autographs. Noted scholars have substantiated this. Professor Frederic Kenyon stated,

> The interval between the dates of original composition and the earliest extant evidence becomes so small as to be in fact negligible, and the last foundation for any doubt that the Scriptures have come down substantially as they were written has now been removed. Both the authenticity and the general integrity of the books of the New Testament may be regarded as finally established.[13]

The great Greek scholar A. T. Robinson explained that "the real concern is with a thousandth part of the entire text."[14] That would make it 99.9 percent free of significant variants. Others have observed that these minor variants do not affect an essential teaching of the Christian church. Even agnostic Bible critic Bart Ehrman (see chap. 5 above) admits: "In fact, most of the changes found in early Christian manuscripts have nothing to do with theology or ideology. Far and away the most changes are the result of mistakes, pure and simple slips of the pen, accidental omissions, inadvertent additions, misspelled words, blunders of one sort or another."[15] So, we securely have 99+ percent of the text and 100 percent of the essential truths of the Christian faith. Hence, we do not need to possess the autographs.

Third, there may be good reasons why God did not preserve the autographs. Knowing the human tendency to worship relics, imagine what would happen to the original Bible breathed out by God! Look what years later happened to the brazen serpent in the wilderness (2 Kings 18:4). Further, knowing the human tendency to distort truth and corrupt doctrine with an alleged divine authority, think of what could happen to the autographs if they fell into the wrong hands. But with the autographs preserved in some 5,700 manuscripts that are spread all over the world, there is no humanly possible way that any essential truth of the Christian faith could be distorted in all these copies.

If Imperfect Copies Are Adequate, Why Not Imperfect Originals?

Perhaps an illustration will help answer this question. It is not difficult to understand the biblical story of God's making a perfect Adam, then allowing him to fall and reproduce other imperfect copies of the original Adam. Now all these copies (descendants) of Adam are 100 percent human and imperfect as we all are. So essential humanity has been preserved even through generations of imperfect copies. Likewise, with Scripture it was essential to have an original that was perfect since a perfect God cannot make an imperfect original. For example, it is inconceivable that a perfect God could have made the first man with a deformed body with cancer growths already on it. But it is not inconceivable that he would make a perfect original man, endow him with free choice, allow him to sin and bring imperfections to his posterity while God, nonetheless, preserves his essential human nature in his posterity. It is for this same reason that God produced a perfect original Bible and yet preserved the copies from all major errors, so as to protect all the essential truths for posterity.

In short, an adequate but imperfect original is not possible for a perfect God to make. There are many things that God cannot do, even with his sovereignty. He cannot change (Mal. 3:6; James 1:13, 17). "He cannot deny himself" (2 Tim. 2:13). He cannot cease being God (Heb. 1:10–12). He cannot break an unconditional promise (Rom. 11:29). He cannot lie (Heb. 6:17–18). And as an absolutely perfect God, he cannot produce an imperfect product either in the realm of truth or morals—because it is contrary to his very nature to do so.

Calling arguments like this "a priori" (DS, 111) or purely "deductive" (136) does not make them invalid or false. They are based on the very revealed nature of God in Scripture, and there is nothing wrong with making logical deductions from biblical truths. The Trinity is such a deduction since nowhere does the Bible explicitly teach in any text that there is one God in essence who is three persons. Rather, it teaches: (1) There is only one God, and (2) there are three persons who are God (i.e., who share this one nature). The doctrine of the Trinity is a necessary logical inference from these two clearly biblical premises. Inerrancy fits into this same category. There are two premises clearly taught in Scripture: (1) God cannot err. (2) The original Bible is the Word of God. The necessary logical conclusion to draw from this is clear: (3) The original Bible cannot err.

Arguing from Alleged Errors and Contradictions in Scripture

McGowan believes that there could be errors in the autographs. He says, "If God is able to use the errant copies ... that we do have, ... why invest so much theological capital in hypothetical originals that we do not have?" (*DS*, 113). He adds, "The autographs (if we could view them) might very well look just like our existing manuscripts, including all the difficulties, synoptic issues, discrepancies and apparent contradictions" (119).

Elsewhere McGowan concludes with Bavinck that "the guidance of the Holy Spirit promised to the church does not exclude the possibility of human error" (*DS*, 158). He seems to be fearful of saying there are "actual contradictions and errors," but it follows from the very logic of his comparison. For the copies have actual errors and contradictions, and God uses them for his purposes. Further, since McGowan claims that the copies are inspired (159), he is faced with the contradictory belief in God-breathed errors anyway. Again, he says that he "reject[s] the implication that thereby the autographs must be inerrant" (124). That certainly means that they can be errant. Again, there is not a "third way." Either the original can have errors, or else they cannot have errors. The undeniable law of noncontradiction demands this conclusion

Before concluding, it will be instructive to examine McGowan's example of an alleged error in the Bible, which he gets from I. Howard Marshall (*DS*, 112). He calls it "*a very good example*" of an error in the biblical text. McGowan alleges that Jairus told Jesus in Matthew 9:18 that his daughter was dead. But in Mark and Luke, Jairus told Jesus she was "at the point of death" (Mark 5:23) but not dead. Luke said she was "dying" but not yet dead (Luke 8:42). McGowan hastily concludes that "there is a *clear contradiction* between the initial words of Jairus as recorded by Matthew and the other Evangelists" (113, emphasis added).

However, there is in actuality no contradiction between anything Jairus is recorded to have said. This apparent discrepancy can be explained by the fact "while he [Jairus] was still speaking, someone from the ruler's house came and said, 'Your daughter is dead'" (Luke 8:49). Matthew did not mention that detail, but included the report of the girl's death in Jairus's request.[16] The fact is that Matthew did not say Jairus said anything that in fact he did not say. He merely combines the two parts of the conversation, thus stressing the point that the girl actually died by that time.[17] Having analyzed some eight hundred alleged contradictions in Scripture in

The Big Book of Bible Difficulties, we have concluded, after a half century of study, that the Bible is without error but the critics are not.

Conclusion

McGowan offers many positive insights into the nature of Scripture that are worth pondering. However, in trying to offer a "middle way" between inerrantist and errantist, he falls into serious errors. For one, he adopts a radical voluntaristic view of God, who is able to utter error in the original manuscripts. This is combined with an unbiblical view of divine accommodation to error, rather than divine adaptation to finitude without error (see chap. 16 below). This is connected with his rejection of an "incarnational" model of inerrancy—a rejection that, if applied consistently to Christ, would lead to the conclusion that even the human words and actions of Christ would not be without sin and error.

As for his offer that Americans forsake their long-standing commitment to inerrancy for the weaker European noninerrancy view, we remind him of the decline of a vital European church based on the noninerrancy view and the greater vitality of the American church based on the inerrancy view. Likewise, where is there a vital group of thousands of scholars (like the ETS) based on the inerrancy of the Bible in Britain or in Europe? In brief, McGowan's proposal to reject the term (and concept) of inerrancy should be graciously but firmly rejected because of its unbiblical, unreasonable, and unorthodox implications. In spite of the above-stated positive aspects of his view, his central theses may seem more broad and attractive (neither of which is a test for truth), but in the end it is a dangerous deviation from the orthodox view of inerrancy taught in the Bible, affirmed by the church down through the centuries, demanded by orthodox theology from time immemorial—which has provided a fruitful basis for a vital Christian church. Hence, rather than tempt one to give up either the concept or term of "inerrancy" to describe God-breathed Scripture, McGowan's gives us more reason to hold on to them.

Sources

Augustine, *On the Predestination of the Saints*

———, *Reply to Faustus*

Ehrman, *Misquoting Jesus*

Geisler, *Baker Encyclopedia*

———, *Systematic Theology*

Geisler and Zuckeran, *Apologetics of Jesus*

Kelly, *Early Christian Doctrine*

Kenyon, *Bible and Archaeology*

McGowan, *Divine Spiration*

Rice, *God-Breathed Book*

Robertson, *Textual Criticism*

Sproul, *Explaining Inerrancy*

Walvoord and Zuck, eds., *Bible Knowledge Commentary*, vol. 2

10

Stanley Grenz and Brian McLaren on Inerrancy

Introduction

The postmodern influence on the evangelical church is highlighted in the emergent church movement. In many ways Stanley Grenz is the grandfather of this movement, and the father is Brian McLaren. So this chapter will concentrate on their view of the origin and nature of Scripture. A few of their followers will be mentioned by way of illustration. First we will briefly state some positive dimensions of their views.

Some Positive Contributions of Postmodern Thought

Like other views, there are many commendable features of postmodern thought. First of all, Grenz, McLaren, and other such church leaders desire to be relevant to the postmodern world in which we live. In line with this is their acknowledgment of the finitude of our understanding of God and of his revelation to us.

Thus, there is understandably a perspectivity to our knowledge. Their pointing out of how the interpreter of Scripture often colors the message in its own subjectivity and colors it with its own tones is well taken. Then, too, the postmodern stress on the need to ground our view of Scripture in a thorough induction of the Bible and take a bottom-up approach is commendable procedure.

Likewise, Grenz and McLaren point to the fact that there is much more than propositional truth in the Bible. There is the power of stories in conveying God's thoughts to us. The Bible contains more than mere descriptive truth. It also has powerful evocative force. In like manner, God desires to transform persons, not just fill our minds with abstract truth. God is surely interested in the concrete application of truths to our lives. Then, too, there is the social dimension and implications of the gospel. God is not interested only in transforming lives but also in transforming society. In short, postmoderns remind those who want to remain "anchored to the rock" that they cannot afford to neglect being "geared to the times."

Postmoderns also rightly remind us that the Bible is not a scientific textbook. Hence, we need not fear that the latest scientific research will upset our true biblical beliefs (Grenz, *Revisioning Evangelical Theology* [*RET*], 116). They also rightly remind us that foundationalism as rooted in Cartesian (and Spinozistic)[1] deductivism is wrongheaded and should not be adopted by evangelicals in their approach to Scripture.

Some Negative Factors in Postmodern Views of Scripture

Generally speaking, postmoderns desire to be creedless. But one cannot avoid doctrine, if only for the reason that this itself is a doctrinal claim. Further, one need only survey their writings to find a multitude of doctrinal claims, albeit not always orthodox ones. Their doctrine of Scripture is no exception.

Stanley Grenz on Scripture

Professor Gordon Lewis of Denver Seminary once told me (Norm) that the Evangelical Theological Society would have done itself a great service by focusing on Professor Grenz's deviant view of Scripture and not just that of Clark Pinnock (see chap. 4). As it turned out, Pinnock slipped through their net, and Grenz slipped off into eternity. Nonetheless, Grenz's view is still alive and is the best effort to provide philosophical underpinning to the emergent church doctrine of Scripture, and thereby it is one of the best ways to understand the foundation of the emergent church movement.

Rejecting the Classical Orthodox View of Scripture

Grenz summarizes quite well the classical view that he rejects: "Evangelical theologians begin with the affirmation that God has revealed himself. This self-disclosure has come through general revelation and more completely in special revelation." Further, "The Holy Spirit preserved some of this special revelation by inspiring biblical writers to inscripturate it. The Bible, therefore, is God's Word. Because the Bible is the inspired Word of God, it is dependable, even inerrant" (*RET*, 116). "Our listening to God's voice [in Scripture] does not need to be threatened by scientific research into Holy Scripture" (116). "The Bible is revelation because it is the [errant] witness to and the [errant] record of the historical revelation of God" (133).

Unfortunately, Grenz rejects the classical approach to inerrancy, claiming, "The construction of bibliology in this manner, 'from above,' as it were, has certain shortcomings" (*RET*, 116). He adds, "We can no longer construct our doctrine of Scripture in the classical manner" (118).

Rejecting Classical Orthodoxy

The postmodern rejection of the classical orthodox view of Scripture is sweeping. It includes a rejection of the correspondence view of truth, a rejection of objective truth, absolute truth, propositional truth, and the inerrant truth in Scripture. This it does in favor of antifoundationalism, relativism, subjectivism, constructionism, nonpropositionalism, Barthianism, and fallibilism. Few views are a more sweeping rejection of the orthodox view of unlimited inerrancy as expressed by the Evangelical Theological Society (ETS) and the International Council on Biblical Inerrancy (ICBI).

Antifoundationalism

Grenz approaches the Bible out of a postmodern antifoundationalist perspective. Like others, however, he wrongly sees all foundationalism as rooted in Cartesian (and Spinozistic) deductivism, which attempts to deduce absolute truth from self-evident principles. However, he ignores a legitimate foundational reductivism, which grounds all truth in irreducible and self-evident first principles like the basic laws of thought.[2]

Along with this, Grenz rejects the traditional rational apologetics based on God's general revelation that Augustine, Anselm, Aquinas, Calvin, and modern followers held.[3] He chides "twentieth-century evangelicals [who] have devoted much energy to the task of demonstrating the credibility of the Christian faith" (*Primer on Postmodernism* [*PP*], 160). But without a rational and evidential apologetic, one is left swimming in the sea of subjectivism.

Grenz contends, "We are in fundamental agreement with the postmodern rejection of the modern mind and its underlying Enlightenment epistemology" (*PP*, 165). While there are sufficient reasons to disagree with some aspects of "enlightenment epistemology," classical foundationalism and a rational apologetic are not among them. Nor is a basic trust in the reliability of sense knowledge about an objectively real world. Therefore, "we ought to commend the postmodern questioning of the Enlightenment assumption that knowledge is objective and hence dispassionate" (*PP*, 166).

However, Grenz threw out the baby of proper foundationalism, which is at the base of the historic evangelical view of Scripture, with the bathwater of rationalistic deductive foundationalism.[4] However, antifoundationalism leads to relativism and subjectivism, which Grenz renames as "post-rationalistic" (*PP*, 167). He does not explain how one justifies using reason to denounce reason per se.

Relativism

Once the foundation for absolute truth is destroyed, relativism and subjectivism follow. Grenz is a victim of this logic. He expresses this relativism as follows: "The Bible is seen, then, not as a finished and static fact or collection of facts to be analyzed by increasingly sophisticated methods, but as a potentiality of meaning which is actualized by succeeding generations in the light of their need" (*RET*, 120). This he sees as the proper understanding of 2 Timothy 3:16–17, which Grenz misinterprets as meaning that God breathed *into* Scripture as he did breathe *into* Adam. In fact, *theopneustos* ("inspired") means to *breathe out*, not to breathe in. Just as Jesus said, every word of Scripture comes "*out of* the mouth of God" (Matt. 4:4 KJV, emphasis added).

Grenz also falls into the self-defeating trap of disclaiming the possibility of objective knowledge of the world or the past. He contends that "we ought to commend the postmodern questioning of the Enlightenment assumption that knowledge is objective and hence dispassionate" (*PP*, 166). He adds, "We affirm the postmodern discovery that no observer can stand outside the historical process. Nor can we gain universal, culturally neutral knowledge as unconditioned specialists" (166). Grenz seems blissfully unaware of his self-defeating claim to have objective knowledge of this allegedly subjective condition.

Postmodern Subjectivism

The next of kin to relativism is subjectivism. Grenz couches his subjectivism in warm-sounding words like "community" and "the voice of the Spirit" in communal illumination. He writes: "We can more readily see the Bible—the instrumentality of the Spirit—as the book of the community" (*RET*, 115). He criticizes classical orthodox Christians who "often collapse the Spirit into the Bible." They "exchange the dynamic of the ongoing movement of the Spirit speaking to the community of God's people through the pages of the Bible for the book we hold in our hands" (117).

Grenz's self-labeled "functional" approach "starts with the role of Scripture within the Christian communities and then draws conclusions from the Bible's normative value" (*RET*, 119). He even reinvents the Trinity in terms of his communal model, declaring that "God is the social trinity—Father, Son, and Spirit" (*PP*, 168). But God is far more than a society of persons. There is only one God, and he has only one *essence*. God is essentially one, not just functionally one as a human community is.

In his communal subjectivity, Grenz also confuses the inspiration of the objective text of Scripture with the subjective illumination of believers in understanding the objective Word. Indeed, he says, "The confession of the inspiration of the Bible is closely intertwined with the experience of illumination" (*RET*, 118).

Likewise, Grenz's rejection of general revelation and reason because of the noetic effects of sin contributes to his subjectivism. He misunderstands Pascal's famous statement about the heart having reasons that reason does not know in a fideistic manner, contrary to Pascal's own use of evidence to support the Christian faith.[5] While Grenz notes that "following the intellect can sometimes lead us away from the truth" (*PP*, 166) he seems oblivious to the fact that following experience can be even worse. After all, the fall affects the whole person. Further, sin may efface the image of God but does not erase it (see Gen. 9:6; James 3:9). And the misuse of reason does not mean there is no proper use of reason.

Deconstructionism

Grenz speaks of the postmodern move from realism, which claims: (1) there is an objective world and (2) it can be known, to constructionism, which denies both. This, he says, leads to rejecting a correspondence view of truth that statements are true if they correspond to reality (see chap. 13 below). Of course, if there is no knowable objective reality to which our thoughts can correspond, then the correspondence view of truth must be rejected. But in this case one must construct one's own truth since there is no objective standard by which one can measure the truth of his statements. One is left swimming in a sea of subjectivism, lost in the subjectivity of one's community. And there is no way to adjudicate between conflicting truth claims of different Christian communities, to say nothing of those of other religions. Grenz and Franke make their position clear in their book *Beyond Foundationalism*.

While Grenz does not wish to totally give up belief in all objective reality (*Renewing the Center* [*RC*], 245–46), nonetheless, he does reject the knowability of a present world by the senses and reason (99–100). Without any serious analysis or argumentation (230–31), Grenz rejects a realistic model and opts for a postmodern reconstruction that focuses on an "eschatological realism" of the world to come. He writes, "The only ultimately valid 'objectivity of the world' is that of a *future*, eschatological world, and the 'actual' universe is the universe as it one day will be" (246). Thus our task is that of deconstructing the traditional view and "constructing a world in the present that reflects God's own eschatological will for creation." In a Wittgensteinian fashion (see chap. 14 below), Grenz opines that "because of the role of language in the world-construction task, this mandate has a strongly linguistic dimension. We participate with God as, through the constructive power of language, we inhabit a present linguistic world that sees all reality from the perspective of the future, real world that God is bringing to pass" (246). Grenz offers no answer to the criticism that affirming the unknowability of present reality is something that he claims to know about present reality.

Nonpropositionalism

Grenz also rejects the traditional orthodox view of propositional revelation. "Our understanding of the Christian faith must not remain fixated on the propositional approach that views Christian truth as nothing more than correct doctrine or doctrinal truth" (*Primer on Postmodernism* [*PPM*], 170). In place of this, he favors what he calls a more "dynamic" view. He rejects the venerable creedal and confessional view that we can make propositionally true statements about God. He insists that "our understanding of the faith must not remain fixated on the propositional approach that views Christian truth as nothing more than correct doctrine of doctrinal truth" (*PP*, 170). One wonders whether Grenz realizes the propositional nature of his doctrinal claim in that statement.

Elsewhere Grenz admits that "right beliefs and correct doctrine are vital to Christian living" (*PP*, 172). But how can we have these without a rationally knowable and propositionally satiable objective reality? Grenz's answer seems to lie in his subordination of the propositional to the experiential. He claims that "sound doctrine is a servant of the Spirit's work in the new birth and transformed life."[6] Doctrine is like a Wittgensteinian language "game" based in the changing experience of the community (*RC*, 246). But here again we are in the quagmire of subjectivism. For reason should be the judge of experience, not the reverse. As Alister McGrath recognized, experience is something that needs to be interpreted, rather than something that is capable of interpreting.[7]

Grenz also claims that "transformed in this manner into a book of doctrine, the Bible is easily robbed of its dynamic character" (*RET*, 114–15). He insists that "the inspiration of Scripture cannot function as the theological premise from which biblical authority emerges" (118). So, in place of the historic belief in the essential authority of the inspired text of Scripture, Grenz proposes a "functional approach [that] moves in a somewhat opposite direction from the canonical" approach (119).

Barthianism

Grenz's view is not essentially different from that of the neo-orthodox theologian Karl Barth. He seems to recognize the similarity of his view in posing this very question: "Is this not simply the older neo-orthodoxy dressed up in new garb?" (*RET*, 124). While he attempts a qualified "no" answer (125), the essence of his view of how revelation and the Bible are related does not differ significantly from that of Karl Barth. For he denies that the Bible is identified with God's revelation. Rather, like Barth, he holds that "the Bible is a divinely appointed channel, a mirror, or a visible sign of revelation."[8] The Bible is not God's words in and of themselves. Rather, "the human words of the Bible are God's Word *to us*" (130, emphasis added).

In support of his position, Grenz mistakenly argues that the Bible nowhere claims that it is the Word of God (*RET*, 131). This is clearly not the case as an examination of only a few texts will illustrate. In John 10:34–35, Jesus uses "word of God," "Scripture [*graphē*]," and "cannot be broken," all reinforcing each other. Second Timothy 3:15–16 does the same by saying that "all Scripture [*graphē*] is breathed out by God" and is identical with the "sacred writings [*hiera grammata*]" that Timothy knew from childhood, namely, the Old Testament. In Matthew 5:17–18 Jesus describes the Old Testament "Law" and "Prophets" as the imperishable

Word of God. Peter declares that the Old Testament prophetic writings come from their ultimate source in God, not by human invention (2 Pet. 1:20–21).

Fallibilism and Barthianism

Citing Berkouwer with approval, Grenz affirms that "our listening to God's voice [in Scripture] does not need to be threatened by scientific research into Holy Scripture" (*RET*, 110). For errors in the Bible are only part of the "scandal" it bears as a human instrument. The Bible is not the Word of God in and of itself but only "to us." Grenz writes, "The Bible is revelation in a functional sense; it is revelatory." Also, "Scriptures are revelation in a derivative sense" (133). Like Barth, the Bible is only a fallible record of or witness to God's revelation in Christ. "The Bible is revelation because it is the *witness* to and the *record* of the historical revelation of God" (133, emphasis added).

The historic view of unlimited inspiration holds that the Bible is without error on whatever topic it touches, science, history, or psychology. Grenz demurs, insisting that "the Bible therefore may not be the kind of authority on the various branches of modern learning that many believers want to maintain" (*RET*, 135). Rather, it is an authority only on matters of salvation.

Brian McLaren on the Inspiration of Scripture

If Grenz is the grandfather of the emergent church movement, then Brian McLaren is the father of it. Al Mohler called McLaren the emerging church's "most influential thinker." *Christianity Today* labeled him the "de facto spiritual leader for the emerging church." Indeed, they gave him the Award of Merit in 2002 for his book *A New Kind of Christian* (*NKC*).

Like other avant-garde Christians, there are many things to admire in his works. They are fresh, original, and relevant. McLaren is the archenemy of traditionalism, legalism, and fundamentalism. He wishes to bring evangelicalism into the twenty-first century. He even claims to have a high view of Scripture. In his book *A Generous Orthodoxy* [*GO*], he says, "I have spent my entire life learning, understanding, reappraising, wrestling with, trusting, applying, and obeying the Bible, and trying to help others to do the same. I believe it is a gift from God, inspired by God, to benefit us in the most important way possible: equipping us so that we can benefit others, so that we can play our part in the ongoing mission of God. *My regard for the Bible is higher than ever*" (original emphasis).

However, as good as this may sound, it is ambiguous at best. For McLaren declared elsewhere: "But for me, . . . opposing it [postmodernism] is as futile as opposing the English language. It's here. It's reality. It's the future. . . . It's the way my generation processes every other fact on the event horizon" (McLaren, *Church on the Other Side* [*COS*], 70). "Why is it so important? Because when your view of truth is changed, when your confidence in the human ability to know truth in any objective way is revolutionized, then everything changes. That includes theology" (69).

Evaluating McLaren by His Friends

Evaluating him by the authors he likes, McLaren has radical leanings. He expresses his liking for scholars of the Jesus Seminar, one of whom told *Time* magazine that after the crucifixion "Jesus' corpse went the way of all abandoned criminals' bodies: it was probably barely covered with dirt, vulnerable to the wild dogs that roamed the wasteland of the execution grounds" (John Crossan). He endorses Steve Chalke's book *The Lost Message of Jesus*, in which Chalke equates the doctrine of substitutionary atonement—the doctrine that "Christ died for our sins," which is the essence of the gospel as defined in 1 Corinthians 15:3—to "a form of cosmic child abuse" (182). Likewise, McLaren placed his approval on Alan Jones's work, who said Jesus should be "reimagined" because his atonement is a "vile doctrine." Why? "Because of the cult of suffering and the vindictive God behind it" (*Reimagining Christianity*, 132). McLaren places his approval on Spencer Burke, who argues that hell does not exist, saying, "The God I connect with does not assign humans to hell" (*Heretic's Guide to Eternity*, 199). Burke adds, "What's more, I'm not sure I believe in God exclusively as a person anymore either. . . . I now incorporate a panentheist view" (195). McLaren declares: "The old show is over, the modern jig is up, and it's time for something radically new. . . . Either Christianity itself is flawed, failing, [and] untrue, or our modern, Western, commercialized, industrial-strength version of it is in need of a fresh look, a serious revision" (*New Kind of Christian*, xxi). As we shall see, this applies to his view of Scripture as well.

The Nature of Inspiration

McLaren gives the following explanation of "What the Bible Really Is":

> The Bible is an inspired gift from God—a unique collection of literary artifacts that together support the telling of an amazing and essential story. The artifacts include poetry, letters, short histories, and other genres that we don't have labels for. Even a familiar category like history needs to be used carefully, because we must avoid imposing modern biases and tastes on these ancient documents: they need to be taken and appreciated on their own terms. The stories these artifacts support cover the amazing career of the descendants of a Middle Eastern nomad named Abraham. It traces their beginnings, growth, settlement, and resettlement through various social structures and economies, through many political arrangements, through good times and bad. This collection is uniquely profitable for teaching, rebuking, correcting, training, and equipping people so they can do good works for God.[9]

It is very difficult to find definitive statements of what he means by the term "inspiration." Those who try to critique his doctrines are vilified as "modern" and "polarizing." But the truth of the matter is that his view is postmodern and polarizing. He does say he no longer believes the "Bible is absolutely equivalent to the phrase 'the Word of God.' . . . Although I do find the term inerrancy useful, . . . I would prefer to use the term inherency to describe my view of Scripture" (McLaren, *The Last Word*, 111). By "inherency" he seems to imply that the Bible merely contains the "Word of God" but is not actually the Word of God itself. In one text he seems to be uncomfortable in even claiming the Bible as authoritative. He writes, "I'm only saying what the Bible says. That oft-quoted passage in 2 Timothy doesn't say, 'all Scripture is inspired by God and *is authoritative*.' It says that Scripture is inspired and useful—useful to teach, rebuke, correct, instruct us to live justly, and equip us for our mission as the people of God" (74).

McLaren sets forth his view of inspiration by the use of an analogy. He says, "I am a human being with a name (plus an assortment of numbers that certify me as a citizen, driver, credit-card holder, phone owner, etc.). Like every other human, I am both a creation of God and a pro-creation of parents who, in partnership with friends and teachers and authors and culture in general, helped make me all I am today." Thus, "The way God willed to create the 'me' I am today, then, like every other human, is through a complex synergy of biology and community and history (plus my own will, choices, and the like)." However, "These parental origins, these organic means, these social and historical contexts, do not decrease in any way the reality of God as my ultimate Creator, the One who through all these many instrumentalities says, 'Let there be a Brian,' and here I am" (*GO*, 161–62).

McLaren believes that "in the same way Scripture is something God has 'let be,' and so it is at once God's creation and the creation of the dozens of people and communities and cultures who produced it. One doesn't decrease the other. One doesn't lessen the other. One doesn't nullify the other" (*GO*, 162).

The notion that the Scripture is God-breathed is not simply the notion that God has "let be" the Scripture similar to the way God "let be" Brian McLaren. The orthodox doctrine is that the very words that compose the Scriptures are the very words that God chose for his revelation (see chap. 14 below). The biblical metaphor—God-breathed—is designed to indicate that God spoke these very words: they were breathed out by God. Parenthetically, it is interesting how McLaren skews the facts to fit the point he wishes to make. In an earlier chapter he criticizes the conservatives for their conflicting and fallible interpretations (*GO*, 162), but in this context he applauds the "Christian community" of "Catholic, Protestant, and Orthodox" Christians for *always* having a "deep feeling and understanding for this integrated dual origin [human and divine] of the Scripture" and for holding on to "both dimensions of the origin of Scripture" (162). This certainly does not sound like a group of "shrill, quarreling voices" who "constantly labeled the interpretations of the fellow Protestants grossly errant" (134).

Rejection of Absolute Truth and Certainty

"Arguments that pit absolutism versus relativism, and objectivism versus subjectivism, prove meaningless or absurd to postmodern people."[10] Elsewhere McLaren adds, "Drop any affair you may have with certainty, proof, argument—and replace it with dialogue, conversation, intrigue, and search" (McLaren and Campolo, *Adventures*, 78). Since we cannot know anything for sure, this gives room for faith. McLaren writes: "Because knowledge is a luxury beyond our means, faith is the best we can hope for. What an opportunity! Faith hasn't encountered openness like this in several hundred years" (*COS*, 173). He says, "If you believe that you absolutely, objectively know the absolute, objective truth, and you know this with absolute certainty, then of course you must debunk anyone who sees differently from you" (25). According to McLaren, "Certainty is overrated. . . . History teaches us that a lot of people thought they were certain and we found out they weren't."[11]

Rejecting Propositional Revelation

McLaren argues that a more effective communication pattern in the postmodern matrix is "the power of story" (*COS*, 90). There certainly is power in a story, especially when it is a true story. But that takes us right back to propositional truth. He "claims that in biblical times there were no modern trimmings like a concern for factual accuracy, corroborating evidence, or absolute objectivity" (80). In this he conveniently ignores texts like Luke 1:1–4, which claim to be objective history based on facts. Likewise, Acts 1:3 speaks of "many proofs" of the resurrection, which gives "assurance to all" (Acts 17:31), and 1 Corinthians 15:12–18 speak of the fact of the resurrection as being indispensible to the Christian faith.

McLaren is emphatic in his opposition to what he characterizes as modernism. He believes that modern Western Christians have actually misrepresented the nature of the Bible: "Because modern Christians loved the Bible, they paid it four compliments, which have damaged as well as enhanced the Bible's reputation" ("The Bible" [TB], 13).

One of the four "compliments" by which modern Christians have misrepresented the Bible is, according to McLaren, "*We presented the Bible as a repository of sacred propositions and abstractions*" (TB, 71). He gives the following as an explanation of what this means:

> Which was natural, for we were moderns—children of the 18th century European Enlightenment—so we loved abstractions and propositions. Our sermons tended to exegete texts in such a way that stories, poetry, and biography (among other features of the Bible)—the "chaff"—were sifted out, while the "wheat" of doctrines and principles were saved. Modern Western people loved that approach; meanwhile, however, people of a more postmodern bent (who are more like premodern people in many ways) find the doctrines and principles as interesting as grass clippings. (71)

That this "compliment" is perceived by McLaren to be a misrepresentation is not a misrepresentation. He says, "These misrepresentations were not malicious" (72), clearly stating that he perceives the notion that the Bible is a repository of propositions to be a misrepresentation.

Opposition to Reason and Certainty

This approach leads to the advice: "Drop any Affair You May Have with Certainty, Proof, Argument—and Replace It with Dialogue, Conversation, Intrigue, and Search" (TB, 78). McLaren apparently sees no inconsistency in his own clarion call against clarity. It would appear that God is not as capable in his Word as McLaren is. He advocates that Bible studies and sermons should not seek clarity because reality is, according to McLaren, "seldom clear, but usually fuzzy and mysterious; not black-and-white, but in living color" (78). The congregation should not aim to capture the meaning of the text but aim for "a text that captured the imagination and curiosity of the congregation" (78). Yet this surely is a false dichotomy. Nothing says that it cannot be both, clearly and accurately capturing the meaning while at the same time stimulating the imagination and curiosity of the congregation.

Not only is truth in general beyond our reach, but so is the truth of Scripture. For we cannot be certain of our interpretation of the Bible. "Well, I'm wondering, if you have an infallible text, but all your interpretations of it are admittedly fallible, then you at least have to always be open to being corrected about your interpretation, right? . . . So the authoritative text is never what I say about the text or even what I understand the text to say but rather what God means the text to say, right?" (NKC, 50). McLaren seems unaware of the self-defeating nature of this statement: "The authoritative text is never what I say about the text or even what I understand the text to say." In brief, he is claiming that he knows the text cannot mean what he knows the text to mean.

Open or Closed Canon?

As for the completeness of Scripture, McLaren seems to have an open-ended canon. He writes: "I can't see church history in any other way, except [that we are] continually being led and taught and guided by the Spirit into new truth" (GO, 193). This flies in the face of the historic Christian views, East and West, of a closed canon.

The ICBI framers said clearly, "We further deny that any normative revelation has been given since the completion of the New Testament writings" (art. 5 of the Chicago Statement).

Salvation Not the Big Story of the Bible

Contrary to the apostle Paul's claim in the classic text on inspiration that Scripture was God-breathed to "make [us] wise for salvation" (2 Tim. 3:15–17), McLaren believes that the "Big Question of the whole Bible" is not the salvation of individuals. He says:

Without focusing on the Big Story, we are tempted to impose alien readings on the Bible. For example, if we reduce the Bible to an elaborate answer to the question, "How does a person go to heaven after he dies?"—if we think this is the Big Question the whole Bible is answering—we'll be prone to misunderstand major parts of the Bible that were written before that question was on anybody's mind (like the entire Old Testament). The Old Testament people were far more concerned about being the people of God *in* this life, not *after* this life. . . . When they performed sacrifices, for instance, they weren't seeking to get a clean slate so they could die forgiven as individuals and go to heaven after they died. To the contrary, they were seeking to remain pure enough as a community to participate in God's twofold promise to them: being blessed by God, and being a blessing to the whole world. (TB, 78–79)

According to McLaren, Old Testament saints did not ask, "How does a person go to heaven after he dies?" He says that in the entire Old Testament, this question was not on anyone's mind. For McLaren, the focus of the Bible is not on salvation but on service—not getting right with God but doing good. But, how can a person be "blessed by God" or be a "blessing to the whole world" unless this means first and foremost that one gets right with God?

Denying Inerrancy

According to McLaren, "For modern Western Christians, words like *authority, inerrancy, infallibility, revelation, objective, absolute,* and *literal* are crucial" (*GO*, 164). He then declares: "Hardly anyone knows about the stories of Sir Isaac Newton, René Descartes, the Enlightenment, David Hume, and Foundationalism—which provide the context in which these words are so important" (164). "Incompleteness and error are part of the reality of human beings" (*COS*, 173). McLaren rejects the view that "the Bible is the ultimate authority, . . . [that] there are no contradictions in it, and [that] it is absolutely true and without errors in all it says. Give up these assertions, and you're on a slippery slope to losing your whole faith" (*GO*, 133–34).

Once again McLaren misrepresents the case. All of these terms, with the possible exception of the term "infallibility," have been used by authors throughout history at least from the time of Augustine. Augustine held to the concept of inerrancy even when it was necessary to resort to allegorical interpretation to avoid what he perceived to be a contradiction. None of these words were invented or found any substantively new connotations during the Enlightenment. Additionally, how does McLaren know what "hardly anyone" knows? And how can he be absolutely certain we should avoid absolutes?

McLaren also declares, "Hardly anyone notices the irony of resorting to the authority of extra-biblical words and concepts to justify one's belief in the Bible's ultimate authority" (*GO*, 164). In one sense, of course, all of the words that we use are nonbiblical since the Bible was not written in English. But he does not merely claim that the words are extrabiblical; instead, he claims that the *concepts* are extrabiblical.

McLaren proposes that it is more reasonable to include a statement like this: "The purpose of Scripture is to equip God's people for good works," than to use "statements with words foreign to the Bible's vocabulary about itself (inerrant, authoritative, literal, revelatory, objective, absolute, propositional, etc.)" (*GO*,

164–65). But not a single one of the words in the statement McLaren sets forth is in the Bible. Now someone will object, "Of course the Bible doesn't contain these English words! He's not saying the Bible must contain these exact English words. What he's saying is that it's more reasonable to use statements that contain the particular meanings, whether expressed in English or in the languages of the Bible that are actually found in the Bible."

If this is what McLaren is saying, then what's the problem? Every single one of the "meanings" of the words he lists as extrabiblical are also found in the Bible! The meaning of the term "authoritative" is found in Isaiah 46:9–10: "For I am God, and there is no other; I am God, and there is none like me, declaring the end from the beginning and from ancient times things not yet done, saying, 'My counsel shall stand, and I will accomplish all my purpose.'" Hebrews 6:18 says, "It is impossible for God to lie." If the Bible is the Word of God, then the concept of inerrancy is in the Bible. We cannot allow the import of what McLaren has said to escape us. He not only says that words like *authority, inerrancy, infallibility, revelation, objective, absolute,* and *literal* are extrabiblical. He also claims that the concepts are extrabiblical: "Hardly anyone notices the irony of resorting to the authority of extra-biblical words and *concepts* to justify one's belief in the Bible's ultimate authority." What he is saying here is that the concepts of authority, inerrancy, infallibility, revelation, objective, absolute, and literal are not concepts that we find in the Bible!

Other Related Issues

The title of this chapter of McLaren's book ought to be changed from "Why I Am Biblical," to "Why Would Anyone Think I Am Biblical?" McLaren presents his beliefs as if they are orthodox Christian beliefs, and he either purposely or inadvertently misrepresents the facts in almost every case, yet he presents these distortions as if they are generally accepted and in complete conformity with the teachings of the Bible.

McLaren's Emergent Followers

Grenz and McLaren are not alone in their denial of the infallibility and inerrancy of the Bible, along with its associated beliefs in propositional revelation, absolute truth, and objective meaning. A number of contemporary emergent leaders, like Rob Bell, have followed suit in denying inerrancy or other important truth.

Conclusion

Postmoderns in general deny an orthodox view of Scripture. The orthodox view of Scripture is rooted in numerous premises denied by postmoderns. They deny absolutism, objectivism, foundationalism, propositionalism, correspondence, and infallibilism—all of which a genuine evangelical view entails, even though these are not always consistently acknowledged or applied.

The Evangelical Theological Society (ETS), which is the largest group of evangelical scholars in the world, following the landmark Chicago Statement (1978) on inerrancy, has heralded this as the standard for understanding the inerrancy of the Bible (see chap. 2 above). Grenz and McLaren definitely fall seriously short of the standard on all major counts. The so-called emerging church is the diverging church since it diverts from orthodoxy on one of its fundamental pillars, the one on which all the others rest.

Scripture is the most foundational of all the fundamental doctrines, since it is the fundamental on which all the other fundamentals rest. And on its view of Scripture, Grenz and McLaren are not only postmodern but are also post-Christian. Their rejection of the classical orthodox view of Scripture is sweeping. It includes a rejection of the correspondence view of truth, a rejection of objective truth, absolute truth, propositional truth, and inerrant truth in Scripture. This is done in favor of antifoundationalism, relativism, subjectivism, constructionism, and Barthianism, nonpropositionalism, and fallibilism.

The so-called emergent church is not emerging; it has already emerged. And what it has emerged into is not Christian in any traditional, historic, or orthodox sense of the words. Indeed, it has emerged from orthodoxy to unorthodoxy, from infallibilism to fallibilism, from objectivism to subjectivism, from absolutism to relativism, and from realism to agnosticism. As Mark Driscoll aptly puts it, "The emergent church is the latest version of liberalism. The only difference is that the old liberalism accommodated modernity and the new liberalism accommodates postmodernity."[12]

DeYoung and Kluck summarize it well. They "have many good deeds. They want to be relevant. They want to reach out. They want to be authentic. They want to include the marginalized. They want to be kingdom disciples. They want community and life transformation." However,

> emergent Christians need to catch Jesus' broader vision for . . . a church that is intolerant of error, maintains moral boundaries, promotes doctrinal integrity, stands strong in times of trial, remains vibrant in times of prosperity, believes in certain judgment and certain reward, even as it engages the culture, reaches out, loves, and serves. We need a church that reflects the Master's vision—one that is deeply theological, deeply ethical, deeply compassionate, and deeply doxological.[13]

Sources

Carson, *Becoming Conversant*
DeYoung and Kluck, *Why We're Not Emergent*
Driscoll, *Confessions of a Reformission Rev.*
Geisler, *Systematic Theology*
Geisler and Howe, *When Critics Ask*
Geisler and Nix, *General Introduction to the Bible*
Grenz, "Nurturing the Soul"

———, *Primer on Postmodernism*
———, *Renewing the Center*
Howe, *Objectivity in Biblical Interpretation*
McLaren, *Generous Orthodoxy*
McLaren and Campolo, *Adventures*
Pascal, *Pensées*
Sproul, *Explaining Inerrancy*

11

Darrell Bock and Robert Webb
on Inerrancy

Introduction

Professors Bock and Webb were chosen here because they are members of a new group of evangelical scholars who believe that they can employ the best of contemporary criticism to aid in showing the authenticity of events in the Gospels, including the resurrection of Christ. Bock and Webb are the coeditors of *Key Events in the Life of the Historical Jesus* [KE], which culminates ten years of study by the Institute for Biblical Research (IBR) Jesus Group. All of the authors consider themselves to be "evangelical" or "orthodox" in their beliefs, and many of them belong to the Evangelical Theological Society (ETS), which demands that they annually sign a statement on inerrancy that declares: "The Bible alone and the Bible in its entirety is the Word of God written, and therefore inerrant in the autographs." Indeed, this society adopted the International Council on Biblical Inerrancy's Chicago Statement as a guide for the meaning of inerrancy (see chap. 2 above). This is relevant to our quest to determine whether the positions held by Bock and the IBR scholars is compatible with such a stand on the inerrancy of Scripture.

Our comments will be divided into two sections. First we will briefly note some commendable aspects of this endeavor. Then we will examine some difficulties and dangers attached to it as it relates to the traditional doctrine of total inerrancy held by the ETS and ICBI framers.

Some Commendations of the Bock-Webb IBR Effort

There are many things about the Bock-Webb endeavor that are commendable, if not noble. First, it is refreshing to see evangelical scholars who are schooled in the tools of the trade in biblical scholarship. Indeed, one cannot help but be pleased with the apologetic desires involved to demonstrate authenticity in the New Testament texts. Then, too, these men are confessedly "evangelical Christians" or "biblically orthodox Christians" (KE, 7). In some respects the IBR group could be called an evangelical response to the notorious Jesus Seminar, whose radical views have riddled the authenticity of the Gospel record. On this point, Bock and company should be commended for their desire to find the historical Jesus. Further, these biblical scholars are admittedly not antisupernatural. Indeed, they do not hesitate to confess belief in the kingpin miracle of Christianity—the resurrection of Christ. In the process of their scholarly efforts, they have unveiled a number of tests for authenticity that are real tools for Christian apologists in their efforts to defend the faith.

We also find it commendable that, unlike many other scholars in the postmodern world, the Bock-Webb volume has not given in to total relativity in their approach to biblical truth (KE, 22–23). Indeed, they chastise postmodern historians for absorbing the object of the historian (to know history) into one's own subjectivity (22–23). Thus they are not averse to making definitive historical statements, such as that Holocaust denials are wrong (31). Nor do they hesitate to say that some reconstructions of the past are better than others. In short, all is not relative. In fact, they point out the self-defeating nature of those who deny that any objective truth can be known about past events (30). They are also correct in pointing out that one must have a context or overall framework by which to interpret history (33).

Most of all, these are scholars who have not given up hope in knowing the actual Jesus of history. Nor do they believe one must cease being a scholar to do so. In fact, right or wrong, they are convinced that by using the acceptable tools of contemporary scholarship, they can fulfill their quest for the historical Jesus. Of course, there are other commendable features of their endeavor, which space does not allow us to elaborate on, but these will suffice to show that these are the efforts of sincere, scholarly evangelicals whose goal is admirable and whose efforts are commendable. This is not to say that there are no difficulties with their positions with regard to the doctrine of inerrancy, which Bock and many others profess to hold. We turn our attention to these now.

Difficulties and Dangers in the Bock-Webb Views

We speak of difficulties and dangers with respect to the traditional view of total inerrancy held by the ETS and ICBI framers' views on inerrancy. Perhaps many of the IBR people do not profess to believe in total inerrancy. If so, this may be an indication that they recognize their methods as incompatible with the ETS and ICBI statements. However, if they do profess to hold to total inerrancy in the traditional sense, then our comments are relevant to them as well.

Some Difficulties with Bock-Webb Views

First we will briefly state several areas in which total inerrantists, such as the framers of the ETS and ICBI statements, have difficulty, such as the following positions: (a) The best we can do is simply paint a "portrait" of the New Testament Jesus (*KE*, 6). (b) We can have no "final word" on the historical Jesus (7). (c) We have only "traces" to go by, not real evidence (13). (d) We can't know past events, only "narrative accounts" (14). (e) We have the puzzle pieces but not the picture on the cover (16). Reconstructing history is not similar to archaeology or geology (17). (f) There is no neutral or objective view of history (20). (g) Gadamer's fusing of two horizons is a helpful way to view how we know the past (29). (h) We begin with subject, not object (33). (i) Science presupposes naturalism (45). (j) Methodological naturalism is an acceptable common ground we have with naturalistic historians (47). (k) The resurrection is not history, even though it may have occurred (49). (l) The New Testament Apocrypha are primary sources (55). (m) The Gospels were written in the 70s and 80s AD. (n) Mark was the first Gospel to be written (55). (o) The Gospels contain redactions in the content of what Jesus said (56–57). (p) There were four stages in the message, including changes, as indicated by Luke 1:1–4 (55–56). (q) The critical method is needed to determine New Testament authenticity (56). (r) Matthew redacted Jesus's words and added the word "church" (in Matt. 16) (65).

Clearly, some of these are more important than others. This is particularly true with regard to the doctrine of inerrancy. We will focus on these in the rest of this chapter.

Some Crucial Problems with Bock-Webb Positions

Of all of the challengeable premises in the Bock-Webb[1] "quest" for the historical Jesus, some more seriously affect the doctrine of inerrancy as formulated by the ETS and ICBI framers. In fact, some of these were directly addressed in the ICBI documents. Let's begin with the dating and order of the crucial New Testament books.

Late Dating of New Testament Books

Late dating is crucial to the redactional views of the New Testament. It takes time for the supposed changes to have happened to the text. The Bock-Webb book posits dates for the Gospels between AD 70 and 90 (*KE*, 55). They suppose four stages: (1) Eyewitnesses observe the events. (2) Oral traditions change the reports as they are retold to others, who in turn tell others. (3) The early collection stage has some who collect and categorize oral traditions, based on the subject matter.

(4) The Gospel composition stage uses material from (a) earlier written Gospels; (b) other early collections, such as the hypothetical Q document;[2] and (c) other oral traditions. On the basis of these stages, the supposed Gospel writers composed their Gospels (55–56).

However, the evidence does not support this view for many reasons. First, it is contrary to the very passage (Luke 1:1–4) they cite to support their view:

> Inasmuch as many have undertaken to compile a narrative of the things that have been accomplished among us, just as those who from the beginning were eyewitnesses and ministers of the word have delivered them to us, it seemed good to me also, having followed all things closely for some time past, to write an orderly account for you, most excellent Theophilus, that you may have certainty concerning the things you have been taught.

It is clear that there are *not* four stages in this text, as Bock-Webb claim. There is one broad stage: the age of the eyewitnesses. Luke the author is a contemporary of the eyewitnesses, and he refers to the earlier books written by eyewitnesses. At most there are two phases of this stage: (a) The "many" (Gk.: two or more Gospels) written by eyewitnesses themselves; (b) Luke's Gospel, written by a contemporary of the eyewitnesses who produces his books as based on eyewitness testimony. Contrary to the Bock-Webb position, Luke 1:1–4 does not mention any oral-tradition stage between eyewitnesses and the works of Luke.[3]

Second, Luke is writing his Gospel well before AD 70. Noted Roman historian Colin Hemer demonstrated (in *Book of Acts*) that Luke wrote Acts before AD 62 because (1) Jerusalem had not yet been destroyed (in AD 70), for if it had, then anyone writing the history of this time and place would have surely mentioned it. Not to mention this momentous event would have been like someone writing the life of President John F. Kennedy after his death in 1963 without any mention of the assassination. (2) Acts gives no hint of the Jewish War with Rome that led to the destruction of Jerusalem that began in AD 66. (3) Also, Acts makes no mention of the Jewish disturbances beginning in AD 64 that led to the war. (4) Acts does not mention the death of the apostle Paul around AD 65. Indeed, he was still alive when the last chapter of Acts was written. (5) Finally, Acts does not mention the death of James the brother of Jesus, whom Josephus documents as dying in AD 62. Hence, Acts must have been written before AD 62, and Luke's Gospel (referred to in Acts 1:1) must have been written before this.

Third, since Luke 1:1 refers to at least two works on the life of Christ that were written before his, these may have been Matthew and Mark. Why? (1) Because almost all New Testament scholars (even critics) believe that Matthew and Mark were written before Luke, and because (2) there are no other Gospels known to exist from this time period. (3) Before Paul died (ca. AD 65) he refers to either Matthew 10:10 or Luke 10:7 in 1 Timothy 5:18, calling it "Scripture." So one (or both) of these two Gospels must have been in existence by that time (before AD 65).

Fourth, other New Testament books claim to have been based on eyewitness testimony (see below). If so, then there was not enough time for the oral tradition and changes to occur that the Bock-Webb redaction hypothesis supposes.

Fifth, some scholars, even critics, have defended early dates for the Gospels, dates in the 40s and 50s AD (see chap. 5 above). William F. Albright, known as the Dean of Archaeology, began his career as a critic of the Bible. But the more evidence that was uncovered, the more he became convinced of the early dates for the Gospels, somewhere between AD 50 and 75 (Albright, "More Conservative View"). Indeed, a noted "Death of God" New Testament scholar, Bishop John Robinson, eventually posited dates for the Gospels as early as the 40s AD (*Redating the New Testament*, 352–54). Finally, a former student of Rudolf Bultmann, Professor Eta Linnemann, rethought her earlier critical views and concluded that the Gospels were written by the eyewitness authors whose names they bear well before AD 70 (see *Is There a Synoptic Problem?* and *Historical Criticism*). But dates before this time, particularly dates in the 40s and 50s, completely destroy the Bock-Webb redaction view. More recently, New Testament critic James Crossley (*The Date for Mark's Gospel*, 2004) argues that Mark may be as early as the late 30s!

The New Testament Basis in Eyewitness Testimony

There is a growing group of scholars who support the New Testament's claim to be based in eyewitness testimony. But if this is so, then the views of evangelical redactionists, like Bock-Webb and company, are wrong. Their view needs more time and a link of oral tradition to get off the ground. Consider first what the New Testament itself claims about being based on eyewitness testimony (emphasis added below): "He who saw it [the crucifixion] *has borne witness*—his testimony is true" (John 19:35). "This is the disciple *who testifies to these things and who wrote them down*. We know that his testimony is true" (John 21:24). "[We proclaim] that which was from the beginning, *which we have heard, which we have seen with our eyes, which we have looked upon and have touched with our hands*, concerning the Word of life ..." (1 John 1:1–3). "This Jesus God raised up, and *of that we all are witnesses*" (Acts 2:32). "Peter and John answered them, ... We cannot but speak of *what we have seen and heard*" (Acts 4:19–20). "*We are witnesses of all that he did* both in the country of the Jews and in Jerusalem. They put him to death by hanging him on a tree, but God raised him on the third day *and made him to appear ... to us who had been chosen by God as witnesses*" (Acts 10:39–41). "... He [Jesus] was buried, ... he was raised on the third day in accordance with the Scriptures, and ... *he appeared to Cephas, then to the twelve. Then he appeared to more than five hundred brothers at one time*, most of whom are still alive. ... Then *he appeared to James, then to all the apostles*. Last of all, ... *he appeared also to me*" (1 Cor. 15:3–8). "How shall we escape if we neglect such a great salvation? It was declared at first by the Lord, and *it was attested to us by those who heard*, while God also bore witness by signs and wonders and various miracles and by gifts of the Holy Spirit distributed according to his will" (Heb. 2:3–4). "We did not follow cleverly devised myths when we made known to you the power and coming of our Lord Jesus Christ, but *we were eyewitnesses of his majesty*" (2 Pet. 1:16). "I exhort the elders among you, as a fellow elder and *a witness of the sufferings of Christ,* as well as a partaker in the glory that is going to be revealed" (1 Pet. 5:1).

It is worthy of note that many of these are claims by the authors of the book to be both apostles and witnesses of the events. Peter, Paul, and John are among them. If this is so, then there is no room for the Bock-Webb evangelical redaction view as described above.

Further, a recent book by Richard Bauckham (*Jesus and the Eyewitnesses*) argues convincingly that the New Testament is based on eyewitness testimony. He concludes that "reading the Gospels as eyewitness testimony . . . honors the form of historiography they are. From its historical perspective, radical suspicion of testimony is a kind of epistemological suicide. It is no more practical in history than it is in ordinary life" (506). Bauckham is not alone in his conclusion. Numerous scholars have come to the same conclusion, including Blomberg (*Historical Reliability of the Gospels* and *Historical Reliability of John's Gospel*), Bruce (*New Testament Documents* and *Jesus and Christian Origins*), Carson and Moo (*Introduction to the New Testament*), Craig (*Knowing the Truth*), Dodd (*History and the Gospels*), Guthrie (*New Testament Introduction*), Habermas (*Historical Jesus*), Hemer (*Book of Acts*), Montgomery (*History and Christianity*), Linnemann (*Is There a Synoptic Problem?*), Metzger (*Text of the New Testament*), Nigel Scotland (*Can We Trust the Gospels?*). In fact, there are several thousand biblical scholars in the Evangelical Theological Society who accept the reliability of the New Testament documents as based on eyewitness testimony!

But if even some of the Gospels and early Epistles are rooted in eyewitness testimony, this destroys the claim of redaction critics, evangelical or not, that there is time between the events of Jesus's life (ca. AD 30–33) and the first accounts of it (at least by the mid 50s) for the kind of molding, changing, and editing (redacting) needed for their hypothesis to even get off the ground, let alone fly after the takeoff.

The Gospel Truths in Paul's Early Epistles

Even the most ardent critics of the New Testament agree that Paul's early Epistles (Romans, 1 and 2 Corinthians, and Galatians) are genuine works of Paul, written between AD 55 and 57. This being the case, Paul confirms the historicity of at least twenty-seven Gospel facts, including Jesus's Jewish ancestry (Gal. 3:16); Davidic descent (Rom. 1:3); virgin birth (Gal. 4:4); command to love one's neighbors (Rom. 13:9); titles of deity (Rom. 1:3–4; 10:9); institution of the Lord's Supper (1 Cor. 11:23–25); sinless life (2 Cor. 5:21); death on the cross (Rom. 4:25; 5:8; Gal. 3:13) for our sins (1 Cor. 15:3; 2 Cor. 5:21; cf. Mark 10:45); burial (1 Cor. 15:4); resurrection on the "third day" (1 Cor. 15:4); postresurrection appearance to the apostles and others, including five hundred people (1 Cor. 15:5–8); and present position at God's right hand (Rom. 8:34). (See chapter 5 for a complete list.)

Several facts are important in understanding the weight of this argument. The apostle Paul was (1) a contemporary of Christ and the apostles. (2) He was an apostle of Christ; he was an eyewitness of the resurrected Christ (1 Cor. 9:1; 15:8). (3) He knew and consulted with members of the twelve apostles on many occasions (Gal. 1–2); his Gospel message was confirmed by all the apostles as authentic (Acts 15). (4) He was trained under one of the great Jewish rabbis of the time, Gamaliel (Acts 5:34; 22:3). (5) He was a onetime zealous antagonist of the Christian faith (Acts 9). For such a one to confirm the basic facts of the sinless life, sacrificial death, and bodily resurrection of Christ is sufficient—apart from the Gospels—to verify the basic historicity of Christ.

The Assumption of Methodological Naturalism

Another disturbing proposal of the Bock-Webb IBR group is the premise of methodological naturalism. Their view allows for and even commends this naturalistic method as a means of finding "common ground" with naturalistic (antisupernatural) scholars. They hope that both groups can join in a common effort to discover the historical Jesus by means of accepting as a working premise the procedure of "methodological naturalism." That is, even those like Bock who believe in the miracles of Jesus, including the resurrection, can nevertheless agree methodologically that history as such does not allow for such events. George Ladd of Fuller Seminary is cited by Bock-Webb as an example. But Ladd asks, "What does history or nature or the totality of human experience know of any bodies that can pass through solid rock? This is historically incredible" (I Believe in the Resurrection, 96). He adds, "What would an observer have seen if he had stood inside the tomb watching the dead body of Jesus?" He answers, "All he would have seen was the sudden and inexplicable disappearance of the body of Jesus" (100). So the resurrection is not an event in history, nor can it be verified by history. It is literally not historical! Bock-Webb do allow that one may go beyond the purely historical and "believe" or "infer" a miracle in view of the data available from history. But the historical method as such does not allow for miracles.

While the Bock-Webb approach criticizes Ernst Troeltsch for stepping beyond "the realm of a historian discussing history and in making ontological and theological claims" (KE, 45), nonetheless the contributors wrongly buy into the "methodological naturalism" implied in Troeltsch and other New Testament critics. They claim that "the 'scientific method' presupposes naturalism" (45). This is the same mistake macroevolutionists make against the science of intelligent design.[4]

First of all, there are two kinds of science: empirical science, which deals with observed regularities in the present; and origin science, which deals with unobserved singularities in the past (see Geisler, Origin Science). So, even if there are no regular occurrences of miracles in the present, this does not mean there was none in the past. Methodological naturalism can be assumed for all regular events in the present, even the ones for which we have no known explanation. But a biblical miracle (like the resurrection) is neither a present nor a regular event. Hence, it is not a logically valid inference to assume that we cannot know by history that such an event occurred in the past.

Second, there are two kinds of causes known to science: natural and nonnatural (or intelligent) causes. For example, the science of archaeology posits intelligent causes for its finds. Also, the science of cryptology has long inferred intelligent causes for codes. Likewise, the science of information theory concludes that there are distinguishable kinds of sounds or symbols that indicate an intelligent cause. So natural causes are not the only kind of causes to posit for events.

Third, likewise, forensic science seeks to know whether there was an intelligent cause for events like a death. But a scientific understanding of origins (whether it is macroevolution or intelligent design) operates like a *forensic* science. When a dead body is found, it cannot be treated like an empirical science, which is based on observation and repetition. For no one saw the death occur, and it cannot be repeated. It is an unobserved singular event. But this does not hinder paleontologists from trying to reconstruct the past based on evidence (fossils, etc.) that remain in the present. Likewise, the fact that historical events were unobserved by present historians and unrepeated in the present does not hinder historians from trying to reconstruct what happened from evidence remaining to the present (like artifacts, writing, etc).

Fourth, most astronomers believe in the singularity of the big bang, even though it was not observed by them nor has it been repeated. And nearly all naturalistic biochemists believe that life began somewhere by spontaneous generation; though unobserved by us and unrepeated by us, that does not hinder them positing that it did occur. In like manner, no one should object to the singularity of a miracle occurring in the past because we do not see miracles occurring regularly in the present. The same is true of history, as Richard Whately showed in sanitizing David Hume's similar objection to miracles (see Whately, *Historic Doubts*). Whately showed that simply because Napoleon's unusual and unrepeated singular victories in the past occurred with no observed examples in the present, this does not hinder historians from reconstructing this history of the Napoleonic exploits.

Further, there is repeated evidence in the present that nonnatural, intelligent causes can produce events that cannot be explained by purely natural causes. It is the science of intelligent design. We know from previous repeated experience that the faces on Mount Rushmore were produced by intelligent intervention, not by natural erosion. The SETI (Search for Extraterrestrial Intelligence) scientists believe that one message from outer space would prove there are intelligent beings there. Cryptology and information theory are alert to more areas where intelligent design, not natural law, can produce an event. More recently, these same principles have been applied to the origin of first life, to demonstrate that the best scientific explanation for the specific complexity in the DNA is the result of intelligence, not purely natural law (see Meyer, *Signature in the Cell*). In like manner, there is no reason why historians cannot uncover some unique events in the past that are best explained by intervention of some nonnatural intelligent force. The resurrection of Christ could be such a historic event.

In brief, even the Bock-Webb methodological naturalism approach begs the question in favor of naturalism. It wrongly assumes, against forensic science and against the evidence, that miracles cannot be known to have occurred in the past by means of the historical method. If this were so, then no unusual events from the past—like the origin of the universe, the origin of first life, or the exploits of Napoleon—could be known, but scholars in the related fields believe that they can be known. By the same token, so could the unusual feats of Jesus of Nazareth be known as well. Indeed, as we showed earlier (in chap. 5 above), there is more historical evidence that Jesus lived, taught, worked miracles, died, and rose from the dead than there is for any other event in the ancient world.

Bock-Webb wrongly believe that they have cleansed the critical-historical method of its naturalistic biases and purified it for appropriate use by evangelicals to find the historical Jesus. But as we have seen, this is as naive as the belief that methodological naturalism as a science, to which they compare their approach (*KE*, 45), will escape the web of naturalistic conclusions. The truth is that, even as they admit, evangelicals who hold the view (like George Ladd) do not believe it leads to the literal body of Christ that lay in the tomb coming back to life again. In short, it does not lead to an orthodox view of the resurrection. At best it leads to a neo-orthodox view of mysterious disappearance by annihilation (or disintegration) of Jesus's body and its replacement by a spiritual body, not of flesh and bones, as shown above. Many young evangelical scholars seem slow to learn that methodology determines theology. And a naturalistic methodology will lead to a naturalistic theology.

Idea of a "Quest" as De Facto Denial of Inerrancy

Inerrantists posit the inspiration and inerrancy of the original text of Scripture. Article 10 of the ICBI Chicago Statement declares: "*We affirm that inspiration, strictly speaking, applies only to the autographic text of Scripture,* which in the providence of God can be ascertained from available manuscripts with great accuracy. We further affirm that copies and translations of Scripture are the Word of God to the extent that they faithfully represent the original" (emphasis added). Indeed, the Bible claims that inspiration (and inerrancy) rests only in this inspired *graphē* (2 Tim. 3:16). As authentic and true as Jesus's actual words were, the claim of the Bible and of inerrantists is that the written Scripture is inspired and inerrant.

However, the whole enterprise of the Bock-Webb and the IBR group is to determine the original and "authentic" words (and acts) of Jesus. But why? True as they are, they are not the authoritative inspired written Word of God. So any quest for these is at best misdirected, if not a de facto denial of the inspiration of Scripture. Why set the Bible aside, even methodologically, and try to go behind it and beyond it to the actual words of Jesus? First of all, as most scholars believe,

Jesus's words were in Aramaic, not Greek. Second, authoritative as they were, they were not inspired Scripture; only the original text of the written Greek New Testament was inspired. So the whole effort is misdirected. Why be in a quest for more prime and primitive sources (oral or written) behind the actual inspired text? This makes sense for nonevangelical scholars who do not believe in the inspiration and inerrancy of the written text of the New Testament. But it does not make real sense for evangelicals to do so. Such an endeavor ignores the divine authority of the autographic text and seeks something behind it that is considered more ultimate. This leads to another problem.

Positing Other Oral and Written Sources Is Misdirected

Another problem with the Bock-Webb evangelical redactionism is that it neglects the role of the Holy Spirit as stated in Scripture. It assumes that the writers of the New Testament had to depend on their fallible memories (if they were eyewitnesses) or else the memories of others who left oral and written traditions. And since, on their late dates for the New Testament, these memories were of events long past (some forty or fifty years later), we cannot be sure of what Jesus's original words actually were in most cases. But this whole assumption is wrong for many reasons, some of which we have already given. First, the critics' dating of the New Testament documents is too late. If Jesus ministered about AD 30 and some NT books were written in the 50s, as even critics agree, then there is only a twentysome-year gap. Second, if this was largely a preliterate culture, as many believe, then memories were much better developed than today. Third, there is evidence that notes were taken at this time on tablets. Fourth, at least one of Jesus's disciples (Matthew the tax collector) was accustomed to taking accurate notes. Fifth, Luke the physician was an educated person who had access to written documents and multiple eyewitnesses to cross-check what he reported. And he has been demonstrated to be accurate in nearly a hundred details (in the book of Acts) that have been confirmed by other sources from the time period. Sixth, the Gospel writers were recording words and events of momentous impact—by their contact with the very Son of God! It is a psychological fact that impact events tend to etch themselves on the mind. Seventh, there was more than one witness to cross-check their memories.

On top of all this, the redaction view ignores the supernatural role of the Holy Spirit. Jesus says, "But the Helper, the Holy Spirit, whom the Father will send in my name, *he will teach all things and bring to your remembrance all that I have said to you*" (John 14:26, emphasis added). It is difficult to see what need there is for redacting, editing, and processing the words of Jesus in canonical Scripture in order to discover or ascertain the authentic original words of Jesus. Either we have them in the New Testament text, or Jesus's promise was wrong and the Holy Spirit has failed. Jesus adds, "When the Spirit of truth comes, he will guide you into all the truth" (16:13). Either we can trust the Holy Spirit to have done his job, or we can reject evangelical redactionism. The two are incompatible.

Errors of Evangelical Redaction Criticism

Modified as it may be, the Bock-Webb view is a form of redaction criticism holding that the New Testament as we have it is the result of a process of changing and molding the original words of Jesus in terms of the life of the believing communities, through which the information passed over the years. As noted above, Bock-Webb see this as four stages:

> (1) Event stage: eyewitnesses observe an event and/or hear a saying; (2) oral tradition stage: eyewitnesses tell others about what they saw and/or heard who in turn tell others; (3) early collections stage: collections of oral traditions are made based on similarity of the subject material or interest of the collector (these collections may have been oral or written); and (4) Gospel composition stage: the Gospel writers use material from earlier written Gospels, other early collections, and other oral traditions to come to their own Gospel. (*KE*, 55–56)

They add, "At any time in this process, it is historically possible and even likely that an event or saying that had been observed or heard was later added to or changed by someone and inserted into the traditioning process at any stage, whether as an oral tradition, a part of an early collection, or a pericope in a written Gospel" (*KE*, 56). This is why they believe that "the critical methods and criteria are needed to ascertain the probability of whether or not—and to what extent—something stated in the written Gospel stage can be traced back to the event stage" (56). Thus the Bock-Webb redaction team proposes criteria to ascertain the authenticity of the Gospel sayings (and events) of Jesus. These include the (1) criterion of multiple attestation (given in more than one place); (2) criterion of multiple forms (given in more than one form); (3) criterion of dissimilarity (i.e., if it is different from Jewish and early Christian material, then it is probably unique to Jesus); (4) criterion of embarrassment (viz., if it is embarrassing to early Christianity, it is probably authentic); and so on.

It is beyond our purpose here to critique these criteria. Indeed, some of them used in the context of eyewitness testimony are helpful tests for authenticity. Our concern is with the very presupposition that supposes these are necessary a half century after the eyewitnesses in order for us to determine what Jesus actually said and what he did not say. There are several serious problems with the way these principles are used by the evangelical redactionists.

First of all, they presuppose against the evidence (cited above) that no Gospels were written by eyewitnesses. Second, they wrongly suppose that "it is historically possible and even likely that an event or saying that had been observed or heard was *later added to or changed* by someone and inserted into the traditioning process at any stage, whether as an oral tradition, a part of an early collection, or a pericope in a written Gospel" (*KE*, 56). If this is true, then the inspired (and inerrant) Gospel record could be misrepresenting what Jesus did or said. The Gospel could be *creating*, not *reporting*, what Jesus said or did. In addition to charging the Gospel record with misrepresenting the facts, this view is clearly contrary to what the ETS and ICBI framers meant by inerrancy. Hence, anyone aware of their expressed meaning could not conscientiously affirm these inerrancy statements.

Incompatibility with the ICBI Statements on Inerrancy

While there is merit to some insights of these evangelical redaction critics, particularly of its apologetic use to establish the authenticity of the New Testament text, taken as a whole the procedure is incompatible with the evangelical stand on the inerrancy of Scripture. Consider the words of the ICBI statements related to this matter, quoted in chapter 2. Some select statements here (with emphasis added) will illustrate our point:

A SHORT STATEMENT

1. *God, who is Himself truth and speaks truth only,* has inspired Holy Scripture. . . .

4. Being wholly and verbally God-given, *Scripture is without error or fault in all its teaching,* no less in what it states about God's acts in creation, about the events of world history, and *about its own literary origins* under God, than in its witness to God's saving grace in individual lives.

THE CHICAGO STATEMENT ON BIBLICAL INERRANCY (1978) ARTICLES OF AFFIRMATION AND DENIAL

Article 11

We affirm that Scripture, having been given by divine inspiration, is infallible, so that, far from misleading us, it is true and reliable in all the matters it addresses. . . .

Article 12

We affirm that Scripture in its entirety is inerrant, being free from all falsehood, fraud, or deceit.

We deny that Biblical infallibility and inerrancy are limited to spiritual, religious, or redemptive themes, exclusive of assertions in the fields of history and science. . . .

Article 13

We . . . further deny that inerrancy is negated by Biblical phenomena such as a lack of modern technical precision, irregularities of grammar or spelling, observational descriptions of nature, the reporting of falsehoods, the use of hyperbole and round numbers, the topical arrangement of material, variant selections of material in parallel accounts, or the use of free citations.

Article 14

We affirm the unity and internal consistency of Scripture.

We deny that alleged errors and discrepancies that have not yet been resolved vitiate the truth claims of the Bible.

Article 15

We . . . deny that Jesus' teaching about Scripture may be dismissed by appeals to accommodation or to any natural limitation of His humanity.

Article 18

We affirm that the text of Scripture is to be interpreted by grammatico-historical exegesis, taking account of its literary forms and devices, and that Scripture is to interpret Scripture.

We deny the legitimacy of any treatment of the text or quest for sources lying behind it that leads to relativizing, dehistoricizing, or discounting its teaching, or rejecting its claims to authorship.

Official ICBI Commentary on the Chicago Statement

The following are important excerpts from the official ICBI commentary on the Chicago Statement on inerrancy (1978).

Article 12 Selections

It has been fashionable in certain quarters to maintain that the Bible is not normal history, but redemptive history with an accent on redemption. Theories have been established that would limit inspiration to the redemptive theme of redemptive history, allowing the historical dimension of redemptive history to be errant. (Sproul, *Explaining Inerrancy* [*EI*], 36)

Though the Bible is indeed *redemptive* history, it is also redemptive *history*, and this means that the acts of salvation wrought by God actually occurred in the space-time world. (37)

Article 13 Selections

When we say that the truthfulness of Scripture ought to be evaluated according to its own standards that means that . . . all the claims of the Bible must correspond with reality, whether that reality is historical, factual or spiritual. (*EI*, 41)

By biblical standards of truth and error is meant the view used both in the Bible and in everyday life, viz., a correspondence view of truth. This part of the article is directed toward those who would redefine truth to relate merely to redemptive intent, the purely personal, or the like, rather than to mean that which corresponds with reality. (43–44)

Article 18 Selections

When the quest for sources produces a dehistoricizing of the Bible, a rejection of its teaching or a rejection of the Bible's own claims of authorship, [then] it has trespassed beyond its proper limits. . . . (*EI*, 55)

We affirm that the text of Scripture is to be interpreted by grammatico-historical exegesis, taking account of its literary forms and devices, and that Scripture is to interpret Scripture. *We deny the legitimacy of any treatment of the text or quest for sources lying behind it that leads to relativizing, dehistoricizing, or discounting its teaching, or rejecting its claims to authorship.* (Art. 18, emphasis added)

By biblical standards of truth and error is meant the view used both in the Bible and in everyday life, viz., a correspondence view of truth. This part of the article is directed toward those who would redefine truth to relate merely to redemptive intent, the purely personal, or the like, rather than to mean that which corresponds with reality. (*EI*, 43–44)

Thus, what Scripture says, God says; its authority is His authority, for He is the ultimate author. . . ." (Packer, "Exposition," 69)

ICBI Commentary on Hermeneutics

Also, an official commentary on the ICBI Hermeneutics Statement (1982), "Explaining Hermeneutics" (EH), was composed. The following are some relevant excerpts from it:

EH on article 13: "We deny that generic categories which negate historicity may rightly be imposed on biblical narratives which present themselves as factual. . . . Some, for instance, take Adam to be a myth, whereas in Scripture he is presented as a real person. Others take Jonah to be an allegory when he is presented as a historical person and [is] so referred to by Christ" (emphasis added).

EH on article 14: "We deny that any event, discourse or saying reported in Scripture was invented by the biblical writers or by the traditions they incorporated" (emphasis added).

EH on article 22: It "affirms that Genesis 1–11 is factual, as is the rest of the book. . . . The denial makes it evident that views which redefine error to mean what 'misleads,' rather than what is a mistake, must be rejected" (EH, 892).

"Thus, what Scripture says, God says; its authority is His authority, for He is the ultimate author" (Packer, "Exposition," 69).

A careful examination of these claims reveals that forms of redaction criticism, as accepted by Bock-Webb, are incompatible with the ICBI view of total inerrancy for many reasons brought out by the highlighted areas. Of particular interest are the following points: (1) It is the Scripture, including every part, that is inspired by God (arts. 6, 8). (2) God chose the very words they used (art. 8). It is the scriptural text that is inspired, not the traditions behind it (art. 10). (3) God does not use deception or falsehoods (art. 12). (4) Inerrancy applies to historical as well as spiritual matters (art. 12). (5) Matters of grammar, figures of speech, arrangement of material, and so forth are part of the providential guidance resulting in an inspired text (art. 13). (6) The Bible is internally consistent and noncontradictory (arts. 14, 15). (7) The biblical author did not invent any sayings or events; they accurately reported them (EH on art. 14). (8) The redemptive events recorded in the Bible are historical (Sproul, *EI*, 37). In the light of these clear affirmations, no evangelical redactionist such as Bock-Webb can affirm them with a clear conscience.

Evangelical Redactionism Contrary to Inerrancy

Evangelicals who have attempted to do redaction criticism have stumbled seriously. One scholar who taught at Bethel College, Robert Geulich, claimed that we could not trust what the Gospel of John recorded as Jesus's statements. Professor Guelich rejected the Gospels as "either biography or memoir" and viewed them merely as "portrait" in which the gospel writer "rearranged, reworked, and even reworded the Gospel tradition." Thus, he said, "We cannot simply assume that the Christ of the Gospels is identical with the Jesus of history."[5] Another scholar, J. Ramsey Michaels, who taught at Gordon-Conwell Seminary, insisted that the Gospels create and not simply report what Jesus said.[6] Grant Osborne of Trinity Evangelical Divinity School originally taught that Matthew "expanded" Jesus's original words in the Great Commission from baptism in the name of Jesus into baptizing in the trinitarian formula of "the Father, and of the Son, and of the Holy Spirit." When called on the carpet for this, he retracted that view and, strangely, claimed that Matthew had actually "contracted" (not "expanded") Jesus's original trinitarian discourses to his disciple.[7] We are not told how he became aware of the unpublished, unquoted, and unknown words of Jesus.

Even Bock-Webb claim that the author of Matthew redacted the original words of Jesus by adding the word "church" in Matthew 16 and 18. We are not told why this could not have been a prediction of Jesus as it is presented. What we do know is that redaction procedure, even in the hands of evangelicals, is a dangerous tool. It comes to radical conclusions that are contrary to total inerrancy as held by the church down through the ages (see chap. 1 above) and expressed in the ICBI statements on the topic.

The Bock Disclaimer

After being criticized for views expressed in the Bock-Webb book, Professor Bock tried to avoid the negative impact by noting that he is only a coeditor and not the author of all the chapters. While this is true, nevertheless Bock is also coauthor of the crucial chapter that is used as the primary basis for our above evaluation, and he must take responsibility for those conclusions. What is more, one can ask why Bock only now informs us that "I prefer to argue that the best explanation for the resurrection is that it was a historical event since other explanations cannot adequately explain the presence of such a belief among the disciples."[8] Why not mention this important fact up front in their lead chapter? Further, why was he so closely associated with such critical views as to be coeditor of the volume and then disassociate from his coeditor and authors when criticized for their radical views? It is like a person being part of a gang that robs a bank, but only after being caught does he insist that he waited in the car and did not actually go into the bank.

Furthermore, even granting Bock's disassociation from the more critical conclusions, the statements he does own reveal how deeply he has bought into the radical presuppositions of the New Testament critics. First of all, he assumes a false dichotomy between using unjustifiably and admittedly "limiting rules" of current critical New Testament scholarship on the one hand, and making "an appeal to inspiration" of the Bible on the other hand.[9] There is a third alternative to establish the historical Jesus, namely, showing that basic books of the New Testament are historically reliable documents. This can be done with a minimum of books such as Luke, Acts, 1 and 2 Corinthians, Romans, and Galatians. As we have shown (in chap. 5 above), there is very strong evidence for the historical reliability of these basic New Testament documents. And if they are accepted as *reliable* per the argument (though not necessarily *inspired* per the argument), then one can argue not only for the *fact* of the resurrection but also for its true *meaning*. We are not left, as are Bock and friends, with a meager twelve-event factual basis with no definitive overall meaning for them—and this after ten years of research and a seven-hundred-page study!

Second, Bock claims that "the problem here is with what history can show, not with the resurrection as an event."[10] But how can we know it is a historical event unless history has shown that it is? This is a false dichotomy since we cannot know the resurrection is a fact of history unless history has revealed it as a fact. We could "believe" or "speculate" that it is true, but we could not *know* it to be so by any historical approach unless history has revealed it to be a fact.

Third, the method Bock employs wrongly assumes that if we start with the Bible as an "inspired" document, then we could only know that an event like the resurrection is a matter of faith but not a fact of history. Besides being based on a false fact/value dichotomy involved in the unwarranted disjunction between the Jesus of history and the Christ of faith, this is a strange logic. Just the reverse is true. For if the Bible is "God-breathed" (what "inspiration" means [2 Tim. 3:16 NIV]), then we can know for certain that if the Bible presents the resurrection (or whatever) as historical, we can say it is historical with the authority of God. Of course, there are different ways to argue that the Bible is inspired, but that is not the point here.[11] Let apologists supply that. The fact is that by whatever way we know that the New Testament is the Word of God, the question of the historicity of Jesus's life, teaching, death, and resurrection are a settled fact. To assume otherwise is to refuse to accept the Scripture as the voice of God.

Fourth, even though he concedes that "theological arguments" can have legitimacy, Bock rejects the use of them in making his case for the historical Christ. But this both reveals an inconsistency and shows a lack of appreciation for the validity of theological argumentation in establishing what really happened and why. For one thing, this is inconsistent with Bock's own claim that the resurrection is "the best explanation" from the known data. But what is this "best explanation" but a theological argument? It is a rational inference based on facts. Furthermore, Bock reveals a tendency, unfortunately shared by too many biblical scholars, that if you want to stick strictly to the facts, then exegesis is virtually the beginning and ending of biblical scholarship. Almost anything beyond that is speculation or faith. However, the history of biblical studies—whether in Augustine, Anselm, Thomas

Aquinas, John Calvin, or the Westminster divines—argues to the contrary. The Westminster Confession of Faith declares that the whole of Christian truth is not always explicitly stated in the Bible but in "the whole counsel of God, . . . either expressly set down in Scripture, *or by good and necessary consequence may be deduced from Scripture*" (in chap. 1, sect. 6, emphasis added).

So there is nothing wrong with accepting, by a "good and necessary" deduction of Scripture, both the fact and meaning of the resurrection of Christ (even though the event itself was not seen by any human being). After all, they saw a dead and buried Jesus, and later they saw an empty tomb and appearances of the same Jesus, alive in the same body, with crucifixion scars and all. The reasonable deduction from this is that this same body had been raised from the dead, just as Jesus said it would be (Matt. 12:40; 17:22; Mark 8:31; 9:31; 10:34; John 2:18–22). This kind of theological reasoning is part of good history. Even with eyewitnesses' testimony, historians include these kinds of reasonable inferences all the time. Indeed, it is even accepted in a court of law in life-and-death matters. In fact, the legal procedure, established over centuries of seeking the truth about past events, is a far better procedure than that accepted by New Testament critics and brings far better results. Legal experts who have used it come to more positive conclusions than those of Bock and friends.[12]

Fifth, Bock speaks of limiting ourselves to "history (at least as normally practiced today),"[13] but this phrase bristles with presuppositions. Two stand out. First, unfortunately, "normally" here means nonsupernatural. Indeed, since the days of Benedict Spinoza and David Hume, an event is not considered historical if it is supernatural. But, as shown here and elsewhere (chap. 5 above), this is neither a common nor a necessary presupposition. Indeed, it is an atheistic (i.e., a-theistic) presupposition, for if a theistic God, such as the God of the Bible who created the universe, exists, then miracles are possible. Hence, to prove miracles are impossible, one would have to disprove the existence of God. Also, the word "history" is used in an unnecessarily limiting manner since Bock has adopted methodology that rules out many of the factual truths of Christ's life, death, and resurrection. The rest, then, is left for mere faith or for the nonhistorical. In short, Bock's view, even with his qualifications, is subevangelical.

Sixth, this reveals the central problem with the whole quest for the historical Jesus. If it were not for their set of false presuppositions, there would be no quest at all. By using common nonantisupernatural procedures for knowing the past, the documents and evidence we have (see chap. 5 above) are more than sufficient for discovering the true Jesus of history. So the best way to find the true Jesus is to reject the principles and procedures of the whole idea of a "quest" to begin with! In brief, since we have the basic historically reliable documents of the New Testament, there is no need for a "quest" since we already have the historical Jesus in the New Testament. What more do we need than twenty-seven books written by eight or nine authors, many of whom are widely accepted (even by critical scholars) to be eyewitnesses or contemporaries of the events?

Finally, a former Bock student and now New Testament scholar, F. David Farnell, sounds a warning, arguing that Bock engages in a kind of doublespeak scholarship.[14] He sees it is an example of putting contemporary scholarship over ancient lordship. He believes that Bock and Webb have subjected the Scripture to hostile alien presuppositions, which reduce the Bible to human categories of probability—implying that there is a definite possibility that events attested in the Bible did not happen—and then they want Bible-believing Christians to commend them for doing good. As such, it reduces the evidential apologetic impact of the Scripture, especially the Gospels, to human categories that subject the Bible to the shifting sands of historical criticism and place great doubt on the events.

While Bock and company believe they have gained a voice among liberals, nonetheless, with their methodological concessions to antibiblical presuppositions, what they have really done is to undermine the authority of the Gospels and in many ways the resurrection itself. A careful examination of their conclusions does not admit the historicity of the resurrection itself—to say nothing of its real meaning—but at best only a historical anomaly of an empty tomb and mysterious encounters and beliefs by his disciples following it. Thus the biblically declared "certainty" (Luke 1:4) on this matter is reduced to probability, and the kingpin of Christian apologetics—the historicity of the bodily resurrection of Christ—is seriously undermined. Indeed, in its full biblical sense and meaning, it is historically unobtainable because their confessed acceptance of this limited critical methodology cannot achieve such conclusions.

In summation, the overall impression that one derives from the Bock-Webb procedure is that only the critical method they employ can achieve true history. In fact, it is all that true history can tell you. The rest is a matter of inference and faith (which a person is welcome to accept if one wishes). However, if you want to be a true scholar, then you must accept a truly scholarly method—like theirs. Any other approach is not truly scholarly. Rather, it is a matter of what William James calls "overbelief." And while anyone is welcome to indulge in overbelief, one should not consider it the result of truly scholarly procedures. Bock-Webb apparently insist that one must accept the rules of the game laid down by true scholars, rules that have bought into methodological naturalism. True, this will not yield all that evangelicals wish to believe, but there is no harm in doing so, in their opinion, and meanwhile we can gain a lot of respect in the academic community by showing that we are capable of using their naturalistic methodology.

In response, we observe that indeed there are crumbs that will fall from the table if we use this critical naturalistic method; one of the larger crumbs is that we can conclude that there was an empty tomb, that the body mysteriously disappeared, and that belief in the resurrection arose in the hearts of the early disciples. Unfortunately, as we have seen, there are several tragic flaws in this thinking. First of all, these crumbs, even the biggest one, fall far short of the literal death and bodily resurrection of Christ narrated in the New Testament. In fact, it is a denial of the true resurrection, by which alone we can be saved (1 Cor. 15:12–19; Rom. 4:25; 10:9). Second, it tends to sacrifice orthodoxy on the altar of academic respectability. Third, it undermines the "certainty" that the New Testament promises with regard to the major events of Jesus's life, including the resurrection (Luke 1:4; Acts 1:3). Fourth, it employs the same kind of logic that leads some evangelicals to accept macroevolution, to deny the historicity of Genesis 1–3, and thereby to undermine crucial evangelical doctrines (Matt. 19:3–6; Rom. 5:12–14; 1 Cor. 15:45–49; 1 Tim. 2:13–14). For there is a striking parallel between this procedure and the scientists who claim that only those who use the true scientific method (the naturalistic one) will come to a truly scientific conclusion, namely, to a naturalistic evolutionary one (see appendix 2).

Conclusion

Evangelicals like those in the Bock-Webb IBR Jesus Group have good intentions and are to be commended for many things listed at the beginning of this chapter. They are sincere, scholarly, and interested in establishing the historicity of Jesus and the authenticity of his acts and statements. Being "evangelical" or "orthodox," they believe in many of the great essentials of Christian orthodoxy, including the resurrection of Jesus. However, they have, knowingly or not, adopted an unorthodox method that undermines the inerrancy of Scripture that many of them profess to hold. This is both unfortunate and unnecessary, given their beliefs in a theistic God who can and does intervene in this world, because such a God is able to inspire an inerrant book, the Bible. Likewise, given that the Gospels and Epistles were written by eyewitnesses, contemporaries, and even apostles of Christ, who promised them supernaturally activated memories (John 14:26) to recall his words, there is no need for redaction criticism. In fact, it is not only unneeded; it is also untrue and dangerous. For its premises and procedures undermine the very divinely authoritative Scripture they confess.

Sources

Albright, "More Conservative View"

Bauckham, *Jesus and the Eyewitnesses*

Blomberg, *Historical Reliability of the Gospels*

———, *Historical Reliability of John's Gospel*

Bock and Webb, *Key Events*

Bruce, *Jesus and Christian Origins*

———, *New Testament Documents*

Carson and Moo, *Introduction to the New Testament*

Craig, *Knowing the Truth*

Crossley, *The Date for Mark's Gospel*

Dodd, *History and the Gospels*

Geisler, *Origin Science*

Guthrie, *New Testament Introduction*

Habermas, *Historical Jesus*

Hemer, *Book of Acts*

Ladd, *I Believe in the Resurrection*

Linnemann, *Historical Criticism*

———, "Is There a Q?"

———, *Is There a Synoptic Problem?*

Metzger, *Text of the New Testament*

Meyer, *Signature in the Cell*

Montgomery, *History and Christianity*

Osborne, "Redaction Criticism"

Packer, "Exposition"

Robinson, *Redating the New Testament*

Scotland, *Can We Trust the Gospels?*

Sproul, *Explaining Inerrancy*

Whately, *Historic Doubts*

PART THREE

REEXAMINATION OF INERRANCY

12

The Nature of God and Inerrancy

Introduction

The nature of God is crucial to the inerrancy debate, as it is to most other theological issues. This will become clear as we see the relation between one's view of God and one's view of inerrancy in the contemporary debate. Bart Ehrman (chap. 5 above), who gave up his evangelical view on inerrancy, also gave up his theistic view of God and became an agnostic. Clearly, believing that the Bible is the inerrant Word of God is not possible for someone who does not even believe in the theistic God of the Bible. Likewise, since the historic view on Scripture's being the inspired Word of God is based on a classical view of God, it is understandable why open theists like Clark Pinnock (see chap. 4), who reject the classical view of God, will deny the view of inerrancy that goes with that classical theistic view. For example, how can the Bible make infallible pronouncements about the future if, as open theists claim, God has no infallible knowledge of the future. The two go hand in hand. Furthermore, individuals such as Kevin Vanhoozer disregard classical theism in favor of a dynamic "communicative theism." He rejects the classical view of God as being sterile and passionless, unable to relate and dialogue in the drama of doctrine (see his *First Theology*, *Drama of Doctrine*, and *Remythologizing Theology*). He then proceeds to use speech-act theory to develop a dynamic view of language and to relate with a dynamic God.

Strangely, some who are not open theists or communicative theists assume a voluntaristic view of God that also undermines inerrancy. For example, Andrew McGowan (see chap. 9) writes: "Inerrantists make an unwarranted assumption about

God. The assumption is that, given the nature and character of God, the only kind of Scripture he could 'breathe out' was Scripture that is textually inerrant. If there was even one mistake in the *autographa*, then God cannot have been the author, because he is incapable of error" (*Divine Spiration*, 113). Thus McGowan says inerrancy is not a legitimate inference from the Bible (115) but is merely an "a priori" argument (131). He further says that "the argument of the inerrantists is that God is *unable* to produce anything other than an inerrant autographic text. . . . I agree with the inerrantists that God *could* have brought into being inerrant autographic texts, had he chosen to do so, but I reject their argument that he *must* have acted in this way" (113–14). He concludes, "I think it is wrong to prejudge the nature of Scripture through some deductivist approach, based on what we believe inspiration must mean, given God's character" (136). We cannot "assume that they must be inerrant because God cannot lie" (137). This could hardly be more clear and, in our view, more faulty.

The connection between God and inerrancy was clearly understood by the founders of the Evangelical Theological Society (ETS). Their sole statement is: "The Bible alone and the Bible in its entirety is the Word of God written, and *therefore* inerrant in the autographs" (emphasis added). The crucial word "therefore" reveals their belief that "inerrant" follows logically and necessarily from who they believed "God" is. For if the "God" of classical theism in whom they believed cannot err, then surely "the Word of God" cannot err. And if "the Bible alone and the Bible in its entirety" is "the Word of God written," then it must be "inerrant" too.

It is well known that all the ETS framers were classical theists. They believed, among other things, that God was infinite, unchangeable, and omniscient, which included his infallible foreknowledge of everything, including all future free acts. Given this view, the logic of their position on inerrancy could be put in such a succinct statement and can be formulated as follows: (1) God cannot err. (2) The Bible is the Word of God. (3) Therefore, the Bible cannot err. Hence, to deny the inerrancy of the Bible, one must deny either premise 1 or 2 or both. That is, one would need either to deny that God cannot err or to deny that the Bible is the Word of God or both. Since both premises 1 and 2 were firmly believed by the ETS framers, inerrancy was just as securely believed to be the "inerrant" "Word of God." It was unthinkable that anyone would deny either premises 1 or 2. For to deny that God cannot err is contrary to the very nature of God! And to deny that the Bible is the Word of God is both unbiblical and Barthian. It was also unthinkable to deny that the Bible was the Word of God, a denial that Karl Barth affirmed. Indeed, in 1983 a member was asked to leave ETS because of his "Barthian" views, which separate the Word of God from the Bible.

Classical and Orthodox View of God and Scripture

The logical connection between classical theism and inerrancy was intact from the very beginning of ETS. And this was rightly so, for as we shall see, the same logical connection between classical theism and inerrancy has existed from the earliest days of the Christian church.

It is well known that the great fathers and teachers of the Christian church, up to and through the Reformation and into modern times, held to both classical theism (see Geisler, *Systematic Theology*, vol. 2) and inerrancy (see Hannah, *Inerrancy and the Church*). Equally important and less well known is that there is a logically necessary connection between the two (see Geisler and House, *Battle for God*).[1] A brief survey of key figures in the history of the church will demonstrate our point. We will begin with the early fathers of the church.

Justin Martyr (d. 165). In his first *Apology* (chap. 65) he referred to the Bible as "the Voice of God." He added, "We must not suppose that the language proceeds from men who were inspired, but from the Divine Word which moves them." Elsewhere he added that "the Holy Spirit of prophecy taught us this, telling us by Moses that God spoke thus" (*JHOG*, 12, 44). This is why Justin could cite the New Testament some 330 (with 266 more allusions) times as the divinely authoritative Word of God.

Irenaeus (130–202). There was only one link between Irenaeus and the apostle John, namely, John's disciple Polycarp. In his famous book, *Against Heresies*, Irenaeus referred to the Bible as "the pillar and ground" of our faith, which was "above all falsehood" and as "Scriptures of truth" (*AHs*, 3:67; 3.5.1). He added that we are "most properly assured that the Scriptures are indeed perfect, since they are spoken by the Rod of God and His Spirit" (Ibid., 2:28.2; 2:35). Thus, he saw the evident connection between the flawless nature of God and the perfect Word of God that he produced.

Clement of Alexandria (158–215). Clement too had no doubt about the connection between his classical view of God and the inerrant Scripture. He writes, "There is no discord between the Law and the Gospel, but harmony, for they both proceed from the same Author . . ." (Westcott, *AISG*, 439). He also spoke of "the Scriptures . . . [which] are valid from their omnipotent authority" (see Geisler, *The Bible*, 31–32). In short, the divine authority of the Bible is derived from the all-powerful nature of God.

Hippolytus (ca. 170–236). This disciple of Irenaeus speaks of the New Testament writers, saying, "These blessed men, . . . having been perfected by the Spirit of Prophecy, . . . were brought to inner harmony like instruments, and having the Word within them, . . . [for] they did not speak of their own power . . . , they spoke that which was [revealed] to them alone by God" (Westcott, *AISG*, 432). So here too, the errorless unity of Scripture came from the God who cannot err.

Augustine of Hippo. There is no doubt that this "medieval monolith" got the point. He repeatedly refers to the Bible as flawless because God was its author. He declares: "I have learned to yield this respect and honour only to the canonical books of Scripture: of these alone do I most firmly believe that the authors were completely free from error" (Geisler, *The Bible*, 40). Why? Because God is "the author of this book" (*Reply to Faustus* 11.5). Hence its words are "the words of God" (*City of God* 10.1) and "infallible Scripture" (11:6). Thus, any apparent error in the Bible must be because "the manuscript is faulty, or the translation is wrong, or you have not understood" (*Reply to Faustus* 11.5).

Thomas Aquinas (1225–74). The greatest theologian prior to the Reformation saw the connection between the classical view of God and the inerrancy of Scripture very clearly. Thomas affirms that "God is the Author of Holy Scripture" (*Summa* 1a.1.10). Hence, "it is heretical to say that any falsehood whatsoever is contained either in the gospels or in any canonical Scripture" (*Exposition on Job* 13, lect. 1). For "a true prophet is always inspired by the spirit of truth in whom there is no trace of falsehood, and he never utters untruth" (*Summa* 2a2ae 172, 6 ad 2). Therefore, "the truth of prophetic proclamations must be the same as that of the divine knowledge. And falsity . . . cannot creep into prophecy" (1a 14.3). Speaking of Scripture, Thomas agrees with Augustine, proclaiming, "I firmly believe that none of their authors have erred in composing them" (1a.1.8).

Martin Luther (1483–1546). The Reformers were no less insistent on the connection between the classical view of God and the doctrine of inerrancy. Luther declares: "This is exactly as it is with God. His word is so much like himself, that the Godhead is wholly in it, and he who has the word has the whole Godhead" (*Luther's Works* [LW], 52:46). Elsewhere he adds, "They do not believe they are God's words. For if they believed they were God's words, . . . they would tremble before them as before God himself" (*LW*, 35:153). In a blisteringly strong passage, Luther writes: "God's Word is God's Word . . . ! When one blasphemously gives the lie to God in a single word, . . . [when] God is blasphemed or called a liar, one blasphemes the entire God and makes light of all blasphemy" (*LW*, 37:26). One thing is certain, Luther can be charged with hyperbole, but he certainly cannot be charged with not seeing the connection between the inerrant nature of God and the inerrant nature of God's Word.

John Calvin (1509–64). Calvin may have been less bombastic, but he was not less clear in seeing the connection between classical theism and total inerrancy. He believed that "the Bible has come down to us from the mouth of God" (*Institutes*, 1.18.4). Therefore, "we owe to Scripture the same reverence which we owe to God; because it has proceeded from Him alone. . . . The Law and the Prophets are not a doctrine delivered according to the will and pleasure of men, but dictated by the Holy Spirit" (Urquhart, *Inspiration and Accuracy*, 129–30). Calvin may be charged (wrongly I believe) with the verbal dictation theory, but he cannot be rightly charged with denying the logical connection between the classical nature of God and the inerrancy of the Word of God. Because God cannot err, the Bible is "the certain and unerring rule" for believers (*Commentaries*, Ps. 5:11). He plainly says, "Nor is it sufficient to believe that God is true, and cannot lie or deceive, unless you feel firmly persuaded that every word which proceeds from him is sacred, inviolable truth" (*Institutes*, 3.2.6).

Charles Hodge (1797–1878). The post-Reformation period is no less convinced of this connection between classical theism and total inerrancy (see McDonald,

Theories of Revelation). This view dominated right up until the late 1800s, when the Old Princetonians—Charles Hodge, A. A. Hodge, and B. B Warfield—defended the historic view of inerrancy.

Charles Hodge argues that "all Protestants agree in teaching that the word of God, as contained in the Scriptures of the Old and New Testaments, is the only infallible rule of faith and practice" (*Systematic Theology*, 1:151). He adds, Protestants hold "that the Scriptures of the Old and New Testaments are the Word of God, written under the inspiration of the Holy Spirit, and are therefore, infallible, and . . . free from all error whether of doctrine, fact, or precept" (151–52). Again, "The infallibility and divine authority of the Scriptures are due to the fact that they are the Word of God; and they are the Word of God because they were given by inspiration of the Holy Ghost" (153–54).

A. A. Hodge and B. B. Warfield. A. A. Hodge, the son of Charles Hodge, and B. B. Warfield joined forces to reaffirm the historic view on inerrancy. They write: "The New Testament continually asserts of the Scriptures of the Old Testament, and of the several books which constitute it, that they ARE THE WORD OF GOD. What their writers said, God said" (*Inspiration*, 29, emphasis original). Hence, "Every element of Scripture, whether doctrine or history, of which God guaranteed the infallibility, must be infallible in its verbal expression" (21–23). Here again, they see the logical and necessary connection between the classical view of "God" and that of the Bible being his infallible and inerrant Word.

It is common knowledge that the framers of the ETS statement on inerrancy and their ICBI successors are heirs of the historic view of the Christian church, as expressed by the Old Princetonians. This is why it came as a great surprise that open theists like Clark Pinnock (see chap. 4 above) would claim to the contrary that one can deny the classical view of God and still hold to inerrancy. As we shall see, the two are incompatible.

Classical Liberal View of God and Denial of Inerrancy

As noted earlier (in chap. 1), the modern controversy on inerrancy began with the Briggs-Warfield debate over the issue. Charles A. Briggs, a professor at Union Theological Seminary in New York City, had denied inerrancy. B. B. Warfield and A. A. Hodge responded strongly with the book *Inspiration* (1881). Warfield added his articles "Inspiration of the Bible" (1894) and "Smith on Inspiration" (1884). The liberal view eventually triumphed in mainline denominations and produced a number of noted proponents like Harry Emerson Fosdick and Harold DeWolf.

The modern denial of inerrancy began with Deism and was eventually incorporated into the church by modernists. Because of their common denial of miracles, they came to the conclusion (logically drawn from their view of God) that the Bible is neither divinely authoritative nor inerrant. After all, how can the Bible be a supernatural revelation from God if he is not a miracle-working God? Likewise, how can there be miraculous acts of God, such as those recorded in the Bible, if there is no God who can act supernaturally? In short, the inerrancy of Scripture is incompatible with a deistic view of God.

Deism flourished in Europe, especially in France and England, and in late eighteenth-century America. Some of the more prominent European Deists were Herbert of Cherbury (1583–1648), the father of English Deism; Matthew Tindal (1656–1733); John Toland (1670–1722); and Thomas Woolston (1669–1731). Immanuel Kant (1724–1804) was an important German (Prussian) Deist. Some of the notable American Deists were Benjamin Franklin (1706–90), Thomas Jefferson (1743–1826), and Thomas Paine (1737–1809).

Thomas Paine (1737–1809). One of the most prominent early American Deists was Thomas Paine. He declares, "I believe in one God, and no more." Like theists, Paine believes that the one God is all-powerful, all-knowing, all-good, infinite, merciful, just, and incomprehensible (Blanchard, *Complete Works of Thomas Paine*, 5, 26, 27, 201). But unlike theists, he rejects all forms of supernatural revelation, believing them to be unknowable. For no human language can be the vehicle of the Word of God (19; cf. 55–56). Thus Paine rejects all claims to a verbal or written revelation from God (6). "The only religion that has not been invented, and that has in it every evidence of divine originality, is pure and simple Deism." In fact, Deism "must have been the first, and will probably be the last that man believes" (6). And for a Deist, "THE WORD OF GOD IS THE CREATION WE BEHOLD: And it is in *this word*, which no human invention can counterfeit or alter, that God speaketh universally to man" (24, 26, 309, emphasis original). In his famous book *The Age of Reason*, Paine lists numerous examples of what he believes to be contradictions and errors in the Bible. It has served as a sourcebook for skeptics and unbelievers since that time.

Thomas Jefferson (1743–1826). Jefferson's form of Deism was more mild than Paine's, but he nonetheless denied miracles. Jefferson believed that there is one God, the Creator, Sustainer, and Manager of the universe. He held that this God is infinitely wise, good, righteous, and powerful. He believed in creation, God's moral law, his providence, and even a day of judgment. He was deistic, saying in an 1822 letter to Benjamin Waterhouse that he was a "Unitarian."

However, Jefferson emphatically rejects the virgin birth of Christ. "The day will come," he says, "when the account of the birth of Christ as accepted in the Trinitarian churches will be classified with the fable of Minerva springing from the brain of Jupiter" (Foote, *Religion of Jefferson*, 49). He also cut the resurrection from his supernaturally sanitized "Bible," accepting only 44 percent of Matthew, 32 percent of Luke, 17 percent of John, and 15 percent of Mark (Fesperman, "Jefferson Bible," 79–80). He ends it with no resurrection, saying only: "Then took they the body of Jesus, and wound it in linen clothes with the spices, as the manner of the Jews is to bury. Now, in the place where he was crucified, there was a garden; and in the garden a new sepulcher, wherein was never man yet laid. There laid they Jesus, and rolled a great stone to the door of the sepulcher, and departed" (Jefferson, *Jefferson Bible*, 146–47).

Jefferson charges the Gospel writers with "forgetting often, or not understanding, what had fallen from Him, by giving their own misconceptions as His dicta, and expressing unintelligibly for others what they had not understood themselves" (*LM*, vii). Jesus's teachings had been rendered "mutilated, misstated, and often unintelligible" (*LM*, 49) by a band of "dupes and impostors" who corrupted the true moral teachings. The worst in this bad lot was the apostle Paul, the "first corrupter of the Doctrines of Jesus."

Harry Emerson Fosdick (1878–1969). Fosdick was a well-known liberal Baptist minister in New York. He claimed that when modern people "get back to the nub of their difficulties, . . . you find it in Biblical categories which they no longer believe—miracles, demons, fiat creation, apocalyptic hopes, eternal hell, or ethical conscience" (*Guide to Understanding*, 5). Fosdick believes this is due to belief in "the evolutionary origin of man, materialistic theories," and other social factors that "tend in many minds to undo what the Hebrew-Christian development did" (97). The result is that "any idea of inspiration which implies equal value in the teachings of Scripture, or inerrancy of its statements, or conclusive infallibility in its ideas, is irreconcilable with such facts as this book presents" (xiv).

Further Fosdick claims that "we are saved by it [modern biblical criticism] from the old and impossible attempts to harmonize the Bible with itself, to make it speak with unanimous voice, to resolve its conflicts and contradictions into strained and artificial unity" (*Guide to Understanding*, 24–25). So "our ideas of the methods of inspiration have changed: verbal dictation, inerrant manuscripts, uniformity of doctrine between 1000 BC and AD 70—all such ideas have become incredible in the face of the facts" (30–31).

Harold DeWolf (1905–86). Professor DeWolf was a Methodist minister and theologian who wrote *The Case for Theology in Liberal Perspective* and *A Theology of the Living Church.* He embraced the typical liberal view of Scripture of his time. He held that "some degree of accommodation to culture seems inevitable unless Christian teaching is to become merely an irrelevant echoing of ancient creeds—which are themselves products of some accommodation to Hellenic thought" (*Case for Theology* [*CT*], 58). There are scientific errors in the Bible: "Plainly the narrator [of Gen. 30:35–43] simply accepted the false science prevalent in his day. Similarly, some or all biblical writers assume the fixity of the earth, the actual movement of the sun and moon from east to west, a space above the firmament reserved for God's dwelling and the demonical explanation of disease. Such views cannot be intelligently accepted as infallible teaching" (*Theology of the Living* [*TL*], 71).

DeWolf concludes, "Strictly speaking, the Bible itself is not the pure Word of God" (*CT*, 17). So "the Bible is by no means infallible" (*TL*, 48). And "in regard to many facts of minor importance, there are obvious contradictions in the Bible" (*TL*, 69). One example given is that "2 Samuel 24:1 tells us that it was by God's command while 1 Chronicles 21:1 says it was by Satan's command" (69).[2]

For DeWolf, "It is evident that the Bible is a collection of intensely human documents" and "many of the moral and religious ideas, especially in the more ancient documents, are distinctly sub-Christian" (*TL*, 73). Thus, when we say the Bible is "inspired," we mean "this doctrine is that the writing of the Bible as a whole was accomplished by an extraordinary stimulation and elevation of the powers of men who devoutly yielded themselves to God's will . . . to convey the truth useful to the salvation of men and of nations" (76).

Given their deistic and Unitarian views of God, with their resultant antisupernaturalism, liberalism understandably rejected both the divine inspiration and inerrancy of Scripture. For a God who cannot supernaturally inspire or preserve Scripture from error certainly cannot produce an infallible and inerrant book. But here again, one's view of God is logically determinative for one's view of Scripture. If there is no supernatural God, then there can be no supernatural Word of God.

Process Theology's View of God and Denial of Inerrancy

The Deism of earlier liberalism was succeeded by process theology in later liberalism under the influence of men like Schubert Ogden and John Cobb. They were influenced by the father of process theology, Alfred North Whitehead, and his most noted student, Charles Hartshorne.

Schubert Ogden (1928–). As a process theologian, Ogden believes that God is not only finite and limited and not omniscient but that God also is in the process of continual growth. Hence, the Bible does not contain infallible predictions. As another process theologian, John Ford, put it, "Prophecy is not prediction, but the proclamation of divine intent. . . . [Thus] God becomes the great improviser and opportunist seeking at every turn to elicit his purpose from every situation" ("Biblical Recital," 1:206). So there is not supernatural intervention by God but simply a divine "lure." As Ogden writes, "Revelation" is nothing new. "What Christian revelation reveals to man is nothing new, since such truths as it makes explicit must already be known to him implicitly in every moment of existence" ("On Revelation," 272).

Nor does God inform man in advance what must occur since God himself must be informed. As another process theologian, John R. Rice, frankly admits, "God, as it were, has to wait with bated breath until the decision is made, not simply to find out what the decision was, but perhaps even to have the situation clarified by virtue of the decision of that concrete occasion" (*Our God-Breathed Book*, 49). In short, God can make no infallible predictions because he has no infallible foreknowledge.

Likewise, Ogden rejects the view that "what the Bible says, God says." He writes: "In Protestant orthodoxy, then, the developed doctrine of the verbal inspiration of the canonical writings entailed the assertion of their uniform authority, . . . that what Scripture says, God says." But "with the emergence of Protestant liberal theology, . . . Scripture neither is nor can be a sufficient authorization for the meaning and truth of theological assertions; this claim was abandoned, never again to be made by those who have led in the subsequent important developments in Protestant theology" ("Authority of Scripture," 257). Since "none of the New Testament writings, in its present form, was authored by an apostle or his disciples, . . . we today must indeed recognize a higher theological authority than the canon of Scripture" (251–52). The Bible has no essential authority but only functional authority "with respect to the end of man's salvation, and so to witnessing to all that is necessary the attainment of that end" (245).

Clearly and confessedly, the neoclassical (process) view of God is an insufficient basis for affirming the total or factual inerrancy of the Bible. Only a classical view of God is sufficient for affirming the inerrancy of the Scriptures. For only in the classical view does God have omniscience and infallible foreknowledge necessary to that conclusion. In short, here again one's view of God is determinative of one's view on inerrancy.

Open Theists' View of God and Denial of Inerrancy

A process kind of view has emerged among some evangelicals who call themselves open theists or freewill theists. Led by the formerly orthodox theologian Clark Pinnock, this view has caused havoc among evangelicals and led to the near dismissal of Clark Pinnock from the Evangelical Theological Society (in 2003). At issue were his new views on inerrancy that emerged in view of his new views on God (see chap 4).

The Open Theist View of God

Along with other open theists like John Sanders and Gregory Boyd, Clark Pinnock believes that God is infinite, all-powerful, and even miracle-working. However, according to open theism, since human beings are free and the future is therefore open, God cannot have infallible foreknowledge of our free actions. This makes infallible predictions of free actions impossible, such as those orthodox theologians have long held are found in the Bible. So this raises the serious question as to whether an open theism view of God is compatible with a statement affirming the infallibility and inerrancy of the Bible. This inevitably led to a vote of ETS on the orthodoxy of Pinnock's position. While a large majority of members (63 percent) believed his view was not consistent with its inerrancy statement, the vote to dismiss him fell short of the two-thirds majority needed, and Pinnock (along with John Sanders) was not expelled from the society.

Earlier citations from Clark Pinnock (see chap. 4) reveal how his open theist view of God relates to the inerrancy of Scripture. Once his view of God is understood, it is clear to see how his deviant view on inerrancy flows from this deviant view of God.

Pinnock's view on the Bible and false prophecy. "Second, some prophecies are conditional, leaving the future open, and, presumably, God's knowledge of it" (*Most Moved Mover* [*MMM*], 50). "Third, there are imprecise prophetic forecasts based on present situations, as when Jesus predicts the fall of Jerusalem" (50). Further, "despite Jesus, in the destruction of the temple, some stones were left one on the other (Matt. 24:2)" (51n66). This was a particularly troublesome statement that Pinnock had to revise in order to save his scalp at the hands of the ETS committee that examined him for his alleged denial of inerrancy.[3]

God is limited and corporeal. Pinnock writes, "Is God in some way embodied? Critics will be quick to say that, although there are expressions of this idea in the Bible, they are not to be taken literally. But I do not believe that the idea is as foreign to the Bible's view of God as we have assumed" (33). "The only persons we encounter are embodied persons and, if God is not embodied, it may prove difficult to understand how God is a person" (34–35).

God's foreknowledge is limited. Pinnock claims, "It is unsound to think of exhaustive foreknowledge, implying that every detail of the future is already decided" (*MMM*, 8). For "though God knows all there is to know about the world, there are aspects about the future that even God does not know" (32).

God changes his mind. "Divine repentance is an important biblical theme" (*MMM*, 43). "Nevertheless, it appears that God is willing to change course" (43). "Prayer is an activity that brings new possibilities into existence for God and us" (46).

God is not in complete control of the world. As another consequence of an Openness View of God, "this means that God is not now in complete control of the world. . . . Things happen which God has not willed. . . . God's plans at this point in history are not always fulfilled" (*MMM*, 36). "Not everything that happens in the world happens for some reason" (47). "As [Greg] Boyd puts it: 'Only if God is the God of what *might be* and not only the God of what *will be* can we trust him to steer us'" (*MMM*, 103).

God undergoes change. "For example, even though the Bible says repeatedly that God changes his mind and alters his course of action, conventional theists reject the metaphor and deny that such things are possible for God" (*MMM*, 63). "I would say that God is *unchangeable in changeable ways*" (85–86)! "God changed when he became creator of the world" (86). Thus, "accepting possibility [in God as open theism does] may require the kind of doctrinal revisions which the open view is engaged in. If God is passible, then he is not, for example, unconditioned, immutable and atemporal" (59n82).

Pinnock admits affinity with process theology. "Candidly, I believe that conventional theists are more influenced by Plato, who was a pagan, than I am by Whitehead, who was a Christian" (*MMM*, 143). This Pinnock says in spite of the fact that Alfred North Whitehead, the father of process theology, denied virtually all of the attributes of the God of orthodox theology, biblical inerrancy, and all the fundamentals of the faith!

Inconsistency of Open Theism with Inerrancy

From an open theism view of God, one cannot logically draw the traditional view of total factual inerrancy. Pinnock's view of Scripture is consistent with his view of the nature of God. There are many reasons the open theists' view about God's foreknowledge is wrong:

It makes infallible pronouncements about the future impossible. First of all, if God has no infallible foreknowledge of future free acts, then he cannot make infallible pronouncements about the future. But the traditional view of total inerrancy does exactly this with the many prophecies in the Bible, most of which involve free actions. As we have seen, open theists try to explain away this problem by denying that these Bible prophecies are real predictions by reducing them to mere probabilistic forecasts. However, this is an unsatisfactory position for several reasons. (1) It is contrary to the very certainty expressed in the contexts of some passages like Isaiah 46:10, where God says that he knows "the end from the beginning." (2) It is contrary to the Bible's teaching that the cross was known by God from the foundation of the world (Rev. 13:8; Acts 2:22–23). (3) It is contrary to the fact that the elect were chosen and known by God before time began (Eph. 1:4; Rom. 8:29; 1 Pet. 1:2). (4) It is contrary to Jesus's statement that he informed them of the happening beforehand so that they would know it was truly a supernatural prediction (John 14:29). Indeed, Isaiah says the same thing in 46:9–10, where it declares emphatically that God knows "the end from the beginning" and even gives the name "Cyrus" of a king 150 years before he was born (Isa. 45:1).[4] In Daniel 2 and 7 God gives the course of the world kingdoms of Babylon, Medo-Persia, Greece, and Rome hundreds of years in advance. Likewise, God predicts through Daniel (in chap. 9) the very time of Christ's death in AD 33 (see Hoehner, *Chronological Aspects*).

It is contrary to the biblical test for a false prophet. The Openness View of God is contrary to the biblical test for a false prophet. Moses declares that one can know a false prophet if their prophecy does not come to pass. He writes: "When a prophet speaks in the name of the LORD, if the word does not come to pass or come true, that is a word that the LORD has not spoken" (Deut. 18:22). The punishment is to be death, the fear of which no doubt dissuaded many would-be prognosticators.

The biblical test for a false prophet refutes the open theists' idea that such statements about the future in Scripture are really not predictions (that can be falsified if they do not come to pass), but merely forecasts that may or may not come to pass without being false. This is directly contrary to what it says, that they are to be given capital punishment "if the word does not come to pass or come true."

It is contrary to the biblical teaching that God can't change his mind. The Openness View claims that God can change his mind. But if this is true, then one cannot be sure that the Bible is infallible, which implies that God cannot change his mind when he makes an utterance. Thus, "It is impossible for God to lie" (Heb. 6:18; cf. Titus 1:2). Indeed, "The Glory of Israel [God] will not lie or change His mind; for He is not a man that He should change his mind" (1 Sam. 15:29 NASB). The God of the Bible cannot go back on his word. He must remain faithful to it "for he cannot deny himself" (2 Tim. 2:13; cf. Rom. 11:29).

An infallible word from God cannot be broken, for that is what "infallible" means. An inerrant word *does not* err, but an infallible word *cannot* err. But if God can change his mind, then the Bible can err. And if the Bible can err, then it cannot be infallible. Strangely, some open theists prefer the word "infallible" to the word "inerrant," when in this sense "infallible" is actually a much stronger term. This is why many unlimited inerrantists, such as the authors, prefer both terms.

It is contrary to God's sovereignty. The Bible affirms that God is in complete control of all that occurs in his universe. Solomon declares that "the king's heart is a stream of water in the hand of the LORD; he turns it wherever he will" (Prov. 21:1). He is *"King of kings and Lord of lords"* (Rev. 19:16). "The Most High rules the kingdom of men and gives it to whom he will and sets over it the lowliest of men" (Dan. 4:17). "So shall my word be that goes out from my mouth; it shall not return to me empty, but it *shall accomplish that which I purpose, and shall succeed in the thing for which I sent it*" (Isa. 55:11; cf. 46:9–11). Christ is "over all creation," including "visible and invisible, whether thrones or powers or rulers or authorities" (Col. 1:15–16 NIV). The angels come before his throne to get their orders to obey (1 Kings 22; Job 1:6; 2:1). For *"at the name of Jesus every knee should bow, in heaven and on earth and under the earth* [evil spirits]" (Phil. 2:10). Even evil angels do his bidding (1 Kings 22:19–22). Even Satan complains, saying to God about Job, "Have you not put a hedge around him and his house and all that he has, on every side? You have blessed the work of his hands, and his possessions have increased in the land" (Job 1:10).

But open theism claims that God is not in complete control of the world, for they believe that when God gave free will to creatures, he thereby gave away some of his sovereignty. But this is as fallacious as assuming that because a teacher gives knowledge to a student, the teacher has lost the knowledge given. Likewise, an omniscient God can give knowledge without losing any knowledge, just as he has given being without losing any of his Being.

On Pinnock's truncated view of sovereignty, God is not in control of the process of divine communications so as to be able to guarantee a perfect product without error. So God's action is reduced to a Barthian idea that there has to be an accommodation to human error, at least to some degree, in order for God to achieve his redemptive goal in revelation. Given this diminished view of God's sovereignty, no errorless Scripture can be guaranteed. But on the classical view of God, by his very nature as a transcendent sovereign, all-powerful, all-knowing Being, God can guarantee in advance that there cannot be any errors in his revealed written Word.

Reasons Pinnock's Openness View of God and Inerrancy Are Not Orthodox

In view of this seriously truncated view of God, it is no wonder that open theists have also had a seriously truncated view of inerrancy. It is plain that open theism is contrary to the ETS statement on inerrancy, which they signed, as well as to the ICBI statement, which defines it for many reasons.

1. The word "God" in the ETS statement is the classical view of God embraced by its framers. But as shown above, Pinnock and others who signed it hold an open theism view, contrary to the ETS statement, which reads: "The Bible alone, and the Bible in its entirety, is the Word of God written and is therefore inerrant in the autographs." So to deny the classical view of "God" in the ETS statement is a denial of the statement's meaning of God, to say nothing of its denial of what is meant by "Word of God" and "inerrant" in the statement, since only the God of classical theism is incapable of error.

2. All the living framers of the ETS statement presented a written statement to ETS leaders insisting that the open theism view on inerrancy was contrary to the meaning of the ETS statement of which they were the framers. But the framers' meaning of the statement is definitive. On a later occasion, when ETS had a request for a Roman Catholic inerrantist to join ETS, he was barred because a living framer (Roger Nicole) recollected that the statement on the "Bible" was meant to exclude Roman Catholics, even though it says nothing about the number of books in the Bible (like "sixty-six books"), or uses the word "Protestant" or any other indicator that it means to eliminate Roman Catholics. One can only wonder about the consistency of eliminating a Roman Catholic who believes in inerrancy as the framers meant it on the basis of one framer's view when at the same time ETS refused to expel a member who did not believe in inerrancy the way the framers meant, on the basis of a statement from every living framer of the ETS statement!

3. The ETS statement equates "the Bible" and "the Word of God written." But Pinnock separates the two, denying the affirmation that "what the Bible says, God says." He rejects Warfield's view that "What the Bible says, God says" (*Scripture Principle*², 264). But this is the orthodox view on inspiration and inerrancy, not only held by the orthodox from at least Augustine to Warfield but also expressed in the ETS and ICBI statements. The ETS statement equates the "Bible" and "the Word of God written." And the ICBI "Short Statement" affirms the same: "2. Holy Scripture, being God's own Word, . . . is of infallible divine authority in all matters upon which it touches: it is to be believed, as God's instruction, in all that it affirms."

4. Pinnock accepts a Barthian view of the Bible: "Barth was right to speak about a distance between the Word of God and the text of the Bible" (*Scripture Principle* [*SP*], 99). But this is clearly contrary to the identity between the Bible and the written Word of God as affirmed by ETS. Indeed, in 1983, speaking of some who held "Barthian" views of Scripture, the minutes of the ETS Executive Committee read: "President Gordon Clark invited them to leave the society." But Clark Pinnock holds an unrecanted Barthian view of Scripture. He flatly states: "Barth was right to speak about a distance between the Word of God and the text of the Bible" (*SP*, 99, emphasis added).

5. The ICBI framers accepted the Old Princetonian view of B. B. Warfield and expressed it in their statement and explanations of it. However, Pinnock denies

the Warfieldian view, insisting that "inerrancy as Warfield understood it was a good deal more precise than the sort of reliability the Bible proposes. The Bible's emphasis tends to be upon the saving truth of its message and its supreme profitability in the life of faith and discipleship" (*SP*, 75).

6. Pinnock rejects the ICBI view as meant by its framers. He writes: "Therefore, there are a large number of evangelicals in North America appearing to defend the total inerrancy of the Bible. The language they use seems absolute and uncompromising: 'The authority of Scripture is inescapably impaired if this total divine inerrancy is in any way limited or disregarded, or made relative to a view of truth contrary to the Bible's own' (Chicago Statement, preamble). It sounds as if the slightest slip or flaw would bring down the whole house of authority. It seems as though we ought to defend the errorlessness of the Bible down to the last jot and tittle in order for it to be a viable religious authority" (*SP*, 127).

7. Pinnock's statements favorable to the ICBI inerrancy provision were based on his misinterpretation of article 13: he wrongly believes it allows for an inerrancy-of-intention view of truth, which he held. However, the ICBI framers were clear to reject this view, defining truth in terms of correspondence to the facts. The official ICBI interpretation of their statement is found in ICBI leader R. C. Sproul's book *Explaining Inerrancy* [*EI*]: "When we say that the truthfulness of Scripture ought to be evaluated according to its own standard, that means for Scripture to be true to its claims it must have an internal consistency . . . and that all the claims for the Bible must correspond with reality, whether that reality is historical, factual or spiritual" (41).

Pinnock clearly rejects the correspondence view of truth for an intentionalist view, affirming that "the wisest course to take would be to get on with defining inerrancy in relation to the purpose of the Bible and the phenomena it displays. When we do that, we will be surprised how open and permissive a term it is" (*SP*, 225). He declares: "All this means is that inerrancy is relative to the [redemptive] intention of the text. If it could be shown that the chronicler inflates some of the numbers he uses for his didactic [redemptive] purpose, he would be completely within his rights and not at variance with inerrancy" (78). But the ICBI framers clearly rejected this, declaring: "When we say that the truthfulness of Scripture ought to be evaluated according to its own standard, that means that . . . all the claims of the Bible must correspond with reality, whether that reality is historical, factual or spiritual" (Sproul, *EI*, 41). It adds, "By biblical standards truth and error is meant the view used both in the Bible and in everyday life, viz., a correspondence view of truth. This part of the article is directed toward those who would redefine truth to relate merely to redemptive intent, the purely personal, or the like, rather than to mean that which corresponds with reality" (Sproul, *EI*, 43–44).

8. Pinnock's view allows for minor errors in the Bible in nonredemptive matters, whereas as the ETS and ICBI statements do not allow for any errors in the Bible. Pinnock writes: "The authority of the Bible in faith and practice does not

rule out the possibility of an occasionally uncertain text, differences in details as between the Gospels, a lack of precision in the chronology of events recorded in the Books of Kings and Chronicles, a prescientific description of the world, and the like" (*SP*, 104). He adds:

> What could truly falsify the Bible would have to be something that could falsify the gospel and Christianity as well. It would have to be a difficulty that would radically call into question the truth of Jesus and His message of good news. Discovering some point of chronology in Matthew that could not be reconciled with a parallel in Luke would certainly not be any such thing. (129)

Pinnock declares, "I recognize that the Bible does not make a technical inerrancy claim or go into the kind of detail associated with the term in the contemporary discussion" (224–25).

By contrast, the ICBI Chicago Statement reads: "We affirm that inspiration, though not conferring omniscience, guaranteed true and trustworthy utterances on all matters of which the biblical authors were moved to write." And in its "Short Statement" it declares: "Being wholly and verbally God-given, Scripture is without error or fault in all its teaching, no less in what it states about God's acts in creation, about events of world history, and about its own literary origins under God, than its witness to God's grace in individual lives." And in article 12 it even goes so far as to say: "We further deny that scientific hypotheses about earth history may be properly used to overturn the teaching of Scripture on creation and the flood." The ICBI commentary confirms this, asserting that "the Bible does have something to say about the origin of the earth, about the advent of man, about creation, and about such matters that have scientific import, as the question of the flood." It rejects the view that "the Bible is not normal history, but is redemptive history with the accent on redemption. . . . Though the Bible is indeed *redemptive* history, it is also redemptive *history*, and this means that the acts of salvation wrought by God actually occurred in the space-time world" (Sproul, *EI*, 36–37). In short, ICBI affirms and Pinnock denies that the Bible is without any error on all matters on which it touches, including history and science, since it is God's Word, and God cannot err on any topic.

9. Pinnock's open theism view allows for myth in the Bible, which is rejected by the ICBI position. He declares: "In the narrative of the fall of Adam, there are numerous symbolic features (God molding man from dirt, the talking snake, God molding woman from Adam's rib, symbolic trees, four major rivers from one garden, etc.), so that it is natural to ask whether this is not a meaningful narration that does not stick only to factual matters" (*SP*, 119). He adds, "On the one hand, we cannot rule legend out a priori. It is, after all, a perfectly valid literary form, and we have to admit that it turns up in the Bible in at least some form. We referred already to Job's reference to Leviathan and can mention also Jotham's fable" (121–22). Further:

When we look at the Bible, it is clear that it is not radically mythical. The influence of myth is there in the Old Testament. The stories of creation and fall, of flood and the tower of Babel, are there in pagan texts and are worked over in Genesis from the angle of Israel's knowledge of God, but the framework is no longer mythical. . . . We read of a coin turning up in a fish's mouth and of the origin of the different languages of humankind. We hear about the magnificent exploits of Samson and Elisha. We even see evidence of the duplication of miracle stories in the gospels. All of them are things that if we read them in some other book we would surely identify as legends. (*SP*, 123)

However, as the previous point has demonstrated, the Bible is God's Word, and as such it cannot err on any topic, major or minor, redemption or otherwise. Peter denies that he uses "myths" when speaking about Jesus's transfiguration (2 Pet. 1:16). The New Testament refers to Adam and Eve, their creation and fall, as literal historical events (Matt. 19:4–5; Rom. 5:12; 1 Tim. 2:13–14). Jonah and the great fish (Matt. 12:40–42) and Noah and the flood (Matt. 24:37–39) are affirmed as literal historical events. To deny this is contrary to the ICBI view on inerrancy.

10. ETS and ICBI rejected Robert Gundry's view of midrash, but Pinnock accepts it. Indeed, Gundry was asked to resign from ETS for his midrash view, which claimed that whole sections of Matthew were not historical. But Pinnock defends this view: "There is no mythology to speak of in the New Testament. At most, there are fragments and suggestions of myth: for example, the strange allusion to the bodies of the saints being raised on Good Friday (Matt. 27:52) and the sick being healed through contact with pieces of cloth that had touched Paul's body (Acts 19:11–12)" (*SP*, 124). He adds, "There are cases in which the possibility of legend seems quite real. I mentioned the incident of the coin in the fish's mouth (Matt. 17:24–27). . . . The event is recorded only by Matthew and has the feel of a legendary feature" (125).

11. Pinnock admits to holding the inerrancy-of-purpose view in contrast to the inerrancy-of-fact position held by the ETS and ICBI framers. In his revised version of *Scripture Principle* (2006), he confesses: "I thus place myself today in an 'inerrancy of purpose' category" (262). "In other words, the Bible may contain errors of incidental kinds, but it teaches none" (264) because its primary purpose is to teach redemptive truth. He clearly says, "The wisest course to take would be to get on with defining inerrancy in relation to the purpose of the Bible and the phenomena it displays" (225).

However, this is contrary to ICBI framers, who said in their official commentary:

By biblical standards of truth and error is meant the view used both in the Bible and in everyday life, viz., *a correspondence view of truth*. This part of the article is directed toward those who would redefine truth to relate merely to *redemptive intent*, the purely personal or the like, rather than to mean *that which corresponds to reality*. For example, when Jesus affirmed that Jonah was in "the belly of the great fish," this statement is true, not simply because of the redemptive significance the story of Jonah has, but because *it is literally and historically true* [i.e., it corresponds to reality]. The same may be said of the New Testament assertions about Adam, Moses, David, and other Old Testament persons as well as about Old Testament events. (Sproul, *EI*, 43–44)

12. Pinnock claims: "I supported the 1978 Chicago Statement of the International Council on Biblical Inerrancy," noting that its famous article 13 "made room for nearly every well-intentioned Baptist" (*SP²*, 266) by defining truth in terms of redemptive intent or purpose. But as just shown in the previous points, this clearly is a misunderstanding of what the ICBI framers meant by inerrancy, as is revealed in its official commentary on the matter by Sproul: truth is defined as "what corresponds to reality," not what is in accord with redemptive intention.

13. Pinnock rejects the prophetic model of inerrancy, that God has spoken Scripture through the mouths of the prophets so that their words are God's words through them. "Paul J. Achtemeier has called attention to the *inadequacy of the prophetic model* for representing the biblical category of inspiration in its fullness—[in his work] *The Inspiration of Scripture*" (*SP*, 232n8, emphasis added). But this prophetic model is precisely what not only inerrancy proponents hold (namely, that the prophets' words were God's words through them); it is also what the Bible claims for itself.

First of all, the nature of a prophet, according to the Bible, is one who is the mouthpiece of God. The Bible describes a prophet in these terms: "I could not go beyond the command of the LORD my God to do less or more" (Num. 22:18). "See, I have made you like God to Pharaoh, and your brother Aaron shall be your prophet" (Exod. 7:1). "He shall be your mouth, and you shall be as God to him" (4:16). "You shall not add to the word that I command you, nor take from it" (Deut. 4:2). "I will put my words in his mouth, and he shall speak to them all that I command him" (18:18). "As the LORD lives, what the LORD says to me, that I will speak" (1 Kings 22:14). "The Lord GOD has spoken; who can but prophesy?" (Amos 3:8). Obeying the prophet's word was obeying God (Isa. 8:5; Jer. 3:6; Ezek. 21:1; Amos 3:1).

Second, the Bible claims to be a prophetic book. The whole Old Testament is considered to be the Law, or the books of Moses (who was a prophet; Deut. 18:15), and the Prophets (Matt. 5:17–18; Luke 24:27). Indeed, the New Testament refers to the whole Old Testament as being prophetic (Heb. 1:1; 2 Pet. 1:2–21). And the New Testament books were also written by apostles and prophets (Eph. 3:3–5; Rev. 22:7–8). Hence, the Scripture as a whole is a prophetic book, for "No prophecy of Scripture was ever produced by the will of man, but men spoke from God as they were carried along by the Holy Spirit" (2 Pet. 1:21). This being the case, then "every word" of Scripture "comes from the mouth of God" (Matt. 4:4). For, as David says, "The Spirit of the LORD speaks by me; his word is on my tongue" (2 Sam. 23:2). Therefore, to reject the prophetic model of Scripture, as Pinnock suggests, is not only to reject the ETS and ICBI views; it is also to reject the plenary (full) verbal inspiration and inerrancy model that the Bible teaches about itself.

Summary and Conclusion

There is a very important connection between one's view of God and one's view of the Bible. The total inerrancy view taught by the church fathers and expressed in the ETS and ICBI statements on inerrancy flows logically from the classical view of God held from the earliest fathers until just before 1900. For unless God is all-powerful and all-knowing (including future free choices), the Bible cannot be the infallible and inerrant Word of God. If God cannot err (because he knows everything), and if the Bible is the Word of God, then it is inescapable to conclude that the Bible is without error in everything it affirms. Thus, deviations from the orthodox view of God will lead to an unorthodox view of Scripture.

A belief in the errancy of the Bible flows logically from truncated views of God, such as are held by Deists, Unitarians, process theology, and open theism. In short, the nature of God is crucial to the inerrancy of Scripture. Nothing short of the classical view of God will serve as a solid basis for belief in the infallibility and full inerrancy of the Bible.

Sources

Archer, *Old Testament Introduction*

Augustine, *City of God*

———, *Reply to Faustus*

Blanchard, *Complete Works of Thomas Paine*

Calvin, *Institutes*

DeWolf, *Case for Theology*

———, *Theology of the Living*

Fesperman, "Jefferson Bible"

Ford, "Biblical Recital and Process Philosophy"

Fosdick, *Guide to Understanding*

Geisler, *The Bible*

———, *Systematic Theology*, vol. 2

Geisler, House, and Herrera, *Battle for God*

Hannah, *Inerrancy and the Church*

Hodge, A., and Warfield, *Inspiration*

Hodge, C., *Systematic Theology*

Irenaeus, *Against Heresies*

Justin Martyr, *Apology*

Luther, *Luther's Works*

Mayo, *Jefferson Himself*

McGowan, *Divine Spiration*

Ogden, "Authority of Scripture"

———, "On Revelation"

Paine, *Age of Reason*

Pinnock, *Most Moved Mover*

———, *Scripture Principle*

———, *Scripture Principle*, 2nd ed.

Rice, *Our God-Breathed Book*

Sproul, *Explaining Inerrancy*

Thomas Aquinas, *Exposition on Job*

———, *Summa*

Urquhart, *Inspiration and Accuracy*

Vanhoozer, *Drama of Doctrine*

———, *First Theology*

Warfield, *Inspiration and Authority of the Bible*

———, "Smith on Inspiration"

13

The Nature of Truth and Inerrancy

Introduction

The nature of *truth* and *error* is crucial to the whole inerrancy debate because inerrantists claim the Bible is wholly true and without error. Others claim the Bible is not wholly *true* and has some *errors*. In both cases, the proponents and opponents have a definition of "truth" and "error" in mind. And many times these are different notions of truth and error. Hence, it is very important to define what these terms mean. For example, if "error" only means what misleads, then what is mistaken but does not mislead would not be an "error." This is precisely the difference between unlimited inerrantists and some limited inerrantists.

Further, the full inerrantists imply that truth is objective, and often those who oppose this hold that truth is either subjective or at least has a subjective element to it. Classical inerrantists believe in propositional truth, while others deny propositional truth, at least as it applies to Scripture. So it is necessary to define our terms before we can meaningfully discuss whether the Bible is true and without error.

Definition of Truth

Inerrantists, such as those who affirm the Evangelical Theological Society (ETS) and International Council on Biblical Inerrancy (ICBI) statements on inerrancy, have in common the everyday meaning of the word "truth," namely, that truth is what corresponds to reality. And error is what does not correspond to reality. "Reality" can be factual reality, for example, like empirical facts in our world. Also,

233

"reality" can also mean nonmaterial reality, like soul, angel, or God. But "reality" in the broad sense used here means "being" or "that which is." Philosophers call this view the "correspondence view of truth." This is made plain in the ICBI Chicago Statement, article 13, and in the official ICBI commentary on it called *Explaining Inerrancy* [EI], by R. C. Sproul, one of the founders of ICBI and a framer of the Chicago Statement.

Article 13 of the Chicago Statement reads:

> We affirm the propriety of using inerrancy as a theological term with reference to the complete truthfulness of Scripture. We deny that it is proper to evaluate Scripture according to standards of truth and error that are alien to its usage or purpose. We further deny that inerrancy is negated by Biblical phenomena such as a lack of modern technical precision, irregularities of grammar or spelling, observational descriptions of nature, the reporting of falsehoods, the use of hyperbole and round numbers, the topical arrangement of material, variant selections of material in parallel accounts, or the use of free citations.

The ICBI Commentary explains: "It is important to note that the word *inerrancy* is called a theological term by Article XIII. It is an appropriate theological term to refer to the complete truthfulness of Scripture. That is basically what is being asserted with the term *inerrancy:* that the Bible is completely true, that all its affirmations and denials *correspond to reality*" (*EI*, 40–41, emphasis added).

Again, the commentary states:

> The first denial that "the Bible ought not to be evaluated according to standards of truth and error alien to its own use or purpose" indicates that it would be inappropriate to evaluate the Bible's internal consistency with its own truth claims by standards foreign to the Bible's own view of truth. When we say that the truthfulness of Scripture ought to be evaluated according to its own standards, that means that *for the Scripture to be true to its claim, it must have an internal consistency compatible with the biblical concept of truth and that all the claims of the Bible must correspond with reality, whether that reality is historical, factual or spiritual.* (41, emphasis added)

Here again "truth" in the claim of inerrantists is to be understood as what "correspond[s] with reality" and "reality" means everything that is, "*whether that reality is historical, factual or spiritual.*" The statement continues,

> "By biblical standards of truth and error" is meant the view used both *in the Bible* and in *everyday life*, viz., *a correspondence view of truth.* This part of the article is directed toward those who would redefine truth to relate merely to *redemptive intent,* the *purely personal* or *the like,* rather than to mean *that which corresponds to reality.* For example, when Jesus affirms that Jonah was in "the belly of the great fish," this statement is true, not simply because of the redemptive significance the story of Jonah has, but *because it is literally and historically true* [i.e., *it corresponds to reality*].

The same may be said of the New Testament assertions about Adam, Moses, David, and other Old Testament persons as well as about Old Testament events.

This is the official view of the ICBI framers, written by one of the framers and published by ICBI as the official commentary on the Chicago Statement. It should eliminate all doubt as to what the ICBI statement means on this important article 13. Hence, those like Clark Pinnock (see chap. 4) who claim they can agree with the ICBI statement but redefine the truth of Scripture in terms of redemptive intent are clearly at odds with what was meant by article 13. And assuming they know about the official ICBI commentary, such claims that they agree with the ICBI stand on inerrancy are disingenuous.

There are many important observations in these statements. First, truth is defined four times as what "corresponds to reality." Second, it explicitly says its affirmation of the correspondence view of truth is in opposition to (a) redemptive-intent views of truth, and (b) views of truth that are "purely personal" or "the like," which would include subjective views of truth. Third, it rules out the midrash and mythological views that dehistoricize the Bible, insisting that the New Testament references to Adam, Jonah, and others are "literally and historically true." Fourth, the statement speaks about the Bible's "internal consistency with its own truth claims." This entails the law of noncontradiction, one of the most foundational of all laws of thought. It also speaks against those who harp against rational attempts to harmonize all biblical truth claims. This is precisely what systematic theology is commissioned to do. God himself cannot violate his own consistent attributes (2 Tim. 2:13) and commands us to "avoid . . . contradictions" (Gk. *antitheseis*) or logical contradiction (1 Tim. 6:20). Mysteries there are (1 Tim. 3:16), which go beyond our ability to comprehend, but nothing in God's revealed truth goes against reason's ability to apprehend these truths (i.e., that is logically contradictory). Finally, a correspondence view of truth does not exclude all personal or subjective applications of truth in a believer's life. It simply insists on defining the core of truth as that which corresponds with reality, whatever that reality may be and to whomever these truths can be applied. Indeed, ICBI sponsored a whole Summit on the application of truth to every area of our lives. The book that resulted from the conference was called *Applying the Scriptures* (ed. Kantzer).

However, whatever else can be said, this official statement on the nature of truth as it is used in the ICBI statement should put to rest any claim made by Pinnock or others that it allows for "redemptive intent" or inerrancy of "purpose" view. Nor does it accommodate to those who deny the complete historical, factual inerrancy of the Bible.

Correspondence View of Truth Used by Philosophers

The question of the nature of truth is not unique to the inerrancy debate. Many noted philosophers, both ancient and modern, have held a correspondence view of truth. The following is a selection from some of those philosophers:

Aristotle (4th cent. BC). "To say of what is that it is not, or of what is not that it is, is false, while *to say of what is that it is*, and of what is not that it is not, is true; so that he who says of anything that it is or that it is not, will say either what is true or what is false" (*Metaphysics* 4.7.1011B.25–30, emphasis added). In short, truth is telling it like it is, and falsity is not telling it like it is.

Aristotle also says:

> Statements and beliefs . . . themselves remain completely unchangeable in every way; it is because the actual thing changes that the contrary come to belong to them. For the statement that somebody is sitting remains the same; it is because of change in the actual thing that it comes to be true at one time and false at another time [e.g., when he stands up]. (*Categories* 5.4a35–4b12)

In short, truth statements do not change, but a new statement about a new state of affairs can be contradictory to another statement about it at another time.

Anselm of Canterbury (1033–1109). In his work on *Truth, Freedom, and Evil,* Anselm defines truth as follows: "All I know is that when a *proposition signifies* that what is the case *is the case,* then it is true and there is truth in it" (chap. 2). Again, "For when a sign signifies the existence of *what does exist* or the nonexistence of what does not exist, then its signification is correct, and it is evident that the correctness exists without which the signification could not be correct" (chap. 13, emphasis added). In short, truth is what corresponds to "what is the case" or what "exists."

Thomas Aquinas (1225–1274). According to Thomas, "Truth is defined by the *conformity* of intellect and thing; and hence to know this *conformity* is to know truth" (*Summa* 1.16.2). Elsewhere he adds, "For all understanding is achieved by way of some assimilation of the knower to the thing known . . . —a harmony we call the *matching* of understanding and thing" (*On Truth* 1.1). Again, "For the meaning of truth consists in a *matching* of thing and understanding. . . . So the notion of truth is first found in understanding, . . . which *corresponds* to the thing and can be expected to *match* it" (1.3, emphasis added).

The italicized words include "correspond" and synonyms of it like "matching" and "conformity." Thomas Aquinas clearly held a correspondence view of truth. The "assimilation" is when the mind takes on the object in an intentional (mental) act and becomes like the object in the process of knowing.

G. E. Moore (1873–1958). The correspondence view of truth was not unique to ancient and medieval times; modern philosophers held it as well. Moore defines truth and falsity as follows: "To say that this belief is true is to say that there is in the Universe a fact to which it *corresponds;* and to say that is false is to say that there is not in the Universe any fact to which it corresponds" (*Main Problems,* 277). He asserts, "When the belief is true, it certainly does correspond to a fact; and when it does not correspond to a fact, then it certainly is false" (279, emphasis added).

Bertrand Russell (1872–1970). Even an agnostic philosopher like Russell accepted the correspondence view of truth. He writes: "A mind, which believes, believes truly when there is a *corresponding* complex. . . . This correspondence ensures truth, and its absence entails falsehood" (*Problems of Philosophy*, 129, emphasis added).

Etienne Gilson (1884–1978). Noted philosopher Gilson supports this view, insisting that

> the definition of truth as an *equation between the thing and the intellect* . . . is a simple expression of the fact that the problem of truth can have no meaning unless the intellect is regarded as distinct from its object. . . . Truth is only the *agreement* between reason which judges and reality which the judgment affirms. Error, on the other hand, is but their disagreement. (*Christian Philosophy*, 231, emphasis added)

Mortimer Adler (1902–2001). General editor of the Great Books series, Adler also defines truth as correspondence. He affirms that "the truth of thought consists in the *agreement or correspondence* between what one thinks, believes, or opines and what actually exists or does not exist in reality that is independent of our minds" (*Six Great Ideas*, 34, emphasis added).

William P. Alston (1921–2009). The linguistic philosopher William Alston also held a correspondence view of truth. He argues that "a statement (proposition, belief) is true if and only if *what the statement says to be the case actually is the case.* . . . Nothing more is required for the truth of the statement, and nothing less will suffice" (*Realist Conception*, 5–6, emphasis added).

This sampling of philosophers from different times and with diverse beliefs is sufficient to show how widespread and persistent the correspondence view of truth is. As we shall see, this is not only true among philosophers but more so among common people.

Correspondence View of Truth Used by Ordinary Persons

Not only do great philosophers define truth as correspondence, but so do other people every day. Consider the common usage of phrases. When we say, "That is not true" or "Tell me the truth" or "Don't hide the truth from me," we are always implying a correspondence view of truth. We expect a person's statements to correspond to the facts. And if they do not, then we believe that they are not telling the truth.

This is supported by the *Webster's Dictionary*[1] definition of "truth," which is based on ordinary usage of the word. The very first definition of "truth" regarding an utterance is "(1): the state of being the case: FACT." Likewise, under "true," Webster says, "(1): being in accordance with the actual state of affairs. . . . (2): conformable to an essential reality."

Certainly we do not accept as true something simply because someone intends it to be true. A trusted friend, with all good intentions, may give us false directions, but we still consider the directions false because they do not correspond with the facts. Neither sincerity nor good intentions are sufficient to determine truth. The truth is that people can be sincerely wrong.

Correspondence View of Truth Used by Courts

Likewise, no court in the land would accept as truth anything but what corresponds to the facts. Swearing to tell the expedient, the whole expedient, and nothing but the expedient, so help me future experience—that would never be accepted by a judge or jury. Only "the truth, the whole truth, and nothing but the truth" is accepted because only it corresponds to reality. And it does not matter whether one replaces the word "expedient" with the words "relevant" or "well-intended" or "personally satisfying" or "what feels good"—it would still not be acceptable by the general public or our legal institutions as "true." The correspondence view of truth is nearly universally understood in common discourse as what is meant by truth.

Life-and-death issues of justice depend on this correspondence view of truth. Otherwise, the innocent would be punished, and the guilty would go free. So a good theory (of truth) is a very practical thing. Ideas do have consequences. And true ideas truly will have good consequences (at least in the long run). So nothing is true because it has good consequences, but what is true will have good consequences, not only in a courtroom but also in life in general.

Correspondence View of Truth Used by Scientists

It is a given in the scientific world that truth is what corresponds to the facts. One's theory is only verified if it corresponds to the way the world really is. Speculation, hypothesis, and theory are allowed, but they are not considered true unless they correspond to the real world. This is why a hypothesis must be tested against the real universe.

Even in forensic science, one's theory about the past must be *in accord with* the way it was in order to be true. The difference is that we do know the past directly but only indirectly. We do not know the past by observation but by projection from what we know in the present. Forensic science is predicated upon the principle of uniformity that "the present is the key to the past." Nonetheless, a statement about the past is only considered "true" insofar as it is believed to *correspond* to the facts in the past.

Likewise, scientific speculations about the future are only considered "true" if they are verified in the future to correspond to the state of affairs predicted by the hypothesis. So, whether science deals with the past, present, or future, its statements are considered true only if they correspond with the facts.

In summary, philosophy, common sense, law, and science conspire together in support of the correspondence view of truth. Likewise, the Bible itself employs the correspondence view of truth.

Correspondence View of Truth Used in the Bible

Since the Bible was written in common language for common people, it should be no surprise that it too employs a correspondence view of truth. There are many lines of evidence to support this conclusion (see Preus, *Inspiration of Scripture*, 24).

1. The command not to bear false witness is based upon a correspondence view of truth. "You shall not give false witness against your neighbor" (Exod. 20:16) depends on the correspondence view of truth. The command implies that any statement that does not correspond to the facts is false.

2. Satan is called "a liar" (John 8:44) because his statement to Eve, "You will not surely die" (Gen. 3:4), did not correspond to what God *really* said: "You shall surely die" (Gen. 2:17).

3. Ananias and Sapphira "lied" to the apostles by misrepresenting the factual state of affairs about their finances (Acts 5:1–4).

4. Joseph's statement to his brothers implies a correspondence view of truth: "Send one of you, and let him get your brother, while you remain confined, that your words may be tested, whether there is truth in you" (Gen. 42:16).

5. Moses commands that false prophets be tested on the grounds that "when a prophet speaks in the name of the LORD, if the word does not come to pass or come true, that is a word that the LORD has not spoken" (Deut. 18:22). This too implies correspondence to reality is what is meant by "true."

6. Solomon's prayer at the dedication of the temple entails a correspondence view of truth: "Now therefore, O God of Israel, let your word [that there will be a temple] be confirmed, which you have spoken to your servant David my father" (1 Kings 8:26).

7. The prophecies of Micaiah were considered to be "the truth" and the false prophets' false words to be lies because the former corresponded with the facts of reality (1 Kings 22:16–22).

8. According to the psalmist, something is considered a "falsehood" if it does not correspond to God's law (truth; Ps. 119:163).

9. Proverbs states, "A truthful witness saves lives, but one who breathes out lies is deceitful" (14:25), which implies that truth is factually correct.

10. Nebuchadnezzar demands of his wise men to know the *facts*, and he considers anything else to be "lying and corrupt words" (Dan. 2:9).

11. Jesus's statement in John 5:33 entails a correspondence view of truth: "You sent to John, and he has borne witness to the truth."

12. In Acts 24 there is an unmistakable usage of the correspondence view. The Jews say to the governor about Paul, "By examining him yourself you will be able to find out from him about everything of which we accuse him" (v. 8). They continue, "You can verify that" (v. 11).

13. Paul clearly implies a correspondence view of truth when he writes, "Having put away falsehood, let each one of you speak the truth with his neighbor" (Eph. 4:25).

14. The biblical use of the word "err" supports a correspondence view of truth, since it is used of unintentional "errors" (cf. Lev. 4:2, 13, 27 NASB, etc.). Certain acts are wrong, whether the trespassers intend to commit them or not, and hence a guilt offering is called for to atone for their "error."

Thus it is clear that the Bible employs and embraces a correspondence view of truth. So it is wrong to speak of a biblical truth that is contrary to a correspondence view. As noted above, even the Ten Commandments imply a correspondence view, as does the test for a false prophet and numerous other things. This is not to say that the term "truth" is limited to correspondence in the Bible. It is not. It often implies trustworthiness as well. Again, a statement is trustworthy only if it corresponds to reality. And correspondence is the basis of trustworthiness.

A Defense of the Correspondence View

Not only is a correspondence view of truth used by philosophers, by everyday persons, by our legal system, by scientists and in the Bible, but it is also undeniable. Consider the arguments for it.

Arguments for a Correspondence View of Truth

First, noncorrespondence views of truth are self-defeating. All noncorrespondence views of truth imply a correspondence view of truth in their very attempt to deny the correspondence view. For example, the claim that "the noncorrespondence view is true" implies that this view corresponds to reality. If so, then the noncorrespondence view cannot even express itself without using the correspondence view of truth.

Second, even opponents of the correspondence view of truth cannot avoid it. In fact, opponents of the view believe that it is false. But by "false" here they mean that it does not correspond with reality. Yet this is exactly what the correspondence view of truth holds.

Third, it is impossible to know that a statement is false without a correspondence view of truth. If a statement does not have to correspond to reality to be true, then any statement could be true. Hence, demonstrating that a statement is false would be impossible unless there was some state of affairs (i.e., "facts") by which it could be known to be false.

Fourth, all communication would break down without a correspondence view of truth. Certainly all factual communication depends on informative statements. But informative statements must be factually true (that is, they must correspond to the facts) in order to inform one correctly. Further, in the final analysis all communication seems to depend ultimately on something being literally or factually true, for we cannot know something (like a metaphor) is not literally true unless we understand what is literal. Given this, it follows that all communication depends in the final analysis on a correspondence view of truth.

Fifth, even the pragmatic theory of truth depends on the correspondence view of truth. The pragmatic theory claims that something is true only if desired results occur. So the results must correspond to one's desires or intentions. But they could not know this without implying that correspondence to a certain state of affairs is necessary for it to be true. So they too imply a correspondence view of truth.

Sixth, even the intentionalist view of truth depends on the correspondence view. For one can only know that the redemptive intent is successful if it works toward salvation. In other words, unless the results correspond to the intent, one does not know it is true. But here again correspondence is necessary, not with facts in the present but with a certain state of affairs in the future.

In brief, not only is the correspondence view undeniable (since the denial purports to correspond with reality), but it also is inescapable since other views of truth depend on it to make sense out of their view. It is similar to the now famous Clintonism: "It depends on what the meaning of 'is' is." The very sentence implies that we know what the meaning of "is" is. Otherwise we would not know the meaning of the last "is" in the sentence. So the meaning of the first "is" is the same as the meaning of the last "is." Likewise, we would not be able either to deny the correspondence view of truth or to affirm an opposing view unless we believed that the correspondence view of truth was the correct view.

Answering Objections to Truth as Correspondence

Objections to the correspondence view of truth come from within as well as from without; they emanate from both Christian and non-Christian sources. The major objections from both sides include the following:

Objection 1. When Jesus said "I am . . . the truth" (John 14:6), he demonstrated that truth is personal, not propositional. This falsifies the correspondence view of truth in which truth is a characteristic of propositions (or expressions) about reality and not about the reality itself.

Reply 1. What Jesus said does not refute the correspondence view of truth. A person can correspond to reality as well as a proposition can. As the Logos (Word), he is the perfect expression of God (John 1:1). As the "exact imprint" (image) of the invisible God (Heb. 1:3), Jesus perfectly corresponds to the Father (John 1:18). He said to Philip, "Whoever has seen me has seen the Father" (14:9). So a person can correspond to another in his thoughts and words (cf. John 14:10), character, and actions. Jesus was all of these in correspondence to the Father. In this sense, persons can be said to be true or to express the truth. Nothing in any of these senses is contrary to a correspondence view of truth. On the contrary, they all depend on it.

Objection 2. The Bible teaches that God is "true" or "truth." It declares that there is only one true God, as opposed to all the false gods (cf. Exod. 20:3; 1 Cor. 8:4–6). Jeremiah declared that "The LORD is the true God" (10:10). Indeed, truth is an attribute of God. Yet there is nothing outside of God to which he corresponds. But according to the correspondence view, all truth is that which correctly represents reality. And since there is nothing outside of God to which he can correspond, then it follows that he is not true, though the Bible says he is (Rom. 3:4).

Reply 2. First of all, the Bible rarely uses the word "true" of God, and when it does it generally means "faithful" or "steadfast." Second, the biblical words for "truth"

(Heb. 'ĕmet; Gk. alētheia) often imply more (not less) than correspondence with reality. They often mean "faithfulness" and are sometimes so translated. Third, "truth" as correspondence relates to God in several ways. (a) First of all, God's words correspond to his thoughts. So God is said to be true in the sense that his Word corresponds to himself and can be trusted. (b) God's thoughts are identical to himself (since God is one indivisible Being of whom we can say many things); this is a kind of perfect "correspondence." In this sense, God is both true (faithful) and "true" to himself in what he says and does (= faithfulness). (c) If truth is understood strictly as what corresponds to another, then in this sense God would not be "true"; he would simply be the ultimate reality to which something else corresponds. (d) Finally, the basic fallacy in this objection is an equivocal use of the definition. If correspondence means correspondence to something *outside* one's self, then of course God cannot be truth but only that ultimate reality to which all truth must correspond. If, on the other hand, correspondence can also be *inside one's self*, then God can correspond to himself in the most perfect way. In this sense, God is truth in a perfect way by self-identity.

Consider the following fallacious thinking: (a) All who submit to the authority of the pope are Roman Catholic; (b) But the pope cannot submit to himself; (c) Therefore, the pope is not Roman Catholic. The mistake here is in the second premise. Contrary to the claim, the pope *can* submit to himself. He simply has to follow the rules he lays down for Roman Catholics. Likewise, God can and does live in accord with his own authority and words. And in this sense he is true to himself, that is, to his own teachings.

Objection 3. There are many other theories of truth. Why accept the correspondence view as the only one? For example, there is the *coherence* theory of truth (what coheres is true), the *pragmatic* theory of truth (what works is true), and the *existential-relevance* theory of truth (what is relevant to my existence is true).

Reply 3. There are many other ways to *test* truth, but with regard to statements, correspondence is the only proper way to *define* truth. For example, the best way to test the truth claim that "this is the best ice cream available" is to try all of them. This is a pragmatic test for truth. However, truth is not defined by its results. It is defined by whether it corresponds to the reality to which it points.

Further, the coherence view is not a definition of truth; it is a subtest for whether the statements are true. If they contradict one another, then they cannot both be true. Even then, it is only a negative test since some things cohere (are not contradictory) but have no truth content since there is no reality to which they correspond. "All husbands are married" is consistent, but as such it is an empty statement if it does not refer to any real husbands.

Likewise, there is a difference between what truth *is* and what truth *does*. Truth is *correspondence*, but truth has certain *consequences*. Truth itself should not be confused with its results or with its application. The failure to make this distinction leads to wrong views of the nature of truth. Something is not true because of its results, even though what is true will have good consequences, at least in the long run.

Objection 4. John 5:31 appears to be an exception. Jesus says, "If I alone bear witness about myself, my testimony is not deemed true." This seems to imply that Jesus's factually correct statements about himself would not be "true."

Reply 4. First, this would not make sense even by an intentionalist's definition of truth, for surely Jesus *intended* to say something true about himself. Second, what is meant in the context of this passage is that a self-testimony alone does not *establish* something as true. As the Bible informs us, the testimony of "two or three [other] witnesses" is needed for a word or testimony to be *established* (Matt. 18:16; cf. John 8:17) and not by one's own word alone. Elsewhere Jesus teaches that his Word alone can be established: "Even if I do bear witness about myself, my testimony is true" (John 8:14), meaning that it is factually correct (corresponds to reality), even if others do not accept it.

Evaluation of the Intentionalist View of Truth

A view of truth that is popular in biblical and theological circles is an intentionalist view of truth. That is, something is true if it has good (redemptive, salvific, spiritual, etc.) intentions. Some have appealed to 2 Timothy 3:15 to justify this view. Paul speaks of the "sacred writings, which are able to make you wise for salvation." He goes on to say that "all Scripture is . . . profitable, . . . that the man of God may be competent, equipped for every good work" (3:16–17). Hence, according to the intentionalist view of truth, the Scriptures are true or profitable not because they correspond to reality but because they bring about a certain result.

Statement of the Intentionalist View of Truth

According to this "redemptive purpose" view, the Bible is only inerrant in its redemptive purpose to save us, but this does not mean that every statement in a text is factually true. Something can have errors in it and still have its edifying effect on our life.

Clark Pinnock held this view, declaring, "*Inerrancy is relative to the intent of the Scriptures,* and this has to be hermeneutically determined" (*Scripture Principle,* 225). Again, "All this means is that *inerrancy is relative to the intention of the text. If it could be shown that the Chronicler inflates some of the numbers he uses for his didactic purpose,* he would be completely within his rights and not at variance with inerrancy" (78). "*The Bible will seem reliable enough in terms of its soteric [saving] purpose*" (104–5).

Jack Rogers of Fuller Theological Seminary affirms this same view, claiming that "a biblical definition of error" is not what involves "incorrectness" but what involves "deception" (Rogers and McKim, *Authority and Interpretation,* 31). Citing Berkouwer with approval, he writes: "It is not that Scripture offers us no information but that the nature of this information is unique. It is governed by the purpose of God's revelation." And God's purpose is redemptive. Hence, "swerving from the truth" of redemption is what constitutes error (431), not factually incorrect statements. "For the purpose of the God-breathed Scripture is not at all to provide scientific gnosis [knowledge] . . . but to witness of the salvation of God unto faith"

(431). For example, citing Berkouwer with approval again, Rogers states, "Paul in the least did not render timeless propositions concerning womanhood" (432). Rather, "religious knowledge was either personal, relational knowledge, or it was not considered worthy of the name knowledge" (434). This is true, he says, because "the purpose of Scripture was to bring us to salvation in Christ. Berkouwer, like Kuyper and Bavinck, was open to the results of critical scholarship in a way that the Princeton theology was not" (429). Thus Rogers rejects the view that "Scripture had come in what seems to us a perfect form" (429). In fact, it is not the form but the function of Scripture (viz., to make us wise to salvation) that is perfect. Thus the truth of Scripture is inspired in its redemptive function of intent. This means that factual mistakes, not essential to salvation, do not really count as errors.

Kevin Vanhoozer (see chap. 8 above) also holds a form of this view in his speech-act theory: truth is not found in an affirmation (or negation), which he calls a locution. Rather, it is found in an illocution, or purpose, for which the author made this affirmation.

Critique of the Intentionalist View of Truth

First of all, many statements can agree with the intention of the author, but they are mistaken nonetheless. "Slips of the tongue" do occur, but they are false. Yet some claim that if a statement is true because it was intended to be true, even if it was mistaken, then it would still be true. But this is absurd. How can mistaken and incorrect statements be true?

Second, if something is true because someone intended it to be true, then all sincere statements ever uttered would be true—even those that were patently absurd! But many sincere people have been sincerely wrong. Hence, the intentionalists' view of truth is inadequate.

Third, the view does not accord with the biblical use of the term "sin" or "error." In the Old Testament there is a sin offering (Lev. 4:2) for unintentional sins. But in an intentionalist view, these would not be sins since they are unintended by the person doing them. Only on a correspondence view of truth does this sin offering make any sense because the violation is unintended and yet is called "sin" (cf. Lev. 4:2, 13, 27, etc.). Certain acts are wrong, whether the trespassers intend to commit them or not; hence a guilt offering is called for to atone for their "error." Of the five times shāgag ("to err") is used in the Old Testament (Gen. 6:3; Lev. 5:18; Num. 15:28; Job 12:16; Ps. 119:67), the Leviticus and Numbers references clearly refer to erring unintentionally. Further, the noun shĕgāgâ ("error") is used nineteen times, and all but two are of unintentional errors (Lev. 4:2, 22, 27; 5:15, 18; 22:14; Num. 15:24, 25 [twice], 26, 27, 28, 29; 35:11, 15; Josh. 20:3, 9).[2] In short, the biblical use of the word "error" does not fit the intentionist view of truth and error.

Evaluation of the Existentially Relevant View of Truth

Following the view of Søren Kierkegaard (1813–55) and other existential philosophers, some have insisted that truth is what is relevant to our personal life or existence and false if it is not. Truth is subjectivity, as Kierkegaard put it. Truth is what is livable. As Martin Buber states and Emil Brunner agrees, truth is found in persons, not in propositions. Other versions of this speak of truth as a personal encounter, or truth as based in personal relationships. There are a number of problems with this definition of truth.

At best, such definitions of truth are misleading or misdirected. At worst, they are mistaken. There is truth about personal relations, but truth itself is not personal. There are truths about subjective experiences, but subjective relations as such are not true. Truth can be enhanced by good relationships and subjective experiences, but these subjective relations are neither the basis for truth nor truth itself.

As we have seen, truth as used by philosophers, everyday persons, courts, science, and in the Bible means that which corresponds to reality. To be sure, it is not only propositions (affirmations or denials) that are true or false. Other expressions, sign language, gestures, attitudes, and actions can all be true or false insofar as they correspond to reality.

First, certainly every Bible student knows that God desires truth to be lived, to be applied to our personal lives. Truth is something we should not only know in our mind, but we should also believe it in our heart (Rom. 10:9) and live it in our lives (James 1:22). However, though truth should be applied to persons, this does not make truth itself personal. Although spiritual truth should be appropriated subjectively, it does not follow that truth is subjective.

Second, not all truth is spiritual truth (i.e., truth needed for our spiritual growth). There are many other kinds of truth, including physical, mathematical, historical, scientific, and theoretical truths. But if truth by its very nature was found only in existential relevance, then none of these could be true. Thus existential or personal relevance fails as a complete definition of truth.

Third, what is true will be relevant, but not everything relevant is true. A pen is relevant to an atheist writer, and a gun is relevant to a murderer. But this does not make the former true or the latter good. A truth about life will be relevant to life. But not everything relevant to one's life will be true.

Important Entailments of a Correspondence View of Truth

Before we discuss the importance of a correspondence view of truth to the inerrancy debate, we need to discuss briefly some of the important entailments of the correspondence view of truth as related to the inerrancy debate. *The first is the objective nature of truth, and the second is the propositional nature of truth.*

Objective Nature of Truth

Understanding truth as that which corresponds to reality entails the objectivity of truth. The reason for this is simple enough. If truth is what corresponds to reality, then there must be some objective reality to which it can correspond. This is even clearer if we state truth as what corresponds to the facts. For there must be some objective facts that truth matches; otherwise it would make no sense to define truth in this manner.

This was made clear by some of the above definitions of truth. For example, Aristotle speaks of truth as "saying" or making a statement about "what is," which is some objective reality. He adds, "Statements and beliefs ... themselves remain completely unchangeable in every way; it is because the *actual thing* changes that the contrary comes to belong to them." This, too, implies that there is some "actual thing" out there about which statements can be made. As noted above, Thomas Aquinas identifies "truth" as "defined by the *conformity* of intellect and *thing*." Again, "truth consists in a matching of *thing*" or *objective reality*. G. E. Moore is even more explicit when he speaks of truth as corresponding to some "*fact*" in the "*universe*." Likewise, Gilson speaks of truth as "an equation between the [objective] *thing* and the intellect," which is not possible "unless the intellect is regarded as *distinct from its object*." Mortimer Adler is clear in saying, "The truth of thought consists in the agreement or correspondence between what one thinks, believes, or opines and *what actually exists or does not exist in reality that is independent of our minds*." Without this external reality, there can be no correspondence view of truth. William Alston rightly points out that "a statement (proposition, belief) is true if and only if what the statement says to be the case *actually is the case*," namely, the objective reality to which the statement corresponds. Not only is truth correspondence; truth is also objective.

Also entailed in the correspondence view of truth is that truth is objective, not subjective. What is true is true for everyone, not just some people. Indeed, evangelical theology is predicated on the premise that the Bible is *the* truth (John 17:17), not just *a* truth. It is God's Word (John 10:34–35), and God cannot lie (Heb. 6:18; Titus 1:2). Hence, God's Word cannot lie. Thus, if Christianity is true, then it is not just true for me, it is true for everyone. It is not just true subjectively, but it is also true objectively. This is the reason why article 6 of the ICBI statement on hermeneutics affirms: "We affirm that the Bible expresses God's truth in propositional statements, and *we declare that biblical truth is both objective and absolute*" (emphasis added). Let's briefly contrast the objective and subjective views of truth:

Objective view of truth	Subjective view of truth
True for everyone	True for me but not for everyone
True everywhere	True only in some places
True all the time	True only sometimes
True absolutely	True relatively

This does not mean, as Aristotle pointed out, that the objective reality cannot change and, hence, what was formerly true of it is no longer true. For when a person stands up, then it is no longer true that they are sitting down. It means that both statements were objectively true when they were made and about the object and time to which they referred.

Likewise, this does not mean that when we say, "It is humid in the jungle," it will be humid everywhere, even in the desert. What it means is that the statement "It is humid in the jungle" is objectively true for everyone everywhere and for all time, not that it is humid everywhere for everyone all the time. It is a statement that corresponds to its object—which is the jungle, and that statement is true everywhere for everyone, even in places where it is arid.

In short, the correspondence view of truth involves the objectivity of truth. There must be an objective reality to which the mind (thoughts or expressions) actually refers. Otherwise, a correspondence view of truth makes no sense.[3]

Propositional Truth

Another entailment of the correspondence view of truth is that truth—which is objective truth—can be put in propositional form. Most of the above-cited philosophers noted this in different ways. They spoke of "saying" the truth or making "a statement (proposition, belief, expression)" about the reality to which that statement referred.

Before we leave the topic, a few comments will be helpful in connection with making truth statements that correspond to reality. As we have shown above, truth as used by philosophers, everyday persons, courts, scientists, and in the Bible means that which corresponds to reality. But it is not only propositions (statements that affirm or deny) that are true or false. Other expressions, sign language, gestures, attitudes, and even actions can all be true or false insofar as they correspond to reality. But whatever way one "thinks," "states," or "expresses" something about objective reality, it follows that truth as correspondence entails the conclusion that truth is propositionalizable, that it can be put into propositions that do apply to that objective reality. This means that every truth contained in the Bible is a propositional truth. In fact, there are no nonpropositional truths in the Bible or anywhere else. For if it is true, then it corresponds to some objective reality, and if it corresponds to objective reality, then it can be put into propositional form.

Yet inerrantists do not claim that every statement in the Bible is a truth statement. Some statements are merely expression of emotion. Others are commands, questions, prayers, and so on. Now it is true (or false) that someone gave a command, but a command as such is not a truth proposition. The command could imply a truth or truths, such as the command to "Believe in the Lord Jesus" (Acts 16:31) implies a lot of truth, such as "Jesus is Lord; he can save; it will be beneficial for you to believe," but the command as such makes no truth claims. This is true of questions, prayers, and stories, all of which may imply certain truth claims. So, while not all the Bible is propositional truth statements, much of the rest of it contains propositional truth, that is, propositionalizable truth claims. And the inerrantists claim that whatever is in the Bible, explicitly or implicitly, claims to be true and is true (i.e., corresponds to reality).

While not everything in the Bible is or contains propositional truth, it nonetheless could be said that all the Bible is sentential revelation since it is all made up of sentences or a string of words[4] that make sense. But not all the sentences are truth statements, since not all of them make truth claims (with affirmations or denials).

Having said this, the denial of the propositional revelation of the Bible is wrong for two reasons. First, the Bible contains a multitude of propositional statements that affirm or deny something as true or false. Second, not everything has to be in the form of a proposition to contain a propositional truth. As just noted, even commands can contain propositional truth. Likewise, questions can contain propositions. So all the truth contained in the Bible is propositionalizable, even if it is not presented in the form of a proposition. Thus the claim of the inerrantist for propositional truth and that the Bible contains propositional revelation of truth is simply another way to claim that everything that the Bible says is true is surely true, and that everything the Bible says is false is surely false. This is sometimes generalized to say, "The Bible is completely true." Even Jesus did this when he said to the Father, "Your Word is truth" (John 17:17).

If truth is objective, as shown above, and if the Bible contains truth claims, then these are objective truth claims. And if truth claims, however couched or expressed in the language of the Bible, can be expressed in propositions, then there is propositional truth in the Bible. This is why article 6 of the ICBI statement on hermeneutics and inerrancy reads: "We affirm that the Bible expresses God's truth in *propositional statements,* and we declare that biblical truth is both *objective and absolute*" (emphasis added). If these truth claims contain revelation from God, then it is meaningful to speak of propositional revelation. If one could successfully argue that language is completely incapable of expressing objective truth, only then would propositional revelation not be possible. But in that case one would challenge the consistency of the opponent of objective propositional truth. Thus in the denial of the correspondence view of truth, the opponent of propositional truth is making a propositional truth statement.

Correspondence View of Truth Important in the Inerrancy Debate

Now that we have defined and defended the nature of truth as what corresponds to reality, we can draw out its significance for the inerrancy debate. Our thesis here is simple: the historic inerrancy view as expressed in the ETS and ICBI statements entails a correspondence view of truth. Thus, those who use an intentionalist view of truth to define inerrancy are really denying inerrancy. One's view of truth is largely determinative of what he believes about inerrancy.

Contrasting Limited and Unlimited Inerrancy

For example, both Jack Rogers and Clark Pinnock can affirm, "The Bible is wholly true and without errors." Indeed, Pinnock claimed to be able to affirm the ICBI inerrancy statement (*SP,* 265–66). Likewise, Rogers can agree that the Bible is error-free. Another contemporary example of the limited inerrancy position is Kevin Vanhoozer, who denies a complete correspondence view of truth (see chap. 8 above). However, all of these men mean something quite different from that of the ETS and ICBI framers. When traditional total inerrantists affirm that the Bible is free from all errors, they mean it is free from error in any statements on any topic, redemptive or not, that corresponds to reality. Thus, when limited inerrantists affirm that the Bible is wholly true, they mean one of several things: (1) It is free of all errors on topics it addresses; (2) it is free of all errors on redemptive matters; or (3) it is free of all errors that would hinder its accomplishing its intended redemptive purpose.

For the sake of discussion, let's call view 1 "unlimited inerrancy" and views 2 and 3 "limited inerrancy." The following chart summarizes some significant differences.

Unlimited inerrancy	Limited inerrancy
Consistent use of correspondence	Inconsistent use of correspondence
Divine adaptation to the finite	Divine accommodation to error
Language of God is descriptive	Language of God is not descriptive
No errors of any kind in Bible	No major or redemptive errors in Bible
All mistakes are errors	Only intentional mistakes are errors

Critiquing the Limited Inerrancy View

It is clear that the framers of both ETS and ICBI statements on inerrancy were unlimited inerrantists. Besides being contradictory to the standard statements on inerrancy embraced by ETS and ICBI, the limited inerrancy view has many serious problems. These include an unbiblical and unjustifiable view of God, of truth, of language, and of the incarnation. Consider the following official statements of ICBI: the Chicago Statement on Biblical Inerrancy's "Short Statement" declares:

1. God, who is Himself truth and speaks truth only, has inspired Holy Scripture. . . .

2. Holy Scripture . . . is of *infallible divine authority* in all matters upon which it touches: it is to be believed, as God's instruction, in all that it affirms. . . .

4. Being wholly and verbally God-given, *Scripture is without error or fault in all its teaching,* no less in what it states about God's acts in creation, about the events of world history, and about its own literary origins under God, than in its witness to God's saving grace in individual lives.

5. The authority of Scripture is inescapably impaired if this total divine inerrancy is in any way limited or disregarded, or made relative to a view of truth contrary to the Bible's own.

The Chicago Statement on inerrancy (1978) includes the following statements on unlimited inerrancy (emphasis added):

Article 3. We affirm that the written *Word in its entirety* is revelation given by God.

Article 6. We affirm that the *whole of Scripture and all its parts,* down to the very words of the original, were given by divine inspiration. *We deny that the inspiration of Scripture can rightly be affirmed of the whole without the parts, or of some parts but not the whole.*

Article 9. We affirm that inspiration, though not conferring omniscience, *guaranteed true and trustworthy utterance on all matters of which the Biblical authors were moved to speak and write.*

Article 11. We affirm that Scripture, having been given by divine inspiration, is infallible, so that, far from misleading us, *it is true and reliable in all the matters it addresses. We deny that it is possible for the Bible to be at the same time infallible and errant in its assertions.* Infallibility and inerrancy may be distinguished, but not separated.

Article 12. We affirm that Scripture in *its entirety is inerrant, being free from all falsehood, fraud, or deceit. We deny that Biblical infallibility and inerrancy are limited to spiritual, religious, or redemptive themes, exclusive of assertions in the fields of history and science. We further deny that scientific hypotheses about earth history may properly be used to overturn the teaching of Scripture on creation and the flood.*

Article 13. We affirm the propriety of using inerrancy as a theological term with reference to *the complete truthfulness of Scripture.* We deny that it is proper to evaluate Scripture according to standards of truth and error that are alien to its usage or purpose.

Article 14. We affirm the unity and internal consistency of Scripture. *We deny that alleged errors and discrepancies that have not yet been resolved vitiate the truth claims of the Bible. We deny that Jesus' teaching about Scripture may be dismissed by appeals to accommodation or to any natural limitation of His humanity.*

In addition, the official ICBI Commentary on the Chicago Statement supports unlimited inerrancy, as in these comments on articles 12 and 13:

> *On article 12.* It has been fashionable in certain quarters to maintain that the Bible is not normal history, but redemptive history with an accent on redemption. Theories have been established that would limit inspiration to the redemptive theme of redemptive history, allowing the historical dimension of redemptive history to be errant. (Sproul, *EI*, 36)
>
> Though the Bible is indeed *redemptive* history, it is also redemptive *history*, and this means that the acts of salvation wrought by God actually occurred in the space-time world. (37)
>
> The denial [in art. 12] explicitly rejects the tendency of some to limit infallibility and inerrancy to specific segments of the biblical message. (36)
>
> *On article 13.* When we say that the truthfulness of Scripture ought to be evaluated according to its own standards, that means that . . . all the claims of the Bible must correspond with reality, whether that reality is historical, factual or spiritual. (41)
>
> "By biblical standards of truth and error" is meant the view used both in the Bible and in everyday life, viz., a correspondence view of truth. This part of the article is directed toward those who would redefine truth to relate merely to redemptive intent, the purely personal, or the like, rather than to mean that which corresponds with reality. (43–44)

Finally, the official commentary on the ICBI inerrancy statement on hermeneutics also supports total inerrancy:

On article 6. We further affirm that a statement is true if it *represents matters as they actually are,* but is an error if it misrepresents the facts.

The denial makes it evident that views which redefine error to mean what "misleads," rather than what is a mistake, must be rejected.

On article 13. We deny that generic categories which negate historicity may rightly be imposed on biblical narratives which present themselves as factual. Some, for instance, take Adam to be a myth, whereas in Scripture he is presented as a real person. Others take Jonah to be an allegory when he is presented as a historical person and [is] so referred to by Christ.

On article 14. We deny that any event, discourse or saying reported in Scripture was invented by the biblical writers or by the traditions they incorporated.

On article 22. [It] affirms that Genesis 1–11 is factual, as is the rest of the book. The denial makes it evident that views which redefine error to mean what "misleads," rather than what is a mistake, must be rejected (Geisler, "Explaining Hermeneutics," in *HI,* 903).

In addition to being contrary to the ICBI statements on inerrancy adopted by ETS, representing the largest group of evangelical scholars in the world, there are strong reasons for rejecting limited inerrancy. Consider the following:

1. *Limited inerrancy often has a diminished view of God.* First of all, many in limited inerrancy views have a diminished view of inerrancy because they have a diminished view of God (see chap. 12 above). They have rejected the classical view of God and, hence, have rejected the classical inerrancy view. After all, if God has no infallible foreknowledge, how can he make infallible pronouncements about the future, which the Bible purports to do? Only an infallible God can produce an infallible book.

2. *Limited inerrancy does not consistently employ the correspondence view of truth.* Many reject a correspondence view of truth, which is entailed in the unlimited inerrancy view. But, as shown above, this view is self-defeating, unbiblical, and contrary to popular, legal, scientific, and even sound philosophical thought. Of course, even limited inerrantists sometimes slip into a correspondence view of truth, as when Fuller Theological Seminary criticized Harold Lindsell for "a handful of mistakes" he made in his book (*Battle for the Bible*) critiquing Fuller Seminary's departure from full inerrancy.[5] For on Fuller's intentionalist view of truth, Lindsell made no errors, since he intended to tell the truth, even if he made some mistakes in the process.

3. *Limited inerrancy is contrary to the claim of Scripture about its own factual accuracy.* As has been shown elsewhere (see Geisler, *Systematic Theology,* vol. 1), the Bible claims its own total inerrancy in many ways: (1) By claiming to be "God-breathed" writings (2 Tim. 3:16 NIV). (2) By claiming to be the Word of God, which cannot err (John 10:35; Matt. 4:4; 5:17–18; 15:5–6; Rom. 3:2). (3) By concluding that the Bible cannot err in anything it addresses. After all, the God of the Bible is omniscient, and an omniscient Mind cannot be wrong about anything it speaks about.

4. *Limited inerrancy rejects the prophetic model of inspiration.* The Old Testament was written by prophets (Heb. 1:1; 2 Pet. 1:20–21). Indeed, Moses was a prophet

(Deut. 18:18), and the whole Old Testament is called the Law (of Moses) and the Prophets (Matt. 5:17–18; Luke 24:27). Even the New Testament was called prophetic "Scripture" (1 Tim. 5:18; 2 Pet. 3:15–16). It came to us from the apostles and prophets of the New Testament (Eph. 3:3–5) and ended with John, who was called a prophet (Rev. 22:9). So, to reject the prophetic model is to reject what the Bible claims for itself, namely, that "every word . . . comes from the mouth of God" (Matt. 4:4). As David says, "The Spirit of the LORD speaks by me; his word is on my tongue" (2 Sam. 23:2). Peter adds, "No prophecy was ever produced by the will of man, but men spoke from God as they were carried along by the Holy Spirit" (2 Pet. 1:20–21).

5. *Limited inerrancy buys into the false view of accommodation.* By their own admission, limited inerrantists buy into a view of divine "accommodation," which allows for error in the Bible. But the God who is truth (Jer. 10:10) and can speak only truth (John 17:17; Rom. 3:4) and for whom it is impossible to lie (Heb. 6:18; Titus 1:2)—this God cannot err. So, despite the fact that God has used human writers, with their vocabularies and styles, the final product is also the very Word of the God who cannot err. But limited inerrantists do not accept this conclusion.

6. *Limited inerrancy rejects the true incarnational model.* The limited view of inerrancy has attempted to co-opt the long-used incarnational model of Scripture to accommodate their unorthodox view (see chap. 16 below). They wrongly argue that since Jesus, God's living Word, was fully human, with all the finitude and mistakes that involves, even so God's written Word is fully human, with all the mistakes and errors that entails.

However, this involves a serious and even heretical view of the incarnation, which in the orthodox view involves a hypostatic union of two natures in one person. So intimate is this union that whatever is done in either nature is done by one and the same person. Hence, it is proper to speak of the Bible as a theanthropic (God-man unity) book, just as Christ is a theanthropic person. Thus, a flaw, imperfection, or error done by Christ in his humanity is also thereby done by one and the same person, who is God! And applying this incarnational model to Scripture yields an absolutely perfect Scripture. For just as Jesus was both God and man without sin or error, even so the Bible is both divine and human without error.

Conclusion

Traditional inerrantists employ a correspondence view of truth, whereas many who reject this view do not. This includes both ETS and ICBI, as their official statements demonstrate. According to a correspondence view of truth, a statement is truth if it corresponds to reality. Historically, this view has been expressed by great philosophers, and practically it is the view of the everyday person. What is more, the correspondence view is used by jurists and scientists. It is also employed in the Bible. In fact, it is undeniable since even the denial of it implies that its view corresponds to reality.

Many who deny the correspondence view of truth speak of truth as what does not mislead and error as what does mislead. However, defining truth as what misleads, rather than as what is mistaken, would mean that almost any sincere statement ever made would be true, even if it was factually incorrect. Also, defining "truth" in terms of the redemptive intent of Scripture leads to the limited inerrantist belief that the Bible is wholly true, even though it may be filled with mistakes. But this intentionalist view of truth is contrary to the Bible, contrary to itself, and contrary to fact.

What is more, limited inerrancy is an attack on the very nature and character of God. After all, if God is omniscient, and the Bible is God's Word, then the Bible cannot contain any errors on any topic it addresses. Why? For the simple reason that an omniscient Mind cannot be wrong about anything.

In short, the nature of truth has strong implications for the whole inerrancy debate. If truth is defined incorrectly, then one can end up, as limited inerrantists do, affirming that the Bible is wholly true even though it has many mistakes in it. In brief, how one defines truth is determinative of what they mean when they say the Bible is true. And from the total inerrantist point of view, a completely true mistake is an oxymoron.

Sources

Adler, *Six Great Ideas*

Alston, *Realist Conception*

Anselm, *Truth, Freedom, and Evil*

Aristotle, *Categories*

———, *Metaphysics*

Fuller Seminary, *Theology, News & Notes*, Special Issue, 1976

Geisler, *Systematic Theology*, vol. 1

Gilson, *Christian Philosophy*

Kantzer, *Applying the Scriptures*

Lindsell, *Battle for the Bible*

Moore, *Main Problems*

Pinnock, *Scripture Principle*

———, *Scripture Principle*, 2nd ed.

Preus, *Inspiration of Scripture*

Rogers and McKim, *Authority and Inspiration*

Russell, *Problems of Philosophy*

Sproul, *Explaining Inerrancy*

Thomas Aquinas, *On Truth*

———, *Summa*

14

The Nature of Language and Inerrancy

Introduction

Unlimited inerrantists believe the Bible is the Word of God. This implies the *whole* Bible is the written Word of God, not just part of it. The view is called plenary inspiration. They also believe that the Bible as a written Word is wholly *without error* (see chap. 13 above). Added to this is their belief that it is an *objective* revelation from God and not merely means by which someone gains a subjective encounter with God. Beneath these beliefs that this is a complete, objective, and errorless revelation of God, there is the belief that it is a *written (verbal)* revelation. This raises the question about the adequacy of human language to convey an objectively true propositional revelation from God.

Two issues are fundamental to this inquiry. First, is language capable of conveying objective meaning and truth? Second, is language capable of conveying objective truth about God? It should come as no surprise that both of these are challenged by Bible critics. First, let's take a look at the inerrantists' claim.

Claiming Adequacy of Human Language to Convey Inerrant Truth

The claim for the adequacy of human language to express divine truth is both implicit and explicit in the claim of inerrantists. We will first examine the implicit claim in the inerrancy statement of the Evangelical Theological Society (ETS).

254

The ETS Statement on Inerrancy

The ETS statement reads as follows: "The Bible alone and the Bible in its entirety *is the Word of God written,* and therefore inerrant in the autographs." While this contains an explicit claim that the Bible is the inerrant Word of God, it also contains an implicit claim that this inerrant truth of God can and is conveyed through human language. For it says that what is "written," in human language, conveys this "inerrant" truth. So inerrantists cannot avoid defending their belief in the adequacy of human language to expresses truth from God. And since "truth" means objective, propositional truth (see chap. 13 above), then it follows that inerrantists also believe that objective, propositional truth statements can be made in human language about God. As we shall see below, this poses a serious problem for the so-called postmodern mind (see Grenz, *Primer on Postmodernism*; Grenz, *Revisioning Evangelical Theology*; Grenz and Franke, *Beyond Foundationalism*; and chap. 10 above). Indeed, it poses a problem for the ancient, medieval, and modern minds as well, but it nonetheless is still a problem. The problem can be simply put: How can God convey infinite truth through finite words to a finite mind?

The International Council on Biblical Inerrancy Statement

The problem of the adequacy of human language to convey divine revelation was recognized by the framers of the ICBI statements. In fact, it comes up in several articles.

Article 3 declares: "We affirm that the *written Word of God* in its entirety is revelation given by God." It adds, "*We deny that the Bible is merely a witness to revelation,* or only becomes revelation in encounter, or depends on the responses of men for its validity."

Article 4 speaks directly to the point: "We affirm that God who made mankind in his image *has used language as a means of revelation. We deny that human language is so limited by our creatureliness that it is rendered inadequate as a vehicle for divine revelation. We further deny that the corruption of human culture and language through sin has thwarted God's work of inspiration.*"

Article 6 says: "We affirm that the whole of Scripture and all its parts, down to the very words of the original, were given by divine inspiration. We deny that the inspiration of Scripture can rightly be affirmed of the whole without the parts, or of some parts but not the whole."

The italicized words reveal an explicit belief in the adequacy of human language to convey divine truth. But as was shown (in chap. 13 above), "truth" is both objective and propositional. Thus inerrantists are committed to believe that human language, regardless of human finitude and fallenness, is capable of communicating objective, propositional truth from God and about God. Here again, this runs contrary to much of contemporary thought, even among some evangelicals.

Challenges to the Adequacy of Human Language
to Convey Objective Divine Revelation

To defend the verbal, plenary inerrancy of the Bible, one must face the contemporary challenges against the ability of language to express objective truth from and
about God. These challenges are generally based around three points: (1) Finite
human language is incapable of communicating objective truth from an infinite
God. (2) Human language cannot convey objective meaning or truth. (3) Fallen
human language cannot convey errorless truth.

The first problem has been around since antiquity. In fact, in some cases it
occasioned the *via negativa* (the way of negation) and mysticism. The second
problem is more acutely modern and gave rise to conventualism, which affirms
the relativity of all meaning. The last problem is theological, rising from a radical
view of human depravity held by neo-orthodox thinkers like Karl Barth.

The Problem of Divine Accommodation

Simply put, the accommodation problem is this: How can a finite mind with
finite language understand infinite Truth (God)? Medieval Christian thinkers
struggled with this issue and presented three alternatives: our knowledge of God
is (1) equivocal (totally different from the way God is), (2) univocal (totally the
same as the way God is), or (3) analogous (similar to the way God is).

Equivocal God-Talk

Plotinus (AD 204/5–270) and the medieval mystics who followed him championed equivocal God-talk called the *via negativa*. According to this view, it is
impossible for a finite mind with finite concepts to understand the infinite God.
God is "wholly other" than anything we experience. Hence, the best we can
do is to say what God is not. That is, we know him only by negating anything
from God that comes from our limited, finite experience. Hence, any positive
attribution of God will not really be of the way God is in his essence but merely
what we attribute to God because he causes this characteristic in creatures. For
example, since God is the cause of all good, we call him "good," but the term is
used equivocally of him. God is not really good the way we understand the term.
So there is only an extrinsic relation (not an intrinsic one) between God (the
Cause) and his effects. The causal connection is like that between hot water and
a hard-boiled egg: there is no real similarity between the effect (solidified) and
the hot water (soft). If one cannot know God in any contentful and objective
way, how then can one know God? The answer of the neo-Plotinian thinkers was
that God is known negatively (through what he is not) and mystically through a
noncognitive subjective intuition that goes beyond all knowledge as we normally
understand the term.

Of course, this view is not acceptable to orthodox Christians, who believe
that both God's revelation in Scripture (special revelation) and God's revelation

in nature (general revelation) have brought us genuine knowledge of God. The basic objection to the *via negativa* is that a person cannot know "not that" unless he knows "that." All negative knowledge presupposes some positive knowledge. Hence, completely equivocal knowledge is no knowledge at all, but this is contrary to both reason and revelation. But once equivocal God-talk is eliminated, there are only two alternatives left: either our language about God is univocal or it is analogical.

Univocal God-Talk

John Duns Scotus (1265–1308) championed the univocal view that our understanding of God must be in terms that have the same meaning when applied to God as they do when applied to creatures. His basic argument was to the point: unless words have the same meaning for us as they have for God, then we are left in total skepticism about God. But both reason and revelation inform us that we can know God. Reason informs us that total skepticism is self-defeating, since we would have to know something about God in order to say we could not know anything about God. And revelation (the Bible) claims to be an objective revelation from God.

As for analogy, Duns Scotus argues convincingly that every analogy must have a univocal element in it, otherwise there would be nothing similar in our knowledge of God. But if it is the univocal element (a sameness) that provides our knowledge about God, then analogous knowledge reduces to univocal knowledge (*Philosophical Writings*).

Analogous God-Talk

Thomas Aquinas was dissatisfied with univocal predications about God for the basic reason that God is infinite and our terms are all finite, and there is an infinite difference between the infinite and the finite. He reasons that to say "John is good" and "God is good," one cannot be applying the term "good" in entirely the same (univocal) way. After all, the term "good" is applied to God infinitely and to John finitely. This is for the simple reason that God is infinitely good and John is only finitely good. The same is true of all other terms that apply to God and creatures. For example, the term "being" applies to God infinitely because he is an infinite Being. But the same term only applies to John finitely since John is only a finite being.

How, then, can this be reconciled with the convincing argument of Duns Scotus that our terms must have a univocal meaning when applied to God and to creatures? The answer is that the terms must be understood in the same sense, otherwise we are left with a totally equivocal understanding of God—which is no understanding of God at all. In short, Duns Scotus was right about the *definition* of the terms used of both God and creatures, but Thomas Aquinas was right about the *application* of these terms. In short, we mean the same things by the term "being" (viz., that which is) when we use it of God or of a creature, but it is applied to God according to his being, which is infinite. So Duns Scotus was right about the *understanding* of the term in a univocal sense, whereas Thomas was correct about the *predication* of the term analogically.

This still leaves an issue to be addressed: How can finite terms have any meaning whatsoever when applied to an infinite Being? "Infinite" means "not finite." So how can a finite term retain any meaning when applied to an infinite God? Isn't there an infinite distance between a finite and an infinite? Thomas's response was that although there is an infinite distance between God and creatures, there nonetheless is not a total lack of similarity. How so? Because God as the infinite Being has created finite beings, and there must be a similarity between an efficient Cause and its effect. God cannot give what he does not have. He cannot produce what he does not possess. God cannot share being with a creature if he has no being to share, just as a teacher cannot share knowledge with students unless he has knowledge to share.

In short, there must be an intrinsic relation between an efficient cause and its effect. In fact, there must be both a similarity and difference between the Creator and his creatures. There must be a similarity because they are both "being": they both are, or exist. Also, there must be a difference because God is an infinite Being and creatures are finite beings. God is Being, and we have being. But what is similar yet different is analogous. Hence, the analogy of being is based on the intrinsic relation of the Creator and his creature, who must be both similar (because he has being) and different (because he is a different kind of being).

To return to the hot-water-and-egg illustration, there is both an intrinsic and extrinsic relation between the hot water and the egg. Hardness in the egg is different from the softness of the water. But hotness in the egg is similar because the water is hot. Heat communicates heat; Being communicates being; Actuality communicates actuality. But the effect must also be different from the Cause (God) because God is infinite, and God cannot make an infinite effect. A created thing can be everlasting from its point of beginning, but it can't be unlimited in every direction. A Creator cannot make another Creator; he can only make a creature. An uncaused Being cannot cause another uncaused being. This being the case, an effect of the Creator, while being similar in being, must also be unlike it since the effect has limitations while the Cause is unlimited.

This brings us to the final question: How can finite terms apply to an infinite Creator without losing all their meaning and content? The answer is clear: only because there is (a) a similarity based on a causal connection, and (b) because all limitations are removed from the term (by the *via negativa*) before it can be appropriately applied to God. But is there any meaningful content left once all limitations are removed from a term? The answer is yes if the term is really an attribute of God and not just a metaphor. For example, God is said to be a "rock" metaphorically because when you remove all finite characteristics from a rock, there is nothing left of its rockiness. But this is not so of metaphysical terms (i.e., terms that really apply to God's nature). For example, if "being" means that which is, and the term is stripped of all its finitude so that we say it is not that which is finite, then and only then can it be applied to God because "that which is" has no intrinsic finitude in its definition. So this univocal definition (as Duns Scotus taught) can be applied to God infinitely and hence analogically to the way it is applied to creatures (as Thomas Aquinas taught) because there are no intrinsic limitations to the meaning of "being." The same is true of "goodness" and other metaphysical attributes of God (see Mondin, *Principle of Analogy*).

Thus, we have seen that finite terms can be used appropriately of an infinite Being. Human language can be used to convey objective truth about the infinite God, but only analogously. And this analogy is based on the real causal relation between an efficient Cause (the Creator) and his effect (the creature). So even though there is an infinite difference between God and creatures, yet there is not a total lack of similarity. For the Cause cannot give what it does not have. Whatever the effect has, it was received from the Cause. But this similarity is only between an efficient cause and its effect. An instrumental cause is not like its effect any more than a fountain pen (an instrumental cause) is like an author, but the ideas expressed in a book are like the author's mind. Likewise, a mosquito is not like the malaria it causes since it is only the instrumental cause (carrier) of the malaria parasite. But malaria parasites are like the malaria parasites they produce through the mosquito. The efficient cause always places its imprint on the effect so that there is some similarity between them. Even when a hammer breaks a mirror, there is a similarity between the efficient cause (motion) conveyed through the hammer (instrumental cause) to the mirror, from which pieces are put in motion because of the moving hammer.

Divine Adaptation to Finitude

There is another important implication here from the real analogy between God and creatures. Not only does it enable us to understand God; it also makes it possible for an infinite mind to condescend and communicate to us in finite language. It is a two-way street: if finite terms can be used for us to understand things about God, then the same medium is a capable channel for God to speak to us. Without this intrinsic similarity between God and creatures, no such communications would be possible.

So, just as objective truth about God can be affirmed (analogously) in Scripture about God, even so God can adapt himself by use of analogous language to speak to us about himself. But in both cases there is nothing that hinders the medium from communicating truth. Thus, in a divine adaptation via language in Scripture, we are receiving objective truth, even if all of the truth about God cannot be communicated. After all, Scripture does speak of God as ineffable (Rom. 11:33; Deut. 29:29): some things we apprehend but do not completely comprehend. So, in a true divine adaptation to our finitude, God does not accommodate himself to our error. As such, what we receive is true, but it is not all the truth (1 Cor. 13:12).

For example, a parent may tell an inquiring three-year-old that babies come from their mommy's tummy. A couple years later, when they ask how the baby got there, the mother may say that daddy placed a seed there, and so on. Sometime later, when asked how daddy placed the seed there, she may tell more of the story. In each case, she is telling the truth but only part of the truth and in terms that the child can understand. At no time does she tell the "stork story," which is false. In like manner, God adapts his truth to our mode of human finitude, but never accommodates his truth to human myths or errors. So, contrary to the contemporary misuse of divine accommodation to err, the infinite Truth can adapt to finite truths, but God's nature as Truth (Jer. 10:10; Rom. 3:4) does not allow him to accommodate to error. We will present more about this as the incarnational model (in chap. 16 below).

The Conventionalist Challenge to Inerrancy

Moving into the contemporary period, with the rise of linguistic studies, inerrancy has gained a new foe. The traditional theory of meaning rooted in Plato and employed by Augustine is facing a serious challenge by a growing relativism in the field of linguistics: conventionalism, which pronounces that all meaning is relative. Since all truth claims are meaningful statements, conventionalism would mean that all truth is relative. But this is contrary to the Christian claim that there is absolute truth, that there are things that are true at all times, in all places, and for all people (see chap. 13 above).

A reaction to Platonic essentialism. Conventionalism is a reaction to Platonism, which (following Plato) claimed that all language has an unchanging essence or form. By contrast, conventionalists believe that all meaning is relative to changing situations. It asserts that meaning is arbitrary and relative to its culture or context. There are no transcultural forms of meaning. Language (meaning) has no form or essence; linguistic meaning is derived from the changing and relative experience on which language is based.

Plato defended a form of essentialism in his dialogue *Cratylus*. Augustine of Hippo did also in his *Principia dialecticae* (AD 384), *De magistro* (389), and *De Trinitate* (394–419). However, he apparently did not hold to the picture theory of meaning (that language pictures meaning),[1] which Ludwig Wittgenstein critiqued in his famous *Tractatus.*

Simply stated, essentialism (also called "naturalism") insists that there is a natural or essential relation between our statements and what they mean. Language is not arbitrarily related to meaning. Rather, there is a one-to-one correspondence between them.

Three names loom large in the contemporary relativizing of meaning: Ferdinand de Saussure, Gottlob Frege, and Ludwig Wittgenstein. Their view, called conventionalism, is widely accepted in current linguistic philosophy.

Ferdinand de Saussure. The forerunner of modern conventionalism was the famous Swiss linguist Saussure (d. 1913). His *Course in General Linguistics* (1916) is still a standard in the field.

Gottlob Frege. Although Frege (d. 1925) wrote relatively little, his teachings, put together from his students' notes, have had a strong influence on the adoption of conventionalism by modern linguists. They are found in *Translations from the Philosophical Writings of Gottlob Frege.*

Ludwig Wittgenstein. Leaning on the works of his predecessors, Wittgenstein (1889–1951) is credited with making conventionalism the dominant view in philosophical and religious thought. His mature view is expressed in his *Philosophical Investigations* [*PI*]. Section 1 presents a critique of "a particular picture of the essence of human language." Wittgenstein rejects the following points from this view: (1) The function of language is to state facts. (2) All words are names (the referential theory of meaning). (3) The meaning of a name is the object denoted. (4) Meaning is taught by ostensive definition (by exhibiting the thing or quality being defined).

He rejects all of these theses as being an oversimplification of language (points 1 and 2); or in the case of point 4, mistaken ("an ostensive definition can be variously interpreted in every case" [*PI* 1.28]); or as in point 3, shown to be absurd by giving examples (e.g., exclamations; *PI* 1.27; 1.39).

Other theses closely connected with "the picture theory of meaning" that come in for criticism are the following: (1) meaning is a matter of producing mental images; (2) analysis of propositions = clarification of propositions (*PI* 1.60); (3) words have a determinate sense.

Wittgenstein offers an alternative view of meaning that employs (1) family resemblances (*PI* 1.67); (2) language games (1.7); and (3) forms of life (1.19, 23, 241; 2.194, 226). Since he rejects both univocal and analogical language (see above), he holds an equivocal view reflected in family resemblances and based on changing experiences. As such, Wittgenstein is one of the strong proponents of conventionalism.

Wittgenstein and Religious Language

In Wittgenstein's earlier work *Tractatus* (*T*), religious language is placed in the realm of the inexpressible. He ends it with the famous line: "That of which you cannot speak, speak not thereof." Religious discourse has no factual meaning. There is an unbridgeable gulf between fact and value—a gulf established by Immanuel Kant. Thus God-talk is nonsense.

It is clear from Wittgenstein's *Notebooks* that things such as a feeling of dependence and the recognition that "to believe in a God means to see that the facts of the world are not the end of the matter" (cf. *T*, 11) are things that Wittgenstein "knows" but are not expressible in language. They are outside the limits of language and thought.

Because things higher and transcendent are inexpressible, this is not to say they are totally incommunicable, for they can be *shown* but not *said.* This is called the doctrine of "showing and saying." An apparent contradiction in the *Tractatus* is found in the fact that, although propositions about language are employed, they nevertheless are strictly speaking nonsense because they are not propositions of natural science. Wittgenstein acknowledges that they are nonsense and thus can only serve as elucidations (6.45). The most generous interpretation to put on this is to treat the *Tractatus* as an example of the doctrine of showing and saying. Otherwise it is inconsistent and self-defeating.

Later in the *Investigations*, Wittgenstein does not directly speak about religious discourse but seems to indicate that praying and theology are legitimate and meaningful linguistic activities. Praying in particular is mentioned as a language game. Since stating facts is only one of a multiplicity of meaningful linguistic activities, this means that there is no a priori bar against the meaningfulness of religious language. It also means that since language games have intrinsic criteria of meaning and religious language is a language game, meaning must be judged by its own standards and not by one imposed upon it. This is a form of semantic fideism.

In his *Lectures and Conversations* [LC], Wittgenstein portrays religious language as having the possibility of being meaningful (as a language game). But it is clear from this work that he holds a noncognitive view of religious language (which could be called "acognosticism" or "acognitivism"), that is, that he rejects any cognitive knowledge in religious language. He recognizes the legitimacy of a form of life that could "culminate in an utterance of belief in a last judgment" (58). He believes that it would be impossible to contradict such a belief, or even to say that it is possibly true.

The only sense in which it might be a blunder is if it is a blunder in the particular system that it is in (*LC*, 59). Such beliefs are not based on evidence: it is purely a matter of faith. However, he would not ridicule those who have such a belief, only those who claim it is based on evidence (e.g., historical apologetics). Belief in these cases is used in an extraordinary way (not in an ordinary way). He writes: "It has been said that Christianity rests on an historical basis. It has (also) been said a thousand times by intelligent people that indubitability is not enough in this case. Even if there is as much evidence for it as for Napoleon. Because the indubitability wouldn't be enough to make me change my whole life" (57).

According to Wittgenstein, religious beliefs have commissive force: they orient our lives. But they are not informative about reality. We are locked in a linguistic bubble. Religious language is meaningful as a language game, but it tells us nothing about God or ultimate reality. God-talk is experientially meaningful, but the God-talk is not really talk about God. God is still the inexpressible. Human language is not capable of making any objectively meaningful statements about God, whether they are univocal or analogical. All meaning is culturally and experientially relative (= conventionalism).

Response to the Conventionalist Challenge to Meaning

The conventionalist challenge to objective meaning is far from definitive. In fact, there are some serious flaws in it. Consider the following critique of conventionalism as a theory of meaning:

1. There is an important difference between a conventionalist theory of *symbols* and a conventionalist theory of *meaning*. Other than natural symbols (like smoke to fire) and onomatopoeic terms (like crash, bang, and boom), whose sound is their meaning, virtually all linguists acknowledge that symbols are conventionally relative. For example, the word "board" has no intrinsic relation to the plank of wood. It can also mean food on the table, as in the sentence "You need to earn your room and board." Further, it can also mean a group of people who sit around a table, as in the sentence "He is a board member." As a matter of fact, different languages have different names for the English word "board." So, it is granted to the conventionalist that symbols or words are conventionally relative in their meaning (i.e., usage).

However, it is an unjustifiable leap to conclude that because *symbols* are culturally relative that all *meaning* is also culturally relative. Words are to sentences what broken pieces of colored glass are to a beautiful stained-glass window of Jesus being crucified. Individual pieces of glass have no intrinsic beauty (e.g., meaning), but when they are put together in the context of the whole picture, they have beauty (e.g., meaning).

2. Perhaps the most severe criticism against conventionalism is that it is self-defeating. For if the statement "All linguistic meaning is conventional" is true, then this statement itself would be relative. But it claims to be an objectively meaningful statement—one affirming that there are no such objectively meaningful statements. It offers itself as a nonrelative statement affirming that the meaning of all statements is relative. The whole case against conventionalism could rest right here, but there is more.

3. Conventionalism rejects the correspondence view of truth. But as was shown earlier (in chap. 13), one cannot deny the correspondence view of truth without using the correspondence view of truth. For conventionalists assume that their view (i.e., conventionalism) corresponds to reality. Indeed, it is self-defeating to claim, as Wittgenstein does, that we have no cognitive knowledge of reality (including God) without assuming that this is a cognitively true statement about God. For either it "shows and says" something cognitively meaningful about God, or it does not. If it does, it is self-defeating for it makes a cognitively meaningful statement about God, and then it cannot deny that these kinds of statements are possible. And if it does not make a cognitively meaningful statement about God, then it leaves us in utter agnosticism. It is in fact an equivocal statement about God. But as Duns Scotus shows, equivocal statements leave us in total skepticism. But total agnosticism is self-defeating since its adherents claim to know that they cannot know anything about God (which implies that they do know something about God).

4. If conventionalism were correct, then no universal statement would translate as a universal statement into another language. But they do. For instance, "All squares have four sides" translates as universally true in other languages. So does "All husbands are married men." But if meaning were only culturally relative, then no such universal transcultural statements would be possible.

5. If conventionalism were true, there would not be any universal truths in any language. But there are. For example, mathematical statements, such as "Four plus four equals eight," are universally true. So also are the basic laws of logic, such as the law of noncontradiction (that contrary propositions cannot both be true at the same time and in the same sense). In fact, no conventionalists can even deny these first principles of thought without using them. For the statement "Opposites can both be true" implies that the opposite of that statement is not true.

6. If conventionalism were true, then we would not know any truth independent of and/or prior to knowing the conventions of that truth in that language. But experiments with little children before they can talk reveal that they can do simple math before they learn to speak. Mathematics may depend on relative choice of symbols to express numbers, but the truths of mathematics are not dependent on any culture. They are true independent of all cultural expressions of them.

7. The laws of logic are not based on human conventions. They are true apart from all linguistic conventions. Logic is not arbitrary. We do not *choose* the laws of logic; rather, we are *ruled* by them. We do not *create* them but merely *discover* them. They are logically prior to and independent of the culture in which they are expressed. Cultures do not think them up or think them up differently. Without the law of noncontradiction, for example, no person in any culture could even think. Even the Zen Buddhist who claims the Tao goes beyond all logic (such as the law of noncontradiction) uses that law to distinguish between the Tao and the non-Tao since they believe they are logically opposite. The fact is that people in every culture, East and West, think *with* the basic laws of logic even before they think *about* them.

8. Conventionalism confuses the immediate *source* of meaning with its ultimate *ground*. The *source* of learning that "All husbands are married" may be social. For example, children may have learned it from their parents or teachers. But the *grounds* for knowing this truth are not social but logical. For like other first principles, the predicate is reducible to the subject. It is true by definition, not by acculturation.

9. If conventionalism were correct, then no meaning would be possible. For if all meaning is based on changing experience, which in turn gets its meaning from changing experience, and so forth, then there is actually no basis for the meaning. An infinite series is no more possible in meaning than it is in causes. Putting off the basis for meaning forever is not the same as finding the basis for it. And a statement without any basis for its meaning is a baseless affirmation. As C. S. Lewis aptly puts it, "You cannot go on 'explaining away' forever: you will find that you have explained explanation itself away" (*Abolition of Man*, 91).

10. Conventionalism has only internal criteria for meaning, such as coherence, but none that transcend our changing cultural experiences. But internal criteria cannot adjudicate meaning conflicts of the same statements made within different worldview contexts. For example, the statement "God is a necessary being" can be interpreted either pantheistically or theistically. Mere internal criteria, such as coherence, cannot determine which of these statements is correct.

11. Conventionalism uses circular argumentation. It really does not *justify* its claims but simply *asserts* them. When a conventionalist is asked for the basis of his belief that all meaning is conventional, he cannot give a nonconventional basis for it because in that case he would no longer be a conventionalist. But if he gives merely a conventional basis for his conventionalism, that is, a relative basis for his relativism, then he argues in a circle.

12. Conventionalists often distinguish between surface and depth grammar to avoid certain problems such as some of those just given. But such a distinction assumes that they have a vantage point independent of language and experience in order to make this distinction. However, conventionalism by its very nature does not allow such a vantage point outside of one's culture and language. Hence, the very distinction they make between surface and depth grammar is not possible on the theory they espouse.

13. No truly descriptive knowledge of God is possible in a conventionalist view of language, since language is simply based in our experience. It tells us only what God *seems to be* (to us) in our experience but not what God *really is* (in himself). It reduces the meaning of "God" to a mere interpretive framework rather than an extracosmic being beyond the world, as we take God to be. In short, it reduces to self-defeating agnosticism or the claim that we know we cannot know anything about the nature of God.

These arguments show that conventionalism is an inadequate theory of meaning. In fact, it is self-defeating since the very statement that all meaning is culturally relative purports to be a meaningful nonculturally relative statement. Such is the fact for all forms of relativism because they stand on the pinnacle of their own absolutes in their attempt to relativize everything else.

Realistic Alternative to Essentialism and Conventionalism

Actually, there are more theories of meaning than two. It is not either essentialism or conventionalism. There is another alternative called realism. It is true that Platonic essentialism turns out to be an unjustifiable form of dogmatism wherein a finite mind has a one-to-one correspondence with an infinite Mind. On the other hand, it turns out, as just shown, that conventionalism is a relativistic overreaction to Platonic essentialism. But there is another alternative that avoids both alternatives without capitulating to theological agnosticism: *realism*.

The Ultimate Basis for All Real Meaning

Realism, certainly theistic realism, contends that meaning is not relative because it transcends our symbols and linguistic means of expressing meaning. Meaning is objective and absolute, not because a given linguistic expression of it is but because there is an absolute Mind, God, who has communicated it to finite minds (human beings) through the common but analogous means of human language, which utilizes a transcendent principle of logic and being common to both God and humans.

Admittedly, without an objective Mind (God), objective meaning would not be possible. But if an objective Mind exists, then objective meaning is possible. Hence, to deny the possibility of objective meaning, one must successfully deny the possibility of God's existence. However, this has been tried unsuccessfully many times (see Geisler, "God, Alleged Disproofs of"). Indeed, as keen thinkers (like Augustine, Thomas Aquinas, Cornelius Van Til, Francis Schaeffer, Greg Bahnsen, John Frame, C. S. Lewis, and others) have shown that, if science or any rational endeavor makes any sense (and it is almost universally believed that they do), then there must be a God to make this possible. For without an absolute Mind, there can be no real (objective) meaning.

The Nature of Objective Meaning

In answering the question "What is the meaning of 'meaning'?" we can point to the meaning of the first word "meaning" in that question. For if the questioner has no idea of what *that* word means, then he does not even know what his question means.

In short, as we shall see, the meaning of "meaning" is what the author means by his word in that sentence and in that context. In order to explain this, it is useful to speak in terms of the traditional six causes. Otherwise, there is a tendency to confuse the issue and miss the meaning of "meaning." First, let's distinguish the six causes and then apply them to the nature of meaning.

1. Efficient cause: that *by which* something comes to be (e.g., a carpenter making a chair).
2. Final cause: that *for which* something comes to be (to sit on one).
3. Formal cause: that *of which* something comes to be (the form or shape of the chair).
4. Material cause: that *out of which* something comes to be (the wood).
5. Exemplar cause: that *after which* something comes to be (the blueprint or pattern).
6. Instrumental cause: that *through which* something comes to be (the tools to make it).

Meaning Found in the Formal Cause

Applying these six causes to the meaning of a written text yields the following analysis of the textual meaning: the writer is the efficient cause, and the writing is the formal cause. Words are merely the material cause, and the final cause is the purpose for which one wrote the text. It is noteworthy that unlike some limited inerrantists, the writing is not the instrumental cause. For it is not that through which meaning is expressed; rather, it is that in which the meaning is expressed:

1. The writer: the *efficient* cause of the meaning of a text.
2. The writing: the *formal* cause of its meaning.

3. The words: the *material* cause of its meaning.
4. The writer's ideas: the *exemplar* cause of its meaning.
5. The writer's purpose: the *final* cause of its meaning.
6. The laws of thought: the *instrumental* cause of its meaning.

Thus the meaning of an intelligible expression, such as a writing, is not found in the meaner (author); he is the efficient cause of the meaning, not its formal cause. The formal cause of meaning is in the writing itself. What is signified is found in the signs that signify it. Verbal meaning is found in the verbal structure and grammar of the sentences themselves. Meaning is found *in* the literary text itself, not in its author (efficient cause) or purpose (final cause) but in its literary form (formal cause). Meaning is not in its individual words (material cause), which as such have no more meaning than broken pieces of colored glass (as compared with the beautiful portrait in a cathedral window formed out of them). Thus it is not the authors of Scripture who are said to be "inspired" (God-breathed) but the *graphē*, the "writing." The authors were "moved" or "carried along" by God (2 Pet. 1:20–21), but it was only their writings that were inspired (breathed-out) by God.

God did not inspire the words in an atomistic way (one by one), but in a holistic way (in meaningful units). For individual words as such have no meaning in themselves; they have only potential meaning. Words have usage in a sentence, which is the smallest unit of meaning. Nevertheless, every word is important insofar as it is a part of what makes up the whole meaning. Changing a part can change the whole meaning.

An example of how individual words as such have no fixed meaning is the word "bark." It has several different meanings (as used in sentences): (1) the bark of a dog is loud, (2) the bark of a tree is hard, or (3) as a figure of speech, as in "Don't bark up the wrong tree." So words have no meaning in themselves. They are only the parts of a whole (the sentence), which has meaning. Likewise, pigments have no beauty as such but are only the parts of a whole that does have beauty in the painting. In like manner, meaning is found in the written text as a whole, not in the parts in and of themselves.

The Locus of Meaning

The locus of verbal meaning is found in the *verba*, the text. Meaning is not found *beyond* the text (in God's mind), *beneath* the text (in the mystic's mind), or *behind* the text (in the author's unexpressed intention or purpose); it is found *in* the text (in the author's expressed meaning). And since meaning (and truth) is found in the text, then, contrary to Kevin Vanhoozer (see chap. 8 above), it is proper to say that the text speaks. Indeed, the Bible speaks this way. In Galatians (3:8) Paul writes of "the Scripture" as "saying" something to Abraham, and in John 7:42 Jesus asks, "Has not the Scripture said?" There is truth in the text, and truth is an affirmation or denial. Hence the text of Scripture speaks the truth. Jesus says to the father, "Your word is truth" (John 17:17). Similarly, we speak of the beauty in a painting. It is not found behind, beneath, or beyond the painting. Rather, beauty is expressed *in* the painting.

All textual meaning (and truth) is *in* the text. The sentences (in the context of their paragraphs, in the context of the whole piece of literature) are the formal cause of meaning. They are the form that gives meaning to all the parts (words, punctuation, etc.). So it is not the author speaking *through* the text of Scripture; it is the author speaking *in* the text. Again, the text is not merely the instrumental cause; it is the formal cause of meaning (and truth). Thus it is proper to say of the Bible, "What the Bible says, God says." Or, simply "God says." A book does speak, not merely authors. Once the author (the efficient cause of meaning) forms the words into meaningful units (which is the formal cause of meaning) in a common medium (language), then these words speak meaningful things. Thus we properly say, "The Bible spoke to me" as I read it. The purpose the author may have for speaking a meaningful sentence is entirely distinct from the meaning itself. The meaning of a sentence can be understood apart from knowing the purpose or significance any author may have in uttering it. Everyone clearly knows what "Don't drink the water in this glass" means, even if they do not know your purpose for saying it (the water may be contaminated). Locating meaning beyond the text in the purpose of final cause is the mistake of the speech-act theory embraced by Kevin Vanhoozer (see chap. 8 above). Vanhoozer says, "Infallibility means that Scripture never fails in its purpose.... Inerrancy, then, is a subset of infallibility; when the Bible's purpose is to make true statements, it does this too without fail" (*Inerrancy of Scripture*, 1). Vanhoozer explains it this way: "Austin distinguishes three components of the total speech act: (a) *the locutionary act* 'is roughly equivalent to "meaning" in the traditional sense,' (b) *the illocutionary act* is what we *do* in saying something, and (c) the *perlocutionary* act is 'what we bring about or achieve by saying something, such as convincing, persuading'" (Vanhoozer, "Semantics of Biblical Literature," 86). In short, the meaning is not found in what the Bible affirms (the locution) but in the purpose for which it affirms it (the illocution). This is why he said of the Bible that "strictly speaking, however, 'it' neither affirms nor addresses; authors do" (Vanhoozer, "Lost in Interpretation?" 106). God speaks through the Bible, but the Bible does not speak. This is an erroneous replacement of the formal cause (the text) with an instrumental cause. But if the meaning is not in the text, then where is it? It is not simply behind the text in the author's mind since there is no way to get at that except by what he expresses. Nor can it be beyond the text in the purpose by which the author affirms these words since purpose does not determine meaning, and furthermore, we have no way to know the author's meaning except from what he says in the text, in surrounding texts, and in parallel texts (context, context, context!).

The Unity of Meaning

Since the meaning of Scripture comes from an objective Mind (God) and is found in an objective text, which uses terms with the same meaning for both God and human beings (see above), then it follows that there is only *one meaning* in a biblical text—the one given to it by the author. Irony or humor is not an exception here since there is only one expressed intention; namely, that it should be taken as a joke (which infuses a double usage of the word or phrase). Of course, there can be *many implications* and applications. Thus the *sensus unum* (one-sense) view is correct when it affirms only one meaning to a text. However, there is a *sense plenior* (full sense) in terms of implications and significances. For example, Einstein knew that $E = mc^2$ (energy equals mass times the speed of light squared), and so does an average high school science student. However, Einstein knew many more implications and much more significance of this than the average high school student does.

Likewise, God sees more implications in a biblical affirmation than does the human author (1 Pet. 1:10–12). However, inasmuch as God inspired the biblical text (2 Tim. 3:16), God sees more implications in it than the human author does. But God does not affirm any more meaning in that text than the human author does. For "whatever the Bible says, God says." That is, whatever the Bible affirms is true, God affirms is true. And whatever the Bible (and God) affirms is false, that is false. They both mean exactly the same thing by the text. There are not two texts, and there are not two meanings of the text. So both the divine and human authors of Scripture affirm one and the same meaning in one and the same text.

Of course, God knows more about the topic than the human author, and God knows more implications of that meaning than the human author. But both God and the human authors mean the same thing by the same words. Texts, including biblical texts, have meaning and many significances. They have one meaning but many implications and applications.

The Objectivity of Meaning

Human languages vary, but a given meaning expressed in them does not change. The same objective meaning can be expressed in a different language. Indeed, it can be expressed in different ways in the same language. This is made possible because there is an objective meaner, an objective means of meaning (logic), and a common medium of meaning (language) between meaner and meanee (reader) that is capable of expressing this meaning. This objective meaning is found in the formal cause (language), which provides the structure or form of meaning. Thus the meaning of God's revelation, whether in Scripture or in nature, is found in an objective expression of the meaner, in a given form of meaning, in a given context of meaning.

Unlike essentialism, which insists upon a one-to-one relation between the meaning and the expression; and unlike conventionalism, which contends there is a many-to-one relation between meaning and language—realism affirms that there is a one-to-many relationship. That is, there is one meaning that can be expressed in many different ways in the same language and in other languages. This is what makes translation possible. Without the one form of objective meaning that can be expressed in different ways, good translations would not be possible.

Although language can and does change, the meaning it expresses does not. The meaning (use) of a word changes from time to time, but the meaning expressed by that word in a sentence at a given time and in a given context does not change. For example, in the King James Version of 1611, the word "letteth" (cf. 2 Thess. 2:7) means "hinders." Today "let" means "allow," the opposite of "hinder." But the *meaning expressed* by the New King James Version (1982) in rendering it as "restrains" is the same as that expressed in the old King James Version (of 1611) when it says "letteth." Usages of words change, but the basic meaning does not.

In short, both essentialism and conventionalism fail as theories of meaning, but they do not exhaust the alternatives. Objective meaning is possible in the context of theistic realism. For if there is an absolute Mind (as in theism), then there can be absolute or objective meaning. The objectivity of truth, which Christianity embraces, is based on the premise that meaning is objective. The conventionalist theory of meaning is a form of semantic relativism; as such, it is unacceptable for an evangelical. Or to put it another way, contemporary evangelicals who, wittingly or unwittingly, buy into a conventionalist theory of meaning will undermine their belief in the factual inerrancy of Scripture. Further, they will thereby undermine the concomitant beliefs in objective truth and propositional revelation (see chap. 13 above).

So human language is not incapable of communicating objective truth. Meaning is not culturally relative, and hence it can convey objective truth. There is, however, another major objection to belief in the Bible as conveyor of inerrant objective truth. It can be described as Barthianism. This involves the belief that error is inherently involved in human depravity and that it is reflected in human culture and human language, including the Bible.

The Challenge of Human Fallenness

There are a number of theological sources of this belief, but the neo-orthodox theologian Karl Barth is the primary source of the others. In brief, this charge claims that error is inherent in the nature of human beings. It is summed up in the famous adage *Errare humanum est*, "To err is human." This view is expressed in the following citations from Barth and some of his followers:

Karl Barth (1886–1968). He affirmed that "there are obvious overlappings and contradictions—e.g., between the Law and the prophets, between John and the Synoptics, between Paul and James" (*Church Dogmatics* [CD], 1/2.509). Why? Because the Bible is a fallible human book. Thus, "the post-biblical theologian may, no doubt, possess a better astronomy, geology, geography, zoology, psychology, physiology, and so on than the biblical witnesses possessed" (*Evangelical Theology*, 31). Why is this so? Because "the prophets and apostles as such ... were real, historical men as we are, and therefore sinful in their actions, and capable and actually guilty of error in their spoken and written word.... But the vulnerability of the Bible, i.e., its capacity for error, also extends to its religious or theological content" (*CD*, 1/2.528–529; 1/1:509).

Emil Brunner (1889–1966). Another neo-orthodox theologian and contemporary of Barth writes: "The word of Scripture is not in itself the word of God but of man, just as the historical appearance of the God-man is in itself that of a man" (*Word of God*, 32). Why? Because the Bible is intrinsically human: "The word of Scripture is not in itself the word of God but of man" (32). So "Scripture is not a formal authority which demands belief in all it contains from the outset, but it is an instrumental authority" by means of which God speaks through its errant pages (*Christian Doctrine of God*, 110). Therefore, "the orthodox view of the Bible . . . is an absolutely hopeless state of affairs. . . . It pleased God to make use of childlike and primitive ideas as an expression of His will" (*Revelation and Reason*, 291). So "at some points the variety of the Apostolic doctrine . . . is an irreconcilable contradiction" (290). Hence, the humanness of the Bible is part of its fallenness, and its errantness is part of its fallenness.

As a result, "the doctrine of the verbal inspiration of Holy Scripture . . . cannot be regarded as an adequate formulation of the authority of the Bible. . . . The Apostolic writings never claim for themselves a verbal inspiration of this kind, with the infallibility that it implies" (*Revelation and Reason*, 127–28). He believes it is "a fatal step" to hold "Scripture as true" to "every single part of Scripture down to the smallest detail" (*Word of God*, 34).

G. C. Berkouwer (1903–96). Under Barthian influence, Berkouwer became the fountainhead of the neoevangelical view of limited inspiration. At the heart of his view is this same mistaken Barthian idea that the Bible is a fallen human book. He too distinguishes between the Bible and the Word of God (*Holy Scripture* [*HS*], 240). He speaks of "organic" inspiration as opposed to a more "mechanical" view (11). Berkouwer insists that inspiration be understood in the light of "the intent" of "the divine message of salvation" (147). Why is it necessary to so narrow the focus of inspiration? Because "the revelation of God entered creation . . . even as far as the humanly weak and ignoble; the Word became Scripture and has subjected itself to the fate of all writing" (199). This fate of human writing is to partake of human error.

For example, he claims that "Paul . . . did not in the least render timeless propositions concerning womanhood" (*HS*, 187) but rather accommodated himself to the false beliefs about women of his day. There are also accommodations to scientific errors (182), to historical errors (181, 185), to worldview errors (182), and even to myths. He goes so far as to say that we "cannot directly take up a position against Bultmann's theological concern with demythologizing" (198). He adds, "If we are dealing with a penetration of story and interpretation, should we not accept a creativity of the evangelists from which 'fantasy' could be distinguished only with great difficulty?" (248).

Jack Bartlett Rogers (1934–). Following his mentor G. C. Berkouwer, Jack Rogers introduces the divine-accommodation-to-error view into evangelicalism. He too calls it "organic" inspiration, which is limited to the redemptive intent of the authors. He writes: "It is no doubt possible to define the meaning of biblical inerrancy according to the Bible's saving purpose and taking into account the human forms through which God condescended to reveal himself" (*Biblical Authority*, 45). These human forms include "errors" (46) in nonredemptive matters, which include accepting negative higher criticism (Rogers and McKim, *Authority and Interpretation*, 393). Again, the Bible is written in fallen human forms and as such will contain the fate of all human writings: error.

 Clark Pinnock (1937–2010). Pinnock agrees with Rogers's inerrancy-of-purpose view (*Scripture Principle*, 262). This allows him to say, "In other words, the Bible may contain errors of incidental kinds, but it teaches none" (264), and to reject the orthodox view that "What the Bible says, God says." He writes, "I now know that Karl Barth had good reason for rejecting the concept of revelation as primarily information" (267). Pinnock clearly states, "Barth was right to speak about a distance between the Word of God and the text of the Bible" (99). He even accepts the Barthian illustration of the Bible being like a scratched record through which comes "the Master's voice" in spite of the imperfections in the record (272). Pinnock then adds another Barthian belief, that the living Word, Christ, is "adequately witnessed to by this sacred text" (272). Once one accepts Barth's premises, it is only a matter of time and logic until one will be forced into Barth's conclusion. The premise is that the Bible is not the written Word of God, and as a human book, it is subject to the fate of all fallen human writings: error.

 Kevin Vanhoozer (1957–). Vanhoozer also holds a form of the accomodation fallacy. He affirms that in the incarnation of Jesus, "his body is considered 'sinful flesh' (Rom. 8:3 RSV) and was made a sin offering (Heb. 10:5–10)" (*Is There Meaning?* 304). He adds, "Jesus' flesh, therefore, was physical, Jewish, sinful [in the incarnation] and spiritual [in the resurrection]" (305). Based on this (faulty) Christology, Vanhoozer develops his (faulty) incarnational analogy as follows: "The body of Jesus is to his meaning ('Christ') as the letter is to the meaning of the text." He continues:

> What is of interest, however, is the way in which the body of Jesus progressively acquires determinate meaning in a series of expanding contexts of descriptions. Such an approach allows me to resist reducing the significance of the body of Jesus to the physical level, just as I will later resist reducing the literal sense to its most primitive level, namely, the empirical objects named by individual words. (305)

Only in this way can we get what he calls "a thick description" of the body of Jesus.

 "Similarly, only when we consider the text as a literary act requiring a number of levels of description can we give an account of what the author is doing in the text" and gather "a sufficiently 'thick description' of the literal sense" (*Is There Meaning?* 305). However, if Jesus is sinful at one state (in the incarnation), then Vanhoozer has gone all the way with Barth here to claim that Jesus's humanness (and by analogy, the Bible's humanness) involves error and even sin!

Response to the Barthian Challenge

Logically speaking, the response is rather simple: the argument has a false premise; therefore the conclusion drawn from it is false. Consider the premises and conclusion:

1. *The Bible is a human book,* written in human languages by human beings, with human vocabularies, and so forth. As such, evangelicals have no problem with this premise, though admittedly some evangelicals have played down the human side of the Bible in favor of the divine and thus made themselves open in practice to the charge of biblical docetism (a heresy that denies Christ's humanity while affirming his deity). Evangelicalism does not embrace biblical docetism and has repeatedly denied it. At best the charge has more weight against some extreme forms of fundamentalism. But even here one is hard-pressed to come up with the name of a single scholar who admits to denying the humanity of Scripture. However, it is the next premise of the Barthian argument and the conclusion they draw from it that are faulty.

2. *Human beings do err.* This statement is true as far as it goes, but it does not go far enough to justify the conclusion. Of course humans do err, but they do not *always* err, nor do humans *necessarily* err whenever they write something. But such a false premise is necessary in order to reach their conclusion.

3. *Therefore, the Bible does err.* The truth is that humans, even without special divine aid, do not always err. Almost anyone can write an errorless book, if the successive pages were: $1 + 1 = 2$; $2 + 2 = 4$; $3 + 3 = 6$; and so on. There are even inerrant phone books in print, where every number is correct. And since it is agreed upon by both sides of the intramural inerrancy debate that God can supernaturally intervene in the world, then there should be no difficulty in concluding that even humans, who sometimes err, did not err when under divine guidance to produce the books of Scripture.

There is, however, a more subtle argument beneath the Barthian charge against inerrancy, and it is more difficult to dissect. It can be stated this way:

1. The Bible is a thoroughly human book.
2. Human beings can err.
3. Therefore, the Bible can err.
4. But a book that can err is not infallible (by definition, "infallible" means to be incapable of erring).
5. Hence, the Bible is not infallible (i.e., incapable of error).

This argument is more difficult to defeat since it does not claim that the Bible *does* err but only that it *can* err. And it is difficult to deny that human beings can err, even when they are not erring. The ability to err seems to flow from their very nature as finite and free beings. How, then, shall we respond?

The most obvious way is to point out that the Bible is, as it claims to be, a coauthored book. Both God and the human authors are responsible for one and the same set of words. There is a divine concurrence with every human word in Scripture so that "What the Bible says, God says." As David puts it, "The Spirit of the LORD speaks by me; his word is on my tongue" (2 Sam. 23:2). Or as Jesus says, what "is written" is "every word that comes from the mouth of God" (Matt. 4:4). Peter writes, "No prophecy was ever produced by the will of man, but men spoke from God as they were carried along by the Holy Spirit" (2 Pet. 1:21). Given this self-description by the Bible of the Bible, which all evangelicals should accept (and most do), then it will follow that both God and the human authors are responsible for all the words in the autographic text. If this is so, then it also follows that there is a kind of "hypostatic" union between the divine and human sides of Scripture in one set of propositions (sentences), just as there is an intimate union between the two natures of Christ, the divine and the human, in one person.

Given this, it follows that each nature is distinct and that each nature retains its own characteristics. So when we ask of one and the same person (Jesus) whether he could get tired, we get two answers: As God, no, he was not able to get tired. But as man, yes, he was capable of getting tired. Likewise to the question as to whether Jesus could have sinned, the answer is no. Likewise, as God, Jesus was not able to sin (Hab. 1:13; Heb. 6:18; Titus 1:2). But as a man, the answer is, yes, he was capable of sinning, for he was really tempted, but he freely chose to not sin (Heb. 4:15; 2 Cor. 5:21; 1 John 3:3).

Likewise, insofar as the Bible is God's Word, it cannot err. It is infallible and incapable of error. But insofar as it is the words of humans (and it is), the Bible can err (but it does not err). So the objection is partially correct: the Bible as a human book is capable of error. But the objection is seriously misdirected because the Bible is also the words of God, who cannot err. Hence, as the Word of God, the Bible cannot err.

The same is true of every event that has both divine and human components. The cross of Christ is said to have been predetermined by God (Acts 2:22–23). And, as such, it must occur. At the same time, Jesus says that he freely chooses it (John 10:17–18). As a human being, he was free to not choose the cross, but he did, saying to the Father freely, "Not what I will but what you will" (Mark 14:36).

In view of this, one must reformulate the logic of divine and human natures of Scripture as follows:

1. God cannot err.
2. The Bible is God's Word.
3. Hence, insofar as the Bible is God's Word, it cannot err.
4. But the Bible is also human words.
5. Hence, insofar as the Bible is human words, it *can err* (but did not).

There is no logical contradiction between "can err" and "cannot err" here since they are not used in the same sense or relationship. In relation to God, they cannot err; but in relation to humans, they can err. The law of noncontradiction is only violated if one affirms and denies the same thing at the same time (which is being done here) *and in the same relationship* (which is not being done here).

The Implications of Barthian Argument from Depravity

Some Barthians seem to imply more than that the Bible is *capable of* erring because it is human and humans are finite. They seem also to argue that depravity *necessitates* an errant Bible. This argument is stronger and more devastating. It can be put like this:

1. Humans are totally depraved, including their culture and language.
2. For depraved human beings, sin and error are unavoidable.
3. The Bible is a thoroughly human book, including its language.
4. Therefore, errors are unavoidable in the Bible.

Clearly, this conclusion is more devastating since logically it makes error (and even sin) unavoidable in the Bible. So this is saying more than that the Bible is not infallible (incapable of error). It is also claiming more than that the Bible is fallible (capable of error). It is claiming that the Bible is inescapably errant. This is a serious charge and deserves serious attention from a traditional inerrantist point of view.

Upon close examination, it appears that the flaw here is in the extreme doctrine of depravity that is being employed. It makes sin necessary and unavoidable. But the Bible says that by God's grace each sin in particular is avoidable (1 Cor. 10:13). As Augustine rightly puts it, depravity means that we have the necessity to die, but only the *propensity* to sin. That is, we all have a sinful nature, which inclines us toward sin but does not necessitate that we sin. Sin in general is inevitable, but each sin in particular is avoidable. If it were not, we would not be responsible for it, but we are responsible. Yet there is no responsibility where there is no ability to respond. The image of God is not erased in fallen humanity but only effaced (Gen. 9:6). Our free will is damaged but not totally destroyed. We are totally depraved in an extensive sense (sin extends to every part of our humanity), but not in such an intensive sense that sin destroys all our rational and volitional faculties.

Nevertheless, we are incapable of initiating or attaining our own salvation (John 15:5; Titus 3:5–6). But we are not incapable of receiving (John 1:12) the gift of salvation (Rom. 6:23). And when a sinner receives God's gracious gift of salvation, the credit does not go to the receiver but to the Giver of the gift (Eph. 2:8–9).

Response to the Barthian View on the Fallenness of Human Language

Some Barthians[2] seemed to reject this more moderate view of depravity in favor of one that makes sin unavoidable and even necessary in fallen human beings. In fact, Barth wrote a book in response to Emil Brunner's question as to whether a person has even the passive capacity to receive God's grace titled *Nein!* [No!]. The Barthian view has devastating consequences on his view of Scripture, and this leads to the following criticisms:

1. *By logical extension, this Barthian view makes the Bible sinful as well as errant.* This is so because if depravity is so penetrating and pervasive in culture and language as to make everything permeated with error, including the human language in the Bible, then by the same logic the fallenness of human language would also make the language of the Bible necessarily sinful as well.

But this is contrary to the Bible's self-claim to be God's *holy* or *sacred* Word (2 Tim. 3:15) as well as its being "breathed out" by God (3:16). Surely we cannot believe that a holy God breathed out an unholy Word. And even on the Barthian view that the Bible is only a human witness to God's personal Word (Christ), there are serious problems. For even they believe that the New Testament is a reliable and apostolic witness about Christ. But if this is so, then how do we know what is reliable and what is not? What criteria do we use to determine this? In truth, we are left with no objective way to determine where the apostolic witness is correct and where it is not.

2. *This Barthian view would make Christ's actual words fallen and errant.* If they are right about the fallenness of human language, then it would make the actual words that Christ spoke into fallen words, even when he was teaching about his holy Father. It would mean that Christ's actual words when teaching about the true God (cf. John 17:3) were permeated by falsehood. This is not to say that Barth would have to believe that we have the exact words of Christ in the New Testament. It is to say that whatever the exact words of Christ were, whatever they are in the New Testament or not, they were penetrated by errors and the sinfulness of all human language. Then, Jesus could not have avoided using profane and even blasphemous language when conveying the saving message of God. This is ludicrous. And if Barthians try to avoid this repugnant conclusion by insisting that God could have supernaturally purified and preserved the words that came from Christ's mouth, then one would ask why God could not also have done this for the writers of Scripture. And if God could do so, they are back to the orthodox view of Scripture, which Barth rejects.

3. *This Barthian view would make Christ sinful.* This fallenness-of-human-language view would, as applied to Christ, either make the Second Person of the Godhead sinful or else lead to a heresy regarding the two natures of Christ. After all, Barthians allegedly hold an orthodox view on the two natures of Christ in one person and the three persons of the Godhead in one God. But if Jesus uttered error and used foul language, then God (in the Third Person, the Second Person, or "via the person of Christ") could commit sin and err. As the apostle Paul would say, "Perish the thought! God forbid!" For after all, if sinful and erroneous things were coming out of Christ's mouth, then the Second Person of the Godhead was doing it. The only way a Barthian could avoid the logic of this is either (1) to fall into a heresy like Nestorianism, where there are two persons in Christ, one human and one divine; or (2) to modify his doctrine of depravity so as not to make sin an unavoidable part of human language. The former alternative is a heresy on the Trinity and two natures of Christ. The latter view opens the door for an evangelical view denying

that language is unavoidably sinful. This alternative points to another Barthian problem and an evangelical solution.

4. *Even on this Barthian view, all human language would not be unavoidably sinful.* Even if the penetration of sin into human language was inevitable, it would not mean that every use of this language necessarily involves sin and error. At most, it would mean that swearing and blasphemy were inevitable parts of human language, not that it was inevitable that every book, sacred or secular, ever written must be penetrated with cursing and blasphemy. One can be aware that there are inevitably such words in the language, but there is no unavoidable necessity that a person must use them. There are plenty of good (and true) words to be used, and an author, even without special divine aid, could choose to use only the good and true ones. How much more could the human authors of Scripture, with the aid of special grace, produce a record without error or profanity?

5. *This Barthian view denies the analogous connection between creatures and the Creator.* Barth's fallen-human-language view denies the necessary analogous connection between our language and the nature of God. It has long been a standard orthodox view (since the early fathers to Augustine to Anselm to Aquinas and on to the Reformers) that the Bible teaches that we can predicate certain attributes to God that really describe him. That is, we can say not only that God is holy but also that God is really holy. We can say not only that God is loving but also that he is actually loving. And despite the debate as to whether God-talk is univocal (as Duns Scotus claims) or analogous (as Thomas Aquinas affirms) or both (as we suggested above), the long-standing standard view of orthodox Christianity has been that our language about God really applies to him. That is, when we affirm that God is good, truth, holy, or loving, these are really true of God: they really correspond to something in God.

By contrast, the Barthian view allows for no such ontological touching point between the Creator and his creatures to be a basis for predications about God's nature. This failure in Barthian theology is manifest in his radical view on the language of Scripture as being not the very Word of God but a fallen human witness to God's personal revelation in Christ. In fact, contrary to what we have presented earlier, Barth himself denies all propositional revelation of objective truth about God. Indeed, the only analogy that Barth leaves room for is "an analogy of faith," in which there is no correspondence between our thoughts and God but only in God's self-revelation to us. But without an analogy based in reality, one is hard-pressed to understand what this could mean other than that God's self-revelation is simply the way God wants us to *think* about him and respond to him, not the way he really *is*.

6. *This Barthian view denies the divine dimension of Scripture, which the Bible affirms about itself.* The Bible affirms about itself that it is the very Word of God. Repeatedly and in many ways, the Bible claims to be not only the Word of God but also the very words of God. We read that "Moses wrote down all the words of the LORD" (Exod. 24:4); Jeremiah is exhorted: "Do not hold back a word"

(26:2); Paul says of the whole Old Testament: "All Scripture is breathed out by God" (2 Tim. 3:16). Jesus says, "The Scripture cannot be broken" (John 10:35) and "It is written: 'Man shall not live by bread alone, but by every word that comes from the mouth of God'" (Matt. 4:4). He declares: "Do not think that I have come to abolish the Law or the Prophets; I have not come to abolish them but to fulfill them. For truly, I say to you, until heaven and earth pass away, not an iota, not a dot, will pass from the Law until all is accomplished" (Matt. 5:17–18). God tells John not to add to "the *words* of the prophecy of this book" (Rev. 22:18).

7. *This Barthian view is contrary to the Bible's nature as a prophetic book.* Contrary to Karl Barth, the Old Testament describes a prophet as a mouthpiece for the very words of God, no more and no less. Also, God asserts about the coming prophet like Moses, "I will put my *words* in his mouth, and he shall speak to them all that I command him" (Deut. 18:18, emphasis added). And God commands Moses, "You shall not add to the word that I command you, nor take from it" (4:2). Micaiah announces, "As the Lord lives, what the Lord says to me, that I will speak" (1 Kings 22:14). Balaam proclaims: "I could not go beyond the command of the Lord my God to do less or more" (Num. 22:18). Yet the entire Bible is considered a prophetic writing. The whole Old Testament is called "Moses [the Law] and . . . the Prophets" (Luke 24:27; cf. 16:31; Matt. 5:17–18).

Likewise, the New Testament church is based on the teachings of "the apostles and prophets" (Eph. 2:20), and the apostle John considers himself among "the prophets" (Rev. 22:6). But given that prophets are considered to be the very mouthpiece of God, and that they deliver the very words of God, nothing more and nothing less, then it is most evident that the Bible claims for itself an identity between its words and God's words. Indeed, David says, "The Spirit of the Lord speaks by me; his word is on my tongue" (2 Sam. 23:2).

8. *This Barthian view is contrary to the interchangeability between what the Bible says and what God says.* The oft-quoted adage, "What the Bible says, God says," is a biblical teaching. Sometimes what God says in the Old Testament is what we read in the New Testament as what Scripture says, as shown below:

What God says . . .	What Scripture says . . .
Gen. 12:3	Gal. 3:8
Exod. 9:16	Rom. 9:17

What Scripture says . . .	What God says . . .
Gen. 2:24	Matt. 19:4–5
Ps. 2:1	Acts 4:24–25
Ps. 2:7	Heb. 1:5
Ps. 16:10	Acts 13:35
Ps. 95:7	Heb. 3:7

What Scripture says . . .	What God says . . .
Ps. 97:7	Heb. 1:6
Ps. 104:4	Heb. 1:7
Isa. 55:3	Acts 13:34
Isa. 6:9	Acts 28:25

For example, in Genesis 12:1–3 we read "Now the LORD said to Abram . . . ," but when this is cited in the New Testament in Galatians 3:8, it says, "The Scripture . . . preached . . . to Abraham, . . . saying . . ." Sometimes it is reversed so that what the Bible said in the Old Testament, the New reads that God said it. This shows the interchangeability of the two phrases. For example, in Genesis 2:24 the author of Genesis says, "A man shall leave his father and his mother." When the New Testament records it in Matthew 19:4–5, we read, "He [God] . . . said, '. . . A man shall leave his father and his mother.'" Likewise, Isaiah (6:8–9) "heard the voice of the Lord saying, '. . . Go, and say to this people,'" but the New Testament puts it this way: "The Holy Spirit was right in saying to your fathers through Isaiah the prophet" (Acts 28:25). This close identity or formal equivalence between what the Bible says and what God says is clearly contrary to the separation of the two by Karl Barth and his new evangelical followers.

In brief, whatever else may be said about the Barthian view, it is clearly contrary to Scripture, which affirms an identity between the Bible and the Word of God. Indeed, the Bible claims to be a prophetic writing such that it conveys the very words of God, no more and no less. Hence there is no way the Bible can be merely a fallible witness to God's personal revelation in Christ. Rather, the Bible claims to be a verbal plenary revelation from God.

Summary and Conclusion

Factual inerrantists claim that the Bible is the written Word of God. They insist that the Bible does not merely *contain* God's revelation but that it also *is* God's revelation. Further, the Bible is not a fallible *witness to* God's personal revelation; instead, the Bible itself *is the revelation* of God. Thus the Bible is an objectively true propositional divine revelation (see chap. 13 above). This entails also the belief that language—the human language in which the Bible is written—is capable of conveying objective divine revelation. Such communication is possible because there is, by way of creation, an analogous relation based in the real causal connection between the Creator and the creature. This similarity in being is not destroyed by the fall, and it makes communication possible between an infinite Being and finite beings since they have something real in common: being (that which is).

Even the fall does not destroy the creature's being. God's image in humanity is effaced but not erased. It is marred but not destroyed. For to destroy being is to send it into nonbeing. Hence, so long as something exists, there is common ground in which the Creator can relate to his creatures. And since God made language that can communicate objective meaning and since humans are rational beings who can understand objective meaning, then it follows that an objectively meaningful and true relation from God in human language is possible.

Many objections have been leveled against such claims from modern times to the present, including mysticism, conventionalism, and Barthianism, with its extreme view of human depravity. However, we have shown that neither human finitude nor fallenness has thwarted God's ability to communicate inerrantly with his creatures, nor our inability to make objectively true statements about God based on his objective, verbal, and propositional revelation to us.

Avoiding both the extremes of Platonic essentialism and modern conventualism, evangelical inerrantism is based in a biblically and philosophically justifiable realism. Our statements about God are not univocally identical to the way he is, nor are they equivocally totally different; yet they are meaningfully and contentfully analogous to the way God is. This analogy is based on real causal relations between Creator and creatures, in which the infinite Being causes finite beings that are similar in their being but different in their kind of being—God is infinite Being, and creatures are finite beings. Being communicates being: God cannot give what he does not have. God cannot produce what he does not possess. Thus the being that God gives to his creatures must be similar to him because he is Being. At the same time, it must be different because we are finite beings and God is infinite Being. Hence, there is a similarity (analogy) between God and creatures. It is this similarity that makes it possible for God to condescend and communicate with us in our language. At the same time it makes us able to speak truth about the Infinite with our finite language. We do this by taking terms that apply to God, stripping them of their finite qualities (by way of negation), and applying the univocal (same) definition of them to God in an analogical way. In this way, our language is an adequate medium for contentful and meaningful God-talk.

Sources

Augustine, De magistro

———, De Trinitate

———, Principia dialecticae

Barth, Church Dogmatics, Volume 1: The Doctrine of the Word of God

———, Evangelical Theology

———, Nein!

Berkouwer, Holy Scripture

Brunner, Word of God

Duns Scotus, Philosophical Writings

Frege, "On Sense and Reference"

Geisler, Baker Encyclopedia

Gilson, Linguistics and Philosophy

Grenz, Primer on Postmodernism

———, Revisioning Evangelical Theology

Grenz and Franke, Beyond Foundationalism

Holy Bible, King James Version

Holy Bible, New King James Version

Lewis, Abolition of Man

Mondin, Principle of Analogy

Pinnock, *Scripture Principle*

Plato, *Cratylus*

Rogers, *Biblical Authority*

Rogers and McKim, *Authority and Inspiration*

Saussure, *General Linguistics*

Thomas Aquinas, *Summa*

Wittgenstein, *Lectures and Conversations*

————, *Notebooks*

————, *Philosophical Investigations*

————, *Tractatus*

15

The Nature of Hermeneutics
and Inerrancy

Introduction

Formally speaking, inerrancy and hermeneutics are distinct. Inerrancy deals with the nature of Scripture, and hermeneutics deals with the interpretation of Scripture. However, in actual practice, the two are closely related. Even the International Council on Biblical Inerrancy (ICBI) statement on inerrancy has a whole article (art. 18) on hermeneutics and alludes to it in many other articles. What is more, those who deny inerrancy often embrace an aberrant hermeneutic. For these reasons it is necessary to discuss the relation of hermeneutics and inerrancy.

The Relation of Hermeneutics and Inerrancy

The ICBI Statement on Hermeneutics and Inerrancy

Realizing the importance of a proper hermeneutic to inerrancy, the ICBI dedicated one whole article to it in its famous Chicago Statement on Biblical Inerrancy (1978). Article 18 reads:

> We affirm that the text of Scripture is to be interpreted by grammatico-historical exegesis, taking account of its literary forms and devices, and that Scripture is to interpret Scripture. We deny the legitimacy of any treatment of the text or quest for

sources lying behind it that leads to relativizing, dehistoricizing, or discounting its teaching, or rejecting its claims to authorship.

This statement makes a clear commitment to the historical-grammatical method of interpreting the Bible. By implication this also means that it is opposed to any method of interpretation that is contrary to this approach to Scripture. And as we will see, deviant views on inerrancy often involve deviant views on hermeneutics.

Other Implications of Hermeneutics and Inerrancy

In addition to the clear commitment to the historical-grammatical interpretation of Scripture, an understanding of what this implies is found in several other articles of the ICBI Chicago Statement on Biblical Inerrancy.[1] One of the most important is that this method is employed in deriving the doctrine of inerrancy itself from Scripture.

Hermeneutics Used to Derive the Doctrine of Inerrancy

Article 15 declares: "We affirm that *the doctrine of inerrancy is grounded in the teaching of the Bible about inspiration.*" This statement implies the necessity to use the historical-grammatical method in order to know what the Bible teaches about its own inspiration and inerrancy.

The same thing is implied in the Short Statement on inerrancy in the ICBI document. It affirms in point 2:

Holy Scripture, being God's own Word, written by men prepared and superintended by his Spirit, is of infallible divine authority in *all matters upon which it touches*: it is to be believed, as God's instruction, in *all that it affirms*; obeyed, as God's command, in all that it requires; embraced, as God's pledge, in all that it promises.

This implies that we can understand what the Bible touches on and affirms. Without the historical-grammatical method of interpretation (affirmed in art. 18), this would not be possible.

Further Defining of the Historical-Grammatical Method

Article 5 further refines what is meant by historical-grammatical (HG): "We affirm that God's revelation in the Holy Scriptures was progressive. *We deny that later revelation, which may fulfill earlier revelation, ever corrects or contradicts it.*"

Article 11 asserts: "We affirm that Scripture, having been given by divine inspiration, is infallible, so that, far from misleading us, it is *true and reliable in all the matters it addresses.*" This reveals that the object of HG is to understand the objective truth of Scripture (see chap. 13 above) in all matters. This includes historical and scientific matters. For article 12 reads:

We affirm that Scripture in its entirety is inerrant, being free from all falsehood, fraud, or deceit. We deny that Biblical infallibility and inerrancy are limited to spiritual, religious, or redemptive themes, exclusive of assertions in the fields of history and science. We further deny that scientific hypotheses about earth history may properly be used to overturn the teaching of Scripture on creation and the flood.

Article 13 further defines the HG method as interpreting the Bible in the light of its own phenomena:

We further deny that inerrancy is negated by Biblical phenomena such as a lack of modern technical precision, irregularities of grammar or spelling, observational descriptions of nature, the reporting of falsehoods, the use of hyperbole and round numbers, the topical arrangement of material, variant selections of material in parallel accounts, or the use of free citations.

Article 2 even implies that HG will yield a belief in *sola scriptura*: "*We affirm that the Scriptures are the supreme written norm by which God binds the conscience*, and that the authority of the Church is subordinate to that of Scripture. We deny that Church creeds, councils, or declarations have authority greater than or equal to the authority of the Bible."

Article 14 makes HG subject to the laws of logic, insisting on "*the unity and internal consistency of Scripture*. We deny that alleged errors and discrepancies that have not yet been resolved vitiate the truth claims of the Bible."

In the years to follow, ICBI gave a more precise definition of the HG method. The statement and scholarly papers on the topic are found in *Hermeneutics, Inerrancy, and the Bible* [*HI*] (1984), edited by Radmacher and Preus. Even though this document is not an official part of the Chicago Statement (1978), it nonetheless does spell out what the ICBI inerrantists held regarding HG hermeneutics and inerrancy. It contains a series of twenty-five articles, with a brief commentary on them (Geisler, "Explaining Hermeneutics" [*EH*], in appendix B of *HI*). Crucial parts of these statements will be alluded to in the following discussion.

Use of Hermeneutics to Deny the Historic Stand on Inerrancy

Our concern here is to look at some contemporary denials of inerrancy and the hermeneutics they use to do so. We begin with Jack Rogers of Fuller Theological Seminary, where the contemporary inerrancy crisis began in the 1960s (see chap. 1).

Jack Rogers's Use of Hermeneutics to Deny or Undermine Total Inerrancy

Jack Rogers of Fuller Seminary, citing G. C. Berkouwer with approval, wrote: "It is not that Scripture offers us no information but that the nature of this information is unique. It is governed by the purpose of God's revelation." And God's purpose is redemptive. Hence, "swerving from the truth" of redemption is what constitutes error (Rogers and McKim, *Authority and Interpretation* [*AI*], 431), not factually incorrect statements. "For the purpose of the God-breathed Scripture is not at all to provide scientific gnosis [knowledge] . . . but to witness of the salvation of God unto faith" (431). For example, citing Berkouwer with approval again, Rogers writes: "Paul in the least did not render timeless propositions concerning womanhood" (432). He claims "a biblical definition of error" is not what involves "incorrectness" but what involves "deception" (31).

Rather, "religious knowledge was either personal, relational knowledge, or it was not considered worthy of the name knowledge" (*AI*, 434). He adds, because "the purpose of Scripture was to bring us to salvation in Christ, Berkouwer, like Kuyper and Bavinck, was open to the results of critical scholarship in a way that the Princeton theology was not" (429).

Following his mentor G. C. Berkouwer, Jack Rogers also introduces the divine-accommodation-to-error view into evangelicalism. He too calls it "organic" inspiration, limited to the redemptive intent of the authors. Rogers writes: "It is no doubt possible to define the meaning of biblical inerrancy according to the Bible's saving purpose and taking into account the human forms through which God condescended to reveal himself" (*Biblical Authority* [*BA*], 45). These human forms include "errors" (46) in nonredemptive matters; thus Rogers accepts negative higher criticism (*AI*, 393). Again, the Bible is written in fallen human forms and as such will contain the fate of all human writings: error.

Clearly Rogers has deviated from the HG hermeneutic as expressed by the ICBI statements and commentary in several ways. Let's consider them briefly:

First, Rogers's view of truth, which HG is designed to discover, is not the factual correspondence view affirmed by ICBI (art. 13). For the official commentary on that article speaks repeatedly of truth as that which "corresponds to reality" (see chap. 13 above). Likewise, error is not a mistake but only what misleads. This too is opposed to what the ICBI framers had in mind in the "Hermeneutical Articles of Affirmation and Denial" (1984 article XIV, hereafter, HA). Article 6 reads: "We further affirm that a statement is true if it represents matters as they actually are, but is an error if it misrepresents the facts." The commentary on this adds, "The denial makes it evident that views [like Jack Rogers's] which redefine error to mean what 'misleads,' rather than what is a mistake, must be rejected" (EH, 892).

Second, for the ICBI framers, truth means that statements about history and science are objectively true, even if they are on topics that are not directly redemptive (see art. 12). Indeed, ICBI later defines the HG hermeneutic as one that unveils "its literal, or normal, sense" (art. 15). It "affirms that Genesis 1–11 is factual, as is the rest of the book" (art. 22). Another article reads: "We deny that generic categories which negate historicity may rightly be imposed on biblical narratives which present themselves as factual" (art. 13). The commentary on this article informs us that it has in view "some, for instance, [who] take Adam to be a myth" and "others [who] take Jonah to be an allegory" (EH, 897).

In short, the literal HG method of interpretation is geared to obtain the objective truth of the text. This includes not only redemptive truths but historical and scientific ones as well. For all truth expressed in the text comes from the God of all truth.

Clark Pinnock's Use of Hermeneutics to Deny Inerrancy

Clark Pinnock is even more explicit in declaring the connection between his Rogers-like hermeneutic of redemptive purpose (see chap. 4 above). He even calls it an inerrancy-of-purpose view (*Scripture Principle* [*SP*], 262). He writes, "*Inerrancy is relative to the intent of the Scriptures,* and this has to be hermeneutically determined" (225, emphasis added here and below). Again, "All this means is that *inerrancy is relative to the intention of the text. If it could be shown that the Chronicler inflates some of the numbers he uses for his didactic purpose,* he would be completely within his rights and not at variance with inerrancy" (78). So the Bible could have factual mistakes and still be redemptively true, according to the intention of the author. Thus "*the Bible will seem reliable enough in terms of its soteric* [saving] *purpose*" (104–5).

This allows Pinnock to say, "In other words, the Bible may contain errors of incidental kinds, but it teaches none" (*SP*, 264). Thus he rejects the orthodox view: "What the Bible says, God says." He states, "I now know that Karl Barth had good reason for rejecting the concept of revelation as primarily information" (267). He clearly says, "Barth was right to speak about a distance between the Word of God and the text of the Bible" (99). He even accepts the Barthian illustration of the Bible being like a scratched record through which comes "the Master's voice" in spite of imperfections in the record (272). Pinnock then adds another Barthian belief, that the living Word, Christ, is "adequately witnessed to by this sacred text" (272).

In this sense, Pinnock's hermeneutic is geared to help the reader to weed out the "scratches" of factual errors and focus on the redemptive message of the Bible. While acknowledging flaws in the Bible, he seems to be blissfully unaware of the flaws in his interpretation of the Bible.

Peter Enns's Use of Hermeneutics to Deny Inerrancy

There are many aspects of Enns's view that are subevangelical (see chap. 6 above). Indeed, they are contrary to the ICBI statements on Scripture and how to interpret it.

Enns says that myth is a proper way to describe Genesis, even though he claims that it also contains history (41, 49). He holds that God adopted the mythical categories within which Abraham thought (53). He also asserts that God transformed the ancient myths to focus on himself (54). Enns also believes it is a fallacious assumption that the Bible is accurate in all details (*II*, 47). He holds, for example, that there was only one cleansing of the temple by Jesus (65), even though the

Gospels list two, at different times: one in Jesus's early ministry (John 2), and another years later (Matt. 21).

Enns also holds that it is a misconception to think that the Bible is unique, unified in outlook (*II*, 16). Also, diverse factual content is not incompatible with theological message (73). There are even inconsistencies in the moral law in the Old Testament (85). Enns believes that "the Bible seems to be relativized" by the culture of the day (*II*, 43). So Israel's laws are culturally relative and not normative (67). Further, the Bible does not contain an objective, unbiased view of history because there is no such thing (*II*, 45).

He holds that all attempts to state the nature of Bible are open to examination (*II*, 48). If this is so, then we are left in agnosticism about what is meant by inspiration and inerrancy. Enns claims that Genesis was not recorded until the first millennium BC (*II*, 52). This means that Moses, who lived hundreds of years earlier, could not have authored or compiled it. He also believes that Samuel and Kings were not written until the fourth or fifth centuries BC (63). This is long after their history ended.

Finally, Enns believes that the Bible is not a timeless how-to book that applies today (*II*, 67). God allows the law to be "adjusted over time" (87). He even criticizes the NIV for assuming inerrancy as a basis of its translation (92).

Enns's Views on Interpreting the Bible

At the foundation of his views on God and the Bible are his views on interpretation. Enns is a proponent of what is called Second Temple hermeneutics (*II*, 117). He believes that the traditional HG is generally a good approach, but "original context" means not only grammar and history but also the hermeneutics of the time (117). Hence, he believes that Daniel was given a deeper meaning of Jeremiah's words about the seventy years (119). The biblical writers dig for deeper "mysteries" in the text (131). In Christ there is a "superfulfillment" of Old Testament texts that were not speaking of him (136). Abraham's "seed" had a double and deeper meaning (137).

Enns also holds that Paul changed an Old Testament text, adding a word and changing the meaning (*II*, 140–42). Nonhistorical tradition is part of the New Testament interpretation of the Old Testament (143). The apostles did not come to view that Jesus is Lord from an objective interpretation of the Old Testament (153). The New Testament takes the Old Testament out of context and puts it in another context, the context of Christ (153). Israel is replaced by the church— God's higher, deeper meaning (154). The HG method is not a normative method (159). God intends more than the human author of the Bible did (160). Like Barth, he believes that the Bible is only a written witness to God's revelation in Christ (161). Christian interpretation goes well beyond scientific markers and objective criteria (162). Proper interpretation is a community activity—a historic community, the family of God. The Bible interpretation is not a fortress to defend but a pilgrimage to take (162). The categories "inerrancy" and "infallible" can never be fully understood (168). We have no absolute point of reference from which to interpret the Bible, stripped of our own cultural context. The incarnational model helps us to see a multidimensional gospel (169). The Bible is not a timeless rule book or owner's manual (169). The available evidence transcends the labels of conservative or liberal (171).

Set beside the ICBI view on hermeneutics and inerrancy stated above from official statements and commentaries, the views of Enns fall significantly short in many areas. In fact, he is a good example of how one's new hermeneutics can undermine the doctrine of inerrancy. It is actually an attack on the venerable historical-grammatical hermeneutics on which inerrancy is based.

Vanhoozer's Statements Undermining Inerrancy

Kevin Vanhoozer of Wheaton College claims to accept the inerrancy of Scripture. However, several aspects of his hermeneutics subtly undermine that claim. A few will be listed here. A more complete treatment of his view is found earlier (in chap. 8 above). Vanhoozer adopts the speech-act theory, which shifts meaning from what the text affirms (a locution) to what he infers the author's purpose was in writing this text (the illocution). As applied to Scripture, Vanhoozer writes: "My proposal, then, is to say both the Bible is the Word of God (in the sense of its illocutionary acts) and to say that the Bible becomes the Word of God (in the sense of achieving its perlocutionary effect)" (*First Theology* [*FT*], 195). To focus on the text apart from its illocution is pure "letterism" or "locutionism" (*Is There Meaning?* 312) since words have no meaning in and of themselves apart from their intended purpose. So the basic unit of meaning is the speech act, not the words of the text (312).

Vanhoozer calls his view "a Trinitarian theology of Holy Scripture." "The Father's activity is locution. God the father is the utterer, the begetter, the sustainer of word. . . . The Logos corresponds to the speaker's act of illocution, to what one does in saying. . . . The Spirit's agency consists rather in bringing the illocutionary point home to the reader and so achieving the corresponding perlocutionary effect—whether belief, obedience, praise or some other" (*FT*, 154–55). So, rather than the locus of the inerrant meaning and truth being in the affirmations of the text (which may be errant), we must focus on the purpose of the author in using those words. The actual affirmation (locution) may be errant (as when Joshua told the sun to "stand still"), but the purpose (illocution) is inerrant. What was the purpose of the text? Vanhoozer claims that "what the author is *doing* in Joshua 9 [sic] is narrating history in order to display how God has made good on his promise to Israel to bestow the Promised Land" ("Lost in Interpretation?" 106–7).

Ironically, it is really Joshua 10, not chapter 9 (as Vanhoozer said). But no doubt Vanhoozer would not consider this an error since his real illocutionary purpose was not to inform us about the actual chapter number!

Defense of the ICBI Statement on Inerrancy

There is no consistent orthodox theology without an orthodox methodology. There is no orthodox doctrine without an orthodox hermeneutic. And this orthodox method of interpretation is called the historical-grammatical hermeneutic (HG). Even the doctrine of inerrancy itself is based on an orthodox HG interpretation of the Bible. Likewise, the early Christian creeds, considered by many to be the standard for orthodoxy (see Geisler and Rhodes, *Conviction without Compromise*, part 1), are a result of using the HG hermeneutic on Scripture (ibid., chap. 17).

Defense of the Historical-Grammatical Hermeneutic

Given the importance of the HG way of interpreting the Bible, a brief explanation of what it means and why it is so crucial to inerrancy is called for. Let us begin by defining what is meant by the HG method.

Definition of the Historical-Grammatical Hermeneutic

The primary challenge to the HG hermeneutic is to its objectivity. It is based on the claims, evident in Enns (above), that subjectivity cannot be avoided in interpreting Scripture. There are many forms of subjectivism in hermeneutics. Since any one of them will undermine the classical doctrine of inerrancy as expressed by ICBI, we will concentrate on defending an objective hermeneutic rather than responding to all the forms of subjectivism.

Basis of an Objective Hermeneutics

The foundation for objectivism in hermeneutics is based firmly in its undeniable nature. Like an objective view of truth (see chap. 13), one cannot deny an objective hermeneutic without affirming it. For to deny objectivity in understanding a text is to imply that there is an objective way to understand that very denial. Indeed, to know that an interpretation is not objective, one must be in possession of an objective interpretation. More about this later, but first let us take a look at the elements that make an objective hermeneutic possible. These include (1) the existence of an absolute Mind (God), (2) the absolute nature of meaning, (3) the analogy between an Infinite understanding and finite understanding, and (4) the ability of finite minds (made in God's image) to understand truths revealed by God.

Existence of an Absolute Mind

The existence of an absolute Mind is a given in the classical view of "God" implied in the ETS and ICBI inerrancy statements, as discussed earlier (in chap. 12 above). A rational defense of this Mind goes something like this: (1) At least one finite mind exists (me), for I cannot deny that I am a thinker without thinking. And I am limited in my thought, or I would not doubt or discover new thoughts, which I do. (2) But the principle of causality demands that every finite thing needs a cause. (3) Hence, it follows that there must be an infinite Mind that caused my finite mind. This is true for two reasons: One, a cause cannot give what it does not have (analogy; see chap. 14 above). Two, the effect cannot be greater than its cause. So if the effect is intelligent, then the Cause must be intelligent. Hence, an infinite Mind must exist. Other inerrantists simply presuppose that such a Mind is a necessary condition for thought, in which we all undeniably engage. Be that as it may, an absolute Mind is absolutely necessary as a ground for absolute meaning.

Absolute Meaning

If there is an absolute Mind, then there can be absolute meaning. The objective basis for meaning is found in the Mind of God. Whatever an infinite Mind means by something is what it means objectively and absolutely. Hence, the existence of objective and absolute meaning is grounded in the existence of an absolute Meaner (God).

Without an absolute perspective, possible only by an absolute Mind, all truth is perspectival; so why should one perspective be considered better than another? Of course, the problem with the claim "All truth is perspectival" is that this is a nonperspectival truth claim; otherwise it could also be relegated to the category of just another relative perspective. Hence, we are back to the possibility of nonperspectival truth claims. But such are only possible if there is an absolute Mind.

Analogy and Meaning

The theistic God of the Bible and classical orthodox theology is capable of conveying thoughts from his Mind to our minds. For not only is this God an infinitely knowing (omniscient) Being; he is also infinitely powerful (omnipotent). But an infinitely powerful God can do whatever is not contradictory. And it is not contradictory for an infinite Mind to convey meaning to finite creatures, since there is a common ground between them in both the undeniable laws of thought and in the similarity (analogy) of being between Creator and creature (see chap. 14 above).

To be sure, an infinite Mind knows things in a much higher way than finite minds do. However, while *how* God knows things is different than how man knows, nevertheless, *what* he knows is similar to what he reveals to mankind. That is, the *thing signified* is the same, but the *mode of signification* is different for God and for us.

The Image of God in Humans

So it is not impossible for an infinite Mind to communicate with a finite mind, since there is common (analogous) ground between them. For it is possible for absolute meaning to be communicated to a finite mind. In short, objective disclosure of objective meaning is possible between an infinite Mind and a finite mind.

However, there remains one question: Can a finite mind *discover* the objective truth that has been objectively *disclosed* to it? It is one thing for an author to disclose the author's thoughts in an objective way (say, in a book), but it is quite another for a reader to be able to discover (understand) what the author has revealed.

The answer to this question is in two parts. First, it is *possible* to know what God has revealed, since all the necessary conditions for knowing the objective meaning expressed by God have been met, as just discussed. Second, whether one will *actually* know the objective meaning that has been objectively expressed will depend on having an objective hermeneutic, a means of understanding this objective meaning.

Principles of Objective Hermeneutics

We should remind ourselves again that there is an important connection between hermeneutics and inerrancy. As noted earlier, we cannot even know the basis for inerrancy in Scripture without the objective HG hermeneutic. Nor can we know the objective meaning of God's inerrant revelation without this objective hermeneutic. What then are the principles of an objective hermeneutic?

Principles of Understanding God's Special Revelation Objectively

Look for the author's meaning, not the reader's. The objective meaning of a text is the one given to it by the author, not one attributed to it by readers. After all, the meaning of the text comes from the meaner of the text (the author). Hence, we must seek what the author meant, if we are going to understand what his text means. So readers should ask what was meant by the author, not what it means to the reader or even to other readers, or to a community and tradition of readers. Once the reader discovers what the author meant by the text, he has obtained the objective meaning of his text. Thus, asking "What does it mean *to me?*" is the wrong question. Likewise, asking, "What has it meant to the traditional Christian community?" is not definitive for the meaning of a text, even though it may be helpful or supportive. Seeking the real meaning of a text anywhere outside of what the author meant will almost certainly lead to a subjective meaning of the text. Asking of the author, "What was meant *by this author?*" will almost certainly lead the reader in the right direction to find the objective meaning of the text.

Look for the author's meaning in what he affirms, not in why (purpose) he affirms it. Another road to hermeneutical subjectivity leads to the author's purpose rather than to his meaning. This was evident in the quotes from Jack Rogers, Clark Pinnock, Peter Enns, and Kevin Vanhoozer (above). They all used a self-confessed inerrancy-of-purpose view (Pinnock, *SP*, 262). But meaning (and truth) is found in *what* the author affirms, not in *why* he affirms it. Purpose does not determine meaning. One can know *what* the author said without knowing *why* he said it. Two examples will suffice to elucidate this point.

If one says, "Come over to my house tonight," there is no difficulty in understanding what is meant, even though the purpose for the invitation is not known. *What* is understood apart from *why*. The meaning is apprehended, even though the purpose is not known. Of course, if the purpose is known, then the statement may take on a whole new *significance*. But meaning and significance are not the same. Meaning deals with "*what?*" and significance deals with "*so what?*" For example, if the purpose of the invitation to come over to my house is to inform you that "You lost a loved one," rather than "You won $10 million," then the significance is seriously different. However, the meaning of the statement "Come over to my house" is identical in both cases.

To offer a biblical illustration, Exodus 23:19 commands the Israelites: "Do not boil a young goat in its mother's milk." The meaning of this sentence is very clear, and every Israelite knew exactly what they were supposed to do. However, the purpose of this command is not clear at all, at least not to us. A survey of a few commentators yields a variety of different guesses as to the purpose of this command: (1) It profaned the Feast of Ingathering. (2) It would cause indigestion. (3) It was cruel to cook it in the milk that nourished it. (4) It was a form of idolatry. (5) It violated the parent-child relation. In other words, nobody seems to know for sure what the purpose was. Yet everyone knows for sure what the meaning is. But if purpose determines meaning, then no one would know what the meaning is. So it is clear that purpose does not determine meaning. *What* is said is clear apart from *why* it was said.

Look for meaning in *the text, not beyond it.* The meaning is not found *beyond* the text (in God's mind), *beneath* the text (in the mystic's mind), or *behind* the text (in the author's unexpressed intention); it is found *in* the text (in the author's expressed meaning). For instance, the beauty of a painting is not found behind, beneath, or beyond the painting. Rather, it is expressed in the painting. All textual meaning is in the text. The sentences (in the context of their paragraphs, in the context of the whole piece of literature, and in their overall worldview context) are the formal cause of meaning. They are the form that gives meaning to all the parts (words, punctuation, etc.). They are the structure that gives meaning to the "stuff" of the text.

As noted earlier, applying the six causes to meaning will help explain the point. Philosophers distinguish six different kinds of causes:

1. Efficient cause: that *by which* something comes to be (producer)
2. Final cause: that *for which* something comes to be (purpose)
3. Formal cause: that *of which* something comes to be (form, structure)
4. Material cause: that *out of which* something comes to be (parts)
5. Exemplar cause: that *after which* something comes to be (pattern)
6. Instrumental cause: that *through which* something comes to be (means, tools)

For example, a wooden table has a carpenter as an efficient cause; to provide something to eat on as a final cause; its structure as a table as its formal cause; wood as its material cause; its blueprint as its exemplar cause; and the carpenter's tools as its instrumental cause.

Applying these six causes to meaning of a written text yields the following analysis: (1) The writer is the efficient cause of the meaning of a text. (2) The writing is the formal cause of its meaning. (3) The words (and punctuation) are the material cause of its meaning. (4) The writer's ideas are the exemplar cause of its meaning. (5) The writer's purpose is the final cause of its meaning. (6) The laws of thought are the instrumental cause of its meaning.

Thus, the meaning of the writing is not found in the meaner; he is the efficient cause of the meaning, not its formal cause. The formal cause of meaning is in the writing itself. What is signified is found in the signs that signify it. Verbal meaning is found in the very structure and grammar of the sentences themselves. Meaning is found *in* the literary text itself, not in its author (efficient cause) or purpose (final cause) but in its literary form (formal cause). Meaning is not in its individual words (material cause).

Words have no meaning in themselves. Words have only usage in a sentence, which is the smallest unit of meaning. But while individual words have no meaning as such, nevertheless words formed by thought into a meaningful whole (e.g., a sentence) do have meaning. So it is entirely appropriate (as opposed to Vanhoozer) to say, "Texts talk," "Books speak," and "The Bible says." The reason for this is that the author has imposed meaning on words in a text, so that the meaning and truth are there in the text. And since truth is an affirmation or denial, it follows that the text speaks. As the Protestant principle of perspicuity affirms, the Bible speaks clearly on its central message. The denial of this, as in Vanhoozer, leaves one with either subjectivity in his interpretation or the need to depend on some external interpreter, such as, the pope, Christian tradition, the Christian community, or the like.

Look for meaning in affirmation, not implication. Another guideline in discovering the objective meaning of a text is to look for its affirmation, not its implications. Ask what the text affirms (or denies), either explicitly or implicitly, not what implications or applications this text may have. This is not to say that implications are not possible or important or true but only that the basic meaning is not found there. Meaning is in what the text *affirms*, not in how it can be *applied*. If the text had no meaning, it would have no implications.

There is only *one meaning* in a text, but there are *many implications* and applications. In this sense the *sensus unum* (one-sense) view is correct. However, there is a *sensus plenior* (full sense) in terms of implications. For example, Einstein knew that $E = mc^2$ (Energy equals mass times the speed of light squared), and so does an average high school science student. However, Einstein knows many more implications of this than the typical high school student.

Likewise, God sees more implications in a biblical affirmation than does the human author (1 Pet. 1:10–12). However, inasmuch as God has inspired the text (2 Tim. 3:16), God sees more implications in it than does the human author. But God does not affirm any more meaning in the text than the human author does. For whatever the Bible says, God says. That is, whatever the Bible affirms is true: whatever God affirms is true. They both mean exactly the same thing by the text. There are not two texts, and there are not two meanings of the text. So both the divine and human authors of Scripture affirm one and the same meaning in one and the same text.

God surely knows more about the topic than does the human author, and God knows more implications of it than the human author. But both God and the human authors mean the same thing by the same set of words in the same context.

In short, God (and the human author) put the objective meaning in the text. And God made humans in his image so that they would be able to understand that objective meaning. That is, God gave us minds like his, using common laws of thought, so that we could understand that objective meaning and truth. And since objective truth is what corresponds to reality (chap. 13 above), then by means of the objective revelation that God gave, we are able to understand the reality about which the text speaks. Further, since truth is objective, it can be put in propositional form. Since all biblical truth is propositional truth (i.e., it can be put in propositional form), inerrantists appropriately speak of the propositional truth of the Bible.

Another way to make this point is that the interpreter should look for meaning in *what* is affirmed (interpretation), not how it can be applied, or significance. There is an important difference between meaning and significance. Both are important, but they are not the same. The true meaning of a text is found in what the author affirms in the texts. Significance is found in the many ways this can be applied. This leads to another important topic.

The Role of the Holy Spirit in Hermeneutics

This is a hotly debated topic, and the outcome is not determinative for what is meant by inerrancy. All evangelicals believe there is a role for the Holy Spirit, but some believe that the Spirit's illumination is necessary for our minds so that we can understand the *meaning* of Scripture, while others believe illumination of our minds is only necessary for understanding the *significance* of Scripture. Certainly, at least the latter is true.

Without any attempt to resolve that intramural debate, what seems clear is that (1) the Holy Spirit is not a substitute for a good hermeneutic; (2) the Spirit of God will not lead one to understand something as true that is contrary to the Word of God; and (3) the Holy Spirit does not bring new content or truth to the illuminating process of understanding Scripture. The Spirit is illuminating our minds to the truth that is there in the text, not bringing new truth to the process not found in the text. (4) The Holy Spirit does not bypass the text to "illuminate" believers to or about God's truth. This would be new *revelation* apart from and in addition to the text of Scripture and not merely a new *illumination* of the fixed revelation in the canon of Scripture. Such new revelation is contrary to the Protestant principle of *sola scriptura* and to the ICBI Chicago Statement (art. 5): "We further deny that any normative revelation has been given since the completion of the New Testament Writings."[2]

Defense of the Historical-Grammatical Hermeneutic

Now that we understand what the HG method of interpretation means and what is implied in it, let us examine the grounds for holding to the HG method.

First, it is actually undeniable in that no one can deny HG without implying it. For example, anyone who denies that "the true meaning of a statement is what the author meant by it" expects the reader to take his meaning of that statement. This is like the argument for the undeniability of objective truth. The very statement "there is no objective truth" is itself an objective truth claim. Likewise, those who claim that "the correct interpretation of a statement is not what the author means by it" nonetheless expect the reader to take the commentators' interpretation of what *they* mean by their own statements.

Second, the HG hermeneutic is the basis for understanding what the Bible teaches about itself. For one could not even know what the Bible teaches about inerrancy (for or against it) without using the HG hermeneutic. The very phrase "about itself" implies that one desires to know what the Bible means, not what we want it to mean.

Third, the HG method is the basis for orthodoxy. Creedal Christianity, the oft-used guideline for orthodoxy, is the result of interpreting the Bible according to the literal, common HG method (see Geisler and Rhodes, *Conviction without Compromise*, chap. 17). In fact, even the denial of orthodoxy uses a literal HG hermeneutic in their denial.

Fourth, although some dispute it, the HG hermeneutic is the one used in the Bible about other parts of the Bible. When Scripture speaks of other events in the Bible, it speaks of them literally. This is true when the New Testament speaks of Old Testament persons, like Adam (Rom. 5:12), Noah (Matt. 24:37–39), and even Jonah (Matt. 12:40–42). Likewise, it is true when it speaks about events, like creation (Matt. 19:4–5), the fall (Rom. 5:12–14), the flood (Matt. 24:37–39), and the exodus (1 Cor. 10:1–3). This is also true of messianic prophecy about Christ's first coming, to be born of a virgin (Isa. 7:14), from the tribe of Judah (Gen. 49:10), the dynasty of David (2 Sam. 7:12–13), suffering for our sins (Isa. 53), and being raised from the dead (Ps. 16; cf. Acts 2:30–32)—all of which were fulfilled literally.

Of course, there are some disputed passages where the New Testament seems to give a spiritual or allegorical interpretation of an Old Testament text. For example, Paul refers to Christ as the "spiritual Rock" that followed Israel in the wilderness (1 Cor. 10:4). But on closer examination, the word "spiritual" (Gk. *pneumatikos*) means not an immaterial body but a physical body having a spiritual source (i.e., God). It was a literal rock from which literal water came, just as the manna was literal manna, which they literally ate, even though it is called "spiritual food" and "spiritual drink" (vv. 3–4). Even a literal human dominated by the Holy Spirit was called "spiritual" (2:13).[3]

Space does not permit a treatment of all the alleged exceptions to this literal interpretation of the Old Testament, and others have done it much better than we can (see the works of Walter Kaiser and S. Lewis Johnson). But the common mistake is forgetting that the New Testament writers often take an implication of the meaning of the Old Testament text while applying it to another referent.

Hosea 11:1 is a case in point: "Out of Egypt I called my son" refers to Israel (the messianic nation) in Hosea. However, Matthew applies it to Christ (the messianic person), who would bring to fruition what that messianic nation was called to do: to bring forth the Messiah. In both cases the *meaning* is the same (since they are both God's "son"), and in both cases their "son" is a literal referent. However, Matthew is drawing an *implication* of that meaning, which Hosea probably did not have in mind when he wrote it. In actual fact, there are no clear undisputed examples in the New Testament of not using a literal HG interpretation or implication of the Old Testament.

Fifth, even nonliteral attempts to interpret the Bible depend on the literal sense to make sense of their method. For to affirm that something is not literal depends on knowing what is literal. The same is true of metaphors and figures of speech. Unless we know what is literally true, we are not able to use nonliteral language to express it. Similarly, in human communication, nonliteral meanings depend on a literal understanding for their meaning. Indeed, no communication makes sense without the literal sense at the basis of it.

Finally, without a literal HG interpretation of a text, one cannot know any objective truth. Like equivocal language (see chap. 14 above), it would leave us in total skepticism. But total skepticism or agnosticism is self-defeating. For the claim that we cannot know anything about God is self-defeating since it claims to know that we cannot know.

Response to the New Hermeneutical Approaches

There is a growing popularity, even among some evangelicals, for what is called Second Temple hermeneutics, meaning Jewish interpretation around the time of Christ, which supposedly influenced New Testament writers. Other forms of interpretation were also adopted that seriously affect the doctrine of inerrancy.

Robert Gundry

In 1983 Robert Gundry was ask to resign from the Evangelical Theological Society because of his use of midrashic interpretation, which led him to deny the historicity of whole sections of the Gospel of Matthew, such as the "wise men" who visited Jesus after his birth (Matt. 2). Gundry writes: "Matthew now turns the visit of the local Jewish shepherds (Luke 2:8–20) into the adoration by Gentile magi from foreign parts" (*Matthew*, 26). He adds, "Matthew has transformed the praiseful return of the shepherds (Luke 2:20) into the magi's flight from persecution" (32). Gundry concludes:

> Clearly, Matthew treats us to history mixed with elements that cannot be called historical in a modern sense. . . . Matthew's subtractions, additions, and revisions of order and phraseology often show changes in substance; i.e., they represent

development of the dominical tradition that results in different meanings and departures from the actuality of events. (623)

How do we know this? By holding that Matthew employs Jewish "midrash" (allegorical) methods of interpretation.

Gundry also argues that one's hermeneutical methodology should not be grounds for dismissal since he has agreed with the doctrinal statement of the society that the Bible is inerrant in all that it affirms. Exactly what it affirms is left entirely to one's hermeneutical method, and inerrancy does not encompass the orthodoxy or unorthodoxy of hermeneutical methods. To show the absurdity of Gundry's position, we asked him whether he believes that anyone who has signed the ETS statement—including people like Origen, Averroes, Karl Barth, and even Mary Baker Eddy (all of whom denied the historicity of parts of the Bible and some of whom denied all evangelical doctrines)—should be accepted as members of ETS. His response was a shocking yes.[4] This points out that whatever formal distinction one can make between inerrancy and hermeneutics, nonetheless in practice they are closely wedded. Indeed, it is methodologically unorthodox.

In fact, the HG hermeneutic is the very basis for knowing that the Bible is inerrant to begin with. And as ICBI was to point out, inerrantists are not making mere formal statements that whatever the Bible happens to address, it does so with no error. Rather, they are concerned about how this inerrant book is interpreted as well. Indeed, the ICBI framers had Gundry in mind when they formulated the Articles on Hermeneutics in their 1984 summit on the topic. Its article 14 reads, "We deny that generic categories which negate historicity may rightly be imposed on biblical narratives which present themselves as factual" (EH, 884).

Clark Pinnock

Pinnock speaks favorably of the Gundry midrash-type view, claiming that "there are fragments and suggestions of myth: for example, the strange allusion to the bodies of the saints being raised on Good Friday (Matt. 27:52) and the sick being healed through contact with pieces of cloth that had touched Paul's body (Acts 19:11–12)" (SP, 124). As a result, Pinnock also denies the historicity of sections of the Bible that are affirmed as true by Jesus or other biblical writers. The ICBI statement clearly affirms that this is contrary to inerrancy.

Pinnock also says, "There are cases in which the possibility of legend seems quite real. I mentioned the incident of the coin in the fish's mouth (Matt. 17:24–27). . . . The event is recorded only by Matthew and has the feel of a legendary feature" (SP, 125). "In the narrative of the fall of Adam, there are numerous symbolic features (God molding man from dirt, the talking snake, God molding woman from Adam's rib, symbolic trees, four major rivers from one garden, etc.), so that it is natural to ask whether this is not a meaningful narration that does not stick only to factual matters" (119). He adds, "We cannot rule legend out a priori. It is, after all, a perfectly valid literary form, and we have to admit that it turns up in the Bible in at least some form. We referred already to Job's reference to Leviathan and can mention also Jotham's fable" (121–22). He adds, "Thus we are in a bind. Legends are possible in theory—there are apparent legends in the Bible—but we fear actually naming them as such lest we seem to deny the miraculous" (122). Pinnock also speaks of legends in the Old Testament: "The influence of myth is there in the Old Testament. The stories of creation and fall, of flood and the tower of Babel, are there in pagan texts and are worked over in Genesis from the angle of Israel's knowledge of God, but the framework is no longer mythical" (123). He adds:

> We read of a coin turning up in a fish's mouth and of the origin of the different languages of humankind [Gen. 11]. We hear about the magnificent exploits of Samson and Elisha. We even see evidence of the duplication of miracle stories in the gospels. All of them are things that if we read them in some other book we would surely identify as legends. (123)

However, the ICBI statement clearly rejects such beliefs as incompatible with inerrancy, affirming in article 18: "We deny the legitimacy of any treatment of the text or quest for sources behind it that leads to relativizing, dehistoricizing, or discounting its teaching, or rejecting its claims to authorship." The official ICBI commentary on this adds, "When the quest for sources produces a historicizing of the Bible, a rejection of its teaching, or a rejection of the Bible's own claims of authorship, it has trespassed beyond its proper limits. . . . It is never legitimate, however, to run counter to express biblical affirmations" (Sproul, *Explaining Inerrancy* [*EI*], 55). But this is precisely what Pinnock did. Indeed, in some cases he went against what Jesus himself affirmed about Scripture by claiming that Jonah (in Matt. 12:40–42) and the flood (Matt. 24:37–39) were legendary and not historical. But article 12 of the ICBI statement says clearly, "We further deny that scientific hypotheses about earth history may properly be used to overturn the teaching of Scripture on creation and the flood."

Peter Enns

Peter Enns's controversial view cost him his teaching position at Westminster Theological Seminary. There are several aspects of his view that undermine the inerrancy of Scripture.

Rejection of a strictly historical-grammatical interpretation. Enns contends that the traditional HG is generally a good approach, but it is insufficient (*Inspiration and Incarnation* [*II*], 159) and not a normative method (159). He believes Daniel was given a deeper meaning of Jeremiah's words about the seventy years' captivity (119). Enns claims that the biblical writers dig for deeper "mysteries" in the text (131). There is a "superfulfillment" in Christ of Old Testament texts that were not speaking of him (136). Abraham's "seed" had double and deeper meaning (137). He sees nonhistorical tradition as part of New Testament interpretation of the Old Testament (143). Nonhistorical tradition is part of New Testament interpretation of the Old Testament (143). New Testament takes the Old Testament out of context and puts it in another context, the context of Christ (153). Further, Enns affirms that the apostles did not come to view that Jesus is Lord from an objective interpretation of the Old Testament (153).

Acceptance of Second Temple hermeneutics. Professor Enns is overly enamored with the alleged Second Temple hermeneutics, which he feels the New Testament writers are making of the Old Testament (*II*, 155). In these New Testament texts, he sees them using a midrash-like nonfactual spiritual embellishment of certain Old Testament passages, such as Paul's allegedly making the rock that followed Israel a midrashic story to emphasize his Christotelic interpretation of the Old Testament. The HG method must be augmented with a so-called Second Temple midrashic view that adds spiritual embellishment to the text (117).

Stress on communal interpretation. Enns claims that Christian interpretation is well beyond any scientific markers or objective criteria (*II*, 162). Indeed, he believes that proper interpretation is a community activity—a historic community, the family of God down through the centuries. The Bible interpretation is not a fortress to defend but a pilgrimage to take (162). Further, he affirms that the categories "inerrancy" and "infallible" can never be fully understood (168). We have no absolute point of reference to interpret the Bible stripped of our own cultural context. The Bible is not a timeless rule book or owner's manual (169).

Acceptance of a relativistic framework. Christian interpretation is well beyond scientific markers of objective criteria (*II*, 162). It is progressive and relativistic. Hence, the terms "inerrancy" and "infallible" can never be fully understood (168). God intended more than the human author of the Bible did (160). We have no absolute point of reference to interpret the Bible stripped of our own cultural context. An incarnational model helps us to see a multidimensional gospel (169). The Bible is not a timeless rule book or owner's manual (169). Thus Enns is unwilling to call his view as either "liberal" or "conservative" (171). As a matter of fact, it should be called neo-Barthian. Enns admits that this is a minority view among evangelicals. He also acknowledges that there are no clear rules to prevent us from taking his Christotelic view too far (162). Further, he is aware that this involves developing "deep intuitions" (102) in order to come to these conclusions. Likewise, he acknowledges that one must reject the traditional HG method of interpretation to do this and come up with multiple layers of meaning (161). Finally, other evangelical scholars have offered alternative interpretations without jettisoning an objective hermeneutic to do so. In brief, Enns's views are unnecessary and subjective, and there are better alternatives.

An Evaluation of Enns's Hermeneutical Views

For a more complete analysis of Enns's view, see the discussion above (in chap. 6). Briefer comments will suffice here. First, Enns is a classic example of what happens when one rejects the sufficiency of the classical HG method of interpretation and buys into a more recent relativistic model. For one cannot deny that objective meaning can be derived from the text without having an objective understanding of the text (see chap. 14 above). Nor can one say that all interpretation is progressive without standing outside the process to make this pronouncement. Further, there is no way to know that God intended a deeper meaning for a given text when all we have is the written text to inform us what God means.

Second, to use other texts to discover this alleged "deeper" meaning does not avoid the problem, for two reasons. First, all we have is the written text to go by. Second, what the biblical text says elsewhere does not add to what another text says; it simply gives us more on this topic. A given text cannot affirm (or deny) any more than that given text affirms (or denies). To claim any more for it is to attempt to read beneath, behind, or beyond the lines, rather than reading the lines. In the final analysis, Enns is not augmenting the HG method of interpretation: he is negating it.

Third, whatever else may be said about Enns's view, it is contrary to the traditional orthodox view on inerrancy. Two articles of the ICBI Chicago Statement speak to the issue of "dehistoricizing" the biblical record. Article 12 reads in part: "We deny that Biblical infallibility and inerrancy are limited to spiritual, religious, or redemptive themes, exclusive of assertions in the fields of history and science." And article 18 affirms: "We deny the legitimacy of any treatment of the text or quest for sources lying behind it that leads to relativizing, dehistoricizing, or discounting its teaching, or rejecting its claims to authorship."

The official ICBI commentary adds, "It has been fashionable in certain quarters to maintain that the Bible is not normal history, but redemptive history with an accent on redemption. Theories have been established that would limit inspiration to the redemptive theme of redemptive history, allowing the historical dimension of redemptive history to be errant." It adds, "The denial [in art. 12] explicitly rejects the tendency of some to limit infallibility and inerrancy to specific segments of the biblical message" (Sproul, EI, 36). In the oral discussion by the drafting committee, Jack Rogers's position was in view here. Later, in the ICBI statement on Hermeneutics and Inerrancy (1984), the oral discussion focused on Robert Gundry: "We deny that any event, discourse or saying reported in Scripture was invented by the biblical writers or by the traditions they incorporated" (EH on art. 14). Also, "We deny that generic categories which negate historicity may rightly be imposed on biblical narratives which present themselves as factual" (EH on art. 13).

Response to Kevin Vanhoozer's Hermeneutic

Vanhoozer is a good example of a bad practice—the practice of taking away with the left hand hermeneutically what one has affirmed with the right hand doctrinally. On the one hand, he affirms inerrancy, saying, "Inerrancy is most appropriate as a description of biblical assertions" ("Lost in Interpretation?" [LI?] 113). He declares that the Bible is "infallible" (92). He rejects Karl Barth's view of Scripture (99). Vanhoozer adds, "Whereas inspiration concerns the origin of the Bible's authority, inerrancy describes its nature. By inerrancy we refer not only to the Bible's being 'without error' but also to its inability to err. . . . Inerrancy, positively defined, refers to a central and crucial property of the Bible, namely, its utter truthfulness" (*Inerrancy of Scripture*, 1).

On the other hand, Vanhoozer undermines the inerrancy that he affirms by the hermeneutic he embraces. For as it turns out, we cannot know what the Bible means merely by what it affirms (locutions). We need to guess at its real meaning through inferences of how the author intended to use these statements (illocutions). So, by importing an alien philosophy of speech-act theory into the text, he undermines the truth of the text. For errors can be present in the affirmations (locutions), and only the guessed illocutions are without error (see chap. 8 above).

Grant Osborne's use of genre determination undermines inerrancy. Grant Osborne, a professor at Trinity Evangelical Divinity School, has a history of adopting contemporary hermeneutical procedures that call into question the inerrancy of Scripture. By use of form criticism, he once held that Matthew embellished Jesus's original words in the Great Commission from baptism "in the name of Jesus" to baptizing in the Trinitarian formula of "the Father, and of the Son, and of the Holy Spirit" ("Redaction Criticism"). When called on the carpet for this, he retracted that view and, strangely, claimed that Matthew had actually contracted (not expanded) Jesus's original words.

More recently Osborne has joined the hermeneutical fad that genre determines meaning. Along with many other scholars, he holds that one must make an upfront genre decision before he can understand what the text means. He writes: "Genre plays a positive role as a hermeneutical device for determining the *sensus literalis* or intended meaning of the text. Genre is more than a means of classifying literary types; it is an epistemological tool for unlocking meaning in individual texts" ("Redaction Criticism"). He is not alone in this procedure; most liberal and postmodern interpreters do the same. Unfortunately, many evangelicals have followed suit. Kevin Vanhoozer is among them (see chap. 8 above).

Professor Thomas Howe wrote a definitive article exposing the fallacy of this thinking ("Does Genre Determine Meaning?"). He asks a penetrating question: "But how can an interpreter attempt to classify a piece of writing into its appropriate genre unless he is able to read and understand what the text is saying prior to deciding its genre?" (4). Reading and understanding a text comes logically before the identification of its genre. The answer is that they must use the normal, customary, HG method of interpreting the text in order to determine the genre. Once determined, the genre can help enhance understanding of the text's significance, but it is not necessary to determine the basic meaning of the text.

In point of fact, using genre to determine meaning is a method, however unwitting, that will undermine the real meaning of a text. For example, if one uses a predetermined genre classification (made outside the text) to determine meaning, then the genre classification of "legend" can be easily imposed on a biblical text because it contains miraculous events. This is no doubt why Clark Pinnock concludes that "the influence of myth is there in the Old Testament. The stories of creation and fall, of flood and the tower of Babel, are there in pagan texts and are worked over in Genesis from the angle of Israel's knowledge of God, but the framework is no longer mythical" (*SP*, 123). He adds, "We read of a coin turning up in a fish's mouth and of the origin of the different languages of humankind. We hear about the magnificent exploits of Samson and Elisha. We even see evidence of the duplication of miracle stories in the gospels. All of them are things that if we read them in some other book, we would surely identify as legends" (123). By a similar fallacious procedure, Wheaton professor Kevin Vanhoozer was led to deny the historicity of Genesis 1–11, including the story of Adam and Eve (see LI? 98–99). This may have been one of the reasons an otherwise orthodox New Testament scholar, Michael Licona, recently denied the historicity of the resurrection of the saints in Matthew 27:51–53.[5]

But this is clearly contrary to the standard understanding of inerrancy meant by the ETS founders and expressed in the ICBI guide that the ETS membership adopted. The famous Chicago Statement on inerrancy declared in article 12:

> We affirm that Scripture in its entirety is inerrant, being free from all falsehood, fraud, or deceit. We deny that Biblical infallibility and inerrancy are limited to spiritual, religious, or redemptive themes, exclusive of assertions in the fields of history and science. *We further deny that scientific hypotheses about earth history may properly be used to overturn the teaching of Scripture on creation and the flood.*

And the official ICBI commentary on that statement reads: "It has been fashionable in certain quarters to maintain that the Bible is not normal history, but redemptive history with an accent on redemption. Theories have been established that would limit inspiration to the redemptive theme of *redemptive* history, allowing the historical dimension of redemptive *history* to be errant" (Sproul, EI, 36). However, "Though the Bible is indeed redemptive history, it is also redemptive history, and this means that the acts of salvation wrought by God actually occurred in the space-time world" (37). In addition, the ICBI statement on hermeneutics and inerrancy adds (EH on art. 13): "We deny that generic categories which negate historicity may rightly be imposed on biblical narratives which present themselves as factual." It adds, "Some, for instance, take Adam to be a myth, whereas in Scripture he is presented as a real person. Others take Jonah to be an allegory when he is presented as a historical person and [is] so referred to by Christ."

Further, the disputed first eleven chapters of Genesis are confirmed as historical by the New Testament, as the following list demonstrates. Each New Testament reference refers to persons and/or events in one of the chapters of Genesis 1–11:

1. Creation of the universe (Gen. 1)—Mark 13:19; John 1:3; Col. 1:16
2. Creation of Adam and Eve (Gen. 1–2)—Mark 10:6; 13:19; 1 Tim. 2:13; 1 Cor. 11:8–9; 15:45
3. God resting on the seventh day (Gen. 1)—Heb. 4:3–4
4. The marriage of Adam and Eve (Gen. 2)—Matt. 19:4–6; Mark 10:7–8; Eph. 5:31; 1 Cor. 6:16
5. The temptation of Eve (Gen. 3)—1 Tim. 2:14; 2 Cor. 11:3
6. The disobedience of Adam (Gen. 3)—Rom. 5:12–19
7. The sacrifices of Abel and Cain (Gen. 4)—Heb. 11:4
8. The murder of Abel by Cain (Gen. 4)—Matt. 23:35; 1 John 3:12; Jude 11
9. The birth of Seth (Gen. 4)—Luke 3:38
10. The translation of Enoch to heaven (Gen. 5)—Heb. 11:5
11. Marriage before the flood (Gen. 6)—Luke 17:27
12. The flood and destruction of humanity (Gen. 7)—Matt. 24:39
13. The preservation of Noah and his family (Gen. 8–9)—1 Pet. 3:20; 2 Pet. 2:5
14. Noah's son Shem and his descendants (Gen. 10)—Luke 3:35–36
15. The birth of Abram (Abraham) (Gen. 11)—Luke 3:34

In view of this, to deny the historicity of these early chapters of Genesis is to deny (a) the inspiration of the New Testament and (b) the authority of Christ who affirmed six of them himself (points 1, 2, 4, 8, 11, and 12).

What is more, denying the historicity of Genesis 1–11 undermines crucial New Testament doctrines that are based on them. This includes the doctrine of marriage (Matt. 19:4–6); the doctrine of the essential equality of men and women who are both in "God's image" (Gen. 1:27; 1 Cor. 11:7–12); the doctrine of the essential unity of the human race (Acts 17:26); the doctrine of the fall of humanity (Rom. 5:12–14) and the doctrine of redemption by the last Adam (1 Cor. 15:45).

Many of those who deny total inerrancy also deny the historicity of much if not all of Genesis 1–11. However, this is not consistent with the evidence that shows that Genesis 1–11 is historically connected with Genesis 12–25. First of all, Genesis 12 begins with a *waw*-consecutive verb ("and he said"), which indicates that what follows is a continuation of chapter 11 and not a break.

Second, the structure of Genesis is connected by the phrase "these are the generations [history] of . . . ," which occurs ten times. Each time this phrase occurs, it narrows the focus to something that has previously been discussed, such as the heavens and the earth (2:4), Adam (5:1), Noah (6:9), Noah's sons (10:1), Shem (11:10), Terah (11:27), Ishmael (25:12), Isaac (25:19), Esau (36:1), and Jacob (37:2). Thus, all of Genesis is presented as historical.

Third, since six of these phrases occur in Genesis 1–11 and four are in Genesis 12–50, it is clear that both sections should be understood in the same way.

Fourth, there is a connective between both sections in Abraham, Sarah, and Lot, whose history begins in the end of Genesis 11 (vv. 27–32) and continues in chapters 12–25.

Fifth, Genesis 12 makes little sense by itself, without the preparatory genealogy given in chapter 11. Only hermeneutical gymnastics could take Abraham, Isaac, and Jacob as historical but not Adam, Noah, Shem, Ham, and Japheth.

Sixth, the New Testament cites indiscriminately from both sections as historical. This was demonstrated above by numerous citations.

Therefore, Genesis 1–11 is just as historical as Genesis 12–50. To deny one is to deny the other, and to affirm one is to affirm the other. Thus, to deny the historicity of Genesis 1–11 is to deny the ICBI inerrancy position of full inerrancy. So evangelicals whose hermeneutic undermines the historicity of Genesis 1–11 are thereby undermining the full inerrancy of the Bible. And with it they are undermining the authority of Christ, the New Testament writers, and many important Christian doctrines based on the historicity of Genesis 1–11.

In short, up-front genre decisions to determine the basic meaning of a text have two serious problems. First, they beg the question. For the historical-grammatical method must be used to determine the meaning first in order to discover its genre. Further, using genre as an up-front determiner of meaning can (and often does) lead to a denial of the historicity and/or supernatural nature of the events.

Summary and Conclusion

There is a close relationship between one's hermeneutics and one's view on inerrancy. First of all, an unorthodox methodology will lead to an unorthodox bibliology. Bad methodology, midrashic interpretation, and so-called Second Temple interpretations lead to bad theology.

Second, false philosophical presuppositions will lead to false theological conclusions. Paul warns readers: "Beware . . . [of] philosophy" (Col. 2:8 NKJV). But we cannot beware of it unless we are aware of it. One of the biggest problems facing the evangelical church today is the unwitting acceptance of false philosophies by biblical scholars, philosophies that ultimately undermine their former theological orthodoxy. To rephrase Plato, until biblical exegetes become philosophers and philosophers become biblical exegetes, there will be no firm foundation for orthodoxy.

Third, only a good hermeneutic leads to good theology. That hermeneutic is the historical-grammatical hermeneutic. It is used by the Bible itself. It was used to form the early creeds, which serve as a basis for orthodoxy. It is used in everyday communications. And it is defensible philosophically because one cannot deny it without using it.

Noted New Testament scholar Professor Robert Thomas summed it up well when he wrote,

> What is the hermeneutical switch that made this switch [into the new hermeneutic] possible? First, and foremost, it is the incorporation of a new first step in the interpretive process, a step called Preunderstanding. In a very subtle way, beginning the exegetical practice with a conscious embracing of the interpreter's preunderstanding

of what to expect from the passage under investigation has transformed evangelical hermeneutics from an objective exercise of letting the passage speak for itself into a subjective exercise of allowing the interpreter to read into a passage the meaning toward which he is inclined. (Thomas, "HN," 290)

In his books *Evangelical Hermeneutics* and *The Jesus Crisis*, he has many more valuable insights on the topic.

Sources

Enns, *Inspiration and Incarnation*

Geisler, *Systematic Theology*

Geisler and Rhodes, *Conviction without Compromise*

Gundry, *Matthew*

Howe, "Does Genre Determine Meaning?" in *Christian Apologetics Journal* (Spring 2007)

Johnson, S., *Old Testament in the New*

Kaiser, *Uses of the Old Testament in the New*

Osborne, "Redaction Criticism"

Pinnock, *Scripture Principle*

Radmacher and Preus, eds., *Hermeneutics, Inerrancy*

Rogers, *Biblical Authority*

Rogers and McKim, *Authority and Inspiration*

Sproul, *Explaining Inerrancy*

Thomas, *Evangelical Hermeneutics*

———, "The Hermeneutic of Noncessationism" in *The Master's Seminary Journal* (Fall 2003)

Thomas and Farnell, eds., *The Jesus Crisis*

Vanhoozer, *First Theology*

———, *Is There Meaning?*

———, "Lost in Interpretation?"

16

The Nature of the Incarnation and Inerrancy

Introduction

Inerrantists have long commented on the relation between God's living Word (Christ) and his written Word (Scripture). They have argued that just as Christ is both divine and human in one person (without sin), even so the Bible has both a divine and human nature without error in one set of sentences. Some have criticized this analogy, pointing to some significant differences between the two. More recently, some have offered a new incarnational model that supports the denial of inerrancy. This model has roots in the neo-orthodox theologian Karl Barth but has also been adopted by some confessed evangelicals. To understand the development of the issue, we begin with the orthodox model.

The Orthodox Incarnational Model of Scripture

Since both Christ (John 1:1; Rev. 19:13) and the Bible (John 10:35; Matt. 15:6) are called the Word of God, it is understandable that a comparison would be drawn between them. Christ is God's revelation in person (John 1:14; 14:9), and the Bible is his revelation in propositions (i.e., in writing). Likewise, since both have divine and human dimensions, the analogy is even more interesting. For according to the orthodox creeds, Christ has both a divine nature and a human nature, being fully God and fully human. Likewise, the Bible is both God's Word and the words of its human authors; it too has both a divine and human dimension. What is more, both

Christ and the Bible are called perfect (Ps. 19:7; Heb. 4:15). What more, then, is needed for a good analogy? Hence, it is not uncommon for orthodox theologians to argue that just as God's personal Word (Christ) is both divine and human in one person, who is without sin, even so God's written Word is both divine and human in one set of propositions, without error. The analogy can be summarized as follows:

The Living Word	The Written Word
The Savior	The Scripture
Divine nature	Divine nature
Human nature	Human nature
One in person	One in propositions (sentences)
Without sin	Without error

In support of the last line, the Bible says that Jesus "was without sin" (Heb. 4:15), that he "knew no sin" (2 Cor. 5:21), that he was "pure" and "righteous" (1 John 2:1; 3:3), and that he "was without blemish or spot" (1 Pet. 1:19).

Likewise, the Bible "is God-breathed" (2 Tim. 3:16 NIV); it "comes from the mouth of God" (Matt. 4:4), "cannot be broken" (John 10:35), and is "perfect" (Ps. 19:7; Heb. *tāmîm*, "without flaw")—the same word used of the Passover lamb, which had to be "without blemish" (Lev. 23:12), as was Christ, our Passover Lamb (1 Cor. 5:7). It means entire, complete, full, and without blemish, as both Christ and the Bible are said to be.

It seems that the analogy is both biblical and reasonable. Just as Christ has two natures, one divine and one human, so does the Bible. For the Bible claims to be a coauthored book so that whatever the prophets wrote, God wrote. As David says, "The Spirit of the LORD speaks by me; his word is on my tongue" (2 Sam. 23:2). And Peter adds, "For no prophecy was ever produced by the will of man, but men spoke from God as they were carried along by the Holy Spirit" (2 Pet. 1:21). What more could be asked for in a good analogy?

This led the ICBI framers to speak of the Bible as a "theanthropic" book, just as Christ is a theanthropic person (both God and man, the God-man). Article 2 of the hermeneutics statement (1984) reads: "We affirm that as Christ is God and Man in one Person, so Scripture is, indivisibly, God's Word in human language. We deny that the humble, human form of Scripture entails errancy any more than the humanity of Christ, even in His humiliation, entails sin." And the ICBI commentary on this adds:

> Here an analogy is drawn between Christ and Scripture. Both Christ and Scripture have dual aspects of divinity and humanity, indivisibly united in one expression.... Both involve the use of fallible human agents. But both produced a theanthropic result; one a sinless person and the other an errorless book.... The denial is directed at a contemporary tendency to separate the human aspects of Scripture from the divine and allow for error in the former. By contrast the framers of this article believe

that the human form of Scripture can no more be found in error than Christ could be found in sin. That is to say, the Word God (i.e., the Bible) is necessarily perfect in its human manifestation as was the Son of God in His human form. (Sproul, *Explaining Inerrancy* [EI], 890)

However, in spite of that affirmation, ICBI considered this to be "an analogy," not a perfect comparison. And in spite of the fact that ICBI acknowledged that "like all analogies, there is a difference" (*EI*, 890), this comparison has come under strong attack by some contemporary evangelical scholars who deny inerrancy.

Defending the Orthodox Model

Andrew McGowan rejects the analogy between Christ and Scripture (see chap. 9 above). First, he argues that unlike Christ, whose two natures are united in one person, there is no such union of the divine and human in Scripture. However, McGowan misses the point, even on his own grounds. For elsewhere he speaks of a coauthorship of Scripture (*Divine Spiration* [DS], 148). He cites with approval the following: "This enables Bavinck faithfully and clearly to emphasize both sides of any orthodox doctrine of Scripture, namely, that God is the author but yet the human beings are the authors" (148). But if the verbal form of Scripture is "breathed out" from God, as McGowan claims it is, then there is a propositional (better, sentential) unity that combines both the divine and human elements of Scripture in one and the same verbal structure.

Even McGowan's own definition of Scripture supports the incarnational model, for he says, "the Holy Spirit caused men to write books and his supervisory action was such that although these books are truly the work of human beings, they are also the Word of God" (*DS*, 43). Again, there is a unity between the human and divine in God's written Word (the Scripture) that is analogous with the union of the divine and human in his living Word (the Savior).

Further, McGowan also argues that the word "divine" does not apply to Scripture as it does to the divine nature of Christ in the incarnation. He writes: "Only God is divine and therefore only God can have a divine nature" (*DS*, 120). But in a very important sense, this is not so. Even Peter affirms that in some real sense we are "partakers of the divine nature" (2 Pet. 1:4). Even the Bible commands us to be like God's moral attributes (Lev. 11:45; Matt. 5:48). McGowan seems to unwittingly answer his own question when he admits that "I am not denying that the Scriptures (like human beings) can share some of the divine attributes" (120). But that is all that is necessary for the analogy to be a good one, namely, to have strong similarities, which it has.

As for the Bible not being God, of course it is not. That is why the incarnational model is only an analogy (similar but not identical). No informed evangelical ever held that the Bible was God and should be worshiped. The Bible is like God in his moral attributes (like truth and holiness), not in his nonmoral (metaphysical) attributes (like infinite and eternal). So God's living Word (Christ) and his written

Word (the Scripture) are similar in that they have a divine and human dimension; these two dimensions are combined in one unity; thus, both are without flaw.

Hence, both God's living Word and his written Word are without flaw in that God's living Word is without sin and his written Word is without error.

In short, the analogy between God's living Word and his written Word is good. The criticisms of it miss the point and thus fail. Even though the Bible is not God, nonetheless, like Christ, it is fully human, yet without flaw. The Bible unites in one set of words what both God and the human authors affirm. Hence, whatever the Bible affirms, God affirms. But God cannot affirm error, and neither can his Word the Bible. The similarity is that they are both the Word of God, not that they are both God.

The Neo-Orthodox Incarnational Model of Scripture

While some evangelicals are denying inerrancy by rejecting the orthodox incarnational model, others are denying inerrancy by using an unorthodox incarnational model. The roots of the denial seem to be found in the writings of the neo-orthodox theologian Karl Barth. This view has been passed on through Berkouwer to Jack Rogers and Clark Pinnock and has been adopted also by Peter Enns, Kevin Vanhoozer, and others (see chaps. 4–11).

Explaining the Neo-Orthodox Incarnational Model

As we will see, there are some significant differences between Barth's incarnational model and the orthodox model. For one, Barth denies that there is a unity or identity between the Bible and the Word of God. For him, the Bible is merely a fallible human witness to the Word of God (who is Christ). However, there is a strong similarity between the neo-orthodox and orthodox views of Christ. Both affirm the full humanity of Christ and the full humanity of Scripture. Based on this, the reasoning seems to go something like this:

1. There is an analogy between Christ and Scripture.
2. This similarity includes the fact that both Christ and Scriptures are fully human.
3. But as fully human, both Christ and the Scriptures partake of human flaws.
4. Hence, the Bible, like Christ, partakes of human flaws.

Karl Barth (1886–1968). Barth believes that "there are obvious overlappings and contradictions—e.g., between the Law and the Prophets, between John and the Synoptics, between Paul and James" (*Church Dogmatics* [*CD*], 1/2.509). Why? Because the Bible is a fallible human book. Thus he wrote that "the post-biblical theologian may, no doubt, possess a better astronomy, geology, geography, zoology, psychology, physiology, and so on than the biblical witnesses possessed" (*Evangelical Theology*, 31). Why is this so? Because "the prophets and apostles as such . . . were real, historical men as we are, and therefore sinful in their actions, and capable and actually guilty of error in their spoken and written word. . . . But the vulnerability of the Bible, i.e., its capacity for error, also extends to its religious or theological content" (*CD*, 1/2.529; 1/1:509).

Emil Brunner (1889–1966). Another neo-orthodox theologian and contemporary of Barth writes: "The word of Scripture is not in itself the word of God but of man, just as the historical appearance of the God-man is in itself that of a man" (Emil Brunner, *Word of God*, 32). Why? Because the Bible is intrinsically human: "The word of Scripture is not in itself the word of God but of man" (32). He adds, "At some points the variety of the Apostolic doctrine . . . is an irreconcilable contradiction" (*Revelation and Reason*, 290). As a result, "the doctrine of the verbal inspiration of Holy Scripture . . . cannot be regarded as an adequate formulation of the authority of the Bible. . . . The Apostolic writings never claim for themselves a verbal inspiration of this kind, with the infallibility that it implies" (127–28). Brunner believes that it is "a fatal step" to hold "Scripture as true" to "every single part of Scripture down to the smallest detail" (*Word of God*, 34).

G. C. Berkouwer (1903–96). Under Barthian influence, Berkouwer has introduced the neo-orthodox incarnational model of Scripture into evangelicalism. At the heart of his view is this same Barthian mistaken idea of the Bible as being a fallen human book. Like Barth, he also distinguishes between the Bible and the Word of God (*Holy Scripture* [*HS*], 240). Thus, incarnationally, as "the revelation of God entered creation, . . . even as far as the humanly weak and ignoble; the Word became Scripture and has subjected itself to the fate of all writing" (199). The fate of human writing is to partake of human error. Thus Paul errs when speaking of womanhood (187). Also, there are incarnational accommodations to scientific errors (182), to historical errors (181, 185), to worldview errors (182), and even to myths (*HS*, 198).

Jack Bartlett Rogers (1934–). Following his mentor G. C. Berkouwer, Jack Rogers introduces the divine incarnational accommodation-to-error view into American evangelicalism. He writes: "It is no doubt possible to define the meaning of biblical inerrancy according to the Bible's saving purpose and taking into account the human forms through which God condescended to reveal himself" (*Biblical Authority*, 45). These human forms included "errors" (46) in nonredemptive matters, which includes accepting negative higher criticism (Rogers and McKim, *Authority and Interpretation*, 393). Again, the Bible is written in fallen human forms and as such will contain the fate of all human writings: error.

Clark Pinnock (1937–2010). Pinnock agrees with Rogers's inerrancy-of-purpose view (*Scripture Principle*, 262). This allows him to say, "In other words, the Bible may contain errors of incidental kinds, but it teaches none" (264). He states, "I now knew that Karl Barth had good reason for rejecting the concept of revelation as primarily information" (267). Pinnock adds, "Barth was right to speak about a distance between the Word of God and the text of the Bible" (99). He even accepts the Barthian illustration of the Bible being like a scratched record through which comes "the Master's voice" in spite of the imperfections in the record (272).

Pinnock then adds another Barthian belief, that the living Word, Christ, is "adequately witnessed to by this sacred text" (272) but not inerrantly expressed. Thus "the Bible does not attempt to give the impression that it is flawless in historical or scientific ways. God uses writers with weaknesses and still teaches the truth of revelation through them" (99). "What God aims to do through inspiration is to stir up faith in the gospel through the word of Scripture, which remains a human text beset by normal weaknesses [which includes errors]" (100).

Peter Enns (1961–). The most explicit and intentional use of the new incarnational model is by Enns. He is correct in positing two important factors of this model: (1) the "full humanity" of Scripture; (2) the unity of the divine and human elements of the Bible. However, he seems to be seriously lacking in his understanding that these elements involve factually and historically incorrect materials (*Inspiration and Incarnation* [*II*], 168). Likewise, he contends that this model handles diversity better (73). Also, it aids us in seeing a multidimensional gospel (169). But this does not escape the charge of hermeneutical relativity, which is self-defeating.

On closer examination, it becomes apparent that by "incarnational model" Enns does not mean what is traditionally meant by orthodox theologians, who make this comparison between Christ and Scripture. For they argue that just as Christ was fully human and without sin, even so the Bible is fully human but without error. After all, both the Savior and Scripture are called "the Word of God." But God can neither sin nor err. Hence, God's Word (living or written) cannot sin or err. Indeed, both are called perfect (flawless) in the Bible.

Further, in his incarnational model, Enns adopts a faulty idea of divine accommodation to error. Although it is acknowledged that historically orthodox theologians have held a divine adaptation to human finitude but not a condescension to human error. But there can be no accommodation to error on God's part. For God cannot err (Titus 1:2; Heb. 6:18). Unfortunately, Enns seems to believe that God can accommodate himself to factually incorrect affirmations (i.e., errors). But this is a denial of the inerrancy of Scripture, a denial manifested in several things he says.

First, he uses some ambiguous terms of the Bible, such as that the Bible is "messy" (*II*, 109) and that Jesus "completely assumed" cultural trappings of the world around him (17). Hence, the Bible cannot be kept from the "rough and tumble drama of human history" (109). But he nowhere clearly disassociates this from implying that there are affirmations in the Bible that entail factual mistakes or misrepresentations. Indeed, at times Enns seems to admit that there are these kinds of errors in the Bible. For example, he holds that the biblical authors really believe there are other gods (i.e., polytheism; 98).

Second, by using a true incarnational model, words and phrases like "messy" (*II*, 109), "completely assumed" cultural trappings of the world around him (17), and entering the "rough and tumble drama of human history" (109) are at best ambiguous, and at worst they veil a denial of the inerrancy of the written Word of God and, by comparison, the sinlessness of the Son of God.

Third, Enns speaks against an apologetic stance that defends the Bible against the charge of error (*II*, 108). If he believes the Bible is inerrant, then he should have no hesitation in trying to defend it against false charges that it is not.

Finally, Enns believes there are inconsistencies in the moral law in the Old Testament (*II*, 85). Even the Mosaic law is inconsistent. He believes that Exodus conflicts with Deuteronomy (87). Enns says that God allows the law to be "adjusted over time" (87). Also, he holds that the NIV translation is wrong for assuming inerrancy as a basis of its translation (92). But what is this but an implied denial of inerrancy.

Kenton L. Sparks. He stresses the humanity of the Bible to the point where error is necessary because it is a human document. However, inerrantists do not deny the humanity of the Bible, but they do deny that it is *necessary* for humans to err. Everyday life confirms that humans are able not to err. There are inerrant exams, phone books, and letters. When it comes to the Scriptures, God is the primary cause, and the human authors are the secondary causes. But it is impossible for a secondary cause to rise above a primary cause. The theological implication is that even though humans are imperfect and have a tendency to err, it does not bleed through to the text of Scripture. Peter affirms this: "For no prophecy was ever produced by the will of man, but men spoke from God as they were carried along by the Holy Spirit" (2 Pet. 1:21). Practically speaking, even God can draw a straight line with a crooked stick!

Sparks claims that Jesus accommodated his teachings to human fallenness when commenting on Matthew 19:1–9. Sparks says,

> In the language of our modern discussion, I would argue that Jesus not only allowed for, but [also] explicitly testified to, Scripture's theological and ethical accommodation to fallen humanity. So if we were at first surprised by the accommodation theology of the church fathers, we need be no longer; indeed, their accommodation theology was apparently in some measure derived from this Gospel text. (*God's Word* [*GW*], 241–42, emphasis added)

Sparks recognizes the christological implications of his claim: "If the critical evidence against the traditional authorial attributions in the Old Testament is as strong as it seems to be, then it is perhaps evangelical Christology—and not critical scholarship—that needs to be carefully reconsidered" (*GW*, 164–65). The implications are that "if Jesus was fully human, as orthodoxy demands, then it is likely that he learned—along with other ancient Jews—that Moses, Isaiah, and Daniel wrote their books, irrespective of factual and historical realities. Moreover, even if Jesus knew the critical fact that Moses did not pen the Pentateuch, it is hardly reasonable to assume that he would have revealed this information to his ancient audience. To the extent that Jesus drew upon his omniscience in everyday life and conversation, it would have been constantly necessary for him to pass up opportunities to tell those around him what he knew" (165).

Response to the Barthian and Neo-Barthian Challenge

Before leaving the topic of incarnation and inerrancy, the roots of the view must be examined more closely. They are found in Karl Barth, and they involve a fallacious view of fallen human nature.

The Barthian Errant View of Human Nature

In short, this view assumes that humanness necessarily involves fallenness. And since the Bible is human, then it too must be errant. Logically speaking, the response is rather simple: the argument has a false premise, and therefore the conclusion drawn from it is false. Consider the premises and conclusion:

1. The Bible is a human book.
2. Human books do err.
3. Therefore, the Bible does err.

As such, evangelicals have no problem with the first premise. The Bible was written by human beings in human languages, with human vocabularies, and human literary styles. So the Bible is thoroughly human. Admittedly some evangelicals have played down the human side of the Bible in favor of the divine and thus in practice made themselves open to the charge of biblical docetism (this was a heresy that denied Christ's humanity while affirming his deity). But evangelicalism does not embrace biblical docetism and has repeatedly denied it.

The second premise is true as far as it goes, but it does not go far enough to justify the conclusion. Humans certainly do err, but they do not *always* err, nor do humans *necessarily* err whenever they write something. But some such false premise is necessary in order to reach their conclusion: "Therefore, the Bible does err."

The truth is that humans, even without special divine aid, do not always err. Almost anyone can write an errorless book, probably a short one for most of us. There are even inerrant phone books in print where every number is correct. If this is possible, with no special divine aid, then there should be no difficulty in concluding that even humans, who sometimes err, did not err when under divine guidance to produce the books of Scripture.

There is, however, a more subtle argument beneath the Barthian charge against inerrancy. And it is more difficult to refute. It can be stated this way:

1. The Bible is a thoroughly human book.
2. Human beings *can* err.
3. Therefore, the Bible can err.
4. But a book that can err is not infallible ("infallible" means to be incapable of error).
5. Hence, the Bible is not infallible.

As noted earlier (in chap. 14 above), there are a number of ways to point out the flaws in this reasoning. The most obvious way is to point out that the Bible is, as it claims to be, a coauthored book. Both God and the human authors are responsible for one and the same set of words. There is a divine concurrence with every human word in Scripture so that "what the Bible says, God says." As David puts it, "The Spirit of the LORD speaks by me; his word is on my tongue" (2 Sam. 23:2). Or as Jesus says, what "is written" is "every word that comes from the mouth of God" (Matt. 4:4). Peter writes, "No prophecy of Scripture was ever produced by the will of man, but men spoke from God as they were carried along by the Holy Spirit" (2 Pet. 1:21).

Given this self-description by the Bible of the Bible, which all evangelicals should accept (and most do), then it would follow that both God and the human authors are responsible for all the words in the autographic text. So the Bible is a theanthropic book. As Christ has a flawless union of the divine and human in one person, even so the Bible has an errorless union of the divine and human in one book. So when we ask of one and the same person (Jesus) whether he could get tired, we find two answers: As God, no, he was not able to get tired. But as man, yes, he was capable of getting tired. Also, to the question as to whether Jesus could have sinned, the answer is no. Likewise, as God, Jesus was not able to sin (Hab. 1:13; Heb. 6:18; Titus 1:2). But as a man, the answer is, yes, he was capable of sinning for he was really tempted, but freely chose not to sin (Heb. 4:15; 2 Cor. 5:21; 1 John 3:3).

Likewise, insofar as the Bible is God's Word, it cannot err. It is infallible and incapable of error. But insofar as it is the words of humans (and it is), the Bible can err (but it does not err). So the objection is partially correct: the Bible as a human book is capable of error even though it does not err. So in the strong sense of the word "infallible" (i.e., incapable of error), the Bible as a human book is not infallible, that is, it is not incapable of error, even though it does not err.

However, this objection is seriously misdirected because the Bible is also the words of the God who cannot err. Hence, as the Word of God, the Bible cannot err. In view of this, one must reformulate the logic of divine-human nature of Scripture as follows:

1. God cannot err.
2. The Bible is God's Word.
3. Hence, insofar as the Bible is God's Word, it *cannot* err.
4. But the Bible is also human words.
5. Hence, insofar as the Bible is human words, it *can err*, even though it does not err.

Of course, as both God's Word and human words, the Bible *did not err.* There is no logical contradiction between "can err" and "cannot err" here since they are not used in the same sense or relationship. In relation to God, the Bible cannot err, but in relation to humans, it can err. The law of noncontradiction is only violated if one affirms and denies the same thing at the same time (which is being done here) *and in the same relationship* (which is not being done here).

The Barthian Errant View of Human Error

Barthians seem to imply more than that the Bible is *capable of* erring because it is human, humans are finite, and finite persons are capable of erring. Hence, the Bible is capable of erring. Also, Barthians seem to argue that depravity *necessitates* an errant Bible. This argument is stronger and more devastating. It can be put like this:

1. Humans are totally depraved, including their culture and language.
2. For depraved human beings, sin and error are unavoidable.
3. The Bible is a thoroughly human book, including its language.
4. Therefore, sin and errors are unavoidable in the Bible.

This conclusion is more serious since it makes error (and even sin) unavoidable in the Bible. It is also claiming more than that the Bible is fallible (i.e., capable of error). It is claiming that the Bible is inescapably errant. This is a serious charge and deserves serious attention from a traditional inerrantist point of view.

On close examination, it would appear that the flaw here is in the extreme doctrine of depravity that is being employed, a doctrine that makes sin necessary and unavoidable. But the Bible says that by the grace of God each sin in particular is avoidable (1 Cor. 10:13). As Augustine rightly put it, depravity means that we have the necessity to die, but only the *propensity* to sin. That is, we all have a sin nature that inclines us toward sin but does not necessitate that we sin. Given our fallen nature, sin in general is inevitable, but each sin in particular is avoidable by the grace of God. If it were not, we would not be responsible for it, but we are. Yet there is no responsibility where there is no ability to respond. The image of God is not erased in fallen humanity but only effaced (Gen. 9:6). Our free will is damaged but not totally destroyed. We are totally depraved in an extensive sense (that sin extends to every part of our humanity), but not in an intensive sense, that sin destroys all our rational and volitional faculties. There are a number of difficulties with this position.

By logical extension it makes the Bible sinful as well as errant. This is so because if depravity is so penetrating and pervasive in culture and language as to make everything permeated with error, including the human language in the Bible, then by the same logic the fallenness of human language would also make the language of the Bible necessarily sinful as well. However, this is contrary to the Bible's self-claim to be God's *holy* or *sacred* Word (2 Tim. 3:15) as well as it being "breathed out" by God (3:16). Surely we cannot believe that the holy God breathed out an unholy Word. And even on the Barthian view that the Bible is only a human witness to God's personal Word (Christ), there are serious problems. For even Barthians believe that the New Testament is a reliable and apostolic witness about Christ. But if this is so, then how do we know what is reliable and what is not? What criteria do we use to determine this? In truth, we are left with no objective way to determine where the apostolic witness is correct and where it is not.

Second, if Barthians are right about the fallenness of human language, then it would make the actual words that Christ spoke into fallen words, even when he was teaching about his holy Father. It would mean that Christ's actual words when teaching about the true God (cf. John 17:3) are permeated by falsehood. This is not to say that Barth would have to believe that we have the exact words of Christ in the New Testament. It is to say that whatever the exact words of Christ were, whatever they are in the New Testament or not, they are penetrated by the errors and sinfulness of all human language. Then Jesus could not have avoided using profane and even blasphemous language when conveying the saving message of God. This is ludicrous. And if Barthians try to avoid this repugnant conclusion by insisting that God could have supernaturally purified and preserved the words that came from Christ's mouth, then one would ask why God could not also have done this for the writers of Scripture. And if God could, then we are back to the orthodox view of Scripture, which Barth rejects.

Third, the Barthian fallenness-of-human-language view would, as applied to Christ, either make the Second Person of the Godhead sinful, or else lead to a heresy on the two natures of Christ. After all, Barth allegedly holds an orthodox view on the two natures of Christ in one person and the three persons of the Godhead in one God. But if Jesus uttered error and used foul language, then God (in the Third Person) could commit sin and error. As the apostle Paul would say, "Perish the thought! God forbid!" For after all, if sinful and erroneous things were coming out of Christ's mouth, then the Second Person of the Godhead was doing it. The only way a Barthian could avoid the logic of this is either (1) to fall into a heresy like Nestorianism, where there are two persons in Christ, one human and one divine; or (2) to modify his doctrine of depravity so as not to make sin an unavoidable part of human language. The former alternative is a heresy on the Trinity and two natures of Christ. The latter choice opens the door for an evangelical view denying that language is unavoidably sinful. This alternative points to another Barthian problem and an evangelical solution.

Fourth, if the incarnation involved the inevitable penetration of sin into human language, then it would mean that every use of this language necessarily involves sin and error. This would mean that swearing and blasphemy were inevitable parts of human language in every book, including the Bible. But this is absurd. For even authors not under special divine assistance can avoid swearing and blasphemy in their writings, as we can in our everyday speech. For even if it is inevitable that such words creep into the human vocabulary, it nevertheless is not inevitable that one uses them when speaking. There are plenty of good (and true) words to be used, and an author, even without special divine aid, could choose to use only the good and true ones. How much more could the human authors of Scripture, with the aid of special grace, produce a record without error or profanity?

Finally, Barth's fallen-human-language view denies the necessary analogous connection between our language and the nature of God. For as was shown earlier (in chap. 14 above), there is an ontological touching point between the Creator and his creatures that serves as a basis for predications about God's nature. Since God is infinite Being and has made finite beings in his image (Gen. 1:27), and since even fallen human beings are still in God's image (Gen. 9:6), marred though it is—there is still a connection in being (reality) for us to know about God through creatures. After all, the only thing an infinite Being can bring into being is a finite being, and both an infinite Being and a finite being have being in common. Hence, by our very nature as creatures of God, we have a common basis for knowing his truth. God does not have to accommodate himself to error in order to communicate with errant beings. He need only adapt himself to our finite being, as he did in the incarnation of Christ and, analogously, as he does in the finite human language of the Bible. Therefore, in the true incarnational model, there need not be (and was not) any sin or error in either Christ or the Bible.

Response to Neo-Barthians' Christological Error

Kenton Sparks's accommodationist view creates a christological crisis (see chap. 7 above). His argument that to err is human is based upon a Gnostic idea that any contact with human fallenness makes error unavoidable. This argument should be rejected for what it is: neo-Gnosticism. Although Sparks argues for the sinlessness of Christ and claims to hold to theological orthodoxy, the logical implications of this view are that Jesus accommodated himself to error and could have accommodated to sin as well! However, this is clearly against the basic New Testament teaching that Jesus did not sin (Heb. 4:15; 2 Cor. 5:21; 1 Pet. 2:22–23; 1 John 3:2–3).

The theological implications of Sparks's view are serious as well. For if it is true, the very teachings of Jesus in human language are tainted with error. Orthodox Christology has never held that the Second Person of the Godhead erred in his human words, but the logic of Sparks's position requires this conclusion. The implications are that the Son of God himself is not the "lamb without blemish or spot" (1 Pet. 1:19); instead, he partook in sin and error, and the saints in heaven will not be freed from their sin and error, in opposition to what the Scriptures teach (1 Cor. 13:10; 1 John 3:2; Rev. 21:4).

However, there is no reason to contend that Christ adhered to this extreme accommodationist position. Rather, orthodoxy has always taught that God has adapted his revelation to human *finitude* and never accommodated it to human *fallenness*. The reason is because it would be contrary to the very nature of God as truth to accommodate to error. So there are two views that must be distinguished: (1) First, God does adapt himself to human finitude, but (2) God does not accommodate himself to human error. Sparks confuses these two.

Summary and Conclusion

Inerrantists have often used an incarnational model, showing the similarity between God's written Word (the Bible) and his living Word (Christ). As the ICBI framers put it, "We affirm that as Christ is God and Man in one Person, so Scripture is, indivisibly, God's Word in human language. We deny that the humble, human form of Scripture entails errancy any more than the humanity of Christ, even in His humiliation, entails sin" (art. 2).

The criticisms of this orthodox incarnational model miss the mark by stressing differences in the analogy with which orthodoxy agrees, such as that the Bible is not God (as Christ is). This is surely true, but it misses the point, namely, the significant similarities between Christ and Scripture nonetheless. For both have a divine and human dimension cojoined in a theanthropic unity, one a person and the other a writing—and both are without sin or error.

Ironically, the new incarnational model is being used to deny the inerrancy of Scripture by insisting that being human entails being errant—for both Christ and Scripture. This, however, is not a biblical historical incarnational model, which involves only a divine adaptation to human finitude but not an accommodation to human error. This unbiblical model is based on a misunderstanding of both human nature and human depravity. To be human or even to be a depraved human does not make sin and error necessary. Being human makes error possible, and being depraved makes sin natural, but neither makes it necessary. The image of God in fallen humanity is effaced, but not erased. By virtue of the analogy between Creator and creature, there is a commonality that makes possible absence of error in God's communication and adaptation to humans in the *incarnation* of his truth in Christ, and in the *inscripturation* of it in Scripture.

Sources

Barth, *Church Dogmatics: A Selection*

Berkouwer, *Holy Scripture*

Brunner, *Revelation and Reason*

———, *Word of God*

Enns, *Inspiration and Inerrancy*

McGowan, *Divine Spiration*

Pinnock, *Scripture Principle*

Rogers, *Biblical Authority*

Rogers and McKim, *Authority and Inspiration*

Sproul, *Explaining Inerrancy*

17

Answering Objections to Inerrancy

Introduction

Numerous objections have been leveled against inerrancy. Most of them have been answered elsewhere in more extensive works (see Archer, *Bible Difficulties*; Geisler and Howe, *Big Book*). However, new ones emerge, and unfortunately the answers to old ones need to be repeated again. Our approach in this chapter will be to give a brief answer to the main objections that have been used as grounds for rejecting the total factual inerrancy of the Bible.

Objections to Inerrancy

1. The Term "Inerrancy" Nowhere Occurs in the Bible

It is true that the *term* "inerrancy" nowhere appears in the Bible, but neither does the word *Bible*. However, the Bible teaches the *truth* of inerrancy, and orthodox Christians accept it. For that matter, neither does the term "Trinity" appear in the Bible, but we do not reject the term for that reason. The question is not whether the term "inerrancy" is in the Bible but whether the truth of inerrancy is taught there. The term is negotiable; the truth is not. Some prefer the phrase "without error." But this is precisely what "in-errant" means: "no error," or "without error."

2. "Inerrancy" Is Not a Good Term Because It Implies Technical Precision

First of all, the term simply means "without error." And there is nothing bad or technical about that phrase. Inerrancy need not mean technical precision, and it does not mean this as defined by ICBI in article 13, which says explicitly: "We further deny that inerrancy is negated by phenomena such as the lack of modern technical precision, irregularities of grammar or spelling, . . . [and] the use of hyperbole and round numbers." What is more, the meaning of a term is determined by its usage in a given context, and "inerrancy" does not mean technical precision when used in a biblical and theological context.

3. Inerrancy Dies the Death of a Thousand Qualifications

Inerrancy is criticized for being too technical a term (objection 2 above). Then, when it is qualified so as to avoid this charge, the critics attack the term for being overqualified. But they cannot have it both ways. McGowan (see chap. 9 above) makes this charge. This objection is odd since elsewhere he actually commends the ICBI statement for making things clearer by having "denials" as well as "affirmations." But these additional negative qualifications make the doctrine even clearer. This allegation is false for two reasons.

First of all, the so-called "qualifications" do not kill it but enhance it and thus keep it alive. In short, they do not negate all meaning in the original claim; they clarify it by negating things from it that do not belong to it.

Second, basically there are not "a thousand" qualifications; there really are only two basic ones: (1) Only the original text is inerrant. (2) Only what is affirmed (directly or indirectly) as true in the text is true and not anything else. The rest of the so-called qualifications are not really qualifications by inerrantists but misunderstandings by noninerrantists. Hence, the rewording is necessary only because opponents have misunderstood or mischaracterized the doctrine. This calls for a denial by inerrantists that helps one to understand what was implied in the original affirmation that everything affirmed as true in the text is true (and everything affirmed as false is false). Just as the early creeds had to grow in order to explain what they meant in earlier more simple forms because later heretics misunderstood, distorted, or challenged it, even so later inerrantists have had to add more "qualifications" to explicate the original meaning as opposed to the heretical challenges of their day.

For instance, it should have been sufficient to simply say, (1) "The Bible is the *Word of God.*" However, since some have denied the obvious, it is necessary to add, (2) "The Bible is the *inspired* Word of God." However, when some use the word "inspired" in a human sense, it is necessary to say, (3) The Bible is the *divinely* inspired Word of God. But since some deny such a book is infallibly true, it is necessary to add, (4) The Bible is the divinely inspired *infallible* Word of God. Likewise, when some claim it is only infallible in intent but not in fact, then it is necessary to clarify that it means, (5) The Bible is the divinely inspired infallible and *inerrant* Word of God. Even here some have argued that it is only inerrant in redemptive matters, hence it is necessary to add, (6) The Bible is the divinely inspired infallible and inerrant Word of God *in all that it affirms on any topic, including historical and factual matters.* And so on. There is no apparent end to this process. Why? Because when someone denies the obvious, it is necessary to affirm the redundant. It is not the inerrantist's fault that he seems to be adding when he is really only explicating what the original statement means. So the inerrantist cannot be blamed for all the alleged "qualifications" (really, further explanations of the original meaning in the light of later denials). It is the opponents of inerrancy that should be blamed for denying the obvious. If "the Bible is the Word of God," then of course it is divinely inspired, infallible, and inerrant on every matter it touches. But if one denies the obvious, then inerrantists must affirm the redundant to make our view clear.

4. Inerrancy Is an Insufficient Term to Describe All That the Bible Is

Strangely, while some critics do not like the term because it is too strong by insisting there are no errors in the Bible, others claim it is too weak. Instead, they prefer words like "infallible," "reliable," or "authentic." After all, there can be inerrant books on math, logic, and telephone numbers, but no one would accept them as the divine authority for all doctrine and practice.

In response, it must be admitted that this object has merit. "Inerrancy" as a term does not cover all that the Bible is. First, it only covers truth statements, and not all statements in Scripture can be reduced to propositional truth (see chap. 13 above). There are exclamations, confessions, commands, memories, and prayers that are not propositions as such. It simply claims that all the claims in the Bible, whether explicit or implicit, are true.

Second, even the truth claims in the Bible, both explicit and implicit, do not tell us as such that they are divinely authoritative or inviolable. Stronger terms, like "infallible" or "divinely authoritative," are needed as well. In the strong sense of the word "infallible," the Bible is both infallible and inerrant. Total inerrantists do not claim that the term "inerrant" says all they want to say about Scripture. They only claim that we dare not say less because it is God's Word, and God cannot err. This is why total inerrantists often use other words, as ETS does when it calls the Bible "the Word of God written." And the ICBI statements speak of the Bible as "divine inspiration," "infallible authority," "infallible divine authority," "inspired Holy Scripture," "God-given Scripture," "authoritative Word of God," and "God's written Word" (see chap. 2 above).

Third, inerrantists are often leery of only the word "infallible" since it is usually taken by limited inerrantist and noninerrantist to mean "not liable to err" or the like. In the strong sense, "infallible" means "not capable of error." In this sense, inerrantists are happy to use the term. But since the meaning of the term is ambiguous, with contemporary usage leaning toward the weak definition, something more is needed, something like the words "inerrant" or "without error."

5. The Term "Inerrancy" Is Not a Good Term Because It Is Negative

By this logic we should also rule out many of the Ten Commandments. The truth is that negative terms are often more clear than positive ones. "You should not commit adultery" is more clear than a more cumbersome attempt to be positive, such as "You should always be faithful to your spouse with respect to your relations with those of the opposite sex."

What is more, the *term* "inerrancy" is negotiable, but the *truth* of inerrancy is not. The phrase "without error" is an acceptable alternative. Of course, this is negative too. Perhaps we should just be negative about the view that does not like negatives.

6. The Doctrine of Inerrancy Is Not Explicitly Taught in the Bible

Neither is the doctrine of the Trinity explicitly taught in the Bible. But inerrancy is taught implicitly and logically, as is the Trinity. Both premises from which inerrancy is the necessary logical conclusion are taught in the Bible. For example, the Bible teaches that (1) it is the Word of God (John 10:35; 2 Tim. 3:16), and (2) the Word of God cannot err (John 17:17; Heb. 6:18). Hence, it follows logically that (3) the Bible cannot err.

The same is true of the Trinity. The Bible teaches that (1) there is only one God (Deut. 6:4; 1 Cor. 8:4), and (2) there are three distinct persons who are God: the Father, the Son, and the Holy Spirit (Matt. 3:16; 28:18–20; 2 Cor. 13:14). Hence, the only logical conclusion is that (3) there are three distinct persons in one and only one God (namely, the Trinity). A doctrine should not be rejected because it is taught in the Bible only implicitly and logically but not explicitly.

The same is true of other essential doctrines like the hypostatic union of two natures, one divine and one human, in the one and only person of Jesus, the Second Person of the Godhead. All the truths that make up this doctrine are in the Bible, such as (1) Jesus is one person; (2) Jesus is fully God; (3) Jesus is fully human. But whereas all the pieces are there, the Bible nowhere explicitly teaches the hypostatic union. Nonetheless, it is a biblically based teaching, being there implicitly.

7. Inerrancy Is Derived Purely Deductively from Other Teachings and Is Not Based in an Inductive Study of Scripture

This objection is similar to the last one, and the response is also similar. Several points should be made. First of all, inerrancy does have a strong inductive basis in Scripture. For both premises from which the conclusion is derived are the result of a complete (perfect) induction of Scripture: (1) God cannot err. (2) The Bible is the Word of God. Both of these truths result from a complete study of all the Scripture. This is called a "perfect induction" in logic since it involves an exhaustive study of the data in limited areas. And perfect induction can come to knowledge that is certain. For example, one can be certain about the truth of the statement "All the coins in my pocket are pennies." Likewise, the Bible is a larger but also finite (limited) area, which one can study exhaustively on given doctrines and come to a certain conclusion. This being the case, both premises on which inerrancy is based are completely inductive, and we can be certain about them.

Second, unless the objectors to inerrancy are going to deny the laws of thought (which is a self-defeating denial), then they must agree that the only logical conclusion from those premises (1 and 2 above) is (3) The Bible cannot err. So the conclusion is a logically necessary inference from two certain premises. In order to deny this conclusion, someone must deny one or more of the premises. But it is simply untrue to argue that the only two premises from which we derive inerrancy are completely inductively based.

Third, to deny logically necessary conclusions from exegetically (inductively) derived truths is also to deny other orthodox doctrines. As shown in the previous point, the orthodox teachings about the Trinity and the hypostatic union of the two natures of Christ in one person are also logically necessary deductions. So too is much of orthodox Christian theology. Thus, to deny the procedure by which we derive the inerrancy of Scripture is to deny the basis of much of orthodox theology.

Fourth, indeed, the fact of the matter is that much of contemporary biblical theology is a repudiation of systematic theology. Many theologians believe that exegesis is the begin-all and end-all of theological study. They think that what one cannot derive from "pure exegesis" of Scripture is not a proper conclusion. Besides being philosophically naive (since even exegesis involves the use of logical thinking and inferences), this view is badly mistaken and misdirected. If applied to nature, it would involve the repudiation of all of science, which attempts to systematically categorize and draw logical inferences from the data of nature. This is also what systematic theology tries to do with the data derived from exegesis of Scripture.

Fifth, it is strange indeed for scholars from a Reformed tradition to hold this "pure" exegesis position. For the Westminster Confession of Faith speaks clearly (in chap. 1, sect. 6) of "the whole counsel of God . . . [is] either expressly set down in Scripture, *or by good and necessary consequence may be deduced from Scripture.*" Hence, it is important to remember that using logic to deduce truths from Scripture is not basing these truths on logic. Logic is only the rational instrument (coming from a rational God and inherent in rational creatures made in his image) that enables us to discover certain truths implied in Scripture.

Finally, as for the objection that one cannot come to any sophisticated or nuanced understanding of what the Bible means as "truth" or "error" by the simple deductive procedures used above, one can readily agree. But then we must quickly point out that such a nuanced view can be achieved by another complete induction of the data (phenomena) of Scripture in conjunction with what is known from God's general revelation. Since we develop this elsewhere (see Geisler, *Systematic Theology* [*ST*], vol. 1, chap. 12) in a complete "theological method," we simply point out here that even in this more refined understanding of what truth and error are, we are still using a combination of inductive study of God's revelation (both in Scripture and in nature) as well as drawing logical inferences from it.

8. There Is No Mention of Inspiration and Inerrancy in the Early Creeds

The early creeds are generally taken as the standard for orthodoxy. If so, then why do they not mention the inerrancy of Scripture? Does this not support the belief of noninerrantists that inerrancy is not an essential Christian doctrine? In response, several things should be kept in mind.

First of all, since creeds generally grew out of the need to defend an essential Christian doctrine that was being denied by some heresy, there was no need for inerrancy to be explicitly mentioned in the early creeds since there was no significant denial of it threatening the Christian church.

Second, the early creeds do imply the inerrancy of the Bible. The inspiration of the Bible (which implies its inerrancy) was commonly accepted by all the orthodox fathers and framers of the creeds (see Hannah, *Inerrancy and the Church*). Given that there were no major challenges to it, it did not have to be further explained or defended.

Third, it is crucial to remember that the belief in a divinely authoritative Bible is everywhere presupposed by the creeds. Almost all of the Apostles' Creed (2nd cent. AD) is made up of phrases that are dependent on the Bible. Likewise, the Nicene Creed (325) uses many of the same phrases and adds explicitly that these truths were "spoken through the prophets." The Chalcedonian Creed (451) uses many of the same phrases from the previous creeds and adds-explicitly that "we have the prophets of the Old [Testament]" and what "the Lord Jesus Christ himself taught" through the apostolic writings in the New Testament. So the divinely authoritative basis for the teaching of the Christian church is evident both implicitly and explicitly in the earliest general creeds of the church. Furthermore, we know from the early fathers that inerrancy was implied in what they mean by divine inspiration (see chap. 1 above and the next point). So, in effect, the early creeds did teach inerrancy.

Fourth, it is well established that the view of the early fathers was strongly in favor of inerrancy. A noted authority on the early fathers, J. N. D. Kelly, characterizes the view of the early fathers, when speaking of Tertullian's view, as being that "Scripture has absolute authority; whatever it teaches is necessarily true, and woe betide him who accepts doctrines not discoverable in it" (*Early Christian Doctrine*, 39). Augustine of Hippo sums up the early fathers well: "If we are perplexed by any apparent contradiction in Scripture, it is not allowable to say the author of this book is mistaken" (*Reply to Faustus* 11.5).

9. The Doctrine of Inerrancy Is a Recent Development, the Result of Rational Apologetics against Modernism

First of all, it would be expected that the defining and defending of inerrancy would be relatively recent since there were no major attacks on the doctrine within the church until relatively recent times. The major objections to inerrancy did not emerge until modern times, particularly after AD 1860 (see chap. 1 above).

Second, there is nothing wrong with being "recent" or "rational" or using "apologetics." God is rational, and he made us as rational creatures in his image (Gen. 1:27). Further, God commands us to "avoid . . . contradictions" (1 Tim. 6:20) and to use our reason in loving him with all our "mind" (Matt. 22:37) as well as giving "a reason" (*apologia*, reasonable defense) for our hope (1 Pet. 3:15). And good apologetics responds to attacks when they occur, whether a long time ago or recently.

Further, the charge is misleading since (1) inerrancy is taught in the Bible, which is as early as you can get. (2) Inerrancy was taught by the early fathers of the church, as well as theologians in the Middle Ages, Reformation, and post-Reformation periods (see Hannah, *Inerrancy and the Church*). (3) The truth is that the denial of inerrancy by those inside orthodoxy is a late invention, appearing in the church only in the last century. (4) Just because a doctrine is articulated and solidified at a certain date does not mean it was not held before that. As with most major doctrines, inerrancy was not as clearly formulated and articulated until it was seriously challenged. It is the denial of what is already believed that calls for a more serious defense of it. Such was the case with inerrancy in the early 1900s.

10. The Doctrine of Inerrancy Is Based on Nonexistent Original Manuscripts

This objection is unfounded for many reasons: First of all, the fact that there are no original *manuscripts* does not mean that we cannot reconstruct the original *texts* with a high degree of accuracy. And the fact that we cannot reconstruct the original *text* with a 100 percent accuracy does not mean that we do not have 100 percent of the doctrinal *truth* of the original text. Neither do we have any original manuscripts for Aristotle, Plato, or most other ancient classics, but this does not mean we cannot know what they taught from good copies of the originals.

Second, as a matter of fact, we have more, earlier, and better copies of the Bible than for any other book from the ancient world (see Geisler, *ST*, vol. 1, chap. 26). Noted scholars have substantiated this. Frederic Kenyon stated:

> The interval between the dates of original composition and the earliest extant evidence becomes so small as to be in fact negligible, and the last foundation for any doubt that the Scriptures have come down substantially as they were written has now been removed. Both the authenticity and the general integrity of the books of the New Testament may be regarded as finally established. (*Bible and Archaeology*, 288–89)

The great Greek scholar A. T. Robertson stated that "the real concern is with a thousandth part of the entire text" (in Warfield, *Introduction*, 22). That would make it 99.9 percent free of significant variants. Others have observed that these minor variants do not affect an essential teaching of the Christian church. Even agnostic Bible critic Bart Ehrman admits: "In fact, most of the changes found in early Christian manuscripts have nothing to do with theology or ideology. Far and away the most changes are the result of mistakes, pure and simple slips of the pen, accidental omissions, inadvertent additions, misspelled words, blunders of one sort or another" (*Misquoting Jesus*, 55). So we can reconstruct up to 99+ percent of the original text, and it contains 100 percent of the essential truths of the Christian faith. Hence, we do not need to possess the autographs.

Third, if the original copy of the Declaration of Independence was lost, it would not mean that we would have to cease existing as an independent nation under God. As long as there was once an original and as long as we still have good copies of it, there is no real problem. The same is true of the Bible.

Fourth, even with the minor errors in existing manuscript copies, we still possess 100 percent of the essential truths of the original text. No reasonable person would refuse to collect the money from a text message that read: "Y#u have won ten million dollars," even though there is an error in it.

11. If Imperfect Copies Are Adequate, Why Not Imperfect Originals?

McGowan asks, "If God is able to use the errant copies . . . that we do have, . . . why invest so much theological capital in hypothetical originals that we do not have?" (*Divine Spiration* [*DS*], 113). To use Barth's analogy, if the master's voice can be understood through a scratched record, why do we need a perfect original? In response, there are several reasons a perfect original is important.

First, an illustration will help answer this question. It is not difficult to understand the biblical story of God's making a perfect Adam, allowing him to fall and reproduce other imperfect copies of the original Adam. Now all these copies (descendants) of Adam are 100 percent human and yet imperfect as we all are. So essential humanity has been preserved even through generations of imperfect copies. Likewise, with Scripture it was essential to have an original that was perfect since a perfect God cannot make an imperfect original. For example, it is inconceivable that a perfect God could have made the first man with a deformed body and with cancer growths already on it. But it is not inconceivable that he would make a perfect original man, endow him with free choice, allow him to sin and bring imperfections to his posterity while God nonetheless preserves his essential human nature in his posterity. For this same reason, God has produced a perfect original Bible and yet preserved the copies of all minor errors so as to protect all the essential truths for posterity.

Second, a merely adequate but imperfect original is not possible for a perfect God to make. There are many things that God cannot do, even by his sovereignty. He cannot change (Mal. 3:6; James 1:13, 17). He cannot deny himself (2 Tim. 2:13). He cannot cease being God (Heb. 1:10–12). He cannot break an unconditional promise (Rom. 11:29). He cannot lie (Heb. 6:17–18). And, as an absolutely perfect God, he cannot produce an imperfect product either in the realm of truth or morals—because it is contrary to his very nature to do so.

Further, calling arguments like this "a priori" (McGowan, *DS*, 111) or purely "deductive" (136) does not make them invalid or false. They are based on the very revealed nature of God in Scripture (see chap. 12 above), and there is nothing wrong with making logical deductions from biblical truths. The Trinity is such a deduction since nowhere does the Bible explicitly teach in any text that there is one God in essence who is three in persons. Rather, it teaches: (1) There is only one God; (2) There are three persons who are God (i.e., who share this one nature). The doctrine of the Trinity is a necessary logical inference from these two clearly biblical premises. Inerrancy fits into this same category. There are two premises clearly taught in Scripture: (1) God cannot err. (2) The original Bible is the Word of God. The necessary logical conclusion to draw from this is clear: (3) The original Bible cannot err.

12. We Don't Need Inerrancy Because the Bible Can Be Reliable, Even if There Are Some Errors in It

This is similar to the last objection, but it is addressed to the all-or-nothing-at-all argument used by some inerrantists. They reason that you cannot trust the Bible in anything unless you can trust it in everything. This is countered by pointing out that a very reliable CPA will make some mistakes, but this does not mean he cannot be trusted in general.

In response, while some unsophisticated inerrantists may make an argument like this, that one little mistake would undermine the reliability of all of Scripture, it is not correct. What they should be saying, and most are saying, is something like this: If a book like the Bible claims to be divinely inspired and inerrant and you find one error in it, then you know for sure that it is not a divinely inspired and inerrant book. This does not mean that there could not be a book that did not claim divine inerrancy yet was a reliable witness to the basic truth of Christianity. What this means is that if your CPA claims divine inspiration and makes one mistake, then you know for sure that his work is not divinely inspired. It does not mean you have to fire him.

13. Belief in Total Inerrancy Undermines Confidence in the Bible

Clark Pinnock hints at such reasoning when he says: "It [the Chicago Statement on inerrancy] *sounds as if the slightest slip or flaw would bring down the whole house of authority. It seems as though we ought to defend the errorlessness of the Bible down to the last jot and tittle* in order for it to be a viable religious authority" (*Scripture Principle*, 127). In short, he argues that if one believes in total inerrancy, it puts him in a state of constant fear that someone will one day come up with a single error, and then he will have to give up his entire Christian faith. It would be a more secure position not to believe in inerrancy but simply affirm the reliability of the Bible. Then minor errors could never undermine one's faith.

In response, several points should be made. First, one could make the same argument about belief in the physical resurrection of Christ. If someone found the physical body of Christ, then our faith would be vain and we would still be in our sins. But this is exactly what Paul says in 1 Corinthians 15:12–19. If our faith in almost anything is meaningful, then it must be confirmable or disconfirmable in some way; otherwise it is not a reasonable faith. For if we don't allow anything to count against it, then it is a blind faith.

Second, besides all that, whether or not a view engenders a sense of security is not a solid ground on which to base its truth. Some views that make us feel secure may be false, and some views that make us feel uneasy may be true. Truth is known by correspondence with the facts, not by feelings of security.

Third, in the case of finding one error in the Bible, unlike the resurrection, it would not destroy the very basis for our faith. There are a couple of fallback positions before that, including limited inerrancy and a general reliability view, before we would have to give up evangelical Christianity. In short, a demonstrated error in the Bible would destroy our view of inerrancy, not the entire basis for the Christian faith.

Fourth, we have good reasons to believe that there are no errors in the Bible. So there is no good reason to fear our faith in inerrancy will be overturned (see Geisler, *ST*, vol. 1, part 2). The good reasons are based on the well-established biblical premises that (1) God cannot err, and (2) the Bible is the Word of God. (3) So the Bible cannot err. In addition, Jesus, who has been confirmed by reliable historical sources to be the Son of God, claims the Bible as the inerrant Word of God (see Geisler and Turek, *I Don't Have Enough Faith*). Further, as will be shown below, no one has ever proved an error in the Bible to date, after thousands of years. So it is not likely that anyone will in the future. Therefore, there is no real reason to fear that our belief in inerrancy will be overthrown, let alone the very basis for Christianity.

14. Inerrancy Is Not an Essential Doctrine and Should Not Be Stressed

First of all, there are different kinds of essential doctrines (see Geisler and Rhodes, *Conviction without Compromise*, part 1). Some doctrines are essential to salvation's being possible, and others are essential to how we *know* salvation is possible (inerrancy fits in this category). In theological language, inerrancy is not a soteriological (salvational) essential, but it is a revelational essential. For without a sure word from God, such as we have in Scripture, we would not have any sure knowledge about salvation.

Second, inerrancy is related to salvation in several ways: (1) Inerrancy is not essential to making salvation *possible*, say, the way the atonement of Christ and his resurrection are (1 Cor. 15:1–7; Rom. 10:9). (2) Further, inerrancy is not essential to make salvation *actual* for an individual. That is, it is not necessary to believe in inerrancy in order to be saved. The gospel is the power of God unto salvation (Rom. 1:16), and believing in the doctrine of inerrancy is not part of the gospel. (3) So inerrancy is not a test of evangelical *authenticity*, but it is a test of evangelical *consistency*. That is to say, one cannot be a consistent evangelical and deny inerrancy. For it is inconsistent to hold that the Bible is the Word of God but yet is not inerrant. (4) Further, it can be argued that inerrancy is essential to evangelical *vitality*. It appears to be a fact of history that belief in inerrancy is part of a vital, growing, evangelistic, and mission-minded Christianity. (5) Even if inerrancy were not essential in any sense, it would not mean that it is not true. But on any significant reckoning, inerrancy is an important doctrine. As such, it has appropriately been called a benchmark doctrine or a watershed belief. Indeed, to deny inerrancy, one has to deny that (a) the Bible is the Word of God, or that (b) God cannot err, or (c) both. For if the Bible is the Word of God (John 10:35; 2 Tim. 3:16), and if God cannot err (Titus 1:2; Heb. 6:18; John 17:17), then it follows necessarily that the Bible cannot err.

15. The Bible Cannot Be Inerrant Because It Was Written by Humans, Who Do Err

This argument does not follow logically for several reasons. First of all, humans do not *always* err. Even without any special divine aid, humans can and do write books without errors—usually short ones. There are, for example, inerrant phone books, where every phone number is right. There are inerrant math books, where every formula is worked out correctly.

Second, there is no contradiction for a perfect God to use imperfect writers as the means to produce a perfect book. Why? Because even imperfect humans can draw a straight line with a crooked stick. How much more can God?

Third, according to the biblical doctrine of inspiration, God was the primary cause of the Bible, and human writers were only secondary causes. "For no prophecy of Scripture was ever produced by the will of man, but men spoke from God as they were carried along by the Holy Spirit" (2 Pet. 1:21; cf. 2 Sam. 23:2). So in the overall process of inspiration, God superintends the process of revelation so as to preserve it from all error (cf. John 14:26; 16:13).

16. The Bible Cannot Be Infallible (Not Able to Err) Because It Is a Human Book, and Humans Can Err

The logic of this objection is as follows: (a) The Bible was written by human beings. (b) Human beings can err. (c) Therefore, the Bible can err. (d) But an infallible book cannot err (since that is what "infallible" means). (e) Hence, the Bible cannot be infallible. However, as strong as this objection may seem, it had a subtle fallacy within it. First of all, it is admitted that insofar as the Bible is a human book, it *can* err. But this does not mean that it *does* err. In fact, it is an error to think so.

However, insofar as the Bible is the Word of God, it cannot err. Since, the Bible is in effect a coauthored book (God being the primary author and humans the secondary authors), one must distinguish in what senses it is without error: (a) As God's Word it cannot err and did not err. (b) As humans' words it can err but did not err. The incarnation is a good example, having both a divine and a human dimension involved. As God, Jesus *could not* make an error in what he taught. As man, he *could have* erred in what he taught (but he did not). But the one and the same person Jesus *did not* err in what he taught. No contradiction is involved.

17. Inerrancy Is Divisive and Divides Christians

This argument has a pragmatic appeal to some, but it is without biblical or logical foundations. (1) First of all, not everything that divides is divisive. Marriage divides one from every other mate in a real sense, but it does not make marriage divisive. (2) If inerrancy is divisive because it divides those for and those against it, then so is believing in any doctrine, including the Trinity, the deity of Christ, his atoning death, and bodily resurrection. But no evangelical would call these divisive doctrines simply because they divide. The truth is that any truth claim divides those who affirm it from those who deny it. That is the very nature of truth that the opposite of it is false. And no one can deny this without dividing his view from those who affirm it. (3) Furthermore, if push comes to shove, it is better to be divided by truth than to be united by error. It is better to be divided by an inerrant Word than to be united by an errant one. Putting unity over orthodoxy will kill orthodoxy every time. (4) Why should those who affirm inerrancy be called divisive because they affirm it rather than those who deny it? Would we call trinitarians divisive because they affirm the Trinity and heretics not divisive when they deny it? It seems to us that if anyone is divisive, then it is those who deny an orthodox biblical teaching and not those who affirm it.

18. Inerrancy Is an Unfalsifiable Belief Since We Have No Original Manuscripts

In response, an important distinction should be made. The inerrancy of the original manuscripts may be unfalsifiable in *practice* right now since we have no original manuscripts. However, inerrancy is falsifiable in *principle* since an original manuscript could be found with an error in it. We have earlier manuscripts in the Dead Sea Scrolls than the time when the New Testament manuscripts were written. Further, inerrancy is also falsifiable in practice if one could find an error in a good copy where there is no dispute about the original. For it is not just the original manuscripts that are inerrant; it is also the autographic text that is also inerrant. For example, a perfect copy of an original manuscript would also be inerrant. Likewise, insofar as the autographic text is preserved in today's Hebrew and Greek texts, it is also inerrant. Thus, finding an error in it would falsify inerrancy. But, as we will show below, no one has succeeded in doing this.

19. If the Autographs Alone Are Inspired, Then Why Did God Not Preserve Them?

McGowan asks: "If textual inerrancy is so vital to the doctrine of Scripture, why did God not preserve the autographs of precise copies of the same?" (*DS*, 109). He adds, "What was the point of God acting supernaturally to provide an inerrant text providentially if it ceased to be inerrant as soon as the first or second copy was made?" (109).

In response, evangelical scholars have long pointed out several things that Mc-Gowan nowhere addresses at any length or really attempts to refute. First, there are important reasons to have a perfect autograph, the foremost of which is that the God of absolute truth cannot utter error (see above). For "It is impossible for God to lie" (Heb. 6:18). The "Spirit of truth" (John 16:13) cannot utter untruths.

Second, since God did not breathe out the copies of the originals, it is possible for them to err. However, God has providentially preserved them as a whole from any substantial error. In short, we have good copies of the original autographs. Third, there may be a good reason why God did not preserve the autographs. Knowing the human tendency to worship relics, imagine what would happen to the original Bible breathed out by God! Look at what happened to the brazen serpent in the wilderness years later (2 Kings 18:4). Further, knowing the human tendency to distort truth and corrupt doctrine, think of what could happen to the autographs if they fell into the wrong human hands. But given that the New Testament autographs are preserved in some 5,700 manuscripts (and the Old Testament in some 10,000 manuscripts), which are spread all over the world, there is no human way possible that any essential truth of the Christian faith could be distorted in all these copies.

20. Belief in Inerrancy Results from an A Priori Assumption That One Brings to the Bible, Not from a Neutral, Presuppositionless Approach to the Text

New Testament critic Bart Ehrman (author of *Misquoting Jesus*) insists that belief in the doctrine of inerrancy does not result from a neutral, objective approach to Scripture but from assuming in advance that it is inerrant before one looks at the text. But this is clearly a misdirected approach for several reasons.

First of all, there is no such thing as a presuppositionless approach to the Bible. Everyone has presuppositions. The only question is whether they are justifiable presuppositions. For example, we must assume the validity of the basic laws of thought as we approach the Bible. For no thought is possible without them. In fact, the most radical and dangerous presupposition one can have is the claim not to have presuppositions.

Second, Ehrman is not without presuppositions. He does not believe in a theistic God, nor does he believe in miracles. These are radical presuppositions. So it is no surprise that he has concluded that the Bible has errors in it since it is both a theistic and supernatural book.

But if God exists, then miracles are possible. As the former atheist C. S. Lewis puts it, "But if we admit God, must we admit miracles? Indeed, indeed, you have no security against it. That is the bargain" (*Miracles*, 109). The reason is simple: if there is a God who can act in creating the world, then he can act in the world he has created. So, basically the issue boils down to whether or not it is reasonable to believe in a creator of the world (for such reasons, see Geisler and Turek, *I Don't Have Enough Faith*). In any event, Ehrman's basic contention is misdirected—there are no neutral, presuppositionless ways to approach Scripture.

Certainly Ehrman's antitheistic and antisupernatural approach to Scripture is far from presuppositionless.

Finally, we have taken pains to show elsewhere that approaching the Bible with a reasonable, historical-grammatical interpretation yields the doctrine of inerrancy (see Geisler, *ST*, vol. 1). For the Bible teaches both that (1) the Bible is the Word of God, and that (2) God cannot err. Given this, it is reasonable to conclude from Scripture that the Bible teaches its own inerrancy.

21. Inerrancy Has Been Falsified by the Many Errors That Have Been Found in the Bible

There have been many attempts to demonstrate that there are errors in the Bible, but none have succeeded for several reasons (see Geisler and Howe, *Big Book*):

1. Most of them confuse difficulty with impossibility. Admittedly, there are many difficulties in the Bible. But to prove an error, it must be demonstrated that there is no possible explanation.

2. The allegations reveal that it is the critics who have made a mistake, not the Bible. In fact, history is replete with examples of critical views that have been wrong. So, while there are no demonstrable errors in the Bible, there are numerous established errors of the critics.

3. Failure to have an explanation for something does not mean it is unexplainable but simply that it is not yet explained. Many things once unexplained in science have since been explained. This favors the belief that an explanation will be found for the rest. The same is true of the Bible.

4. The assumption that something is unexplainable (such as a contradiction in nature) would stop progress in science. Likewise, the assumption of error in the originals would stop progress in Bible research. So, too, the assumption of inerrancy has heuristic value: it prompts further investigation.

5. Since the list of unexplained problems in science (and in the Bible) has decreased over the years, this favors the presumption that others will be explained in the future. This presumption favors both the scientists and the inerrantists. For many things once unexplained are now explained.

6. In the final analysis, Augustine's dictum is the best to follow: "If we are perplexed by any apparent contradiction in Scripture, it is not allowable to say, The author of this book is mistaken; but either [a] the manuscript is faulty, or [b] the translation is wrong, or [c] you have not understood" (*Reply to Faustus* 11.5).

Answering Allegations of Error in the Bible

There are many allegations of error in the Bible, but there are no demonstrations of error. Rather, every known attempt reveals an error of the critic, not an error in the Bible. For in every case there is a possible explanation. Hence, in no case is there a necessary demonstration of error. The following list of attempts illustrates our point. These examples were chosen because they have been used by critics to deny inerrancy and because they contain the most difficult allegations made against inerrancy (for a more exhaustive treatment, see Geisler and Howe, *Big Book*).

Allegation 1. Genesis says the sun was not made until the fourth day (Gen. 1:14–19). Yet there was "evening and morning" and "light" from the first day (1:2–5).

Response. (1) First, there was light from the first day when God says, "Let there be light," and there was both "evening and . . . morning" (1:3). (2) Nevertheless, the light holders (sun, moon, and stars) did not become visible until the fourth day. This is a common phenomenon even today. On a foggy or cloudy day, we can see light and the difference between day and night, even when the sun is not visible. (3) Apparently for the first few days of creation, the sun was not visible because of some kind of cloud barrier (perhaps vapor from the earth still cooling) that was removed by the fourth day, when God made the sun appear. This fits with the command "Let there be lights in the expanse" (1:14). The Hebrew word *ʿāsāh*, "made" (1:16), can mean "made to appear" or "revealed."

Allegation 2. Genesis has contradictory accounts of creation. In Genesis 1 land animals are created (1:25) before humans are created (in 1:27). But Genesis 2:19 indicates that the land animals were created after Adam, when he named them. This is a contradiction in the order of creation.

Response. (1) First, these two accounts are not contradictory but complementary. Genesis 1 gives the outline and chronological order, showing that the creation of animals was first. (2) Genesis 2 gives a more topical and detailed account, leading up to the naming of the animals. (3) In Genesis 1 the animals are *created* before man. In Genesis 2 they are *named* after man is created. (4) Genesis 2 does not say the animals were created after man was created. It simply says that God brought them to Adam, and he named the animals, which God had already created (2:19). Again, the error is in the critics, not in the Bible.

Allegation 3. The Bible says (in Gen. 4:16–17) that Cain has a wife and children. But there is no one else to marry since there is only Adam, Eve, and Cain left after Cain kills Abel (4:8–15).

Response. (1) It is not true that there is no one else to marry since Adam and Eve have "other sons and daughters" (Gen. 5:4). (2) Adam lives for eight hundred years after he had Seth (5:4). And one can produce a lot of offspring in eight hundred years! So there were many other women to marry, including sisters, cousins, and even nieces. (3) At this time it was not yet forbidden to marry one's close relatives for two reasons. First, there was no one else to marry back at the beginning. Second, the law forbidding incest came much later (in Lev. 18). We know today that incest can produce genetic deformities. But no doubt no such genetic deformities had yet developed at the beginning.

Allegation 4. Mathematics has demonstrated that the circumference of a circle is 3.1459 times the diameter and not three times, as represented in the Bible (2 Chron. 4:2). This is clearly an error in the Bible.

Response. (1) This is not an error; it could be a round number, which inerrancy allows for (see the ICBI Chicago Statement on inerrancy, art. 13). (2) Again, the Bible is written for average, everyday persons. And for average, everyday purposes, pi (π) is about three. (3) Even scientists round off pi to a limited number of decimal points since it goes on indefinitely when calculated. In fact, no matter how many decimal points it is carried out, it would still be imprecise since there would still be an infinite number of decimals left to go, if one wants to be technical. (4) The fact is that the Bible sometimes uses round numbers. Luke says Jesus was "about thirty years of age" (Luke 3:23) when he began his ministry. And the Bible should be judged by its own standards, which were the standards of the day, and not by some modern, technical standards, contrary to those standards. The ICBI statement declares: "We further deny that inerrancy is negated by Biblical phenomena such as a lack of modern technical precision . . . [and] the use of hyperbole and *round numbers . . ."* (emphasis added).

Allegation 5. Joshua speaks of the sun "stand[ing] still" (Josh. 10:12). But modern science has proved that the sun does not move around the earth but that the earth moves around the sun. Hence, the Bible has a scientific error here.

Response. (1) First of all, it is not unscientific to say that they saw the sun stand still or that it rises, which Joshua said earlier (Josh. 1:15). (2) Even contemporary meteorologists speak every day of "sunrise" and "sunset." Looking at the blazing evening western sky, no scientist says to his wife: "Honey, look at the beautiful earth rotation!" (3) This is observational language, and from a point of view on the surface of the earth, this is exactly what someone observes. The statement is not antiscientific: it is nonscientific. Again, ICBI (art. 13) clearly says, "We further deny that inerrancy is negated by Biblical phenomena such as a lack of modern technical precision, irregularities of grammar or spelling, *observational descriptions of nature . . ."* (emphasis added). The Bible is written for the ordinary people from the ordinary person's point of view, and as such it is perfectly accurate. We are not told how God performed this miracle. But an omnipotent Being would have no problem. A God who can create the universe (Gen. 1:1) would have no problem in doing this miracle.

Allegation 6. There are several numerical errors in the Bible. For example, 1 Kings 4:26 says that Solomon had forty thousand horse stalls, but the parallel passage in 2 Chronicles 9:25 says he had four thousand stalls. Likewise, 2 Kings 8:26 (KJV) says that Ahaziah was only twenty-two years old when he began to reign, but 2 Chronicles 22:2 says he was forty-two years old. Clearly these both cannot both be true. At least one must be an error.

Response. (1) These seem to be real errors since they appear to be talking about the same things. (2) However, inerrantists do not claim there are no copyists' errors in the text that we possess. The ICBI inerrancy statement says: "We affirm that inspiration, strictly speaking, applies only to the autographic text of Scripture" (art. 10). (3) These copying errors are relatively rare and do not affect any essential teaching of Scripture. (4) In fact, in most cases we know which one is right from the context or from other Scriptures. So in no way do these relatively few and minor errors affect the doctrine of inerrancy. (5) Most anyone who has received the following message would happily collect their money: "Y#U HAVE WON TEN MILLION DOLLARS." For even with the mistake, 100 percent of the message comes through. And the Bible has fewer copyists' errors than this message has.

Allegation 7. Biblical authors affirm the once-held ancient view that the atmosphere is not basically empty but is a solid dome. Job says that God "spread out the skies" like "a cast metal mirror" (37:18). Indeed, the Hebrew word for "firmament" (*rāqîa*', as in Gen. 1:17 NKJV) is defined in the standard Hebrew dictionary (Brown, Driver, and Briggs) as a "solid" object.

Response. (1) First, it is true that the root meaning (etymology) of *rāqîa*' was a solid object, yet meaning is not determined by *origin* but by *usage*. For example, the word "board" was originally a solid plank but now can refer to a group of persons, such as a "board" of trustees. (2) Further, *rāqîa*' means to beat out or spread out, as metal is thinned out when beaten. It is correctly rendered "expanse" (cf. Exod. 39:3; Isa. 40:19 NIV, NASB). Second, Isaiah 40:22 says that God "stretches out the heavens like a curtain," which fits with the idea of an expanding universe. (3) The Bible speaks of rain as falling through the sky (Job. 36:27–28), which is not possible through a solid object. (4) Finally, Job does not say the skies *are* a metal mirror but only that they are *like* one in their strength (endurance). This should not be taken any more literally than saying God is like a strong tower (Prov. 18:10) when he is pure spirit (John 4:24).

Allegation 8. Leviticus 11:5–6 says a rabbit "chews the cud," but science has proved they do not. Cows do, but rabbits don't. So, the Bible is wrong here.

Response. (1) Rabbits do not chew the cud in the modern technical sense (of ruminants, which usually have four stomachs), but they do have a thorough chewing action that looks similar and falls within the nontechnical meaning of the Hebrew term for chewing the "cud" (Heb. *gērâ*), whose root (*gārar*) means "to drag, to drag away." Rabbits do practice refection or reingestion (chewing their droppings). Even the famous scientist Linnaeus originally classed rabbits as ruminants because of their similar chewing motion. (2) The Bible does not use modern technical categories but those useful for an average observer, who could see by this chewing motion whether it was an unclean animal or not. The Bible employs the same observational language when it speaks of "sunrise" and "sunset." The ICBI inerrancy statement declares (in art. 13): "We further deny that inerrancy is negated by Biblical phenomena such as a *lack of modern technical precision* [and] ... *observational descriptions of nature*" (emphasis added).

Allegation 9. In Matthew 10:9–10 (NIV) Jesus says, "Do not take ... a staff [for your journey]," but Mark 6:8 says Jesus charges them to "take nothing for their journey except a staff." Which is right? Both can't be correct?

Response. Mark declares that they should take nothing except a staff, which a traveler would normally have. But Matthew says they are not to acquire an *extra* staff. In short, travel light, with the one staff a person normally has along. These are not contradictory instructions. This understanding is supported by the fact that Matthew also records that Jesus says, Don't take "two tunics" (Matt. 10:10). Obviously he was including the one they had on and only forbidding them to take an extra one.

Allegation 10. Matthew 8:5 says "a centurion came forward to him, appealing to him." But Luke 7:6 says "the centurion sent friends" to speak to Jesus. Which is it? One account contradicts the other.

Response. (1) Both are true; the centurion speaks through his official representatives. (2) The same thing occurs today when the secretary of state speaks as the official representative of the president. The president speaks through the secretary of state. Likewise in the Gospels, the centurion is speaking through his official representatives.

Allegation 11. The Bible makes a scientific error when it says, "The mustard seed ... is the smallest of all seeds" (Matt. 13:31–32). Science knows that certain orchid seeds are the smallest of all known seeds. This is a particularly important problem text since it is listed by Dan Fuller as a basis for rejecting the factual inerrancy of the Bible (see chap. 1 above). And with his influence, Fuller Seminary has moved away from their original inerrancy position.

Response. A careful look at this charge reveals that it is based on the classic fallacy of taking a text out of context. The context for Jesus's statement is given in the text. He says only that the mustard seed is the smallest one *"that a man took and sowed in his field"* (Matt. 13:31, emphasis added). He never says it is the smallest in the whole world. Here again, the critic errs, not the Bible. Sadly, this error was influential in a major seminary's rejection of the inerrancy of Scripture.

Allegation 12. The inscription on Jesus's cross was listed four different ways. Which one is correct?

Matthew 27:37: THIS IS JESUS, THE KING OF THE JEWS.

Mark 15:26: THE KING OF THE JEWS.

Luke 23:38: THIS IS THE KING OF THE JEWS.

John 19:19: JESUS OF NAZARETH, THE KING OF THE JEWS.

[Together: THIS IS JESUS OF NAZARETH, THE KING OF THE JEWS]

Response. The error of the critic here is in assuming that a partial report is a false report. Each has the essential part of it. Most reports on most topics are only partial. More could have been said. No report says anything false (i.e., contrary to fact), such as, "This is Thutmose from Cairo, the King of the Egyptians."

Allegation 13. Andrew McGowan (see chap. 9 above) claims this as "a very good example" of an error in the biblical text. In Matthew 9:18 Jairus tells Jesus that his "daughter has just died." But in Mark and Luke, Jairus tells Jesus she is only "at the point of death" (Mark 5:23; cf. Luke 8:42). McGowan concludes that "there is a clear contradiction between the initial words of Jairus as recorded by Matthew and the other Evangelists" (*Divine Spiration*, 113).

Response. (1) First, there is no contradiction between Jesus's initial and final statements since "while he was still speaking, someone from the ruler's house came and said, 'Your daughter is dead'" (Luke 8:49). (2) After that it is correct to say, as Matthew (9:18) records, that Jairus says, "My daughter has just died." Matthew does not report that Jairus says anything that in fact he does not say. He merely combines the two parts of the conversation, thus stressing the point that the girl has actually died by that time. This is an acceptable literary practice called collation. The ICBI inerrancy statement allows for such literary practices (in art. 13). Only a rigid literalistic interpretation of the text (which McGowan himself rejects) would argue to the contrary. Again, the critics wrongly impose on the Bible standards contrary to the practice of its day. At the same time, they insist that we must understand the Bible in terms of historic and literary cultural settings. But this is inconsistent.

Allegation 14. There are two opposing accounts of the death of Judas. Matthew (27:5) says Judas "hanged himself." But Acts (1:18) declares that "falling headlong he burst open in the middle and all his entrails gushed out."

Response. Both of these can be true. First, Judas hangs himself. Then, sometime after this his body is discovered, the rope cut (since it is forbidden to touch a dead body), and the body falls on sharp rocks and bursts open. Or the body has decayed enough that it breaks loose from the rope on its own. At any rate, the two accounts are speaking of two different events. The first one tells how he dies, and the second informs us of what happens later. No contradiction has been demonstrated since a possible explanation is available.

Allegation 15. Matthew (28:2, 5) says there is *one* angel at the tomb. But John (20:12) says there are *two* angels there. Both can't be true.

Response. First of all, it is a mathematical certainty that wherever there are *two*, there is always *one*. It never fails! Matthew does not say there is *only* one angel there at one and the same time that there are two. Mary sees two, "one at the head and one at the feet" of where Jesus has lain (John 20:12), because only she "stooped to look into the tomb" (20:11). If this is exactly the same event, perhaps "the women" (plural in Matt. 28:5) only see one angel from their angle of vision at the tomb. Since the angels speak in unison ("*they* said to her" [John 20:13]), perhaps it sounds like one voice to the other women, who see only one of the angels. So understood, this alleged discrepancy would vouch for the integrity of each eyewitness as reporting exactly what they see and hear. On the other hand, these may not refer to exactly the same event but to a later appearance to Mary (see order of resurrection next).

Allegation 16. The order of the resurrection accounts is contradictory in the Gospels. Some have Peter first. Others have Mary first and Peter later, and so on.

Response. The following is a plausible order of events that harmonizes all the accounts of the postresurrection events:

1. Early on the Sunday morning after Jesus's crucifixion, Mary Magdalene, Mary the Mother of James, Joanna, and Salome go to the tomb with spices to anoint

Jesus (Matt. 28:1; Mark 16:1; Luke 24:1; John 20:1). Finding the tomb empty, Mary Magdalene runs to Peter and John to tell them someone has taken the body of Jesus (John 20:2).

2. The other women enter the tomb, where an angel (Matt. 28:5) who has a companion (John 20:12; Luke 24:4) tells them Jesus has risen and will meet the disciples in Galilee (Matt. 28:2–8; Mark 16:5–8; Luke 24:4–8). On their hurried return in trembling and astonishment (Mark 16:8) yet with great joy (Matt. 28:8), they say nothing to anyone along the way (Mark 16:8) but go back to the disciples and report what they have seen and heard (Matt. 28:8; Mark 16:10; Luke 24:9–10; John 20:2).

3. Meanwhile, after hearing Mary Magdalene's report, Peter and John run to the tomb (John 20:3–4), apparently by a different and more direct route than the women took, since they do not run into the women returning from the tomb (see point 2 above). John arrives at the tomb first (20:4). He peers into the tomb and sees the grave cloths but does not enter (20:5). When Peter arrives, he enters the tomb and sees the grave cloths (20:6). Then John enters, sees the grave cloths and the folded head cloth in a place by itself, and believes (John 20:8). After this, by the same route they return to the place the other disciples are staying (John 20:10) and so do not meet the women.

4. Arriving after Peter and John leave, Mary Magdalene goes into the tomb (for a second time) and sees the angels (John 20:13). *She also sees Jesus* (appearance no. 1; John 20:11–14) and clings to him and worships him (John 20:11–17). She then returns to the disciples (John 20:18; Mark 16:10).

5. While the other women are on their way to the disciples, Jesus *appears to them* (no. 2). They take hold of his feet and worship him (Matt. 28:9–10). Jesus asks them to tell his disciples that he will meet them in Galilee (Matt. 28:10). Meanwhile the guards are bribed and told to say that the disciples stole his body (Matt. 28:11–15).

6. When Mary and the women find the disciples, they announce that they have seen Jesus (Mark 16:10–11; Luke 24:10; John 20:18). After hearing this, Peter probably rushes to find Jesus, and *Peter sees him* (no. 3) that day (1 Cor. 15:5; cf. Luke 24:10).

7. The same day Jesus *appears to Cleopas and another unnamed disciple* (maybe Luke; no. 4) on the road to Emmaus (Mark 16:12; Luke 24:13–31). He reveals himself to them while eating with them, and he tells them he has appeared to Peter (1 Cor. 15:5; Luke 24:34, which may mean either that the two tell the eleven that Jesus has appeared to Peter, or that when the two see the eleven, the latter are saying that the Lord has appeared to Peter).

8. After Jesus leaves them, they return to Jerusalem, where Jesus *appears to the ten disciples* (Thomas being absent: John 20:24; no. 5), showing his scars and eating fish (Mark 16:14; Luke 24:35–49; John 20:19–24).

9. After eight days, *Jesus appears to the eleven disciples* (Thomas now present; no. 6). He shows his wounds and challenges Thomas to believe. Thomas exclaims, "My Lord and my God!" (John 20:28).

10. *Jesus appears to seven of his disciples* (no. 7) who have gone fishing in the Sea of Galilee (John 21:1). He eats breakfast with them (21:2–13), after which he restores Peter (21:15–19).

11. *Then Jesus appears to five hundred brothers* at one time (1 Cor. 15:6; no. 8).

12. After this he *appears to all the apostles* in Galilee and gives them the Great Commission (1 Cor. 15:7; Matt. 28:18–20; no. 9).

13. Then Jesus appears to James (1 Cor. 15:7; no. 10), probably in Jerusalem.

14. Later in Jerusalem, *he appears to all his apostles* (1 Cor. 15:7; no. 11), presenting many convincing evidences to them (Acts 1:3), including eating with them (1:4). He answers their last question (1:6–8) and then ascends into heaven (Mark 16:15–20; Luke 24:46–52; Acts 1:9–11).

15. Several years later, on the road to Damascus, *Jesus appears to Saul* of Tarsus (Acts 9:1–8; 1 Cor. 9:1; 15:8; no. 12), later known as the apostle Paul.

Allegation 17. There is a contradiction in two of the accounts of Paul's conversion. One says Paul's companions hear the voice (Acts 9:7), another that they do *not* hear the voice (22:9). Both use the same Greek word (*akouō*). But both can't be true.

Response. (1) This is not an uncommon occurrence. It occurs regularly at our house when my (Norm's) wife calls from the other end of the house, and I say, "I can't hear you." I clearly hear *the sound* but do not hear the *meaning* of her words. The word for "hear" is commonly used in these two different senses in speech today, as it was in the first century. (2) Since Luke claims to be a careful writer (see Luke 1:1–4) and is known as such (see Hemer, *Book of Acts*), it is evident that he saw no contradiction between his two accounts. Otherwise, he would not have recorded it that way. Hence, neither should we see them as contradictory.

Allegation 18. Some say Jesus is wrong in Mark 2:26 in mentioning Abiathar as high priest instead of Ahimelech. Jesus says that when David ate the consecrated bread, Abiathar was high priest. Yet 1 Samuel 21:1–6 mentions that the high priest at that time was Ahimelech. This difficulty is of particular importance because Bible critic Bart Ehrman (see chap. 5 above) claims that his inability to explain this was a key factor in opening his eyes to the errancy of the Bible (*Misquoting Jesus*, 8–10).

Response. Samuel is correct in stating that the high priest was Ahimelech at the time David ate the bread. However, this does not mean that Mark was wrong in mentioning Abiathar. There are many possible ways that both may be true.

First of all, there are a few early manuscripts that omit the phrase "in the days of Abiathar." This would eliminate the problem, though most scholars do not believe this was the original reading.

Second, given the current text, there are still several other possible solutions to the difficulty. For one, Mark may have given the name of the more famous of the two, who, though not then high priest, nonetheless was at the tabernacle at that time. He may have been an assistant to his father at the time, as Eli's sons were to him (1 Sam. 4:4).

Further, since it is only said to have been "in the *days* of Abiathar" (v. 26), it does not necessarily imply that Abiathar was high priest at the time. Later, when

King Saul had Ahimelech killed (1 Sam. 22:17–19), Abiathar escaped and went to David (v. 20) and became the high priest. So, even though Abiathar was made high priest after David ate the bread, it would still be correct to speak of David as eating the bread "in the *days* of Abiathar." After all, Abiathar was alive when David did this and soon afterward became the high priest, after his father's death. Thus it would have been during the *time* of Abiathar, but not during his *tenure* in office.

Further, noted Greek expert A. T. Robertson suggests that "it is possible that both father and son bore both names (cf. 1 Sam. 22:20; 2 Sam. 8:17; 1 Chron. 18:16), Abiathar [being] mentioned though both [were] involved" (*Word Pictures*, 1:273).

Also, the word "time" or "days" is not in the Greek text. It is literally *epi Abiathar*, "upon Abiathar," and could be a Greek idiom, as Robertson suggests. Finally, "a plausible explanation is to render the introductory phrase: 'in the passage about Abiathar, the high priest' (cf. parallel phrase in Mark 12:26). This was a customary Jewish way of indicating the section of the Old Testament where a desired incident could be found" (see Grassmick in *Bible Knowledge Commentary*, ed. Walvoord and Zuck, 2:114).

In short, there are many ways the passage can be viewed without charging it with an error. Hence, when possible and even plausible solutions to biblical problems are readily at hand, some of which are held by noted Greek scholars, then one can only wonder what moves critics to "see" errors where they do not necessarily exist. From a philosophical perspective, antisupernatural and antitheistic presuppositions are often a contributing factor.

Summary and Conclusion

Many objections have been leveled against the doctrine of total inerrancy. Those who object to the term "inerrancy" fail to make their point. For the term as defined by ICBI is not only appropriate but also descriptive of what the Bible actually teaches and the evidence shows. Further, by analogy with science, there are good reasons for holding to an inerrant original revelation from God. For the study of God's revelation in nature (general revelation) should be assumed to be non-contradictory. And given our finitude, to say nothing of our fallenness, it can be expected that we will have difficulties with God's revelation in Scripture (special revelation). What is more, it is reasonable to assume for both revelations that we will be able to explain more of the difficulties as time goes on. Given the above, it is reasonable to assume that there is no error in either revelation but only in our understanding of it.

Indeed, assuming no error in both revelations has heuristic value: it prompts further investigation and the progress of both areas of study. Conversely, to assume an error in the original Scripture (or nature) is counterproductive and stultifies research. Having analyzed some eight hundred alleged contradictions in

Scripture in *The Big Book of Bible Difficulties*, we have to concur. We found that after a half century of study, no one has demonstrated an error in the Bible, but there are numerous examples of the errors of critics. Again, one cannot improve on the words of Augustine: "If we are perplexed by any apparent contradiction in Scripture, it is not allowable to say, The author of this book is mistaken; but either [1] the manuscript is faulty, or [2] the translation is wrong, or [3] you have not understood" (*Reply to Faustus* 11.5).

Sources

Archer, *Bible Difficulties*

Augustine, *Reply to Faustus*

Ehrman, *Misquoting Jesus*

Geisler, *Systematic Theology*, vol. 1

Geisler and Howe, *Big Book*

Geisler and Rhodes, *Conviction without Compromise*

Geisler and Turek, *I Don't Have Enough Faith*

Hannah, *Inerrancy and the Church*

Hemer, *Book of Acts*

Kelly, *Early Christian Doctrines*

Kenyon, *Bible and Archaeology*

Lewis, *Miracles*

McGowan, *Divine Spiration*

Robertson, *Textual Criticism*

———, *Word Pictures*, vol. 1

Schaff, *Creeds of Christendom*, vol. 2

Walvoord, ed., *Bible Knowledge Commentary*, vol. 2

Epilogue

A Brief Review of the Issue

With the dawn of the twenty-first century, the historic view on the inerrancy of Scripture has faced formidable challenges. A major disruption occurred when the noted evangelical Clark Pinnock (*Scripture Principle*) challenged the traditional view of unlimited inerrancy in favor of a limited inerrancy that allows for errors in nonredemptive matters (see chap. 4 above). This led to a vote to expel him from ETS, which fell just short of the two-thirds majority needed to dismiss him from the society.

Meanwhile, many young evangelicals trained in contemporary higher criticism by modern and postmodern schools have grown increasingly dissatisfied with the traditional view of unlimited inerrancy, which was embraced by Warfield, the ETS founders, and ICBI. Many of them had joined ETS since the society made a conscious decision not to challenge the consistency of each member's views with what the ETS framers meant by the statement. Instead, each member was allowed to have one's own interpretation of the ETS statement: "The Bible alone and the Bible in its entirety is the Word of God written, and therefore inerrant in the autographs."

Inevitably, this "open" view on membership has led to two camps within ETS and within inerrantists in general. The vast majority of ETS (80 percent) voted (in 2003) to accept the ICBI Chicago Statement as the ETS definition of what is meant by inerrancy: it means unlimited inerrancy, that the Bible is totally without error in any matter on which it speaks (see Geisler, ed., *Inerrancy*). As the ICBI Short Statement put it, "Holy Scripture, being God's own word, written by men prepared and superintended by his Spirit, is of infallible divine authority *in all matters upon which it touches*" (emphasis added).

The other camp contains those who do not believe in unlimited inerrancy as meant by the ETS and ICBI framers. This came to light in 1976 when the ETS

Executive Committee confessed that "some of the members of the Society have expressed the feeling that a measure of intellectual dishonesty prevails among members who do not take the signing of the doctrinal statement seriously." Further, an ETS Ad Hoc Committee recognized this problem when it posed the proper question in 1983: "Is it acceptable for a member of the society to hold a view of [a] biblical author's intent which disagrees with the Founding Fathers and even the majority of the society, and still remain a member in good standing?" The society never said no. And the subsequent vote not to expel Pinnock (63 percent) reveals that a large percentage of the members do not believe it is necessary to hold to unlimited inerrancy as the ETS and ICBI framers meant it.

We set the scene for our discussion by providing the background (chap. 1), formation (chap. 2), and influence (chap. 3) of the widely heralded ICBI Chicago Statement on Biblical Inerrancy, which was adopted as a guide by ETS, the largest evangelical theological society in the world. However, the dissenters are growing. We have discussed a whole range of the dissenters, including Clark Pinnock (chap. 4), Bart Ehrman (chap. 5), Peter Enns (chap. 6), Kenton Sparks (chap. 7), Kevin Vanhoozer (chap. 8), Andrew McGowan (chap. 9), Stanley Grenz and Brian McLaren (chap. 10), and Darrell Bock and Robert Webb (chap. 11). From this emerged the crucial issues about the nature of inerrancy itself (chap. 12), the relation of truth to inerrancy (chap. 13), the relation of language to inerrancy (chap. 14), the relation of hermeneutics to inerrancy (chap. 15), the relation of the incarnation to inerrancy (chap. 16), and an attempt to answer the major objections to inerrancy (chap. 17).

Now Hear the Conclusion of the Whole Matter

The issue of the erosion of inerrancy has been carefully examined. Several questions were posed at the outset: Can this view of total inerrancy be reaffirmed for the twenty-first century? Does the ICBI statement need to be revised or even discarded? Is it possible to be a biblical scholar and still believe in unlimited inerrancy? After reviewing all major arguments pro and con, our considered response is that we can and should reaffirm inerrancy for a new generation.

After careful examination, we have concluded that the real problem with contemporary deviations from inerrancy is not factual but philosophical. We have already discussed this in our ICBI book titled *Biblical Errancy: Its Philosophical Roots* (1981). Things have not changed with the exception that new philosophies appear on the scene that also undermine inerrancy. It is not that new facts or evidence have been found that makes the historical view of total inerrancy incredible. It is because new philosophies have been imbibed by the new generation of scholars, some wittingly and some not, that are incompatible with a traditional view of inerrancy. Some of these new ideas come from the philosophy of meaning, some from the philosophy of language, and some from the philosophy of hermeneutics. But at root they are all philosophical problems.

I (Norm) spoke about this in my presidential address to the Evangelical Theological Society (in 1998), which was published in the *Journal of the Evangelical Theological Society* (March 1999): "Beware of Philosophy: A Warning to Biblical Scholars." The exhortation still stands, the casualties still mount, and sadly many of the people discussed in this book are among them.

My academic advice has not changed. How can good, godly, and scholarly persons avoid the pitfalls of adopting philosophies that undermine the historic evangelical stand on inerrancy? My advice is the same: (1) Avoid the desire to become a famous scholar. (2) Avoid the temptation to be unique. (3) Do not dance on the edges. (4) Steer right to go straight. (5) Do not trade orthodoxy for academic respectability. (6) Reject any methodological inconsistency with the Bible or good reason.

My spiritual advice still holds when there is a conflict: (1) Always choose lordship over scholarship. (2) Do not allow morality to determine methodology. (3) Do not allow sincerity to be a test of orthodoxy. I would also add two more: (4) Do not choose fraternity over orthodoxy. (5) Do not choose unity over orthodoxy. Of course, often both terms of these pairs are possible, but in the final analysis, it is better to be divided by the truth than to be united by error. And though we should strive for both orthodoxy and scholarship, it is better to be known for one's orthodoxy than to be lauded for one's scholarship at the expense of one's orthodoxy.

Although no doctrinal statement is perfect and incapable of improvement, we have found no reason to make any significant revisions in the Chicago Statement on Biblical Inerrancy formulated by nearly three hundred scholars, adopted by the Evangelical Theological Society as such, and incorporated in essence by the largest Protestant denomination in America, the Southern Baptist Convention, as well as by numerous other evangelical groups. Most of the contemporary deviations from inerrancy were taken into consideration by the ICBI statement and its official commentaries and subsequent statement and commentary on hermeneutics (see *Hermeneutics, Inerrancy, and the Bible*), which provide guidelines for the very issues being raised today by the "new generation." These include responses to relativism, pluralism, naturalism, antipropositionalism, and even the new hermeneutic deviations undermining the inerrancy of Scripture. Hence, the authors invite others to join them in reaffirming inerrancy for a new generation.

Signers of the ICBI Chicago Statement on Biblical Inerrancy

INTERNATIONAL COUNCIL ON BIBLICAL INERRANCY
P.O. Box 13261, Oakland, California 94661 · Phone (415) 339-1064

LIST OF SIGNERS
of the
CHICAGO STATEMENT ON BIBLICAL INERRANCY

Wm. Ackerman	Donald K. Campbell	Eldon R. Fuhrman
Jay E. Adams	Greg Cantelmo	Frank E. Gaebelein
John N. Akers	J. William Carpenter	Richard B. Gaffin, Jr.
Robert L. Alden	D. A. Carson	Kenneth O. Gangel
Brooks Alexander	Stephen M. Clinton	Alden A. Gannet
Rev. Russell T. Allen	Edmund P. Clowney	Verne Garrison II
Gleason L. Archer	Robert S. Coleman	William N. Garrison
Hudson T. Armerding	Harvie M. Conn	Arthur E. Gay, Jr.
Robert L. Atwell	W. Robert Cook	Norman L. Geisler
Edward D. Auchard	E. Clark Copeland	George Giacumakis, Jr.
Hermann J. Austel	Allan Coppedge	Duane T. Gish
Greg L. Bahnsen	Winfried Corduan	Omar Gjerness
James M. Baird	Vic Cowie	W. Robert Godfrey
Kenneth L. Barker	W. A. Criswell	John E. Grauley
William S. Barker	William C. Crouse	William T. Greig, Jr.
Alexander Barkley	Linward A. Crowe	Jay H. Grimstead
David A. Barnes	Scott Eugene Daniels	Robert Gromacki
Thomas G. Barnes	John J. Davis	Wayne Grudem
Daniel L. Barnett	Wilber T. Dayton	Stanley N. Gundry
Cal Beisner	G. Waldemar Degner	David E. Hall
Richard P. Belcher	Daniel F. DeHaan	Francis H. Hall, Jr.
William E. Bell, Jr.	Peter DeJong	Pearl Crosby Hamilton
Warren S. Benson	Bruce A. Demarest	Mark M. Hanna
Bobb Biehl	William Dennison	R. Laird Harris
Thomas F. Blanchard	Robert K. DeVries	Wendell C. Hawley
Henri A. G. Blocher	James B. DeYoung	William G. Hay
Edwin A. Blum	C. Fred Dickason	Jack W. Hayford
Stuart Boehmig	Raymond B. Dillard	Steven A. Hein
Carl W. Bogue	David V. Dissen	Howard G. Hendricks
James M. Boice	David R. Douglass	Alverda Hertzler
James A. Borror	Duane A. Dunham	Bartlett L. Hess
David A. Bowen	Robert J. Dunzweiler	Albert A. Hiebert
James L. Boyer	Ralph Earle	D. Edmond Hiebert
William R. Bright	Daniel L. Edmundson	Paul M. Hillman
Arthur C. Broadwick	Stanley E. Edwards	David L. Hocking
Harold O. J. Brown	Leroy O. Eger	Harold W. Hoehner
Stephen W. Brown	Allan C. Emery, Jr.	Donald E. Hoke
Walter F. Brunn	Ted W. Engstrom	Henry W. Holloman
James M. Buchfuehrer	Wallace A. Erickson	David F. Holsclaw
Jon Buell	Howard A. Eyrich	Russell E. Horton
Harold H. Buls	Jelle Faber	William G. Houser
J. Buraga	Julius E. Farup	Karen C. Hoyt
Donald W. Burdick	John S. Feinberg	John J. Hughes
David Burnham	Paul D. Feinberg	Horace Hummel
John A. Burns	Harold D. Foos	Morris A. Inch
Russ Bush	John M. Frame	Herbert J. Jantzen

January 1, 1979

The original document is located in the Dallas Theological Seminary Archives.

LIST OF SIGNERS - Continued   Page 2

W. Maxey Jarman
Gene L. Jeffries
Irving L. Jensen
Robert T. Jensen
Rosemary M. Jensen
A. Wetherell Johnson
Alan F. Johnson
Dennis E. Johnson
Elliott E. Johnson
G. L. Johnson
Arthur P. Johnston
Martha L. Johnston
Wendell G. Johnston
David C. Jones
Norman L. Jones
James B. Jordan
Walter C. Kaiser, Jr.
David E. Kelby
D. James Kennedy
Homer A. Kent, Jr.
Eugene R. Kerr
William F. Kerr
Joseph N. Kickasola
Dennis F. Kinlaw
Fred H. Klooster
George W. Knight, III
Hendrik Krabbendam
Charles W. Krahe
Samuel R. Külling
Robert G. Lambeth
Donald H. Launstein
Merritt E. Lawson
Francis Nigel Lee
James T. Lester
Samuel Leuenberger
Gordon R. Lewis
Walter L. Liefeld
Hal Lindsey
Art Lindsley
Calvin D. Linton
George H. Livingston
George W. Long
Marvin L. Lubenow
William F. Luck
Caryl McCarty
Thomas E. McComiskey
Josh P. McDowell
Richard T. McIntosh
J. Robertson McQuilkin
John MacArthur, Jr.
John MacArthur, Sr.
Allan A. MacRae
E. William Male
W. Harold Mare
Trueman M. Martin, Jr.

James Earl Massey
Erich Mauerhofer
Richard R. Melick, Jr.
Billy A. Melvin
David Merk
Robert Metcalf
Gerald Metz
John S. Meyer
Darrow L. Miller
Jimmy A. Millikin
John J. Mitchell
John L. Mitchell
Elmer J. Moeller
James M. Moran
J. P. Moreland
Henry M. Morris
Daniel R. Morse
W. Donald Munson, Jr.
Douglas M. Muraki
John W. Murray
Lloyd R. Nelson
Mark Neuenschwander
John C. Neville, Jr.
Robert C. Newman
David R. Nicholas
Roger R. Nicole
William E. Nix
Boyd E. Nixon
Emilio Antonio Nunez
John W. Nyquist
Stanley Obitts
Harold J. Ockenga
Heinrich M. Ohmann
Stephen F. Olford
Kay Oliver
Juan Carlos Ortiz
Raymond C. Ortlund
James I. Packer
Luis Palau
Edwin H. Palmer
Luis L. Pantoja, Jr.
Majlis L. Parke
Donald B. Patterson
Dorothy Patterson
Paige Patterson
Richard D. Patterson
J. Barton Payne
Philip Barton Payne
Sue Perlman
Douglas W. Petersen
Vern S. Poythress
Paul Pressler
Klemet I. Preus
Robert D. Preus
Rolf Preus

Earl D. Radmacher
Robert G. Rayburn
K. Reddy
Robert L. Reymond
Arthur K. Robertson
O. Palmer Robertson
Bill Rogers
Cleon Rogers
Moishe Rosen
Joseph F. Ryan, Jr.
Charles C. Ryrie
Robert L. Saucy
Franky Schaeffer V
Robert W. Schaibley
F. Richard Schatz
Rick Scheideman
Dale A. Schlack
Dale Schlafer
Eckhard Schnabel
Theodore W. Schubkegel
Samuel J. Schultz
Lubbertus Selles
Norman Shepherd
Joseph R. Shultz
Stephen E. Slocum, Jr.
C. Don Smedley
Elmer B. Smick
A. E. Wilder Smith
Charles E. Smith
Charles R. Smith
Paul B. Smith
Wayne R. Spear
R. C. Sproul
John A. Sproule
James A. Stahr
Hardy W. Steinberg
Bruce C. Stewart
Donald D. Stewart
William R. Storer
Richard L. Strauss
Robert B. Strimple
Everald H. Strom
Samuel H. Sutherland
G. Aiken Taylor
Jerry Taylor
Robert L. Thomas
Michael B. Thompson
James A. Thomson
Donald Tinder
James R. Tony
Dick L. Van Halsema
J. Robert Vannoy
Paul M. Vigress
Jerry Vines
Frederick G. Wacker, Jr.

The original document is located in the Dallas Theological Seminary Archives.

LIST OF SIGNERS - Continued   Page 3

Roger Wagner
Larry L. Walker
Wilber B. Wallis
Leon F. Wardell
Gilbert B. Weaver
Ed A. Weise
David Wells
Carl E. Wenger
John W. Wenham
Dean O. Wenthe
Waldo J. Werning
Walter W. Wessel
John C. Whitcomb
Gene R. White
John H. White
Paul S. White
Luder G. Whitlock, Jr.
Bruce H. Wilkinson
David Williams
James A. Wilson
George Winston
John A. Witmer
George F. Wollenburg
A. Skevington Wood
Laurence W. Wood
John D. Woodbridge
Lewis H. Worrad, Jr.
Martin H. Woudstra
Paul O. Wright
Edwin M. Yamauchi
Ronald Youngblood

Appendix 2

Inerrancy,
Theistic Evolution,
and BioLogos

Introduction

One of the more militant and mission-driven organizations dedicated to an anti-inerrancy position is BioLogos. The members are intractably committed to theistic evolution and thereby opposed to the historic Christian stand on the inerrancy of the Bible. Consider this recommendation of the group, issued by a noted British New Testament scholar, N. T. Wright, the bishop of Durham: "Christians and secularists alike are in danger of treating 'Darwin vs. the Bible' as just another battlefront in the polarized 'culture wars.' This grossly misrepresents both science and faith. BioLogos not only shows that there is an alternative, but actually models it. God's world and God's word go together in a rich, living harmony."[1] More recently, a former creationist and evangelical Old Testament scholar Bruce Waltke has jumped ship and become a theistic evolutionist. He told the BioLogos Forum (in a March 24, 2009, release) that "if the data is overwhelmingly in favor of evolution, to deny that reality will make us a cult, ... some odd group that is not really interacting with the world. And rightly so, because we are not using our gifts and trusting God's Providence that brought us to this point of our awareness."[2] He subsequently resigned from Reformed Theological Seminary in Orlando, Florida.

BioLogos Founder: Francis Collins

BioLogos was founded by Francis Collins, the physician and geneticist known for spearheading the Human Genome Project and the discovery of disease genes. The organization consists of scientists, theologians, and other persons with one clear agenda—to move evangelicals toward a full embrace of evolutionary theory. They claim that their purpose is to "explore, promote, and celebrate the integration of science and the Christian faith." In regard to the doctrine of inerrancy, they argue that the "evidential threshold" has been crossed, and they insist that the Bible has come up short. The biblical writers were simply trapped within the limits of their own ancient cosmology and observations.[3]

The Commitment to Theistic Evolution

The starting point for BioLogos is their intractable commitment to theistic evolution, which they define as follows:

> BioLogos is most similar to Theistic Evolution. Theism is the belief in a God who cares for and interacts with creation. Theism is different than *deism*, which is the belief in a distant, uninvolved creator who is often little more than the sum total of the laws of physics. Theistic Evolution, therefore, is the belief that evolution is how God created life. Because the term evolution is sometimes associated with atheism, a better term for the belief in a God who chose to create the world by way of evolution is BioLogos.[4]

BioLogos scholars claim that they "take both the Bible and science seriously, and seek a harmony between them that respects the truth of each. By using appropriate biblical and theological scholarship BioLogos believes that the apparent conflicts that lead some to reject science and others to reject the Bible can be avoided."[5] Some of the noted theologians who embrace this position include Peter Enns, Kenton Sparks, N. T. Wright, Bruce Waltke, Alister McGrath, and John Polkinghorne.

Arguments for Theistic Evolution and Responses

BioLogos embraces many of the traditional arguments in favor of theistic evolution, believing that they can accommodate the biblical text to the latest discoveries in science. Some of these include the following:

Logically, God Could Have Used Theistic Evolution

A common argument used by theistic evolutionists, including BioLogos, is that there is no inherent contradiction between theism and evolution. If a theistic God is able to perform miracles, surely he could guide the necessary changes required for evolution to occur.

Response

However, this is not really an argument for theistic evolution. At best, it is an argument for the logical *possibility* of theistic evolution. It is an argument for what God *could have* done, not what God *did do*. One must still carefully examine both God's special revelation in the Bible and his general revelation in nature to see what God actually did do. As we shall see, the evidence is lacking in both domains for theistic evolution. As someone declares, "It may be a beautiful theory, but it is destroyed by a brutal gang of facts."

The Creation Account Is an Accommodation to the Ancient Mesopotamian Accounts

To accommodate macroevolution and Genesis, one must reject the traditional historical-grammatical understanding of Genesis. BioLogos does this by appealing to ancient mythology. These scholars argue that the ancient Mesopotamian cultures did not understand "in the beginning" (Gen. 1:1) to mean "from the very outset"—where there was first "nothing" and then God brought all things into being from nothing. Genesis 1 refers not to the origin of the material universe but to how those preexisting materials are now designed to function. Today most scholars translate Genesis 1:1 as "When God began creating" or something like that.[6]

Response

This is a futile attempt to accommodate Scripture to a prevailing scientific theory—a procedure with a long and fatal history. First, it is contrary to good science, which supports a more literal understanding of Genesis. Francis Collins himself refers to the supernatural creation of the universe by God: "The Big Bang cries out for a divine explanation. It forces us to the conclusion that nature had a definite beginning. I cannot see how nature could have created itself. Only a supernatural force that is outside of space and time could have done that" (*Language of God*, 67). Agnostic astronomer Robert Jastrow declares, "Now we see how the astronomical evidence leads to a biblical view of the origin of the world; . . . the chain of events leading to man commenced suddenly and sharply at a definite moment in time, in a flash of light and energy" (*God and the Astronomers*, 14). The fact is that the physical universe is not eternal. Space, time, and matter had a beginning. This is the conclusion of most astrophysicists. If so, then one is left with either the absurd conclusion that nothing produced something or with the conclusion that a supernatural force brought the universe into existence. Even the great skeptic David Hume says, "I never asserted so absurd a proposition as that something could arise without a cause" (*Letters of David Hume*, 1:187). So there is no real reason from modern science to reject a literal understanding of Genesis 1.

As for God's other revelation, the Bible, there are strong reasons to believe that Genesis 1:1 was the creation from nothing of the entire material universe. (1) While the Hebrew word for "creation," *bārā'*, does not necessarily mean to create from nothing (cf. Ps. 104:30), nevertheless Genesis 1:1 says, "God created the heavens and the earth" (the whole universe), and puts this "in the beginning." The natural sense of this is that *bārā'* means creation ex nihilo in this context. So in this context it does refer to the original creation. (2) One of the oldest extrabiblical recorded statements on creation known to archaeologists, over four thousand years old, makes a clear statement on creation ex nihilo: "Lord of heaven and earth: the earth was not, you created it, the light of day was not, you created it, the morning light you had not [yet] made exist" (Pettinato, *Archives of Ebla*, 259). (3) Creation from nothing is clearly expressed in the intertestamental book of 2 Maccabees 7:28 (RSV), which declares of Genesis 1: "Look at the heaven and the earth and see everything that is in them, and recognize that God did not make them out of things that existed." (4) The inspired New Testament text implies creation ex nihilo when it refers to God as saying, "'Let there be light,' and there was light" (Gen. 1:3; 2 Cor. 4:6). For light literally and apparently instantaneously came into existence where previously it did not exist. (5) Psalm 148:5 declares: "Let them [angels] praise the name of the LORD! For he commanded and they were created."

In the New Testament, (6) Jesus affirms: "And now, Father, glorify me in your own presence with the glory I had with you before the world existed" (John 17:5). Similarly, the phrase "before the ages" appears in 1 Corinthians 2:7 and 2 Timothy 1:9. Obviously, if the world had a beginning, then it did not always exist. It literally came into existence out of nonexistence. (7) In this same way, every New Testament passage that speaks of the "beginning" of the universe assumes creation ex nihilo (cf. Matt. 19:4; Mark 13:19). (8) Romans 4:17 asserts creation ex nihilo in very clear and simple terms: "God . . . gives life to the dead and calls into existence the things that do not exist." (9) In Colossians 1:16 the apostle Paul adds, "For by him [Christ] all things were created, in heaven and on earth, visible and invisible." (10) In the Apocalypse, John expresses the same thought, declaring, "You created all things, and by your will they existed and were created" (Rev. 4:11). So, from Genesis to Revelation, the Bible declares the doctrine of God's creation of everything else that exists, other than himself, out of nothing.

Literary Devices of Genesis Can Accommodate Modern Science

Many theistic evolutionists believe that the poetic features of Genesis warrant an allegorical interpretation of the text. They argue that a literalistic understanding leads to an inappropriate handling of the genre of the text. For example one writer says:[7]

> Evening and morning are declared for three days without a sun. Evening and morning have meaning only in the context of the earth rotating about its axis adjacent to the sun. Without a fixed light source, there is no evening or morning. To say [that] God himself was the source of light is insufficient, for this would require that God was "off" prior to Day 1, and that he was fixed in one position and not omnipresent until Day 4. The standard reply is that this is an expression of a 24-hour day as it

would be observed for the rest of time. Which is to say, a figurative interpretation is called upon to support a literal interpretation.

Hence, a literal interpretation of Genesis cannot be reconciled with known scientific discoveries.

Response

First of all, Genesis 1 is not Hebrew poetry. It has no poetical couplets typical of Hebrew poetry, as seen in Job, Psalms, and Proverbs, such as, "Righteousness exalts a nation, but sin is a reproach to any people" (Prov. 14:34).

Second, even if it has an overall parallel between the first three days and the last three, this does not mean it is not speaking of literal events. Many literal events are spoken about in Job and Psalms in poetic form such as Israel in the wilderness (Ps. 90), the captivity (Ps. 137), the destruction of the temple (Lam. 1), the exodus and experiences in the wilderness (Ps. 78). Even Job is presented as a real person (cf. Ezek. 14:14, 20), from a real place called Uz (Job 1:1; cf. Gen. 10:23), who really suffered and was rewarded by God (James 5:11).

Third, there is no contradiction between a literal interpretation of Genesis 1:1 and modern science. God creates light on the first day (Gen. 1:3). It was possibly because of a vapor barrier that made it impossible to see the actual sun until the fourth day (Gen. 1:14), just as we can tell the difference between day and night on a foggy day even when we cannot see the sun.

Fourth, even agnostic Robert Jastrow declares: "Now we see how the astronomical evidence leads to a biblical view of the origin of the world" (*God and the Astronomers*, 14). It is strange indeed when biblical scholars are taking Genesis allegorically and agnostic astronomers are taking it literally!

Fifth, given that the Bible is the best interpreter of the Bible, there is every reason to believe that Genesis 1:1 refers to the original creation ex nihilo of the whole material universe (see above). Indeed, Jesus himself refers to Genesis 1 as the original creation. He mentions a time period from "the beginning of the creation that God created until now" (Mark 13:19). It is difficult to take this reference to "the beginning of the creation" as anything but the original creation out of nothing.

Finally, there is no scientific or biblical reason to deny the basic literal understanding of Genesis 1–3. Indeed, not only does the rest of the New Testament take it as literal, but major Christian doctrines also are based on a literal understanding of Genesis 1–3. (1) Jesus refers to Adam and Eve as literal persons (Matt. 19:4–5) and bases his teaching on lifelong monogamy between two literal persons, a male and female, on a literal understanding of Genesis 1–3. (2) The apostle Paul also takes Genesis literally when speaking about the roles of men and women in the church (1 Tim. 2:13–14; 1 Cor. 11:2–3). (3) Romans 5:12–14 takes a literal understanding of Genesis 3 as a basis for his teachings on human depravity and why all people literally die. He writes, "Just as sin came into the world through one man, and earth through sin, and so death spread to all men because all sinned. . . .

Yet death reigned from Adam to Moses." No serious exposition of this passage can deny that Paul is affirming a literal Adam, a literal Moses, and literal death for all humans. (4) Adam is listed as the literal head of a literal genealogy that includes Abraham, David, and Christ (Luke 3). (5) Even in the Old Testament, Adam is the first in a literal genealogy that goes from the beginning up to David (1 Chron. 1). (6) Paul compares a literal Adam with the literal Christ as the first and last Adams, the respective heads of the race (1 Cor. 15:45).

In short, denying the literal interpretation of Genesis on creation, as the BioLogos people do, is contrary both to God's general revelation in nature and to his special revelation in Scripture. And denying the literal understanding of Genesis is contrary to the way the rest of Scripture understands Genesis; such a denial *undermines many important Christian doctrines based on that literal understanding of Genesis!*

Many Famous Church Theologians Accommodated Science and the Bible

Many of the BioLogos advocates claim that theologians such as Augustine, Thomas Aquinas, and Calvin accommodate their interpretations of the biblical text to the science of their day. Hence, contemporary theologians should accommodate the biblical text to fit with the scientific discoveries of our day.[8] Failure to do so will result in a poor interpretation of the text and ridicule by unbelievers.

Response

First, all the theologians cited had a basically literal understanding of Genesis 1–3. None of them agreed to pagan mythological interpretation of the text. In fact, all of them believed in the factual inerrancy of Scripture. Regarding the books of Scripture, Augustine declares: "Of these alone do we most firmly believe that the authors were completely free from error" (*Letters* 82.3). And he wrote a commentary on the "literal" understanding of Genesis. Thomas Aquinas insisted that "it is heretical to say that any falsehood whatsoever is contained either in the gospels or in any canonical Scripture" (*Exposition on Job* 13, Lect. 1). For "A true prophet is always inspired by the spirit of truth in whom there is no trace of falsehood, and he never utters untruths" (*Summa* 2a2ae, 172, 6 ad 2). Calvin believed that every word of Scripture on every topic was inspired and even charged Servetus with heresy for, among other things, denying a geographical detail in Scripture!

Second, the fact that some theologians in the past tried to accommodate the Bible to the scientific understanding of their day does not prove that they were right. Nor, we might add, does the fact the BioLogos people accommodate to macroevolutionary views of our day prove that they are right. Errors have been made on both sides of this issue. Flat Earthers were wrong in using the phrase "the four corners of the earth" (Rev. 20:8) to support their view, and so were geocentrists in using Joshua 10 ("The sun stood still") to support their view. On the other hand, as we shall see below, macroevolutionists are wrong in trying to force Genesis 1–3 to fit into their preconceived notions. One must always be careful not to read prevailing scientific views of the day into Scripture, especially when they are contrary to the clear teaching of Scripture and undermine important Christian doctrines.

Third, a hint at why Christians who are in science sometimes too quickly cave in to the prevailing science of the day in contradiction to the clear teaching of Scripture is found in the BioLogos statement that "failure to do so will result in . . . *ridicule by unbelievers*" (emphasis added). Peer pressure is a powerful pressure. The desire to be accepted is a very human trait. This is no different in academic circles. In fact, evangelicals, including theistic evolutionists, too often trade orthodoxy for academic respectability.

God Continues to Be Active in the World by Furthering the Process of Evolution

Theistic evolutionists, opposed to naturalists, argue that God is the cause of macroevolutionary changes in species. One writer says, "A proper understanding of theism implies [that] God has endowed nature with a certain degree of freedom. In much the same way that humans can act freely in the world, nature itself has an inherent liberty. This is not to say that nature has a mind of its own, but only that nature is not restricted to a machine-like, predetermined evolution."[9] Second, "It is thus perfectly *possible* that God might influence the creation in subtle ways that are unrecognizable to scientific observation. In this way, modern science opens the door to divine action without the need for lawbreaking miracles. Given the impossibility of absolute prediction or explanation, the laws of nature no longer preclude God's action in the world. Our perception of the world opens once again to the *possibility* of divine interaction."[10] Third, according to BioLogos, failure to believe in this type of divine interaction leads to the uninvolved, disinterested god of Deism.

Response

First of all, one is puzzled at the scientifically unorthodox view that Nature has "an inherent liberty," which God can apparently persuade to do things contrary to a regular pattern. Besides undermining science, which is based on regular laws, this sounds strangely similar to the process theology of Lewis Ford in his book *The Lure of God*, which is totally contrary to the traditional evangelical view of a theistic God.

Second, be that as it may, the emphasized word in the BioLogos quote about the "possible" is problematic: "It is thus perfectly *possible* that God might influence the creation in subtle ways." The possible does not demonstrate the probable or the actual. Anything that is not contradictory is possible, but this is a long shot for demonstrating the plausibility or even probability of the view.

Third, the view that "God might influence or 'lure' the creation in subtle ways that are unrecognizable to scientific observation" is not even science: it is pure speculation. How can what is "unrecognizable to scientific observation" be science? And if it is pure speculation, then how can this be held out as a good ground on which we must reject the literal interpretation of Genesis 1–3?

Fourth, it is indeed strange and ironic that BioLogos would charge creationists who believe in repeated intervention into the natural world with the title of "Deism." The truth is that the BioLogos God is the ultimate in a deistic[11] kind of God since he produces only one act of creation in the beginning and has not supernaturally intervened again since that time! If there were ever a deistic kind of God, then this is it. For God only really made one creative act in the beginning, and he does not make another after that time. He simply preplanned and preprogrammed everything that would follow for the development of life by a Darwinistic mechanism after that time.

Intelligent Design and Irreducible Complexity

BioLogos argues for the gradual change and natural selection of irreducibly complex structures.[12] They do not deny the complexity of these structures. In fact, they argue for the complexity of the inner middle connecting bones in fish, the bacteria flagellum, and the human eye. But they deny that all of the complex parts are required for the structure to be operable. They claim:

> Although we don't have the eye intermediates preserved in stone the way we can see the simpler assembly of the parts of the mammalian middle ear, we do have a vast array of eye structures in the animal kingdom, any one of which might appear to be irreducibly complex but which, in fact, has been put together through a set of processes that has included exaptation, co-option, step-by-step adaptation and some redundancy at various stages along the way. Indeed, these eye structures themselves are likely intermediates. Everything changes as it passes through the eons of time. This is the legacy of creation through the process of natural selection.[13]

Response

First of all, the admission that "we don't have the eye intermediates preserved in stone" is a telling one. Why? Because geology is the only evidence of what *did happen* in the past; all the rest, at best, is only what *could have happened*. And as we will see below, the fossil evidence does not support evolution.

Second, microbiologist Michael Behe, who started the intelligent design revolution, in *Darwin's Black Box*, has subsequently answered all these objections.[14] The truth is that there is no observable, repeatable process known to science that can produce irreducible complexity such as even the first one-cell animal had. The fact that there were animals with a light-sensitive cell does not disprove the irreducibly complex nature of a human eye. The truth is that even with 90 percent of an eye, a human is still blind. All the parts must be there at the same time in order for one to see. Nor does the fact that some parts of an organism are used in other organisms prior to the irreducibly complex use in another organism prove macroevolution. It may show only a common creator, not a common ancestor. Crucial parts of a car (like a distributor) are found in early cars, but this is no proof that a sophisticated sports car evolved by natural selection from it, nor that the distributor is not an irreducibly complex part of a contemporary gas engine because it was also found in a Model T.

Third, evolutionists have no answer for the origin of the first self-replicating cell. Even the notorious atheist Richard Dawkins admits that a one-celled animal has enough DNA information crammed into it to fill a thousand sets of an encyclopedia! Macroevolutionists have no natural explanation for this or for the origin of any other complex organism. The only cause known to humans that can produce this kind of genetic information is an intelligent one. Even former atheists Sir Fred Hoyle, who tried to discover a natural explanation, finally concluded that "biochemical systems are exceedingly complex, so much so that the chance of their being formed through random shuffling of simple organic molecules is exceedingly minute, to a point indeed where it is insensibly different from zero." So, there must be "an intelligence, which designed the biochemicals and gave rise to the origin of carbonaceous life" (Hoyle and Wickramasinghe, *Evolution from Space*, 3, 143).

Further, not only has Francis Collins ignored the landmark work of Meyer in *Signature in the Cell*, but he has also refused to dialogue with him on the topic. Along with the work of William Dembski (in *Design Inference* and, with Wells, *Design of Life*), the argument for intelligent design has provided the only reasonable (observable, repeatable) scientific explanation for the origin of both irreducible complexity and specified complexity of life. The macroevolutionary speculation has not provided a scientific explanation for either the origin of first life or of new life-forms. As Phillip Johnson demonstrates (in *Darwin on Trial*), without a naturalistic philosophical presupposition, the Darwinian hypothesis collapses, whether or not there was a God at the beginning of it.

Collins and Junk Genes

Elsewhere Collins argues that junk DNA in apes and humans is evidence that it is mutational junk in DNA since it has no known function. However, first of all, this is the fallacy of arguing from ignorance. Second, Luskin and Gage list thirteen known functions of the junk DNA ("Reply to Francis Collins," 226). Third, some scientists now speak of them as "gems among junk" and call for a "new conceptual framework" (Gibbs, "The Unseen Genome," *Scientific American*, November 2003). Finally, this fallacious argument for evolution is like the old one from vestigial organs—organs that had no known use and that evolutionists assumed were a hangover from earlier evolutionary processes. In Darwin's day there were some 180 vestigial organs. Today the list has shrunk to about six, and there are some known functions for these. Even if one believed, as Collins does, that God used evolution to create all life-forms, Collins should know that God does not make junk.

Evolution and the Second Law of Thermodynamics

The proponents at BioLogos know that many nonevolutionists use the second law of thermodynamics to argue against evolution. Because disorder, or entropy, increases or stays the same over time, and evolution requires that an increase of order occur for new species to arise, evolution violates the second law of thermodynamics. The BioLogos proponents disagree with this argumentation for two reasons:[15]

Misunderstanding of the second law of thermodynamics. Critics claim that "this objection is grounded in a misunderstanding of the second law, which states that any isolated system will increase its total entropy over time. An isolated system is defined as one without any outside energy input. Because the universe is an isolated system, the total disorder of the universe is always increasing."[16]

> With biological evolution however, the system being considered is not the universe, but the Earth. And the Earth is not an isolated system. This means that an increase in order can occur on Earth as long as there is an energy input—most notably the light of the sun. Therefore, energy input from the sun could give rise to the increase in order on Earth including complex molecules and organisms. At the same time, the sun becomes increasingly disordered as it emits energy to the Earth. Even though order may be increasing on Earth, the total order of the solar system and universe is still decreasing, and the second law is not violated. [17]

Response. First of all, this argument does not explain the origin of the universe, which is a closed and isolated system, by their definition. But the second law calls for a supernatural cause to produce the whole universe. For if the amount of useable energy is decreasing in the whole universe, then the universe must have had a beginning. And the law of causality demands that whatever comes to be must have had a cause. Combine this with the anthropic principle (see Gonzalez and Richards, *Privileged Planet*), which argues that the universe was fine-tuned from the very beginning for the emergence of human life, and it is reasonable to conclude that the universe had an intelligent cause.

Second, the mere fact that the earth is receiving energy from beyond it (from the universe) does not mean that this energy or force can produce specified complexity such as we have in first life and new life-forms. For example, a force outside a checkerboard (like a hand under it and punching it) does not thereby demonstrate that intelligent moves can be made. What the macroevolutionists must show is that there is an intelligent force outside of the universe that can produce irreducible or specified complexity. But, of course, this is precisely what intelligent design proponents say, and it is contrary to the Darwinian type of macroevolution proposed by Francis Collins and the BioLogos people.

Misapplication of the Second Law of Thermodynamics

According to critics, "To claim that evolution violates the Second Law of Thermodynamics is also grounded in a misunderstanding of where the law applies. Nobody has ever figured out how to apply the second law to living creatures. There is no meaning to the entropy of a frog. The kinds of systems that can be analyzed with the second law are much simpler."[18]

A living organism is not so much a unified whole as it is a collection of subsystems. In the development of life, for example, a major leap occurred when cells mutated in such a way that they clumped together so that multicellular life was possible. A simple mutation allowing one cell to stick to other cells enabled a larger and more complex life-form. However, such a transformation does not violate the Second Law of Thermodynamics any more than superglue violates the law when it sticks your fingers to the kitchen counter.[19]

The implication is that order can arise from disorder. They conclude by saying, "The Second Law of Thermodynamics also has interesting implications for cosmology, as it requires that [the] universe began in a highly ordered state."[20]

Response

First of all, even if the second law did not apply to living cells, it would not thereby prove macroevolution. As we just saw, not every force outside of living things is capable of producing specified complexity in them.

Second, the second law can be applied to life since it demands that everything in the physical universe is tending toward disorder. But as we move to higher levels, the origin of life and new life-forms manifest more and more order. And the order is not just any kind of order, such as a hurricane generates. It is specified order, such as a human language and a DNA. But no force of nature produces such an order. So the theoretical arrow of evolution is swimming upstream against the arrow of the second law. No force known to humanity that can produce specified complexity is capable of swimming against the current of thermodynamics except that of intelligence.

Third, mutations and natural selection do not produce specified complexity. All known natural forces, even over long periods of time, produce more randomness and disorder. For example, dropping red, white, and blue confetti from an airplane never produces the American flag on a field. And dropping from higher elevations (which give it more time), no matter how high you go, will not help specify it into an American flag. Only intelligence can do that.

Fourth, random mutations do not produce more complex information. To begin with, most mutations are harmful or lethal. And those that occur do not produce more complex forms of life. They garble the information. For instance, making random mutations on the poem "Mary Had a Little Lamb" may produce "Mary had a little lamp" and "Mary sad a little lamp," but it will never produce Shakespeare's *King Lear*. Only an intelligent being can take the same alphabet parts contained in "Mary Had a Little Lamb" and produce a higher and more complex piece of literature.

The same is true of natural selection. Unlike artificial selection, it never produces higher and more complex forms of life. First of all, it is a principle of *survival* of old forms of life, not a principle for the *arrival* of new higher forms of life. Further, Darwin wrongly compared it to artificial selection, but the two are opposite in almost every major way—thus making it a false analogy. For in artificial selection (AS), one has an aim or an end in view, but natural selection does not. In AS one chooses desired individuals to crossbreed, selecting them by the characteristics one seeks to perpetuate or enhance. Not so in nature. Further, in AS one protects them and their offspring by all means possible, keeping them from the operation of natural selection, which would speedily eliminate many freaks. In AS one continues an active and purposeful selection until reaching, if possible, the chosen goal. But nothing of this kind happens, or can happen, through the blind process of differential survival, which is wrongly labeled natural selection. As the renowned Harvard zoologist Louis Agassiz said in his landmark review of Darwin's *On the Origin of Species*: "[Darwin] has lost sight of the most striking features, and the one which pervades the whole, namely, that there runs throughout Nature unmistakable evidence of thought corresponding to the mental operations of our own mind; ... no theory that overlooks this element can be true to nature" ("Agassiz on the Origin of Species").

The Fossil Record

BioLogos proponents claim that the fossil record can provide evidence of evolutionary theory by showing the forms and features of species through time.[21] They claim, "The fossil record provides a unique view into the history of life by showing the forms and features of species through time. This is particularly important for evolution because it shows the changes in species across long periods of the Earth's history; it provides insight into the evolutionary tree."[22]

Response

On the contrary, the fossil record does not support macroevolutionists. Even Darwin admits this and simply hopes that the future finds will fill in the gaps, but it has not. He writes, "Geology assuredly does not reveal any such finely graduated organic change, and this is perhaps the most obvious and serious objection which can be urged against the theory [of evolution]" (*On the Origin of Species*, 152). But in over 150 years since Darwin, the fossil record has not filled in the gaps. In fact, to quote one famous scientist, Sir Fred Hoyle, "The fossil record leaks like a sieve"! (a chapter title by Hoyle and Wickramasinghe, *Evolution from Space*). The former Harvard paleontologist and evolutionist Stephen Jay Gould says, "The evolutionary trees that adorn our textbooks have data only at the tips and nodes of their branches."[23] Even his colleague Niles Eldredge says, "Most families, orders, classes, and phyla appear rather suddenly in the fossil record, often without anatomically intermediate forms" (*Macroevolutionary Dynamics*, 22). Colin Patterson, once head paleontologist for the British Museum, declared:

> I fully agree with your comments on the lack of direct illustrations of evolutionary transitions in my book. If I knew of any, fossil or living, I would certainly have included them. So, much as I should like to oblige you by jumping to the defense

of gradualism, and fleshing out the transitions between the major types of animals and plants, I find myself a bit short of the intellectual justification necessary for the job. (letter cited by Guste in "Plaintiff's Pre-Trial Brief")

More recently, David M. Raup, Curator of Geology, Field Museum of Natural History in Chicago, writes:

> We now have a quarter of a million fossil species but the situation hasn't changed much [since Darwin]. The record of evolution is still surprisingly jerky and, ironically, *we have even fewer examples of evolutionary transitions than we had in Darwin's time.* By this I mean that some of the classic cases of Darwinian change in the fossil record, such as the evolution of the horse in North America, have had to be discarded. . . . So Darwin's problem has not been alleviated in the last 120 years and we still have a record which does show change but one that can hardly be looked upon as the most reasonable consequence of natural selection. ("Conflicts between Darwin and Paleontology," 25, emphasis added)

Answering Questions about Inerrancy and Theistic Evolution

While theistic evolution is logically possible, it nonetheless is scientifically improbable (as shown above) and, as will be shown below, biblically untenable. There are many reasons it is incompatible with the Bible.

Contrary to a Literal Interpretation of the Bible

As was shown above (in chap. 15), the correct interpretation of any document, including the Bible, is the "literal," or historical-grammatical, interpretation. It is self-defeating to deny it. It is the way the inspired New Testament interprets the Old Testament. Indeed, it is the natural, normal, everyday way to approach a document. Indeed, as shown above, the New Testament writers repeatedly and consistently referred to the first chapters of Genesis as literal, space-time history. However, the BioLogos people have to take the early chapters of Genesis as myth, poetry, or allegory in order to make the view of macroevolution fit with the Bible.

Contrary to the Bible's Own Understanding of Genesis 1–3

As shown above, the rest of the Bible takes Genesis 1–3 to be literal, historical, space-time events. This is not only true about Adam and Eve but also about the means by which they appeared here. This is evident from many facts. First is the affirmation that humans came from dust and will return to dust (Eccles. 3:20; Ps. 90:3). Second, the New Testament declares that God created a literal Adam and Eve (Matt. 19:4). Third, Paul asserts that Eve came from Adam (1 Tim. 2:13; 1 Cor. 11:8–9). Fourth is the fact that Adam died and all humans will die because of him (Rom. 5:12). Fifth is the fact that Eve was tempted by Satan (1 Tim. 2:14). If macroevolution is correct, then we must not only reject all these teachings, but we must reject the inspiration of the Bible as well. In short, BioLogos leads to a denial of the inspiration and inerrancy of the Bible.

Contrary to a Contextual Understanding of Genesis 1–2

There are many things in the text of Genesis itself that are opposed to macro-evolution. First, the repeated use of the words "create" and "made" imply a direct intervention by God into the world (Gen. 1:1, 16, 21, 25, 27). Second, the words "God said" imply an act of creation by fiat: God simply speaks, and things come to be (cf. Gen. 1:3). Indeed, this is how the New Testament understands this act (cf. 2 Cor. 4:6). Third, the words "God formed the man of dust from the ground" imply a molding process by God (Gen. 2:7). Fourth is the fact that humans came from the dust directly and not from animals, as evolutionists say. Fifth, that humans return to dust (as they literally do after death) vouches that they came from dust to begin with (Eccles. 3:20). Sixth, that each animal reproduces "according to its kind" (Gen. 1:24–25) implies a created stability of each type of created thing. Seventh is the fact that Eve is created directly from Adam's rib (Gen. 2:21–23), not indirectly from animals through a long process. All these facts (along with the New Testament confirmation of them as literal) speak against any kind of macroevolution, theistic or not.

Contrary to the Historic Understanding of the Inerrancy of Scripture

With the exception of Origen, who was unorthodox on a number of doctrines,[24] virtually all the great fathers in the history of the church up to modern times held to a literal creation and the historicity of Adam and Eve. This was codified by the most widely accepted statement on inerrancy in the world, the famous Chicago Statement on Biblical Inerrancy, and by its framers in many further statements. Consider the following that the same thing is implied in the Short Statement on inerrancy in the ICBI document. It affirms in point 2:

> Holy Scripture, being God's own word, written by men prepared and superintended by his Spirit, is of infallible divine authority in *all matters upon which it touches*: it is to be believed, as God's instruction, in *all that it affirms*; obeyed, as God's command, in all that it requires; embraced, as God's pledge, in all that it promises.

Article 11 asserts: "We affirm that Scripture, having been given by divine inspiration, is infallible, so that, far from misleading us, it is *true and reliable in all the matters it addresses*" (emphasis added in all these quotes). This reveals that the object of historical-grammatical exegesis is to understand the objective truth of Scripture (see chap. 13 above) in all matters. This includes historical and scientific matters. For article 12 reads:

> We affirm that Scripture in its entirety is inerrant, being free from all falsehood, fraud, or deceit. *We deny that Biblical infallibility and inerrancy are limited to spiritual,*

*religious, or redemptive themes, exclusive of assertions in the fields of history and science.
We further deny that scientific hypotheses about earth history may properly be used to
overturn the teaching of Scripture on creation and the flood.*

Some ICBI scholarly papers on the topic are found in *Hermeneutics, Inerrancy*
[*HI*], edited by Radmacher and Preus. It contains a series of twenty-five hermeneutical articles (HA), with a brief commentary on them (in appendix B). Crucial
parts of these statements will be alluded to in the following discussion.

For ICBI framers, truth means that statements about history and science are
objectively true, even if they are on topics that are not directly redemptive (HA,
art. 12). Indeed, ICBI later defines the historical-grammatical hermeneutic as one
that unveils "its literal, or normal, sense" (HA, art. 14). It "affirms that Genesis
1–11 is factual, as is the rest of the book" (HA, art. 22). Another article reads: "We
deny that generic categories which negate historicity may rightly be imposed on
biblical narratives which present themselves as factual" (HA, art. 13). The commentary on this article informs us that it has in view *"some, for instance,* [who] *take
Adam to be a myth"* and *"others* [who] *take Jonah to be an allegory"* (*HI*, 897). These
affirmations place *the BioLogos people well outside the historic, orthodox Christian
view on Scripture.*

Conclusion

The BioLogos movement poses a major threat to the inerrancy of Scripture for many
reasons. First and foremost, it accepts a macroevolutionary view that is inconsistent
with a historical-grammatical interpretation of Scripture. Second, by denying a
literal understanding of Genesis 1–3, it thereby undermines many important New
Testament teachings based on this literal understanding of Genesis, including the
depravity of humans (Rom. 5:12), the basis for a monogamous marriage (Matt.
19:4), the divinely appointed order in a family (1 Cor. 11:3) and in the church
(1 Tim. 2:12–13). Even more seriously, it undermines the authority and deity of
Christ, who understood Genesis 1–3 as literal (Matt. 19:4; 24:38–39; Mark 13:19).

The problem with theistic evolution is that it is an "easy" solution to the problem of the conflict between prevailing contemporary scientific views and a serious
literal, historical understanding of Scripture. Rather than challenging the philosophical and scientific basis of the evolutionary hypothesis, it is a whole lot easier
to save one's academic reputation and job by just agreeing with it. However, the
price paid for this "easy" solution is too high. And it is unnecessary. For there is
a credible, albeit not widely accepted, alternative that is credible science without
forsaking the inspiration and inerrancy of Scripture: the intelligent design movement. Too often down through the years, evangelicals have forsaken orthodoxy
for academic respectability. The BioLogos movement, sincere as it may be, is an
example of this kind of danger.

Sources

Agassiz, "Agassiz on the Origin of Species"

Augustine, *Letters*

Behe, *Darwin's Black Box*

Collins, *Language of God*

Darwin, *On the Origin of Species*

Dembski, *Design Inference*

Dembski and Wells, *Design of Life*

Eldredge, *Macroevolutionary Dynamics*

Gibbs, "The Unseen Genome"

Gonzalez, *Privileged Planet*

Guste, in "Plaintiff's Pre-Trial Brief"

Hoyle and Wickramasinghe, *Evolution from Space*

Hume, *Letters of David Hume*

Jastrow, *God and the Astronomers*

Johnson, *Darwin on Trial*

Luskin and Gage, "Reply to Francis Collins"

Meyer, *Signature in the Cell*

Pettinato, *The Archives of Ebla*

Raup, "Conflicts between Darwin and Paleontology"

Thomas Aquinas, *Exposition on Job*

————, *Summa*

Notes

Foreword

1. John Henry Newman, *Sayings of John Henry Newman* (London: Burns and Oates, Ltd.), 18.

Prologue

1. By "total inerrancy" is meant generally that the Bible is without error on any matter it addresses, whether it is redemptive, historical, or scientific. By "limited inerrancy" is meant that the Bible is only without error on redemptive matters but not necessarily other matters it discusses.

Chapter 2: Formation of the ICBI Chicago Statement on Inerrancy

1. The Chicago Statement is available online and in many works including Norman L. Geisler, *Inerrancy* (Grand Rapids: Zondervan, 1979), 493–502.

Chapter 5: Bart Ehrman on Inerrancy

1. Ehrman believes that this diversity should caution modern claims to the authority of the Bible because clearly people interpreted the text differently. One of these faith communities came from a second-century Gnostic named Heracleon, who wrote a commentary on the Gospel of John (*MJ*, 28). Gnosticism was recognized as a heretical group by the "orthodox" Christians. The presence of the commentary reveals that they held to a high view of Scripture. But they clearly disagreed with the "orthodox" Christians about the fundamentals of the faith. Hence, we cannot know which interpretation of the Bible is true Christianity, according to Ehrman.

2. Ehrman says, "Some of these manuscripts are inexpensive, hastily produced copies; some were actually copied onto reused pages (a document was erased and the text of the New Testament was written over the top of erased pages); others are enormously lavish and expensive copies, including some written on purple-dyed parchment with silver or gold ink" (*MJ*, 88).

3. For a defense of absolute truth against relativism and agnosticism, see chap. 13 on "The Nature of Truth and Inerrancy."

4. Kostenberger and Kruger show that Bauer tried to prove his thesis by investigating the four major geographical centers of Christianity: Asia Minor, Egypt, Edessa, and Rome. His conclusion was that in Asia Minor there was diversity between Peter and Paul's theology, and among the churches in Revelation. In Egypt there was an early presence of Gnostic Christianity alongside other churches, each believing they represented orthodoxy. In Edessa, he argued, Marcion's view of Christianity constituted the earliest

form of orthodoxy. Finally, he contends that Rome imposed its form of Christian orthodoxy simply because that church ultimately gained political and doctrinal superiority (*HO*, 25–26).

5. For a full treatment against the Bauer-Ehrman thesis, see Kostenberger and Kruger, *Heresy of Orthodoxy.*

6. As for the allegation that Jesus misinterpreted the Old Testament, others have handled this objection more comprehensively (see S. L. Johnson, *Old Testament in the New*; Kaiser, *Uses of the Old Testament in the New*). Our comments are in chap. 14 below. What is even more problematic is his assumption that Jesus, the Son of God (who taught with all authority in heaven and on earth [Matt. 28:18–19]), could err in his interpretation of the Bible.

7. See "Bart Ehrman's Millions and Millions of Variants, part 1 of 2."

8. For a defense of apparent contradictions in the Bible, see Geisler and Howe, *Big Book.*

9. For a complete response to the many aspects of the problem of evil, see Norman L. Geisler, *If God, Why Evil?* (Minneapolis: Bethany House, 2010).

Chapter 7: Kenton Sparks on Inerrancy

1. Kenton Sparks endorses Thom Stark's popular-level book *The Human Faces of God: What Scripture Reveals When It Gets God Wrong (and Why Inerrancy Tries to Hide It)* (Eugene, OR: Wipf & Stock, 2011). However, his work is largely a rehash of long-since refuted charges against the inerrancy of Scripture. Also, both Sparks and Stark offer many similar false claims about the nature of God, especially relating to the problem of evil and inerrancy. These have been addressed in this chapter and other sections throughout the book. Further, Thom Stark, while claiming to be within the ranks of Christendom, actually denies essential doctrines such as the deity of Christ and affirms unorthodox views of the nature of God and Scripture.

2. For a treatment of the topic of miracles, see Geisler, *Systematic Theology*, 1:43–63.

3. Sparks quotes Augustine's *Literal Interpretation of Genesis*: "It is a disgraceful and dangerous thing for an infidel to hear a Christian, presumably giving the meaning of Holy Scripture, talking nonsense on these [cosmological] topics, and we should take all means to prevent such an embarrassing situation, in which people show up vast ignorance in a Christian and laugh and scorn" (AI, 5). He quotes the Genesis commentary of Thomas Aquinas: "One should adhere to a particular explanation [of Scripture] only in such a measure as to be ready to abandon it, if it be proved with certainty to be false; lest Holy Scripture be exposed to ridicule of unbelievers, and obstacles be placed to their believing" (AI, 5).

4. Sparks borrowed the term "verbal idols" from Vanhoozer's book *Is There Meaning?* (459). Vanhoozer believes that an approach that sees the text as a source of knowledge in itself does not encapsulate the fullness of Scripture (see chap. 8 below for a critique of Vanhoozer). Instead, Vanhoozer argues for an approach that sees "texts as communicative acts characterized by intention, illocution, and efficacy" (459).

5. Circular arguments function by assuming the conclusion in one of the premises.

6. Scripture recognizes that God is perfect (Matt. 5:48), that God cannot lie (Titus 1:2; Heb. 6:18), and that God cannot "deny himself" (2 Tim. 2:13).

7. Thomas Aquinas says, "Now God is the first principle, not material, but in the order of efficient cause, which must be most perfect. . . . Hence, the first active principle must needs be most actual, and therefore most perfect" (*Summa* 1.4.1).

8. The inerrancy position reserves perfection to the original autographs. The affirmation of art. 10 says, "We affirm that inspiration, strictly speaking, applies only to the autographic text of Scripture, which in the providence of God can be ascertained from available manuscripts with great accuracy. We further affirm that copies and translations are the Word of God to the extent that they faithfully represent the original."

9. Jesus affirms that David wrote Ps. 110 (Matt. 22:44–45) and that Moses wrote Lev. 13 (Matt. 8:4). John affirms that Isaiah wrote both sections of Isaiah (John 12:38–42). Jesus and NT writers make many more attributions of authorship.

10. For a full defense of the Christology of Christ, see the section on Christology in Geisler, *Systematic Theology*, vol. 2.

11. There are some three hundred verses in the Bible confirming the basic facts of creation recorded in Genesis 1. Indeed, Jesus himself affirms the creation of Adam and Eve (Matt. 19:4–5), as does the apostle Paul (see 1 Tim. 2:13).

12. http://www.albertmohler.com/2010/08/16/.

Chapter 8: Kevin Vanhoozer on Inerrancy

1. Please see Dr. Kostenberger's review of Vanhoozer's *Drama of Doctrine* at http://www.biblical foundations.org/theology/the-drama-of-doctrine. Dr. Vanhoozer's response can be found at http://www.biblicalfoundations.org/theology/vanhoozer-responds-to-my-review.

2. It should be noted that evangelical scholar G. K. Beale, in his work *Erosion of Inerrancy in Evangelicalism*, expresses concern about Vanhoozer's critiques of the traditional view of inerrancy when he states, "Some scholars at noteworthy institutions, however, now believe that with the passing of some thirty years, the Chicago Statement is outdated in some very important respects, and some of these institutions do not discourage their faculty from having a critical view of important elements of the document" (19–20).

Furthermore, in the footnote on page 19, he elaborates upon those who believe this document is outdated when he states, "E.g., see K. Vanhoozer, 'Lost in Interpretation? Truth, Scripture, and Hermeneutics,' *JETS* 48 (2005): 89–114, who offers critiques of what he considers the traditional view of inerrancy but does not give any substantive criticism of the Chicago Statement; however, note his rather pedantic criticism of the Chicago Statement's Article XI, 'It [the Bible] is true and reliable in all matters it addresses': 'Strictly speaking, however, "it" neither affirms nor addresses; authors do' (ibid., 106). But I doubt whether the Chicago Statement meant to downplay either human or divine authorship here; rather they were using an accepted stylistic convention for referring to such authorship in the Bible. One can easily recall, for example, Billy Graham's repeated refrain in his evangelical sermons, 'The Bible says . . . ,' not to speak of Jesus's own repeated reference 'Scripture says . . .' (John 19:37; so also John 7:38, 42; 19:28)." Perhaps, ironically, Vanhoozer, who criticizes inerrancy as too literal of an approach and as underemphasizing different genres of Scripture, should realize that he may be misinterpreting the genre of this expression used in the Chicago Statement; i.e., he takes it much more literally than was intended.

In a letter from R. C. Sproul to me (William Roach) about Vanhoozer's statement, he says: "But you asked particularly the question regarding Vanhoozer's statement where he distinguishes between what the Bible addresses and what men or authors do. His statement, strictly speaking, *it* doesn't affirm or address anything; only authors do. This is worse than pedantic. It's simply silly. When we're talking about the Bible, the inerrancy position makes it clear that the Bible is a book written by human authors, which authors address various matters. And whatever these authors address within the context of sacred Scripture, while under the supervision of the Holy Spirit, carries the full weight of inerrancy. It would seem to me that if somebody is trying to avoid the conclusions that the Chicago Statement reaches regarding inerrancy, it's a far reach to avoid them by such a distinction. In the final analysis, the distinction is a distinction without a difference." June 30, 2010.

3. For a detailed discussion of this realistic theory of meaning, which is neither Platonic essentialism nor Wittgensteinian conventionalism, see O'Callaghan, *Thomistic Realism*.

4. No contemporary American scholar has done more to further the *sensus unum* view than Walter Kaiser, whom Vanhoozer only mentions in passing (LI? 90). See Kaiser, ed., *Classical Evangelical Essays in Old Testament Interpretation* (Grand Rapids: Baker, 1972); Kaiser, *Toward an Exegetical Theology* (1981); *Uses of the Old Testament in the New* (1985), and, with M. Silva, *Biblical Hermeneutics* (1994).

5. Even the noninerrantist Kenton Sparks recognizes this error with speech-act theory and Vanhoozer when he says, "A Speech Act theorist (like Vanhoozer or Ward) will admit that this is wrong by modern scientific standards but will also point out that the 'Speech Act' of the biblical author—the thing he was trying to accomplish in Genesis—had nothing to do with science. Hence the author's errant cosmology was not an error in his discourse. Variations on this theme focus on the genre of the Bible, suggesting, for instance, that Genesis is not a book of 'bad science' so much as a book of myth or saga that teaches

good theology. In essence, if Scripture appears to be wrong, we've simply misunderstood the kind of discourse that it is" (AI, 9).

6. Vanhoozer offers an extended defense of the need for tradition in interpreting the Bible in DD, 115–85. Space does not allow a critique of this here. It will suffice here to say that, whatever merit it has, it certainly demonstrates that he does not believe in sola Scriptura and perspicuity in the traditional sense.

7. For a defense of *sola scriptura* and inerrancy, please see "'Sola Scriptura' in History and Today" by J. I. Packer in *God's Inerrant Word: An International Symposium on the Trustworthiness of Scripture*, ed. John Warwick Montgomery (Minneapolis: Bethany House, 1974), 43–62.

Chapter 9: Andrew McGowan on Inerrancy

1. The same basic material in this chapter appears also in an article by Norman L. Geisler, "An Evaluation of McGowan's View on the Inspiration of Scripture," *Bibliotheca Sacra* 167, no. 665 (January–March 2010).

2. McGowan agrees with Herman Bavinck more than almost any other author, saying, "My argument, then, is that Herman Bavinck... offers the finest model for an evangelical doctrine of Scripture" (DS, 212).

3. See Sproul, *Explaining Inerrancy*, 31.

4. For a defense of the correspondence view of truth, see chapter 13.

5. Geisler, *Systematic Theology*, vol. 1.

6. It is acknowledged that many orthodox theologians have used the word "accommodation" to mean adaptation to finitude, but it is denied that they mean this to include error or sin. However, since the term "accommodation" now carries this connotation for many, I recommend that we speak of divine "adaptation" to finitude and leave the word "accommodation" for the neo-orthodox (and neo-Gnostic) view of God acquiescing to error in the Bible.

7. We argue that the Bible "cannot" err insofar as its divine dimension is concerned and "did not" err insofar as its human dimension is concerned.

8. See Rice, *Our God-Breathed Book*, 9.

9. For a treatment of the many ways in which Jesus uses reason and evidence to substantiate his claims, see Geisler and Zuckeran, *Apologetics of Jesus*.

10. Augustine, *On the Predestination of the Saints* 5.

11. Kelly, *Early Christian Doctrine*, 39.

12. See Augustine, *Reply to Faustus* 11.5.

13. Kenyon, *Bible and Archaeology*, 288.

14. Robertson, *Textual Criticism*, 22.

15. Ehrman, *Misquoting Jesus*, 55.

16. See Walvoord and Zuck, eds., *Bible Knowledge Commentary*, 2:40.

17. For McGowan to insist that it is an error because Matthew's record represents the ruler as saying it at a different time is an example of the very "literalistic" view he elsewhere deplores in inerrantists. Further, it begs the question by assuming that conflation is not a legitimate literary style, which the ICBI view on inerrancy allows.

Chapter 10: Stanley Grenz and Brian McLaren on Inerrancy

1. Spinoza in particular had a deductive system built on the model of Euclid's geometry: he began with allegedly self-evident axioms and tried to deduce from them absolutely certain conclusions about all of reality.

2. Traditional theists depend on certain undeniable first principles (like the laws of logic) on which all thought is based and to which rationally valid thinking could be reduced. But, contrary to modern foundationalism (like Spinoza), one could not deduce from these principles alone anything true about the real world. All knowledge of the real world begins in sense experience (see Geisler, *Thomas Aquinas*, chap. 6).

3. For a discussion of general revelation, see Geisler, *Systematic Theology*, vol. 1, chap. 4.

4. Not all inerrantists claim to be foundationalist, but virtually all inerrantists are foundationalist in that they believe that the basic laws of thought (like the law of noncontradiction) are indispensible to all thought, including all theological thought.

5. Pascal, *Pensées*, sect. 1, chaps. 14–15; sect. 2, chaps. 11–12, 16–18.

6. Grenz, "Nurturing the Soul," 39.

7. Alister McGrath, "Theology and Experience," in the *European Journal of Theology* 2, no. 1 (1993): 67.

8. Grenz is citing Donald Bloesch with approval in *Revisioning Evangelical Theology*, 131.

9. McLaren, "Missing the Point: The Bible," in McLaren and Campolo, *Adventures in Missing the Point*.

10. Brian D. McLaren, "The Broadened Gospel," in "Emergent Evangelism," *Christianity Today* 48 (November 2004): 43.

11. Greg Warner, "Brian McLaren," *Faithworks*, www.faithworks.com/archives/brian_mclaren.htm; as quoted in John MacArthur, "The Perspicuity of Scripture: The Emergent Approach," *The Master's Seminary Journal* 17, no. 2 (Fall 2006): 141–58, online at http://www.tms.edu/tmsj/tmsj17g.pdf.

12. Mark Driscoll, *Confessions of a Reformission Rev.* (Grand Rapids: Zondervan, 2006), 21.

13. DeYoung and Kluck, *Why We're Not Emergent*, 247–48.

Chapter 11: Darrell Bock and Robert Webb on Inerrancy

1. Since Bock and Webb are the editors, we use their names to represent the views in general, realizing that not every author contributing to this book agrees with everything in every essay.

2. Bock-Webb assume documents like the alleged "Q." For a critique of this hypothetical document, see Geisler, "Q Document," in *Baker Encyclopedia*; and Eta Linnemann, "Is There a Q?" in *Bible Review* (October 1995).

3. This is not to say the gospel was not preached earlier (between c. 30 and 50 AD). It was (see Acts 2–15). Nor is it to say there were no early creeds (cf. 1 Cor. 15). There were (see also 1 Tim. 3:16). The apostles had early oral as well as written authority (2 Thess. 2:2). It is only to say that there was no prolonged oral period of forty-plus years, supposed by redaction critics, in which content was reshaped and changed by the later church after the time of the eyewitnesses.

4. See Norman Geisler, *Creation in the Courts: Eighty Years of Conflict in the Classroom and the Courtroom* (Wheaton: Crossway, 2007), chaps. 8–9.

5. Robert Guelich, "The Gospels: Snapshots or Portraits of Jesus' Ministry" (paper presented at the Evangelical Theological Society in 1978).

6. J. Ramsey Michaels, Servant and Son: Jesus in Parable and Gospel (Atlanta: John Knox, 1981).

7. Grant Osborne, "Redaction Criticism," JETS 19, no. 2 (1976): 73–85. See also JETS 21, no. 2 (June 1978): 117–30.

8. See Bock's response: http://www.amazon.com/Events-Life-Historical-Jesus-Collaborative/dp/0802866131.

9. Ibid.

10. Ibid.

11. See *God's Inerrant Word: An International Symposium on the Trustworthiness of Scripture*, ed. John W. Montgomery (Minneapolis: Bethany House, 1974), esp. chap. 11 by R. C. Sproul, "The Case for Inerrancy: A Methodological Analysis," 242–61.

12. See Thomas Sherlock, *The Tryal of the Witnesses of the Resurrection* (London: J. Roberts, 1729); Attorney Frank Morison, *Who Moved the Stone?* (New York: Century, 1930); Montgomery, *History and Christianity* (1964); and Lee Strobel, *The Case for Christ* (Grand Rapids: Zondervan, 1998).

13. See Bock's response: http://www.amazon.com/Events-Life-Historical-Jesus-Collaborative/dp/0802866131.

14. Taken from an important forthcoming series by F. David Farnell, "Three Searches for the 'Historical Jesus' but No Biblical Christ": Part 1, "The Rise of the Searches," *The Master's Seminary Journal* 24, no. 1 (Spring 2012); Part 2, "Evangelical Participation in the Search for the 'Historical Jesus,'" *The Master's Seminary Journal* 24, no. 1 (Spring 2013).

Chapter 12: The Nature of God and Inerrancy

1. In addition to God's infinity, immutability, and full omniscience, classical theists also believe in God's eternality and simplicity. However, the discussion here is centered on omniscience and immutability since they are crucial to inerrancy.

2. Actually, 1 Chron. 21:1 does not say it was by Satan's "command" but simply says it was "incited" by Satan. It does not occur to DeWolf that God in his sovereignty uses even evil forces to accomplish his will (see Job 1).

3. One ETS member suggested to him that this could be a figure of speech meaning "total destruction." If so, then it would be unnecessary to take it as a false prediction by Jesus. This provided an out for Pinnock.

4. Critics have tried to avoid this by dating this section of Isaiah (40–66) later, but this fails because Jesus and the inspired New Testament writings (see John 12:38–41) refer to both sections of Isaiah as from one and the same prophet, who lived long before Cyrus was on the scene. Further, no one has ever discovered a separate manuscript for a later Isaiah, and there are literary indicators that link the two sections of Isaiah into one book (see Archer, *Old Testament Introduction*).

Chapter 13: The Nature of Truth and Inerrancy

1. *Webster's Ninth New Collegiate Dictionary* (Springfield, MA: Merriam-Webster, 1985). Of course, truth can also be used in the sense of fidelity or trust, but we count statements as truth because they correspond with the facts, not the reverse.

2. Only Eccles. 5:5 and 10:5 could be understood as using *shĕgāgâ* to refer to intentional errors, but in Leviticus it clearly means an unintentional error.

3. In the case of God's self-knowledge, the object of his knowledge is identical to the subject, but it is an objective reality nonetheless. This is also true of our own self-knowledge. However, in the case of our knowledge of God and of the world, the object is outside of the subject.

4. There are no one-word sentences since all one-word sentences (like, "Go") imply at least two words (viz., ["You] go.").

5. In Fuller Theological Seminary, *Theology, News & Notes*, Special Issue, 1976.

Chapter 14: The Nature of Language and Inerrancy

1. Many believe that this passage in Augustine's *Confessions* (1.8), which Wittgenstein critiqued, was not embraced by Augustine but only offered for consideration, since he rejected it elsewhere (in *De magistro*).

2. By "Barthian" we mean some followers of Barth but not necessarily Barth himself, whose view on some of these issues changed over time and is not always clear.

Chapter 15: The Nature of Hermeneutics and Inerrancy

1. Emphasis is added in all the following quotes to stress hermeneutical aspects of them.

2. This does not mean that the Holy Spirit cannot guide a believer on thoughts and actions relevant to living the Christian life and yet not specifically addressed in the Bible. But the Spirit of God never leads the children of God contrary to the Word of God that the Spirit inspired for them.

3. For more extensive comments on this point, see Michael Licona, *The Resurrection of Jesus* (Downers Grove, IL: InterVarsity Press, 2010), 204–16.

4. See Robert H. Gundry, "A Surrejoinder to Norman Geisler," *Journal of the Evangelical Theological Society* 26 (March 1983): 109–15, esp. 114.

5. Michael R. Licona, *The Resurrection of Jesus: A New Historiographical Approach* (Downers Grove, IL: InterVarsity Academic, 2010), 185–86, 552–53, 556.

Appendix 2: Inerrancy, Theistic Evolution, and BioLogos

1. Quoted on the website of The BioLogos Forum, http://www.biologos.org/news-events, accessed June 9, 2011.

2. "Why Must the Church Come to Accept Evolution?" The BioLogos Forum, March 24, 2010, http://biologos.org/blog/why-must-the-church-come-to-accept-evolution.

3. From http://www.albertmohler.com/2010/08/16.

4. From http://biologos.org/questions/biologos-id-creationism.

5. From http://biologos.org/resources/leading-figures.

6. From http://biologos.org/blog/genesis-creation-and-ancient-interpreters.

7. From http://biologos.org/blog/biblical-and-scientific-shortcomings-of-flood-geology-part-2.

8. Sparks quotes Thomas Aquinas in his Genesis commentary as saying, "One should adhere to a particular explanation [of Scripture] only in such a measure as to be ready to abandon it, if it be proved with certainty to be false; lest Holy Scripture be exposed to the ridicule of unbelievers, and obstacles be placed to their believing." Augustine shared similar concerns in his Genesis commentary: "It is a disgracefully and dangerous thing for an infidel to hear a Christian, presumably giving the meaning of Holy Scripture, talking nonsense on these [cosmological] topics, and we should take all means to prevent such an embarrassing situation, in which people show up vast ignorance in a Christian and laugh it to scorn" (Sparks, AI, 5–6).

9. From http://biologos.org/questions/evolution-and-divine-action.

10. Ibid., emphasis added.

11. Really, it is more of a process panentheistic view, which like deism is naturalistic.

12. See http://biologos.org/questions/complexity-of-life.

13. Ibid.

14. See "Responses to Critics," www.arn.org/authors/behe.html.

15. See http://biologos.org/questions/evolution-and-the-second-law.

16. Ibid.

17. Ibid.

18. Ibid.

19. Ibid.

20. Ibid.

21. See http://biologos.org/questions/fossil-record.

22. Ibid.

23. Stephen Jay Gould, "Evolution's Erratic Pace," Natural History 5 (May 1977): 14.

24. Origen was a universalist, holding that we all eventually will be saved. He denied the full deity of Christ. He denied the physical resurrection of Christ, claiming it was a spiritual body. And he forsook the literal interpretation for an allegorical one, thus denying the historicity of sections of the Bible, including the early chapters of Genesis.

Bibliography

Achtemeier, Paul J. *The Inspiration of Scripture: Problems and Proposals*. Philadelphia: Westminster, 1980.

Adler, Mortimer. *Six Great Ideas*. New York: Thirteen, 1982.

Agassiz, Louis. "Prof. Agassiz on the Origin of Species." *American Journal of Science and Arts*, 2nd ser., 30 (June 30, 1860): 142–54.

Albright, William F. "Toward a More Conservative View." *Christianity Today* 7 (January 18, 1963): 4–5.

Alston, William P. *A Realist Conception of Truth*. Ithaca, NY: Cornell University Press, 1997.

Anselm of Canterbury. *Truth, Freedom, and Evil: Three Philosophical Dialogues*. Edited and translated by Jasper Hopkins and Herbert Richardson. New York: Harper & Row, 1967.

Archer, Gleason, Jr. *Encyclopedia of Bible Difficulties*. Grand Rapids: Zondervan, 1982.

———. *A Survey of Old Testament Introduction*. Revised, expanded ed. Chicago: Moody, 2007.

Aristotle. *Categories*. In *The Basic Works of Aristotle*, edited by Richard McKeon. New York: Random House, 1941.

———. *Metaphysics*. In *The Basic Works of Aristotle*. Edited by Richard McKeon. New York: Random House, 1941.

———. *On Interpretation*. In *The Basic Works of Aristotle*, edited by Richard McKeon. New York: Random House, 1941.

Augustine of Hippo. *Augustine: Earlier Writings*, edited by J. H. S. Burleigh. Library of Christian Classics. Philadelphia: Westminster, 1953.

———. *City of God*. In vol. 2 of *Nicene and Post-Nicene Fathers*, edited by Philip Schaff. 1st series. 14 vols. 1886–94. Repr., Grand Rapids: Eerdmans, 1952.

———. *De Trinitate* [On the Trinity]. In vol. 3 of *Nicene and Post-Nicene Fathers*, edited by Philip Schaff. 1st series. 14 vols. 1886–94. Repr., Grand Rapids: Eerdmans, 1952.

———. *On the Predestination of the Saints*. In vol. 5 of *Nicene and Post-Nicene Fathers*, edited by Philip Schaff. 1st series. 14 vols. 1886–94. Repr., Grand Rapids: Eerdmans, 1952.

———. *Principi Della Dialettica*. Como, Italy: Gruppo Amici del Liceo Volta, 1985.

———. *Reply to Faustus the Manichaean*. In vol. 4 of *Nicene and Post-Nicene Fathers*, edited by Philip Schaff. 1st series. 14 vols. 1886–94. Repr., Grand Rapids: Eerdmans, 1952.

Austin, J. L. *How to Do Things with Words*. Cambridge, MA: Harvard University Press, 1975.

Baptist Faith and Message: A Statement. 2000. http://www.sbc.net/bfm/bfm2000.asp.

Barth, Karl. *Church Dogmatics, Volume 1: The Doctrine of the Word of God*. Edited by G. W. Bromily and T. F. Torrance. Translated by G. T. Thomson and Harold Knight. Edinburgh: T&T Clark, 1956.

———. *Church Dogmatics: A Selection*. With an introduction by Helmut Gollwitzer. Translated and edited by G. W. Bromiley. New York: Harper Torchbooks, 1961.

———. *Evangelical Theology*. Grand Rapids: Eerdmans, 1992.

———. *Nein!* [No!]. Eugene, OR: Wipf & Stock, 2002.

Bauckham, Richard. *Jesus and the Eyewitnesses.* Grand Rapids: Eerdmans, 2008.

Beale, G. K. *The Erosion of Inerrancy in Evangelicalism.* Wheaton: Crossway, 2008.

Behe, Michael. *Darwin's Black Box.* New York: Free Press, 2006.

Berkouwer, G. C. *Holy Scripture.* Translated by Jack Rogers. Grand Rapids: Eerdmans, 1975.

Blanchard, Calvin. *The Complete Works of Thomas Paine.* Chicago: Donohue Brothers, 1920.

Blomberg, Craig. *The Historical Reliability of the Gospels.* Downers Grove, IL: InterVarsity Press, 1987.

———. *The Historical Reliability of John's Gospel.* Downers Grove, IL: InterVarsity Press, 2001.

Bock, Darrell L., and Robert L. Webb, eds. *Key Events in the Life of the Historical Jesus: A Collaborative Exploration of Context and Coherence.* Grand Rapids: Eerdmans, 2010.

Boice, James M. *Foundations of the Christian Faith.* 4 vols. Downers Grove, IL: InterVarsity Press, 1978–81. Rev. ed. as 1 vol. 1986.

Bright, Steve. "Nostradamus: A Challenge to Biblical Prophecy?" *Christian Research Journal* 25, no. 2 (2002). http://www.equip.org/PDF/DN088.pdf.

Bruce, F. F. *Jesus and Christian Origins outside the New Testament.* Grand Rapids: Eerdmans, 1974.

———. *The New Testament Documents: Are They Reliable?* Downers Grove, IL: InterVarsity Press, 1960.

Brunner, Emil. *The Christian Doctrine of God.* Vol. 1. Translated by Olive Wyon. London: Lutterworth, 1949.

———. *Revelation and Reason.* Philadelphia: Westminster, 1946.

———. *The Word of God and Modern Man.* Translated by David Cairns. Richmond: John Knox, 1964.

Bultmann, Rudolf. *Kerygma and Myth: A Theological Debate.* New York: Harper Collins, 2000.

Burke, Spencer. *A Heretic's Guide to Eternity.* San Francisco: Jossey-Bass, 2006.

Bush, L. Russ, and Tom J. Nettles. *Baptists and the Bible.* Chicago: Moody, 1980.

Calvin, John. *Calvin's Commentaries.* 22 vols. Edited by David W. Torrance and Thomas F. Torrance. Grand Rapids: Eerdmans, 1972.

———. *Institutes of the Christian Religion.* 2 vols. Edited by John T. McNeill. Translated by Ford Lewis Battles. Library of Christian Classics 20–21.

Philadelphia: Westminster, 1960.

Carson, D. A. *Becoming Conversant with the Emerging Church.* Grand Rapids: Zondervan, 2005.

Carson, D. A., and Douglas Moo. *Introduction to the New Testament.* 2nd ed. Grand Rapids: Zondervan, 2005.

Chalke, Steve, and Alan Mann. *The Lost Message of Jesus.* Grand Rapids: Zondervan, 2004.

Collins, Francis. *The Language of God.* New York: Free Press, 2006.

Craig, William Lane. "The Evidence for Jesus." http://www.leaderu.com/offices/billcraig/docs/rediscover2.html.

———. *Knowing the Truth about the Resurrection.* Rev. ed. Ann Arbor, MI: Servant Books, 1981.

Darwin, Charles. *On the Origin of Species.* Original, 1859. Edition of 1872, http://www.infidels.org/library/historical/charles_darwin/origin_of_species. New York: Signet Classics, 2003.

Dembski, William. *The Design Inference.* Cambridge: Cambridge University Press, 1998.

Dembski, William, and Jonathan Wells. *The Design of Life.* Richardson, TX: Foundation for Thought and Ethics, 2007.

DeWolf, Harold. *The Case for Theology in Liberal Perspective.* Philadelphia: Westminster, 1959.

———. *A Theology of the Living Church.* New York: Harper, 1960.

DeYoung, Kevin, and Ted Kluck. *Why We're Not Emergent.* Chicago: Moody, 2008.

Dodd, C. H. *History and the Gospels.* West Yorkshire, UK: Pomona Press, 2008.

Duns Scotus, John. *Philosophical Writings.* Translated and introduced by Allan B. Wolter. Indianapolis: Bobbs-Merrill, 1962.

Edwards, Paul, ed. *The Encyclopedia of Philosophy.* Detroit: Macmillan Reference, 2006.

Ehrman, Bart. *Misquoting Jesus: The Story behind Who Changed the Bible and Why.* San Francisco: HarperSanFrancisco, 2005.

Eldredge, Niles. *Macroevolutionary Dynamics.* New York: McGraw-Hill, 1989.

Enns, Peter. *Inspiration and Incarnation.* Grand Rapids: Baker Academic, 2005.

Fesperman, Charles. "Jefferson Bible." *Ohio Journal of Religious Studies* 4 (October 1976): 78–82.

Foote, Henry Wilder. *The Religion of Thomas Jefferson.* Boston: Beacon, 1947; repr. 1960.

Ford, Lewis S. "Biblical Recital and Process Theology." *Interpretation* 26 (1972).

———. *The Lure of God: A Biblical Background for Process Theism*. Philadelphia: Fortress, 1978.

Fosdick, Harry Emerson. *A Guide to Understanding the Bible*. New York: Harper & Brothers, 1948.

Frege, Gottlob. "On Sense and Reference." Translated by Peter Geach. In *Translations from the Philosophical Writings of Gottlob Frege*, edited by Peter Geach and Max Black. Oxford: Basil Blackwell, 1960.

Fuller Seminary. *Theology, News & Notes*, Special Issue, 1976.

Geisler, Norman L. "Accommodation." In *Baker Encyclopedia of Christian Apologetics*. Grand Rapids: Baker, 1999.

———. "God, Alleged Disproofs of." In *Baker Encyclopedia of Christian Apologetics*. Grand Rapids: Baker, 1999.

———. *The Battle for the Resurrection*. Nashville: Thomas Nelson, 1989.

———. *The Bible: Decide for Yourself*. Grand Rapids: Zondervan, 1982. Repr., Eugene, OR: Wipf & Stock, 2004.

———, ed. *Biblical Errancy: An Analysis of Its Philosophical Roots*. Grand Rapids: Zondervan, 1981. Repr., Eugene, OR: Wipf & Stock, 2004.

———. "Explaining Hermeneutics: A Commentary on the Chicago Statement on Biblical Hermeneutics Articles of Affirmation and Denial." In *Hermeneutics, Inerrancy, and the Bible*, edited by Earl D. Radmacher and Robert D. Preus. Grand Rapids: Academie Books, 1984. http://biblesanity.org/chicago2.htm.

———, ed. *Inerrancy*. Grand Rapids: Zondervan, 1980.

———. *Popular Survey of the New Testament*. Grand Rapids: Baker, 2007.

———. *Systematic Theology*. 2 vols. Minneapolis: Bethany House, 2002–3.

———. *Thomas Aquinas: An Evangelical Appraisal*. Grand Rapids: Baker, 1991. Repr., Eugene, OR: Wipf & Stock, 2003.

———. "Truth, Nature of." In *Baker Encyclopedia of Christian Apologetics*. Grand Rapids: Baker, 1999.

Geisler, Norman L., and J. Kerby Anderson. *Origin Science: A Proposal for the Creation-Evolution Controversy*. Grand Rapids: Baker, 1987.

Geisler, Norman L., and Joshua M. Betancourt. *Is Rome the True Church?* Wheaton: Crossway, 2008.

Geisler, Norman L., and Winfried Corduan. *Philosophy of Religion*. Eugene, OR: Wipf & Stock, 2003.

Geisler, Norman L., and Joseph Holden. *Living Loud: Defending Your Faith*. Nashville: Broadman & Holman, 2002.

Geisler, Norman L., and H. Wayne House with Max Herrera. *The Battle for God*. Grand Rapids: Kregel, 2001.

Geisler, Norman L., and Thomas Howe. *The Big Book of Bible Difficulties*. Grand Rapids: Baker, 2008. Previously published as *When Critics Ask*. Wheaton: Victor, 1992.

Geisler, Norman L., and William E. Nix. *A General Introduction to the Bible*. Chicago: Moody, 1986.

Geisler, Norman L., and Ron Rhodes. *Conviction without Compromise*. Eugene, OR: Harvest House, 2008.

Geisler, Norman L., and Frank Turek. *I Don't Have Enough Faith to Be an Atheist*. Wheaton: Crossway, 2004.

Geisler, Norman L., and Patrick Zuckeran. *The Apologetics of Jesus*. Grand Rapids: Baker, 2009.

Gibbs, W. Wayt. "The Unseen Genome: Gems among the Junk." *Scientific American* (November 2003).

Gilson, Etienne. *The Christian Philosophy of St. Thomas Aquinas*. South Bend, IN: University of Notre Dame Press, 1994.

———. *Linguistics and Philosophy*. South Bend, IN: University of Notre Dame Press, 1988.

Glueck, Nelson. *Rivers in the Desert: A History of the Negev*. Philadelphia: Jewish Publication Society, 1969.

Gonzalez, Guillermo, and Jay W. Richards. *The Privileged Planet: How Our Place in the Universe Is Designed for Discovery*. Washington, DC: Regnery Publishing, 2004.

Greenleaf, Simon. *An Examination of the Testimony of the Four Evangelists*. London: A. Maxwell & Son, 1847.

Grenz, Stanley. "Nurturing the Soul, Informing the Mind." In *Evangelicals, Scripture: Tradition, Authority, and Hermeneutics*, edited by Vincent Bacote, Laura C. Miguelez, and Dennis L. Okholm. Downers Grove, IL: InterVarsity Press, 2004.

———. *A Primer on Postmodernism*. Grand Rapids: Eerdmans, 1996.

———. *Renewing the Center: Evangelical Theology in a Post-Theological Era*. 2nd ed. Grand Rapids: Baker Academic, 2006.

———. *Revisioning Evangelical Theology*. Downers Grove, IL: InterVarsity Press Academic, 1993.

Grenz, Stanley, and John R. Franke. *Beyond Foundationalism*. Louisville: Westminster John Knox, 2001.

Grinbank, Mariano. "Bart Ehrman's Millions and Millions of Variants: Part l of 2." Posted September 16, 2010. http://www.truefreethinker.com/articles/bart-ehrman%E2%80%99s-millions-and-millions-variants-part-1-2.

Gundry, Robert H. *Matthew: A Commentary on His Literary and Theological Art.* Grand Rapids: Eerdmans, 1982.

———. *Sōma in Biblical Theology.* Grand Rapids: Academie Books, 1987.

Guste, William J., Jr. In "Plaintiff's Pre-Trial Brief" for the Louisiana Trial on Creation and Evolution. June 3, 1982.

Guthrie, Donald. *New Testament Introduction: The Gospels and Acts.* London: Tyndale House, 1965.

Habermas, Gary. *The Historical Jesus: Ancient Evidence for the Life of Christ.* Joplin, MO: College Press, 1996.

Hannah, John D., ed. *Inerrancy and the Church.* Chicago: Moody, 1984.

Hemer, Colin. *The Book of Acts in the Setting of Hellenistic History.* Winona Lake, IN: Eisenbrauns, 1990.

Henry, Carl. *The Uneasy Conscience of Modern Fundamentalism.* Grand Rapids: Eerdmans, 1947.

Hodge, Archibald A., and B. B. Warfield. *Inspiration.* Philadelphia: Presbyterian Board of Publication, 1881. Repr., Grand Rapids: Baker, 1979.

Hodge, Charles. *Systematic Theology.* 3 vols. New York: Scribner, 1872. Repr., Grand Rapids: Eerdmans, 1940.

Hoehner, Harold. *Chronological Aspects of the Life of Christ.* Grand Rapids: Zondervan, 1978.

Holy Bible: English Standard Version. Wheaton: Crossway Bibles, 2001.

Holy Bible: King James Version. Oxford: Oxford University Press, 1611.

Holy Bible: New King James Version. Nashville: Thomas Nelson, 1982.

Howe, Thomas A. "Does Genre Determine Meaning?" *Christian Apologetics Journal* 6, no.1 (Spring 2007): 1–19.

———. *Objectivity in Biblical Interpretation.* Longwood, FL: Advantage Books, 2004.

Hoyle, Fred, and Chandra Wickramasinghe. *Evolution from Space.* London: J. M. Dent & Sons, 1981.

Hume, David. *The Letters of David Hume.* Edited by J. Y. T. Greig. 2 vols. Oxford: Clarendon, 1932.

Irenaeus. *Against Heresies.* In vol. 1 of *The Ante-Nicene Fathers,* edited by Alexander Roberts and James Donaldson. Boston: Christian Literature Publishing, 1885. Repr., Grand Rapids: Eerdmans, 1952.

Jastrow, Robert. *God and the Astronomers.* New York: W. W. Norton, 1978.

Jefferson, Thomas. *The Jefferson Bible: The Life and Morals of Jesus of Nazareth.* Boston: Beacon Press, 1989.

Johnson, Phillip E. *Darwin on Trial.* Downers Grove, IL: InterVarsity Press, 2010.

Johnson, S. Lewis. *The Old Testament in the New: An Argument for Biblical Inspiration.* Grand Rapids: Zondervan, 1980.

Jones, Alan. *Reimagining Christianity: Reconnect Your Spirit without Disconnecting Your Mind.* Hoboken, NJ: John Wiley & Sons, 2005.

Jones, Timothy Paul. *Misquoting Truth: A Guide to the Fallacies of Bart Ehrman's Misquoting Jesus.* Downers Grove, IL: InterVarsity Press, 2007.

Justin Martyr. *Apology.* In vol. 1 of *Ante-Nicene Fathers,* edited by Alexander Roberts and James Donaldson. Boston: Christian Literature Publishing, 1885. Repr., Grand Rapids: Eerdmans, 1952.

Kaiser, Walter C. *Toward an Exegetical Theology: Biblical Exegesis for Preaching and Teaching.* Grand Rapids: Baker, 1981.

———. *The Uses of the Old Testament in the New Testament.* Chicago: Moody, 1985.

Kaiser, Walter C., and M. Silva. *Introduction to Biblical Hermeneutics: The Search for Meaning.* Grand Rapids: Zondervan, 1994.

Kantzer, Kenneth, ed. *Applying the Scriptures.* Grand Rapids: Academie Books, 1987.

Kelly, J. N. D. *Early Christian Doctrine.* New York: Harper & Row, 1960.

Kenyon, Sir Frederic. *The Bible and Archaeology.* New York: Harper, 1940.

———. *Our Bible and the Ancient Manuscripts.* Revised by A. W. Adams. 4th ed. New York: Harper, 1958.

Kostenberger, Andreas J., and Michael J. Kruger. *The Heresy of Orthodoxy: How Contemporary Culture's Fascination with Diversity Has Reshaped Our Understanding of Early Christianity.* Wheaton: Crossway, 2010.

Ladd, George. *I Believe in the Resurrection.* Grand Rapids: Eerdmans, 1975.

———. *The New Testament and Criticism.* Grand Rapids: Eerdmans, 1967.

Lewis, C. S. *The Abolition of Man.* New York: Macmillan, 1947.

——. *Miracles: A Preliminary Study.* New York: Macmillan, 1969.

Lindsell, Howard. *The Battle for the Bible.* Grand Rapids: Zondervan, 1976.

Linnemann, Eta. *Historical Criticism of the Bible: Methodology or Ideology?* Grand Rapids: Baker, 1990.

——. *Is There a Synoptic Problem? Rethinking the Literary Dependence of the First Three Gospels.* Grand Rapids: Baker, 1992.

Luskin, Casey, and Logan Paul Gage. "A Reply to Francis Collins's Darwinian Arguments for Common Ancestry of Apes and Humans." In *Intelligent Design 101: Leading Experts Explain the Key Issues.* Edited by Wayne House. Grand Rapids: Kregel, 2008. http://www.ideacenter.org/stuff/contentmgr/files/640ee5bfb01620f5eacd6675a51bc119/miscdocs/id101_franciscollinsrebuttal.pdf.

Luther, Martin. *Luther's Works.* Edited by Jaroslav Pelikan and Helmut Lehmann. 55 vols. Minneapolis: Fortress Press; St. Louis: Concordia, 1957–86.

——. *Works of Martin Luther.* 6 vols. Philadelphia: Muhlenberg Press, 1915–43.

Marsden, George. *Reforming Fundamentalism: Fuller Seminary and the New Evangelicalism.* Grand Rapids: Eerdmans, 1987. Repr., 1995.

Mayo, Bernard. *Jefferson Himself.* Charlottesville: University of Virginia Press, 1942. Repr., 1970.

McDonald, H. D. *Theories of Revelation: An Historical Study, 1700–1960.* 2 vols. in 1. Twin Brooks Series. Grand Rapids: Baker, 1979.

McGowan, Andrew T. B. *The Divine Spiration of Scripture.* Nottingham, UK: Apollos, 2007.

McLaren, Brian D. *The Church on the Other Side.* Grand Rapids: Zondervan, 2000.

——. *A Generous Orthodoxy.* Grand Rapids: Zondervan, 2004.

——. *The Last Word and the Word after That.* San Francisco: Jossey-Bass, 2005.

——. "Missing the Point: The Bible." In *Adventures in Missing the Point,* by Brian D. McLaren and Tony Campolo. Grand Rapids: Zondervan, 2006.

——. *A New Kind of Christian.* San Francisco: Jossey-Bass, 2001.

McLaren, Brian D., and Tony Campolo. *Adventures in Missing the Point.* Grand Rapids: Zondervan, 2006.

Metzger, Bruce. *The Text of the New Testament.* New York: Oxford University Press, 1964.

Meyer, Stephen. *Signature in the Cell.* New York: HarperOne, 2009.

Mohler, Albert. "The Inerrancy of Scripture: The Fifty Years' War . . . and Counting." http://www.albertmohler.com/2010/08/16.

Mondin, Baptista. *The Principle of Analogy in Protestant and Catholic Theology.* The Hague: Nijhoff, 1963.

Montgomery, John Warwick, ed. *God's Inerrant Word: An International Symposium on the Trustworthiness of Scripture.* Minneapolis: Bethany House, 1974.

——. *History and Christianity.* Downers Grove, IL: InterVarsity Press, 1964.

Moore, G. E. *Some Main Problems of Philosophy.* New York: Collier, 1962.

Nicole, Roger, ed. *Inerrancy and Common Sense.* Grand Rapids: Baker, 1980.

O'Callaghan, John. *Thomistic Realism and the Linguistic Turn.* South Bend, IN: University of Notre Dame, 2003.

Ogden, Schubert. "The Authority of Scripture for Theology." *Interpretation* 30, no. 3 (July 30, 1967): 242–60.

——. "On Revelation." In *Our Common History as Christians,* edited by John Deschner, et al. New York: Oxford University Press, 1975.

Osborne, Grant. "The Evangelical and Redaction Criticism: Critique and Methodology." *Journal of the Evangelical Theological Society* 22, no. 4 (December 1979): 305–22.

Packer, J. I. "Exposition on Biblical Hermeneutics." In *Hermeneutics, Inerrancy, and the Bible,* edited by Earl D. Radmacher and Robert D. Preus. Grand Rapids: Academie Books, 1984.

Pascal, Blaise. *Pensées.* Edited and translated by Roger Ariew. Indianapolis: Hackett Pub., 2005.

Pettinato, Giovanni. *The Archives of Ebla: An Empire Inscribed in Clay.* New York: Doubleday, 1981.

Pinnock, Clark H. *Biblical Revelation: The Foundation of Christian Theology.* Chicago: Moody, 1971.

——. *A Defense of Biblical Infallibility.* 1967. Repr., Phillipsburg, NJ: P&R Pub., 1977.

——. *The Most Moved Mover.* Grand Rapids: Baker, 2001.

——. *The Scripture Principle.* San Francisco: Harper & Row, 1984. 2nd ed. Grand Rapids: Baker Academic, 2006.

Plato. "Cratylus." In *The Collected Dialogues of Plato,* edited by Edith Hamilton and Huntington Cairns. New York: Pantheon, 1964.

Preus, Robert. *The Inspiration of Scripture*. Edinburgh: Oliver & Boyd, 1955.

The Proceedings of the Conference on Biblical Inerrancy. Nashville: Broadman, 1987.

Radmacher, Earl, and Robert D. Preus, eds. *Hermeneutics, Inerrancy, and the Bible*. Grand Rapids: Academie Books, 1984.

Ramsay, Sir William. *St. Paul the Traveler and the Roman Citizen*. 3rd ed. New York: G. P. Putnam's Sons, 1898.

Raup, David M. "Conflicts between Darwin and Paleontology." *Field Museum of Natural History Bulletin* 50 (January 1979): 22–29.

Rawlings, Harold. *Trial by Fire: The Struggle to Get the Bible into English*. Wellington, FL: Rawlings Foundation, 2004.

Reu, Johann M. *Luther and the Scriptures*. Columbus, OH: Wartburg Press, 1944.

———. *Luther and the Scriptures*. St. Louis: Concordia, 1980.

Rice, John R. *Our God-Breathed Book: The Bible*. Murfreesboro, TN: Sword of the Lord, 1969.

Robertson, Archibald Thomas. *An Introduction to Textual Criticism of the New Testament*. Nashville: Broadman, 1925.

Robinson, John A. T. *Redating the New Testament*. 1976. Repr., Eugene: Wipf & Stock, 2000.

———. *Word Pictures in the New Testament*, vol. 1. Nashville: Broadman Press, 1930.

Rogers, Jack B., ed. *Biblical Authority*. Waco: Word Books, 1978.

Rogers, Jack B., and Donald K. McKim. *The Authority and Interpretation of the Bible*. San Francisco: Harper & Row, 1979.

Russell, Bertrand. *The Problems of Philosophy*. London: Bibliobazaar, 1912.

Saussure, Ferdinand de. *A Course in General Linguistics*. London: Collins, 1974.

Schaeffer, Francis. *No Final Conflict: The Bible without Error in All That It Affirms*. Downers Grove, IL: InterVarsity Press, 1975.

Schaeffer, Francis, et al. *The Foundation of Biblical Authority*. Edited by James M. Boice. Grand Rapids: Zondervan, 1978.

Schaff, Philip. *Companion to the Greek Testament and the English Version*. 3rd ed. New York: Harper, 1883.

———, ed. *The Creeds of Christendom*. Vol. 2. 6th ed. New York: Harper & Row, 1931. Repr., Grand Rapids: Baker, 1983.

Scotland, Nigel. *Can We Trust the Gospels?* Exeter: Paternoster Press, 1979.

Sheler, Jeffery L. "Is the Bible True?" *U.S. News and World Report*, October 25, 1999.

Sparks, Kenton. "After Inerrancy: Evangelicals and the Bible in a Postmodern Age." http://biologos.org/projects/scholar-essays.

———. *God's Word in Human Words: An Evangelical Appropriation of Critical Biblical Scholarship*. Grand Rapids: Baker Academic, 2008.

Sproul, R. C. *Explaining Inerrancy: A Commentary*. Oakland: International Council on Biblical Inerrancy, 1980. 4th printing. Orlando, FL: Reformation Trust, 2002. Reissued as *Can I Trust the Bible?* Lake Mary, FL: Reformation Trust, 2009.

Sproul, R. C., John Gerstner, and Arthur Lindsley. *Classical Apologetics: A Rational Defense of the Christian Faith and a Critique of Presuppositional Apologetics*. Grand Rapids: Zondervan, 1984.

Thomas, Robert. *Evangelical Hermeneutics: The New Versus the Old*. Grand Rapids: Kregel, 2002.

———. "The Hermeneutic of Noncessationism." *The Master's Seminary Journal* (Fall 2003).

Thomas, Robert, and F. David Farnell, eds. *The Jesus Crisis: Inroads of Historical Criticism into Evangelical Scholarship*. Grand Rapids: Kregel, 1998.

Thomas Aquinas. *The Literal Exposition on Job*. Translated by Anthony Damico. Atlanta: Scholars Press, 1989.

———. *On Truth*. Translated by J. V. McGlynn. Chicago: H. Regnery, 1952–54.

———. *Summa theologica*. 60 vols. Edited by O. P. Gilby. New York: McGraw-Hill, 1966.

Tozer, A. W. *Knowledge of the Holy: The Attributes of God, Their Meaning in the Christian Life*. New York: HarperOne, 1978.

Urquhart, John. *Inspiration and Accuracy of the Holy Scriptures*. London: Marshall; Kilmarnock, UK: John Ritchie, 1895. http://www.archive.org/details/theinspirationac00urquuoft.

Vanhoozer, Kevin J. *The Drama of Doctrine: A Canonical-Linguistic Approach to Christian Theology*. Louisville: Westminster John Knox, 2005.

———. "The Inerrancy of Scripture." http://www.theologynetwork.org/biblical-studies/getting-stuck-in/the-inerrancy-of-scripture.htm.

———. *First Theology: God, Scripture, and Hermeneutics*. Downers Grove, IL: InterVarsity Press, 2002.

———. *Is There Meaning in This Text?* Grand Rapids: Zondervan, 2009.

———. "Lost in Interpretation? Truth, Scripture, and Hermeneutics." *Journal of the Evangelical Theological Society* 48, no. 1 (March 2005): 89–141. http://www.etsjets.org/files/JETS-PDFs/48/48-1/48-1-pp089-114_JETS.pdf.

———. "The Semantics of Biblical Literature: Truth and Scripture's Diverse Literary Forms." In *Hermeneutics, Authority, and Canon*, edited by D. A. Carson and John Woodbridge. Grand Rapids: Academie Books, 1987. Repr., Grand Rapids: Baker, 1995.

———. "The Voice and the Actor: A Dramatic Proposal about the Ministry and Minstrelsy of Theology." In *Evangelical Futures: A Conversation on Theological Method*, ed. John Stackhouse Jr. Grand Rapids: Baker, 2000.

Walvoord, John F., and Roy B. Zuck, eds. *The Bible Knowledge Commentary: An Exposition of the Scriptures*. 2 vols. Wheaton: Victor, 1983–85.

Warfield, A., and Hodge. *See* A. Hodge and Warfield.

Warfield, B. B. *The Inspiration and Authority of the Bible.* Edited by Samuel G. Craig. Philadelphia: P&R Pub., 1948. Essays drawn from *Revelation and Inspiration.* New York: Oxford University Press, 1927.

———. "The Inspiration of the Bible." *Bibliotheca Sacra* 51 (1984): 614–40.

———. *An Introduction to the Textual Criticism of the New Testament.* London: Hodder & Stoughton, 1886.

———. "Professor Henry Preserved Smith on Inspiration." *Presbyterian and Reformed Review* 5 (1894): 600–653. Repr. as *Limited Inspiration.* Phillipsburg, NJ: P&R Pub., 1961.

Weaver, Richard. *Ideas Have Consequences.* Chicago: University of Chicago Press, 1948.

Westcott, Brooke, and John A. Hort. *The New Testament in the Original Greek.* 1881. Repr., Charleston, SC: Nabu Press, 2010.

Whately, Richard. *Historic Doubts Relative to Napoleon Bonaparte.* In *Famous Pamphlets*, ed. H. Morley. New York: Routledge, 1890.

Wittgenstein, Ludwig. *Lectures and Conversations on Aesthetics, Psychology, and Religious Belief.* Edited by Cyril Barrett. Berkeley: University of California Press, 1966.

———. *Notebooks: 1914–1916.* Edited by G. H. von Wright and G. E. M. Anscombe. Translated by G. E. M. Anscombe. 2nd ed. Chicago: University of Chicago Press, 1979.

———. *Philosophical Investigations.* New York: Macmillan, 1953.

———. *Tractatus logico-philosophicus.* Translated by D. F. Pears and B. F. McGuinness. London: Routledge & Kegan Paul, 1961.

Woodbridge, John. *Biblical Authority: A Critique of the Rogers/McKim Proposal.* Grand Rapids: Zondervan, 1982.

Norman L. Geisler (PhD, Loyola University of Chicago) is Distinguished Professor of Apologetics and Theology at Veritas Evangelical Seminary in Murrieta, California. He is the author of more than seventy books, including the *Baker Encyclopedia of Christian Apologetics*.

William C. Roach (MA, Southern Evangelical Seminary) has served as a research assistant to Dr. Norman Geisler and is an ordained minister, active speaker, and writer. He is currently a PhD student at Southeastern Baptist Theological Seminary and resides in Wake Forest, North Carolina.